*On the Margins
of Art Worlds*

# Institutional Structures of Feeling

George Marcus, Sharon Traweek,
Richard Handler, and Vera Zolberg, *Series Editors*

---

# On the Margins
# of Art Worlds

*edited by*
*Larry Gross*

Westview Press
*Boulder* • *San Francisco* • *Oxford*

*Institutional Structures of Feeling*

Copyright © 1995 by Westview Press, Inc.

Published in 1995 in the United States of America by Westview Press, Inc., 5500 Central Avenue, Boulder, Colorado 80301-2877, and in the United Kingdom by Westview Press, 12 Hid's Copse Road, Cumnor Hill, Oxford OX2 9JJ

Library of Congress Cataloging-in-Publication Data
On the margins of art worlds / edited by Larry Gross.
    p.   cm. — (Institutional structures of feeling)
  Includes bibliographical references.
  ISBN 0-8133-1679-0
  1. Communication in art.   2. Art—Social aspects.   I. Gross,
Larry.   II. Series.
N72.S605   1995
701'.03—dc20

94-39071
CIP

Printed and bound in the United States of America

The paper used in this publication meets the requirements
of the American National Standard for Permanence of Paper
for Printed Library Materials Z39.48-1984.

10     9     8     7     6     5     4     3     2     1

# Contents

# Preface

During the late 1980s, the near-worship of artistic genius produced auction sales of works by Vincent Van Gogh and Pablo Picasso for tens of millions of dollars, over $15 million for a painting by Jasper Johns, and record prices for works by many other deceased and even living masters. At the same time, it was no longer controversial in academic and intellectual circles to maintain that art works are the products of what Howard Becker has termed collective activity carried out within loosely defined art worlds:

> Works of art, from this point of view, are not the products of individual makers, "artists" who possess a rare and special gift. They are, rather, joint products of all the people who cooperate via an art world's characteristic conventions to bring works like that into existence. Artists are some sub-group of the world's participants who, by common agreement, possess a special gift, therefore make a unique and indispensable contribution to the work, and thereby make it art. (1982: 35)

The concept of the art world—with its central focus on the collective, social, and conventional nature of artistic production, distribution, and appreciation—confronts and potentially undermines the romantic ideology of art and artists still dominant in Western societies.

In contrast to this romantic image, the sociological art world perspective emphasizes similarities rather than distinctions between artistic and other activities. As Becker's pioneering work showed, there is enormous explanatory power to be gained by this approach. It is not necessary to deny that artworks are in some ways special and are different from other products of human activity nor to argue that artists are in no significant sense different from other workers who produce goods and services. But treating the production of art as work and artists as workers and examining the conditions under which these activities take place illuminates much that is obscured by the dictates of romantic individualism.

We might also ask what happens if we consider the arts from within the framework of communication theory; after all, the arts are generally assumed to be forms of communication. We might say that artists are the "sources" who "encode" works of art (i.e., "messages") that are "decoded" by audiences. But this terminological exercise leaves many questions unanswered: Who is permitted or required to be an artist? Which objects or events are considered to be works of art? Who is eligible to be among the audiences for these works? And what do the processes of creation and appreciation consist of? These questions may be approached from many perspectives—psychological, historical, and sociological among them—with differing consequences for how answers are sought and found.

The chapter that begins this collection puts the marginal role of the so-called fine or high arts in historical perspective, asking why modern Western societies have come to view the arts as a preserve for elites from which most citizens are estranged. Key to understanding this development are the ideology of individual talent and the concomitant demand for constant innovation, a demand that undermines the communicative capability of artworks. The analysis presented here suggests a historical and sociological context within which the study of art worlds might be fruitfully pursued.

The art worlds perspective represented in these original studies asks about the social arrangements that determine the recruitment and training of artists, the institutional mechanisms governing distribution and influencing success or failure, the processes of innovation within art worlds, and the emergence of new formations around new media and new players. The contributors further share a focus on borderline cases and questions; on actions, transactions, and transitions at the margins of art worlds. Just as the study of visual perception has been enriched by research conducted at the borders of visual processes (such as the numerous investigations of optical illusions that reveal much about "normal" perception) so too have we much to learn about the normal functioning of art worlds from the study of marginal movements and moments. Indeed, the dynamic relationship (oftentimes the struggle) between the margins and centers of artistic production has of late become a focal concern in art worlds themselves.

Controversies surrounding critical incidents illuminate many of the otherwise invisible art world rules, procedures, and practices. Transitions across the border into art worlds, through the recruitment, training, and socialization of aspiring artists (and their subsequent career paths) have much to tell us about the aesthetic values and biases that are obscured by the romantic ideology of artistic genius. Looking at art worlds organized around marginal media—amateur photography, video, graffiti—reveals patterns of interaction and evaluation strikingly reminiscent of those found in the fine art mainstream.

Controversies arise when innovators confront established art worlds (McLoughlin); when avant-garde works acceptable in elite venues are imposed on unappreciative citizens as public art (Slavin); when the introduction of photography provides amateurs with the technical ability to rival the skill of painters and when various groups of photographers create works that might be candidates for aesthetic appreciation (Inglesby, Griffin, Preston).

Conflicts arise when women confront the endemic sexism of the male-dominated elite art world and find themselves torn between the diverging strategies of assimilation and separatism (Kauffman); when Polish artists trained in a nonmarket system in which graphic arts were considered equal in status to painting find themselves confronted in New York with a gallery-based art world that relegates most graphic arts to the second-class status of commercial art (Warchol); when a graduate film program that cultivates directorial talent and personal vision nevertheless needs to prepare its graduates for a profession over-equipped with contenders for scarce spaces at the top (Henderson).

The mechanisms of art world recruitment and the negotiation of status and hierarchy are apparent as emerging artists enter the mainstream market system of galleries, dealers, and collectors (Warchol), but they can also be found in the marginal context of graffiti artists—wall writers—with its clearly articulated standards and its hierarchy of stars (Drew). Related art world adjustment mechanisms appear in the assimilation of animation cels as salable artworks (under the marked term *animation art*) in the institutionalized routines of collectors, dealers, auction houses, and museums (Mikulak). Finally, Native American artists making the transition to "external" markets and to novel media raise questions about Native American identity as well as art (Leuthold).

The research represented in this volume was conducted by graduate students at the Annenberg School for Communication of the University of Pennsylvania. By approaching the study of art worlds within the context of communications studies these scholars were at once free from the disciplinary boundaries that separate the study of art into social, historical, and aesthetic domains and at the same time obliged to follow the threads of their questions wherever they led them, without resorting to the security of those same disciplinary constraints. Together, they reflect the rich potential, indeed the necessity, of interdisciplinary approaches that combine empirical investigation and theoretical analysis for a deeper and more nuanced understanding of the workings of art worlds.

I have worked with all of these researchers—as teacher or adviser—and my understanding of art worlds has benefited from the fruits of their labors. I am grateful for the opportunity to have taught and learned from such gifted and dedicated scholars. These projects also benefited from the teaching and advice of my Annenberg School colleagues, in particular Carolyn Marvin, Paul Messaris, and Charles Wright as well as Charles Bosk of Penn's sociology department.

I am also grateful to those who fashioned the environment in which these efforts flourished: to Walter Annenberg, who founded and has consistently supported a broad-based and intellectually adventuresome school; to George Gerbner, who recruited a diverse, interdisciplinary faculty united by their belief in the centrality of communications to the understanding of the human condition, and who encouraged a young psychologist to follow his intellectual and moral instincts wherever they led; and to Sol Worth, who engaged me in an exciting conversation that began the day we met, continued until his untimely death, and still enriches my life. I am also grateful to colleagues beyond the Annenberg School who stimulated and influenced my efforts to combine the study of art and social science; the title of this collection is a friendly wave to Howard Becker and Barbara Herrnstein Smith. I have been lucky as an academic in my colleagues and students, and I hope that these chapters convey some of the pleasure I have found in the study of art worlds.

*Larry Gross*

# 1

# Art and Artists
# on the Margins

## LARRY GROSS

ART IS A TERM THAT HAS BEEN USED in too many ways and been applied to too many phenomena to have a simple or consistent meaning. However, common patterns can be discerned. Works of art seem generally to be considered communicative acts, and therefore we can adapt the shorthand definition of a communicative event as involving a *source* who *encodes* a *message* that is *decoded* by a *receiver;* in the case of the arts each of these terms takes on special properties: an *artist creates* a *work of art* that is *appreciated* by an *audience.*

Not all messages are considered art, and not everyone who produces a message is considered an artist. Art is the product of human creative skill, but because not all manufactured products are given this honorific title, other criteria must be involved in this designation. In its modern use the term is applied primarily to the products of a set of activities known collectively as the *fine arts*. Some of these were presided over by Muses postulated by the ancient Greeks: poetry, dance, tragedy; others (for example, painting, sculpture, and architecture) were joined to the concept of fine arts through a long process that culminated in the eighteenth century and was codified in Diderot's *Encyclopedie* and the newly emerging philosophy of aesthetics (Kristeller, 1990a). More recently the practitioners of new media—photography, film, video—have aspired to be included in this honored grouping.

The modern Western designation of the *fine,* or *high,* arts expresses a distinction drawn between these exalted domains of cultural production and others that might reasonably be included but are disqualified on various grounds. Most notably excluded are those performers and products whose appeal may be too broad—the *popular,* or *low,* arts—or too utilitarian, such as crafts. It has often been noted that these exclusions follow—and reinforce—lines of class and gender privilege. In other periods and cultures, as is well-known, such distinctions have not been made or have been derived from other social and ideological formations.

In some contexts and cultures artists are valued for their virtuosity in exercising conventional skills, with the greatest accolades for performances that approach the ideal realization of the conventional form; in others, aesthetic norms emphasize innovativeness and individuality, with an implicit expectation of radical innovation as the badge of genius. Each of these positions carries implications for the communicative role of the arts in society. These two definitional poles coexist in our time, although the balance is clearly tilted toward the latter. Art is generally assumed to result from the extraordinary technical abilities and personal qualities of its makers, unhampered by pragmatic considerations of utility. Although wide disparities among cultures and periods appear in their concepts of who can and should be defined as an artist and in the recruitment, training, and treatment of these individuals, in the modern West it is assumed that unique individual attributes—generally called talent—mark those eligible for the role of artist.

## THE BIRTH OF THE ROMANTIC ARTIST

European societies in the fifteenth and sixteenth centuries underwent a series of radical transformations. These upheavals, which are partially identified by the labels of the Renaissance, originating in southern Europe, and the Protestant Reformation, originating in northern Europe, can be seen as resulting in part from the political and economic developments associated with the decline of feudalism and the stirrings of bourgeois capitalism and in part from the technological revolution embodied in the invention of printing.

Among the legacies of this period is the Western preoccupation with the individual as the focus of theological, moral, political, economic, and social concern. Protestantism emphasizes the inescapably individual relation of each person to the deity, and the political and social philosophies of modern Western societies locate in individual citizens fundamental rights and obligations that define their relationship with both the state and their fellow citizens.

In the realm of the arts these shifts are reflected in the increasing focus on the individuality of the artist and of artistic creation. The seeds planted in the Renaissance bore fruit in the eighteenth century and gave birth to the romantic concept of the artist.

> For the first time, the term "creative" was applied not only to God but also to the human artist, and a whole new vocabulary was developed to characterize the artist and his activity although there were some partial or scattered precedents to be found in ancient and Renaissance thought. The artist was guided no longer by reason or by rules but by feeling and sentiment, intuition and imagination; he produced what was novel and original, and at the point of his highest achievement he was a genius. (Kristeller, 1990b: 250)

A great work of art thus came to be defined as the product of creative genius that transcends tradition and convention in the fulfillment of its inspiration.

Achievement in art comes to be identified with innovation, as the artist's genius is manifested in the originality of style and execution. Following this conceptualization artists in Western cultures have been expected, in keeping with the spirit of romanticism, to prove their worth by expressing a personal and unique vision. The resulting pattern of constant innovation in the arts undermines their ability to embody the common experiences and meanings of the society, to serve the central communicative functions of socialization and integration—roles now assigned to the domain of the "popular" arts and the mass media. Artists came to see themselves as the avant-garde, the "frontier scouts" of culture, moving ahead of their contemporaries into uncharted territories where they undergo privation and sacrifices as they suffer under the ambivalent burdens of genius, only to be redeemed by the recognition of posterity. This peculiarly romantic model of the artist as quintessential outsider, set off from society by the special traits of talent and genius, both justifies and maintains the alienation of art from "real life" and the ambivalence that typically characterizes the relationship between artists and audiences.

## THE RESERVATION

The majority of the population in modern industrial societies does not view the arts as central, essential institutions in any personal, individual fashion. That is, for most of us the activities and products associated with the arts are generally outside the mainstream of our daily lives and important concerns.

As I have noted, the term *art,* or *the fine arts,* in the modern sense, came into currency in Europe only in the 18th century. Arguably, the term became conceivable as the common rubric for a diverse class of activities and products partially in response to their increasing irrelevance to the lives of most people. As these various objects and events moved to the periphery of Western culture, their common characteristics became more visible, their differences less noteworthy—hence their ability to shelter comfortably under a common umbrella. To use a metaphor, this process of cultural realignment resulted in the banishment of the arts to a *reservation* on the psychological periphery of Western culture.

By using the image of a reservation I do not mean to imply a dry wasteland at the geographic boundary of our world. I am speaking of a reservation in the sense that we tend to view the arts as institutions that exist at the fringe of society. These are cultural "spaces" that real people *visit* in their spare, fringe time but that only fringe, spare people inhabit in their *real* time. The arts can be said to exist on a reservation, therefore, because their "territory" is foreign to the majority of the population, is visited briefly by a minority as a leisure-time tourist attraction, and is lived in by a tiny minority of special people. Only those with special qualifications (genetic or temperamental) are considered eligible for (or condemned to) full-time residency on this reservation.

It may help to clarify and convey the import of this metaphor if I extend it a bit further. There is another reservation that is adjacent to that on which the arts reside; the two even appear to overlap at points. This reservation contains another institution that has also moved to the periphery of modern Western culture: religion. Again, I use the image to reflect the fact that most people see religion as an activity-institution to be visited in their spare, leisure time and as the full-time occupation-residence of special, somewhat peculiar people. As with the arts, those called or chosen for full-time participation are singled out by special qualifications of soul or temperament. In both cases there is a common tendency to view such cultural specialists—artists and clerics—with a mixture of respect and contempt. They are granted a degree of respect because of their special abilities and their somewhat mysterious status as dwellers in a non-mundane realm. They may also, however, be objects of disdain for that very quality of being removed from real life.

Needless to say, this wasn't always so. Throughout most of Western history, and in most non-Western societies even today, it would be inaccurate to say that religion and the arts (the rubric itself would be inappropriate) occupy positions at the fringe of real life. Certainly, many of their practitioners may have been viewed as special in a variety of ways. However, the activities and products we lump together under these headings can generally be seen in the center of life and consciousness, often joined together. The common observation that art and religion seem to "go together" in many cultures of the past and the non-Western present can be traced to their joint roles as carriers and articulators of these cultures' basic beliefs about the nature of things and about the moral order.

At one time what we call religion was *the* institution that served to explain the way things were in this world and why, as well as how people were meant to behave. The means used to articulate and disseminate these explanations were often those of the arts. Religion and art were intertwined for good reason: They both dealt with matters of great importance—communal and cosmic order. As religion ceased to be the prime source of basic knowledge and value for most people, the arts ceased to be the vehicle of the symbolic functions that integrate and maintain social reality. They became a specialized province of largely meta-communicative creation and appreciation; in a fundamental sense they *don't matter.*[1]

The qualifications for living on these reservations are similar. One needs to have special qualities, what in both cases is frequently called a *vocation.* One is called—motivated by a sense of inner necessity to give up the world of "normal" people and follow a different path. In the case of art the calling is defined by the mysterious spark of talent, even genius, that sets one outside (above?) the mainstream. Children are quick to absorb the contradictory messages they encounter about the arts: They are valued and scorned at the same time, treated with respect yet suspicion, fundamentally alien to the real business of life. Encounters with art take on a pass-fail overtone in which one's innate potential is being assessed. Not surprisingly, most give up, relinquishing any claim to membership in the communicative community of the arts.

## FIRST ENCOUNTERS, LASTING LESSONS

When asked general questions about the arts, most Americans voice the proper pieties as readily as they claim to believe in God and to attend church faithfully. In a 1992 survey conducted for the National Cultural Alliance and reported in the *New York Times* on March 1, 1993, 87 percent of the 1,059 adults questioned said the arts and humanities are life enriching, and 84 percent described them as a means of self-fulfillment. Yet in the same survey, 57 percent said the arts and humanities played only a minor role in their lives as a whole, and 41 percent said they had little to do with their daily lives. In similar surveys, overwhelming proportions have rated the arts as a very important part of life, yet as few as 5 percent said they visit museums or art galleries, and only 6 percent said making art is a leisure activity in which they can participate (Trend, 1992: 1).

The pattern is familiar: The vast majority of adults regard the arts with feelings of inadequacy, incomprehension, and indifference. In brief, most members of our culture view the "arts reservation" as foreign territory to which they have no passport and little inclination to visit. Why should this be so?

One explanation of why adults seem so "deficient" in relation to the arts might be that the raw material is unsuited for transformation into a better product. If few adults are inclined or able to participate competently in artistic enterprises, this may simply reflect the fact that few children arrive with the potential to acquire competence in the arts. Possibly it is the nature of things that only a lucky few possess the essential ingredient—talent—that will permit them to scale the walls and play in the garden, and the best we can hope from society is that it not erect any further barriers that might stifle this talent in its rare appearances. Artistic competence and performance, by this view, are the province of the gifted, and the rest of us can only aspire to join the audience and benefit from their achievements.

There is, however, another possible explanation. Perhaps the capacity to acquire competence in the symbolic modes we associate with the arts is not rare but widespread, and it may wither for lack of nourishment. Is it possible that we are all born with sufficient potential to develop substantial competence in these modes but that we encounter them in a fashion that discourages most children through self-fulfilling assumptions of incapacity? On what basis could we support this argument?

First, there is the point made by ethnomusicologist John Blacking: "Because there are some societies whose members are as competent in music as all people are in language, music may be a species-specific trait of man" (1973: 34). Although it might be argued that such musical societies represent concentrations of inbred talent, it seems as likely, to quote Blacking again, that "the functions of music in society may be the decisive factors promoting or inhibiting latent musical ability" (1973: 35).

In all societies adults are competent in the lexical and social-gestural modes;

those few who are not are invariably defined as deficient—retarded, disturbed, or foreign—and treated accordingly (Gross, 1974). Although everyone will not be equally skillful or creative in his or her native tongue, by early childhood we have all acquired substantial competence in a highly complex symbol system. Why does this not occur in the case of other symbolic modes, at least in our culture?

There is a common pattern in the way children encounter music, say, in those societies Blacking was referring to and the way children encounter language in *all* societies. In both cases they are born into contexts where it is assumed that *everyone* will acquire music/speech, and they are surrounded by competent adult performers who treat their early performative efforts as potentially meaningful and respond to them as such.

In contrast, in our society children typically encounter the arts in contexts where most adults (1) are themselves incompetents, (2) assume that only a genetically chosen few will acquire competence and at least tacitly convey the message that the child is not necessarily expected to get anywhere, and (3) are incapable of responding to the child's beginning efforts in any discriminating fashion (as they would in the case of speech), thus dampening any sense that these modes are vehicles of shared meaning. Imagine the consequences if we assumed that only those possessing special talent would learn to speak.

Our commonsense genetic theory of artistic ability is further reinforced by the observation that artistic competence *does* seem to run in families—parents who actively engage in music seem more likely than others to have children who develop musical skills. But notice that such families are the most likely to possess the characteristics of "musical" societies and all speech communities: Everyone engages in a symbolic mode, and it is implicitly conveyed to children that they are expected to join in.

Encountering the arts in circumstances in which few adults manifest competence or expect it in the child, and the arts do not function as common carriers of cultural knowledge, which thus reinforces their marginal status. And, as has been repeatedly demonstrated, this status is reflected in the tenuous position of the arts in education—arts teachers are the last hired, first fired.

## TEACHING ART AS NONCOMMUNICATION

Viewing the arts as the province of exceptional persons gives them the attributes of value associated with scarce resources. In this case that means we concentrate heavily upon those characteristics of artistic performances and products that most clearly manifest scarcity: the *unique* contributions of the *individual* artist that, almost by definition, will be *innovative* (else how could they be unique?). Thus we put a premium on novelty and make our concept of creativity synonymous with originality.

These core notions of what art is, or should be, often show up in discussions of early art education. For example, in her successful textbook *Teaching Art to Chil-*

*dren*, Blanche Jefferson explicitly and insistently connects the individuality and uniqueness she associates with adult artists to the approach she advocates for art education in primary schools:

> In their studios, artists work independently. This high degree of independence has been identified with art since time began. Each creates works of a highly personal and original nature, and this gives us the tremendously varied and interesting world of art. For example, Picasso works alone in his studio following his own ideas and knowledge, and applying his own critical judgment to his work. These same working conditions are a fundamental aspect of high quality art education. . . . Art is based upon the individuality of the person doing the art. In fact, every child is required and expected to work differently from every other. Therefore, if each child is *not* working in a personal and original way, it is *not* art. (1970: 1, 28)

This emphasis on individuality creates a serious problem for those who believe the arts are media of communication through which members of a culture create and share knowledge, belief, and feeling. Namely, the very essence of communication is that it is grounded in *shared* ways of articulating—conventions and codes—and cannot easily cope with radical innovation. In Claude Levi-Strauss's phrase, "We would never manage to understand each other if, within our society, we formed a series of coteries, each one of which had its own particular language, or if we allowed constant changes and revolutions to take place in language, like those that we have been able to observe now for a number of years in the fine arts" (Charbonnier, 1969: 60).

Parents, schools, and peers convey in a variety of forms the message that art isn't quite "real" and that its ambivalent, peripheral status is appropriate to those who are "called" to it. For those children who do manifest a strong interest and ability in an art form, it is often quickly apparent that others are able to offer them little help. Parents and other adults tend to respond to children's art with generalized, nondiscriminating support (or, in some cases, indifference) that undermines any communicative component. It didn't take long for me, at age six or seven, to realize that my parents' response did not differentiate between artwork I produced that I thought was good and work I knew wasn't; it all went up on the refrigerator door art gallery. In the same way, I understood very well my father's sympathetic comment that although being involved in art was nice, I did need to understand that it wasn't possible to make a living at it (I was about seven at the time and not yet pressed to make a living).

Similarly, children probably draw certain conclusions from the contrast between the almost obligatory "individualism" expected by art teachers like Blanche Jefferson and their peers' views about performance in sports (something that is clearly important). When something really matters, there is a right way to do it, and the boundaries of the permissible are clearly marked. Yet it is in such contexts that children are likely to experience the satisfactions of acquiring a socially valued skill through repetitive practice and interaction with skilled practitioners (Gross, 1973). Sports are far more likely than art to provide children with the aesthetic pleasures of mastery and competence in a shared endeavor. Certainly, some children will quickly achieve a markedly greater level of skill, but differentials in performance need not condemn the less skillful to passivity and exclusion (although in our mass society most people are now cast in the role of passive receiver in sports as well as in the arts).

As long as we place a heavy premium on the importance of talent in the determination of who will be expected to succeed in the acquisition of artistic skill, we erect a hurdle most children will fail to surmount. The issue here is whether the search for talent is in fact an appropriate criterion for setting educational priorities.

The acquisition of sophisticated competence in any symbolic mode requires an enormous investment of time and effort. The basic modes we all learn absorb most of our time and energies as infants, but, of course, we do not assess the activities of young children in terms of productivity. Beyond infancy, however, time is a scarce commodity and must not be squandered too freely on the acquisition of nonremunerative skills (as my father informed me).

In preindustrial periods of Western culture, when handicraft was the major mode of production, the arts were seen in a favorable light by those whose children showed the glimmerings of talent. In such situations it makes more sense to expect that if everyone learns the basic skills, those with unusual ability will be more readily identifiable, than to assume the truly talented will somehow reveal themselves without any particular training. (As we will see, some of this view did survive into the industrial age.)

In the age of the industrial middle classes, training in the arts is largely a luxury of the affluent; far from being a source of income, it is a sign of wealth. Training in the appreciation of art, however, is the middle-class goal; the number of individuals willing to undertake the difficult and hazardous attempt to become self-supporting artists is very small.[2] Even smaller is the number who succeed.

We are faced, then, with a situation in which our respect for artistic talent causes us to cast a narrow rather than a broad net over succeeding generations of children and then to bemoan the fact that so few are engaged with the arts. In John Fowles's phrase, "An artist, as we understand the word today, is someone who does by nature what we should all do by education." The prospect seems bleak indeed with respect to art education as successive generations of children encounter the barriers placed around the reservation and lose interest in gaining entrance for more than brief, perfunctory visits.

## CONTRASTING CASES

The marginal status of the arts in modern Western societies may be further illuminated through contrast with some of the tribal societies that fulfill the conditions enumerated earlier as those most likely to encourage the acquisition of skill in the various symbolic modes. I have cited John Blacking's conclusion that "music may be a species-specific trait of man." This is based on his extensive study of the Venda of southern Africa, who believe "that all normal human beings are capable of musical performance" (1973: 34). Blacking notes that music is a constant feature of Venda life: "The Venda learn to understand the sounds of music as they understand speech" (1973: 40).

Although the Venda expect everyone to be musically competent, they do not deny the existence of individual differences in musical ability. This is not a situation where, in the words of W. S. Gilbert, "when everyone is somebody, then no one's anybody."

> The Venda may not consider the possibility of unmusical human beings, but they do recognize that some people perform better than others. Judgment is based on the performer's display of technical brilliance and originality, and the vigor and confidence of his execution. . . . In applauding the mastery of exceptional musicians, the Venda applaud human effort, and in being able to recognize mastery in the musical medium, listeners reveal that their general musical competence is no less than that of the musicians whom they applaud. We should remember that the existence of Bach and Beethoven depends on discriminating audiences as much as on performers. (Blacking, 1973: 46–47)

Another example of a society in which the arts are viewed as part of the common repertoire comes from Daniel Crowley's description of the Chokwe of the Congo (1971). Here again we find the recognition of singular abilities and the existence of semiprofessional status in a society of amateurs:

> Every home possessed a few objects decorated beyond function, and nearly every village had two or three pieces of impressive quality. . . . Most Chokwe are able to make some of these objects for themselves, while others are almost always purchased from a professional. . . . The only artist who made his living exclusively by the sale of his products was the potter Kalandjisa. Otherwise all the artists with whom we worked carried on farming and tended sheep and goats as the major source of their livelihood. . . . Virtually every village had at least one practicing artist of more than routine skill, and most had several in different media, while every home had at least one object of merit by Western standards. (Crowley, 1971: 316–318)

A final example is provided by the Akan of Ghana, described by J.H. Kwabena Nketia as a people for whom "the enjoyment or satisfaction which a social occasion gives to the participants is directly related to its artistic content—to the scope it gives for the sharing of artistic experience through the display of art objects, the performance of music, dancing, or the recital of poetry" (1973: 82). The focal role of the arts in Akan social life does not, however, isolate a distinct class of artists apart from their fellows: "It is important to emphasize here that while the musician is recognized in Akan society as a person whose gifts and services are needed by the community, he is not treated or regarded in a class apart from the rest of the members of his society. Nor can he himself find means of expressing his musicianship by working in isolation from everybody else. On the contrary, it is as a member of a group that it is believed he can make his distinctive contribution" (Nketia, 1973: 83). Given this, we are not surprised to find that the Akan, like the Venda and the Chokwe, differentiate among the degrees of ability manifested by various members of their group. Despite their emphasis on group participation in musical performances, "distinctions are made between different grades of performers, on the basis of levels of performance skill coupled with knowledge and ability or skill" (Nketia, 1973: 83).

Nketia's description of musical training among the Akan gives an extended illustration of the principles I've noted as essential for the widespread cultivation of symbolic competence and the integration of artistic talent in society.

> As far as it is known, the principle of musical education has always been that of *slow absorption* through exposure to musical situations and active participation, rather than formal teaching. The very organization of traditional music in social life enables the individual to acquire his musical knowledge in slow stages, to widen his experience of the music of his culture through the social groups into which he is progressively incorporated and the activities in which he takes part. . . . It seems safe to conclude, then, that the perpetuation of tradition has depended very largely on the opportunities created in a community for learning through participation, through imitation and slow absorption, rather than on institutional methods. Musical instruction is part of what students of culture have come to describe as the enculturative process. Traditional instruction thus includes all the means by which an individual, during his entire lifetime, assimilates the musical traditions of his culture to the extent that he is able to express himself in creative efforts and in performance in terms of that tradition. (Nketia, 1973: 87–89)

The relevance of the Akan example for our own situation is not missed by Nketia, as he observes the consequences for the Akan of their acculturation into Western values. Noting that "a change in social organization such as we find now minimizes the chances of learning by participation," he concludes that the cumulative effect of over a hundred years of Western education, which removes the child from the traditional enculturative process, may be that "one may become a mere spectator, having missed the opportunity of learning through participation" (Nketia, 1973: 89–90).

## CHILDHOOD, ART, AND EDUCATION

The roots of our present ambivalence about the arts and their relation to the education of children can be traced to conflicting tendencies inherent in Western views of art and of childhood. The period that witnessed the migration of art to an honored but marginal position on the periphery of culture also experienced the impact of romantic notions of childhood. Kant left an enduring legacy for our views of art by opposing the aesthetic to the utilitarian, defining art by its lack of any practical purpose; Rousseau shaped our views of childhood with his image of the child as a creature of nature uncorrupted by society. In the two centuries since these ideas became part of our cultural perspective, we have seen repeated use of the child as a metaphor for the artist. When Baudelaire presents the child as the pure archetype of the "painter of modern life" (Schapiro, 1978: 63), he is not suggesting that the child is a skilled creator but, rather, is emphasizing the importance of the child's innocent but intense sensations of discovery.

The enduring influence of romanticism in Western culture has made this Rousseauian attitude a cornerstone of our view of the arts and has shaped our understanding of the conflict between convention and individualism in art. The fifteenth and sixteenth centuries saw the emergence of individualism as a force that changed art and religion; in the late eighteenth century romanticism raised the role of individualism in art to a new level through its emphasis not on the skill of the artist but on the artist's unique personal vision. Art was seen as an expression of this vision; in Zola's famous dictum, "a work of art is a bit of nature seen through a temperament": "The substitution of an expressive for a mimetic theory of the arts put a new emphasis on the authenticity of the emotions expressed and, consequently, on the artist's sincerity and integrity. Spontaneity, individuality and 'inner truth' came in this way to be recognized as the criteria by which all works of art, literature and music, of all periods and countries, should be judged" (Honour, 1979: 20).

Sincerity and integrity were often demonstrated, it appeared, by distortions of form or color, perspective or handling. Awkwardness in drawing could be seen as evidence of sincerity, as when the symbolist painter and critic Maurice Denis wrote in 1895, "I call awkwardness this sort of maladroit affirmation through which the personal emotion of an artist is translated outside of accepted formulas" (quoted in Shiff, 1978: 363). It is not hard to understand how contemporary educators began to look at children's drawings with new interest.

Although we might reasonably assume that children have been drawing for millennia, we have little evidence that anyone paid much attention to their efforts; when they did, it seems invariably to have been the precocity of the child that was noted (as in the apocryphal account of Giotto as a young shepherd, discovered drawing on a rock with a piece of stone by the artist Cimabue; cf. Kris and Kurtz, 1979). The Italian art theorist Corrado Ricci reported that his interest in children's art began one day in the 1880s when he was on his way to the University of Bologna. It began raining, and Ricci took shelter under a portico. As he was waiting, he noticed that the walls were covered with drawings at various heights. The lowest row, and to him the most charming, was made by the youngest children, he reasoned; the highest by the oldest. This discovery led him to form an interest in children's drawing and to write *L'Arte dei Bambini* (1887), the first interpretation of the way children draw people. Shortly afterward, James Sully published his *Studies of Childhood* (1895), and in 1897 Franz Cizek opened his Juvenile Art Class in Vienna, the first school to base its instructional techniques on the concept of "child art."

These pioneers of art education were not, however, the only voices urging that children should be educated in art; they can be contrasted with a group of educators who espoused with equal fervor a very different point of view. If the first group was impressed with the innocent creativity of the child—as exemplified by Ricci's preference for the scribblings of the youngest of the graffitists—the second group was determined to treat art as a subject to be taught like any other but also as a particularly important subject because it saw education in art as a precondition for industrial success: "The universal importance of instruction in drawing was not fully recognized until the products of the arts and industries of the various nations met each other at the World's Fairs. It then became evident that most raw materials receive their value in social interchange through form only; and that therefore the education of form, according to aesthetic principles, is the first condition for the successful development of industry, as well as for the elevation of taste in general" (Langl, 1875: 5). Professor Langl's report "Modern Art Education" was part of the Austrian Official Report on the Vienna World's Fair of 1873, and in the introduction to the U.S. edition, Charles Stetson drew a clear lesson for the United States: "Europe is putting into her industries millions of men and women trained in art and science, but especially in art; and she is making vast and systematic efforts to elevate as well the public taste as that of the artisans. We can do no less; we can meet such competition only in kind; our people must be educated in art" (Stetson, 1875: xxxiv).

But Stetson knew his urgings were in conflict with the prevalent views of art, and he tried to counter the objections he expected, claiming "it is no degradation of art, as the same thing is no degradation of geometry, to make it subserve the cause of industry; that is only making art perform a portion of its legitimate work" (Stetson, 1875: xxxviii). The core of the resistance, however, was not the sacred inviolability of art divorced by Kantian dogma from the corruption of utility; there was also the romantic vision of the artist's unique sensibility, of art as the product of individual talent. As Stetson knew, "Those who regard art mainly or wholly as a matter of feeling believe it cannot be taught as other things are taught" (Stetson, 1895: xxxviii–xxxix). Thus, he anticipated objections

from those who look upon art as something peculiarly divine. They are shocked when one talks of making art contribute to the daily wages of the artisan, to the volume of trade, to national prosperity, and the sinews of war. . . . They also believe that instruction in neither industrial nor fine art can be reduced to fixed principles and methods, and so believe that art cannot be taught in schools as other things are taught. Consequently they take delight in telling how impossible it is to do what the great masters have done, instead of attempting to show how the great masters actually went to work to secure their wonderful results. (Stetson, 1875: xxxvii)

Stetson and his colleagues won the battle but lost the war. Between the 1870s and the beginning of World War I, training in pictorial media indeed became an established curricular subject—of 996 city school systems in the United States surveyed in 1907, 99.7 percent reported that manual and mechanical drawing was a mandatory subject in the public elementary schools (Bailey, 1909)—and the growth of the high school and of technical schools during the same period also expanded the overall time devoted to training in visual media. However, the role that was forecast for the arts in industrial competition did not turn out quite the way Stetson had expected. He granted that "Americans have especially distinguished themselves in devising labor-saving machinery, and have been abundantly rewarded for thus cheapening production," but he confidently assumed that the route to ultimate industrial success led in another direction: "It is taste especially which can contribute to the value of innumerable manufactures; which always tends to enhance, never to diminish, prices" (Stetson, 1875: xxiv). As the history of industrial production shows, however, Frederick Taylor and Henry Ford were better prophets than Charles Stetson, and U.S. industrial supremacy was built on the economies of scale rather than the achievements of artistic design.

By the end of the nineteenth century, the educational methods espoused by those who sought to "treat instruction in drawing and art as a matter which can be subjected to reason, and [be] treated according to true pedagogical principles" (Stetson, 1875: xxxv) came under attack by the first generation of "progressive" educators, who argued that these methods paid insufficient attention to the developing needs of the individual child. Progressive education as a whole tended to wane after the 1920s, to return again with renewed vigor in the 1960s (cf. Cremin, 1961). In the area of art education, however, progressive approaches did not decline but continued to expand, dominating the field after World War II.

The strength of the progressive position in shaping arts education policy can be seen, perhaps, in the claim of its most influential proponent, John Dewey, that whereas in "traditional" education "the subject matter . . . consists of bodies of information and skills that have been worked out in the past," in progressive education "to imposition from above is opposed expression and cultivation of individuality; to external discipline is opposed free activity; to learning from texts and teachers, learning through experience" (1938: 17–19). This way lies Blanche Jefferson.

The undisputed sincerity of this progressive position nonetheless reinforces the isolation of the arts from the things that really matter and further weakens the basis for art education. To the extent that art education is seen as a realm for purely individual expression and development, for which shared standards do not apply, then all that children, teachers, parents, and the rest of us have to fall back on—besides a trivializing solipsism (if it feels good, it must be good)—is the mystery of talent and vocation.

### THE TALENT TRAP

Here we arrive at a dilemma that is still very much with us: the conflict between our deep-seated and abiding romantic belief in the necessity of unusual talent and unique individuality for the emergence of artistic ability and the uncomfortable realization that we aren't sure how to recognize or cultivate talent when it appears.

As a society made up of people who are mostly unsure of their judgment in the arts and who are aware of their own lack of skill, we perpetuate a contradictory set of views that trap most of us into dropping out. The progressive position we at least vaguely adhere to does not provide us with any standards by which to judge performance. The (Blanche) Jeffersonian ideology of uniqueness has a leveling effect that discourages discrimination—here, indeed, if every child is somebody, then no child is anybody. Lacking an alternative basis for judgment, then, in the most general sense—and this applies for children around nine to twelve years old—"photographic realism is the commonplace criterion for being a good artist. The ubiquity with which this standard is upheld and the relatively low priority given to drawing instruction result in most children giving up on artistic expression in despair and disgust" (Pariser, 1989: vol. 1, 260).

Thus it is that inside most adults in our society there hides a nine-year-old, who only emerges when and if the adult is forced to try to draw something. Most of the time we are not even aware of the existence of this vestigial nine-year-old we carry around, and our abiding sense of alienation and insecurity about the arts is kept under control by the simple device of staying away from the reservation to which the arts are confined.

It is also important to understand that the ideology of talent and individuality as the passport to the reservation is congruent with the institutional structure of the official, elite art worlds. These professional art worlds (Becker, 1982) are structured mostly around (supposedly) singular artists whose talent, vision, and, of course, products are the focal points of economic speculation for a complex group of dealers, critics, museum curators, collectors, and art historians. The entrepreneurial role of contemporary artists requires them to achieve a distinctive and marketable individuality, and this in turn supports the romantic view of the artist as creating out of a personal vision. As Meyer Schapiro noted in 1937, "Modern artists . . . consider their art a free projection of an irreducible personal feeling, but must form their style in competition against others, with the obsessing sense of the originality of their work as a mark of its sincerity" (1978: 188).

The solution to the problem would seem to lie in radical changes in the ways our culture conceives of both art and education. But in another perspective, we may be unnecessarily narrow if we focus only on the limits of art education. *Most* of what our children encounter in their schooling fails to engage them in a very meaningful way. To create the conditions for real education in art would likely require a radical restructuring of our educational priorities and methods. A program for early education that focuses on the acquisition of competence in primary modes of thought and action—lexical, iconic, musical, logico-mathematical—understood as communicative systems (Gross, 1974) could make possible a fuller employment of human potential than we now achieve.

The "health" of a culture may not depend upon the degree to which all its members are competent in each of these modes—a division of labor may be both more adaptive and more responsive to a natural variability of native potential. It will, however, depend upon the ability of each member to acquire sufficient mastery to experience the basic, "self-actualizing" satisfactions that give meaning and lasting value to one's life. I contend that such satisfactions have the characteristic Ruth Benedict and Abe Maslow termed *social synergy*—that is, they transcend conflicts between the interests of the individual and the interests of society by valuing most highly the inherently abundant, rather than the inherently scarce, resources upon which most of our notions of value and wealth are based.

The achievement of satisfaction through the acquisition of inherently scarce resources (for example, material wealth) will have the effect of weakening some of the ties that bind together and support the members of a society as it inevitably reduces the amount of resources available to others. But the satisfactions attendant upon the mastery and exercise of symbolic skills are based on inexhaustible resources—knowledge and information, art and beauty, love and affection. Unlike material wealth, knowledge is increased when it is shared. These resources and the pleasures they bring are limited only by the social, symbolic, and emotional competence of human beings and by their willingness and opportunity to invest the effort required to achieve, maintain, and extend that competence. Information and art can be made into scarce resources; they can be secreted, hoarded, and their material value thus increased. But they can only be multiplied through social interaction and sharing; the atomization of culture will not feed its continued growth.

### NOTES

1. Carol Duncan, writing about her experiences teaching art history in an elite college, refers to her students' puzzlement at "the general tendency of modern society to consign creative activity to the ambiguous position of something both very important (more meaningful than common experience and highly status-conferring) and not important at all (totally useless and irrelevant to 'real,' material values)" (1993: 136).

2. Youthful investment of time and energy in the acquisition of potentially marketable skills is more likely to be found today on the basketball court and among members of garage rock bands than in art studios and music conservatories.

### REFERENCES

Bailey, H. T. [1909] *Instruction in the Fine and Manual Arts in the United States: A Statistical Monograph.* Washington, D.C.: U.S. Bureau of Education Bulletin: 6.
Becker, Howard S. [1982] *Art Worlds.* Berkeley: University of California Press.
Blacking, John [1973] *How Musical Is Man?* Seattle: University of Washington Press.
Charbonnier, Georges [1969] *Conversations with Claude Levi-Strauss.* London: Jonathan Cape.

Cremin, Lawrence [1961] *The Transformation of the School: Progressivism in American Education, 1876–1957.* New York: Knopf.

Crowley, Daniel J. [1971] "An African Aesthetic." In Carol Jopling, ed., *Art and Aesthetics in Primitive Societies.* New York: Dutton, pp. 315–327.

Dewey, John [1938] *Experience and Education.* New York: Collier.

Duncan, Carol [1993] "Teaching the Rich." In *The Aesthetics of Power: Essays in Critical Art History.* New York: Cambridge University Press, pp. 135–142.

Gross, Larry [1973] "Art as the Communication of Competence." *Social Science Information* 15.

———. [1974] "Modes of Communication and the Acquisition of Symbolic Competence." In D. R. Olson, ed., *Media and Symbol.* Chicago: University of Chicago Press, pp. 56–80.

Honour, Hugh [1979] *Romanticism.* New York: Harper and Row.

Jefferson, Blanche [1970] *Teaching Art to Children.* 3rd edition. Boston: Allyn and Bacon.

Kris, Ernst, and Otto Kurtz [1979] *Legend, Myth and Magic in the Image of the Artist.* New Haven: Yale University Press (original edition 1934).

Kristeller, Paul [1990a] "The Modern System of the Arts." In *Renaissance Thought and the Arts.* Princeton: Princeton University Press, pp. 163–227 (original publication of article 1951–1952).

———. [1990b] "Afterword: 'Creativity' and 'Tradition.'" In *Renaissance Thought and the Arts.* Princeton: Princeton University Press, pp. 247–258 (original publication of article 1983).

Langl, Joseph [1875] *Modern Art Education: Its Practical and Aesthetic Character Educationally Considered.* Boston: L. Prang and Co.

Nketia, J.H. Kwabena [1973] "The Musician in Akan Society." In Warren d'Azevedo, ed., *The Traditional Artist in African Societies.* Bloomington: Indiana University Press, pp. 79–100.

Pariser, David [1989] "Child Art." In Erik Barnouw, ed., *International Encyclopedia of Communications.* New York: Oxford University Press, vol. 1, pp. 258–262.

Ricci, Corrado [1887] *L'Arte dei Bambini.* Bologna: Zenichelli.

Schapiro, Meyer [1978] *Modern Art: 19th and 20th Centuries.* New York: George Braziller.

Shiff, Richard [1978] "The End of Impressionism: A Study in the Theories of Artistic Expression." *Art Quarterly.*

Stetson, Charles B. [1875] "Introduction." In Joseph Langl, *Modern Art Education: Its Practical and Aesthetic Character Educationally Considered.* Boston: L. Prang and Co.

Sully, James [1895] *Studies of Childhood.* London: Longmans, Green and Co.

Trend, David [1992] *Cultural Pedagogy: Art/Education/Politics.* New York: Bergin and Garvey.

# ❧ 2 ❧

# Negotiating
# the Critical Discourse:
# The Armory Show Revisited

## MOIRA MCLOUGHLIN

The critic as interpreter owes his existence to the alienation and antipathy, and not to the sympathy, which most people bring to the great works of art.

(Hauser, 1982: 473)

To STAND BEFORE WHAT ARNOLD HAUSER has called the "great works of art" is, for many gallery visitors, to become aware of the very act of looking. Counseled prior to viewing a work, the visitor self-consciously searches for those marks of creativity and genius already established outside his or her own experience. As art's audience, we search for what we have already learned we will see. Inheritors of a particular aesthetic discourse, we know both what to look at and what to look for. The layers of evaluation that have been shaped by a multitude of individuals have settled to transparently encase the work and to inform how the work should be approached. The evaluative history of a work becomes an integral element in both contemporary and future reception: Each viewer approaches a work through a filter of earlier evaluation. This history constructs a unique discourse that locates the work within the particular aesthetic, social, and political concerns of its audience and becomes a critical factor in our perception. The critic, in providing an audience with materials necessary for the "appreciation" of art, also produces the very conditions of its engagement.

The premise of this study is that the transparent nature of the evaluative discourse is what allows it to be perceived by its reader as an objective vocabulary within which a work is to be studied. The critical evaluation, in the form of the art historical text, critical review, or exhibition catalogue, takes on the appearance of "evidence" for a particular reading of art history. Michael Baldwin,

Charles Harrison, and Mel Ramsden (1981) have noted, "They [critics and con-
noisseurs] have been allowed to decide not just *what* will stand the test of time,
but what that residue is to be seen *as*" (p. 435). These texts are, therefore, extremely important contributors to the self-consciousness brought to the viewing
by an audience member.

As a receiver of art, the gallery visitor is encouraged to decipher the subjective
code, to isolate within form and content, value and meaning. However, rarely
acknowledged is the idea that the critical tools provided for deciphering are
themselves cultural constructs, determined by distinct judgments of value. A
failure to "understand" an artwork could also be viewed as the inability of the
viewer to integrate an evaluative history into contemporary reception. This study
looks at the critical response inherited by an audience for use in deciphering a
work as itself a primary text—that is, not simply as a crystal reflection of an innate value but as a product of the concerns of a professional audience, the critic.

## CONSTRUCTION OF THE TRANSPARENT
## CRITICAL TEXT

Audience studies carried out in art galleries and museums have shared the conclusions of educators and sociologists that competence in the artistic code that
structures the evaluative discourse is the "basic precondition for the creation or
comprehension of symbolic meaning" (Gross, 1974: 57). Legitimization of a formal discourse and the necessity of mediation require a highly defined code, inac-
cessible without education and exposure. Education is the "deciphering stencil"
applied to a work of art, disclosing "signification at different levels according to
the degree to which the individual has mastered the code" (Bourdieu, 1968: 592).
It is argued that only with repeated exposure to artworks and history can a student interiorize and integrate the structuring code and thus become so fluent as
to be able to create an independent evaluation using the language of the current
evaluative discourse. Access to the "legitimate" culture is, thereby, effectively limited, and control by a few is preserved.

As a substitute for education and exposure, audiences are offered the critic,
fluent in the discourse, who constructs from his or her experience an evaluation
designed for consumption by a larger audience. As Barbara Herrnstein Smith
(1988) has noted, to evaluate a work of art is "to estimate its potential value for
others" (p. 13). However, as the critic's "ability to make that estimation increases
in time with general and specific knowledge" (Smith, 1988: 13), the acquisition of
this education makes the critic increasingly less like members of the audience.
The critical writing then becomes less an evaluation to be shared than a lesson to
be taught. Evaluation is presented as fact, unchallenged in its reception. Evaluative language takes on the appearance of description or explanation: unquestion-

able, authoritative, and transparent. This particular language has become the medium on which many gallery visitors depend for information about a work. Unfamiliar with the codes of art, the visitor turns to labels, catalogues, art historical texts, and reviews for the "meaning" of a work. A particular reading, modeled within the current discourse, *becomes* both what the picture is to express and an active builder of the very discourse that provides authority and legitimacy.

Continued control of the formal aesthetic discourse by the critic requires that its subject be made at once more complex, to ensure the need for a mediator, and more simple, so as to convince the reader that, in fact, mediation is successful. In writing the critical review, a multitude of possible evaluations are reduced by the critic to a single, seemingly objective value. The proposed classification of the object as "art" is posited first, and then those characteristics that satisfy this categorization are isolated and constructed into a single definition of the object. The statement is, however, couched within a complex discourse, access to which is limited to the few who are educated in the codes that constructed it. As the quote from Hauser that opened this chapter suggests, the adoption of an evaluative discourse determined by an "expert" has been necessitated by the isolation of art within a formal aesthetic discourse removed from the immediate concerns of our culture, thereby denying any possibility of "sympathy." Sympathy demands familiarity; it requires an active understanding of the nature of the object.

## THE ARMORY SHOW

This study looks at the negotiation of the aesthetic discourse through a particular and highly contested event: the 1913 Armory Show. The show was the first large-scale exhibition of modernism in the United States and was responsible for unprecedented challenges to, and a reexamination of, the American art world's boundaries and definitions. The exhibition was sponsored by the Association of American Painters and Sculptors, a group that came into being in frustrated response to the absence of exhibition space for the moderns, European or American. Earlier splinter groups from the National Academy had attempted to establish alternative art organizations and exhibitions, but none were extant in 1913. Only three small galleries (Alfred Stiegltiz's "291," the Folsom Gallery, and the Madison Gallery) had, by February 1913, presented the works of moderns such as Matisse, Picasso, and Brancusi. The exhibitions, however, drew little or no press coverage.

The original concept behind the Armory Show was to stage a large and comprehensive exhibition of what the association believed to be the most progressive painters and sculptors working in the United States. (Members of the association were automatically included in this definition.) However, the interest of the organization's president (Arthur P. Davies) in the European moderns took him and the group's secretary (Walter Kuhn) to exhibitions in Germany, France, Holland,

and England in search of works to include in an expanded show. It was the European works acquired on the trip that became the center of critical and public attention.

The works exhibited were primarily French, as the organizers believed Paris to be the heart of the modernist revolution. The works of Gauguin, Van Gogh, and Cézanne were well represented. Other modern artists who received considerable attention from the press included Duchamp, Matisse, Picabia, and Brancusi. The works of the German expressionists were omitted, dismissed by Davies and Kuhn as "adapters" and "imitators" of the French, with little significance for the future of modernism. The Italian futurists, who insisted upon being exhibited as a group, were refused, rejected by Davies as "feeble realists." English painting was not widely represented, as the organizers believed the work exhibited little force and showed no "substantial development." Finally, because of the shortage of travel time, the only Russian artist to be included was Kandinsky.

The U.S. section was a representation of the works of association members, including works by both Kuhn and Davies. The European acquisitions were met with considerable resentment from many association members, who feared their own works might suffer from a comparison with those of the foreign artists. However, because Davies had made arrangements for their inclusion, and he was the only member capable of raising the necessary funds to mount the show in a short time, the situation was accepted with reservation by the majority of association members.

The Armory Show's organizers attempted to ease the shock of the moderns by putting together a comprehensive look at modernism and its artistic lineage (Figure 2.1). The exhibition was set up so works by what were called modernism's predecessors "explained" the moderns as a natural outgrowth of an identifiable and logical tradition. The physical setting reflected Davies's chart, suggesting that art is progressive, moving unmistakably toward its future, and, it is hinted, requiring the sacrifice of stability. The show, in its construction of an explanatory exhibition, strove to convince its audience that the values that had been ascribed to art were not shattered but transformed. Frederick James Gregg, who wrote the show's catalogue, argued that "the moral is that there is nothing final in art, no last word and that the main thing is not to be taken in on one hand, and not to be blind on the other" (cited in Kuhn, 1972: 25).

Nothing Gregg could write, however, was sufficient to cushion the shock of the works and the indignation of many of the critics. The public responded slowly at first, but attendance rose dramatically in the third week of the exhibition as word of mouth and the writings of critics spread. The audience arrived to be both shocked (the room housing the cubist works was quickly dubbed the "Chamber of Horrors") and entertained. Art teachers indignantly guided classes through the "vulgar, lawless and profane" works of art, until the organizers claimed their outspoken rejections were upsetting fellow visitors. The crowds became so thick that the price of admission in the mornings was raised from 25 cents to one dollar

| Classicists | Realists | Romanticists |
|---|---|---|
| Ingres | Courbet | Delacroix |
| Corot | Manet | Daumier |
| Puvis de Chavannes | Monet | Redon |
| Degas | Sisley | Renoir |
| Seurat | Pissaro | |
| | Signac | |
| | Cassatt | |
| | Lautrec | |
| | Morisot | |
| Cézanne | Cézanne | |
| | | Van Gogh |
| Gauguin | | Gauguin |
| Matisse | | |
| Post-Impressionists | | |
| Cubists | Futurists | |
| Picasso | (feeble realists) | |
| (classic) | | |

FIGURE 2.1  Arthur Davies's Chronological Chart Outlining the Growth of Modern Art, *Arts and Decoration* 3 (March 1913), p. 150.

in order to provide the "serious" public with an opportunity to study the works. Public officials in both New York and Chicago (where the show later moved) tried unsuccessfully to have the show closed as a menace to public morality. The exhibition, despite abundant negative response, had successfully introduced "modernism" into the art vocabulary of twentieth-century Americans.

The focus of analysis in this study is 126 critical reviews of the Armory Show, located in four art periodicals, nine review magazines, and five New York newspapers.[1] The periodicals were studied for the year preceding and following the show, and newspapers were followed from January to June 1913. Included in the sample were reviews of the show as well as articles that addressed the artists, the works, and issues regarding post-impressionism, cubism, and futurism.

### NEGOTIATING AESTHETIC BOUNDARIES

However it was cushioned, modernism could *not* be accommodated within the confines of the evaluative criteria of the dominant discourse. For the public and for the large majority of critics, these works looked like nothing they had seen or read of before. The rage and derision expressed in the negative reviews of the

Armory Show are at first glance unlikely and extreme reactions to paintings and
sculpture one can, at will, leave behind or choose not to see. A work, if considered inadequate in technique, creativity, or sincerity, could more efficiently be
dismissed if its critics chose *not* to acknowledge it in any sense, positively or neg-
atively. This point was made by a visitor to the Armory Show in a letter to the
*New York Evening Post:* "Left severely alone by the press, the wretched eclipse
brought on by them would have been of but brief duration. But they have already
caused mischief" (Bloor, 1913: 8). Smith (1988) noted that a work that is not discussed, reviewed, or cited will quickly disappear from sight, to survive, if at all, as
a physical relic: "One of the major effects of prohibiting or inhibiting explicit
evaluation is to forestall the exhibition and obviate the possible acknowledgment
of divergent systems of value and, thus to ratify, by default, established evaluative
authority" (p. 29).

Response to the European moderns at the Armory Show emerged from a frustrated inability to locate the works within a familiar history. The audience was
unable to turn to trusted art historians for clues as to how the works of artists
such as Cézanne and Duchamp should be approached. The critics of 1913 were
*the* evaluative authority who supplied to the public the vocabulary and references
for their judgments. And although many of the critics ridiculed and rejected the
works, none chose to ignore them. The question to ask the Armory Show critics,
then, is what motivated such an outpouring of denial (and, consequently, an encouragement of attendance) when a critical "freeze" would have more effectively
reduced the visibility of the exhibition.

Many of the arguments put forward here are greatly indebted to the "method-
ological prescription" of Baldwin, Harrison, and Ramsden (1981), founded on the
premise that "what a work of art means is determined by what it is *possible* that it
means" (p. 439). To preserve the evaluative discourse adopted and their own position as authorities, critics must assume or maintain "that the particular functions they expect and desire the class of objects in question . . . to perform are
their intrinsic function" (Smith, 1988: 40). The critical discourse is inevitably informed by both past and contemporary ideas and beliefs about what art is and
what functions it might serve. The critic's reading highlights those features or
qualities that can be seen as potentially fulfilling the preconceived evaluation.
The artwork is measured against all others like it. If it is discovered that there is no
other like it, it must be determined whether the work is an extension of the tradition
or a departure from it and whether the definition of art, as previously known, can be
preserved. Leo Steinberg (1972) wrote that one way for the critic to cope with the
"provocation of novel art" is to "rest firm and maintain solid standards" (p. 63). The
conviction must be maintained that "only those innovations will be significant
which promote the established direction of advanced art" (Steinberg, 1972: 63).

In discussing his own negative first reactions to the target paintings of Jasper
Johns, Steinberg (1973) proposed that the experience of losing control is the confused response to being asked to "applaud the destruction of values which we still

cherish" (p. 224) without being clearly offered a reason for the sacrifice or a substitute value. He stated that the paintings had placed him in the position of evaluating in the "absence of available standards" (1973: 224). This sentiment is one that recurs in studies that have addressed critical reception, and I suggest it can pose a serious obstacle to the study of the "plight" of the critic or the public.

In his history of the Armory Show, Milton Brown (1963) presented a similar argument, expressing the view that the critics "for the defense" could not base their evaluations on "accepted standards of artistic judgment" and were obliged to establish a "whole new set of values" (p. 150). Available standards are *not* absent; they are very much entrenched within the evaluative discourse brought to the viewing. The discomfort and disorientation experienced on first viewing a Johns or a Duchamp is evidence that "available standards" are being put into play and are rejecting the works as incompatible. Like appreciation and acceptance, rejection is active rather than passive, requiring the engagement of the adopted evaluative discourse. The absence of standards would preclude any involvement with the work, making even the judgment of "absurd" impossible. Steinberg (1973) asserted, "Modern art always projects itself into a twilight zone where no values are fixed" (p. 224). The "perpetual anxiety" induced by new art threatens a fixed and authoritative discourse and challenges aesthetic indifference. The anxiety is born, however, not from an "absence of standards" but from the demand that those standards be confronted. As Smith (1988) has observed, the critic's sense of control over the aesthetic environment falters when the categories by which experience has been organized prove inadequate.

Also to be challenged is Brown's (1963) argument that the attack on modernism in 1913 was brought about by an "irrational" attachment to the past and an "ignorance" of the new art movement and its "goals and intentions" (p. 83). He related that the critics "arose like knights to protect the sacred house of art from an imagined affront" (1963: 83). I contend that there was nothing "imagined" about the threat posed by modernism. As has been argued earlier, the dismissal of modernism does not necessarily imply an inability to understand the art or a hallucination about "imagined affronts" but, rather, represents a profound appreciation of the potential ability of modernism to disrupt the conservative position in the art world. Critics of the Armory Show could genuinely fear the European artists, for their work suggested the existence of a public (albeit a small one in 1913) that might not rely on the critics' evaluations. "Art" for this potential public could no longer be discussed within the confines of the evaluative criteria of the dominant discourse. The discourse is modified, and new concerns and qualities become significant, reflecting shifts in the perceived function of art and the makeup of its public. Despite implications that modernism was an invasive "virus," with its origins outside the social order defined by its critics, the vehement denial that met the European works suggests that the critics worried that a public *could* be discovered within their world—a public that must be warned of the insidious, but irrelevant, nature of the work.

## A COMMON DISCOURSE
## FOR DIVERGENT VOICES

Earlier histories of the Armory Show have defined its impact and influences in the terms of its detractors. However, my study revealed that although opposition was predominant and particularly impassioned, supportive voices were heard in all but four of the twenty periodicals studied. It is vital that this balance be reintroduced into the show's history. The debate must not be seen simply as individual differences of opinion over particular works or artists but as power struggles over the domain in which the works should be discussed, struggles over how art is defined and by whom. A *New York Globe and Commercial Advertiser* critic wrote, "I have never heard a crowd of people talk so much about meaning and about life, and so little about technique, value, tone, drawing and perspective" (Hapgood, 1913b: 8).

The language adopted most by the critics—its themes and metaphors—emphasized concern for control over art's boundaries. Negative reviews concentrated on the preservation of what was consistently referred to as a "shared language"—shared by artists, critics, and audiences. What was perceived as modernism's unregulated individualism threatened to deny the audience (and, most important, the critic) access to the work through the known vocabulary. Supportive reviews argued for the extension of that language so it might accommodate and recognize the new vocabulary of modernism. What has been the greatest weakness of earlier Armory Show histories is their failure to recognize that what was being argued in these reviews was *not* simply polar positions but a shared evaluative discourse challenged by modernism and the preservation of an aesthetic order in which each critic had claimed a stake. Study of 126 critical reviews in newspapers, art journals, and review magazines revealed that evaluative criteria and descriptive language were common property put to very different uses in defense of particular positions: boundaries constructed with shared materials drawn from the dominant discourse but situated on very different lines.

Study of the reviews addressed the interpretive methods most often employed in the construction of the critical evaluation. Particular themes and language emerge regularly as the evaluative criteria used in both positive and negative responses. Rather than concentrating on judgments of individual artists or on those made by particular critics, I contended that an emphasis must be placed not on differences but on those criteria or concerns *shared* by the critics, regardless of their judgment. The illumination of those issues disputed and those agreed upon points out the characteristics assigned to a "valuable" work of art and the perceived function of that work.

I concentrate here on what was perhaps the most fascinating use of language in the re-creation of aesthetic boundaries. Critics developed measures of the artists' physical and spiritual health and repeatedly employed metaphors equating the artwork with the human body, as a possessor of mental and physical attributes and defects. Diagnoses of the state of the creative artists' health, of the effect the artwork might have on its audience, and of the health of the artwork abounded in the critical texts. The paintings and sculptures were discussed as if they were biological organisms subject to physical and mental changes. Hutchins Hapgood (1913c) noted, "Thousands of persons had approached these silent things as if they were human temperaments, expressing their passionate convictions about experience" (p. 9).

My attention was drawn to this association in an article by Kate Flint (1983) in which she argues that late nineteenth-century English art criticism often assumed a normative approach in its discussion of artworks that employed "pairs of opposites used elsewhere to define the human Victorian subject" (p. 60). Playing on the same "associations of approval and disapprobation" noted by Flint, Armory Show critics utilized opposites that included life-death, health-illness, growth-decay, sanity-insanity, decorum-aggression, and sophistication-primitivism. As willful bodies it could be argued that individual works were responsible for the continued existence of art and were capable of its destruction and regeneration.

The possession of "life" or "vitality" was a criterion prized by the show's critics; it appeared in half of the texts. As Brown (1963) noted in his history of the show, standards of "good" and "bad" were replaced with new standards of "life" and "death" (p. 151). The analysis included in this category language that made reference to the presence or absence of "life" in the work. In addition, adjectives or metaphors that refer to traits that provide or take away life were noted. Christian Brinton (1913) wrote, "Paintings and sculptures are living organisms, which must reflect the aims and aspirations of the time" or lose their acquired humanity to become "sterile and soulless formulae" (p. 33).

The living, vital work was capable of generating an ongoing aesthetic. Sharing the metaphor but not the judgment of modernism, Duncan Phillips (1913) diagnosed the works as "impotent," implying an inability to reproduce and ensure the future of art's "life." Count deDragon (1913) described the Armory Show as an exhibition of "the really artistically virile work of the modern artist" (p. 12). If the modernist aesthetic did persevere, its detractors insisted it would mark the end, rather than the continuation, of the art world. Kenyon Cox (1913a) predicted that should the post-impressionists and cubists influence the development of the dominant aesthetic, there would ensue a "reaction against the classic and the traditional and art would cease to exist" (p. 10).

In his defense of modernism, Guy Pene du Bois (1913) gave clear voice to the notion of a life cycle for the being "art": "They are born, reach maturity and then, the life gradually fading out of them, they begin the downward slide to death" (p. 152). Maturity was characterized by the possession of vitality, spirit, and creative energy. The works lived if they addressed the aesthetic and social concerns of their audience. Walter Pach (1914) described cubism as "living ideas embodied in form" (p. 861). Charles Caffin (1913a) argued in the *New York American* that the "great public's interest is in life and it is only interested in art so far as the latter expresses what it knows and feels of life" (p. 8). The concerns of the critics and their readers differed, of course, so that Brinton (1913) could write of Van Gogh that his painting "throbs with creative energy" (p. 30), and James Britton (1913) described the work of the classicist Pierre Puvis de Chavannes as "alive with the spirit of classical antiquity" (p. 3). Vitality was associated in the reviews either with the continuation of valued traditional representation or with the growth and rediscovery of the "spirit" or "force" of art, freed from the "meticulous elaboration of academic practice" (Brinton, 1913: 30).

Critics also disagreed in their ideas of what the "cause of death" for an artwork had been. Hapgood (1913c) identified the National Academy as a "huge morgue in which stiffened corpses had been shown in decent and decorous fashion" (p. 9). Cause of death: suffocating traditional values and techniques that failed to generate new and vital painting and sculpture. *International Studio* cited a similar process and warned that art might finally die "for want of exercise" ("The Lay Figure: On Art Crazes and Their Meanings," 1913: 350). Like the human body it paralleled, the artwork required stimulation and nourishment in order to continue. Walter Cabot (1913) argued, "To detach art from life is to starve it" (p. 594). Cox (1913a) also used the metaphor of nourishment but designated art as nourishment for its human audience rather than a subject in need of sustenance. Limited to a diet of modernism, the audiences' appreciation of art would perish, for their "stomachs [would] revolt against this rubbish . . . not fit for human food" (p. 10). Phillips (1913) continued the accusations, condemning Matisse as a creator of "poisonous" paintings (p. 79).

Modernism's detractors repeatedly accused the works of being unable to sustain vitality in art or in its audiences' appreciation. Precisely the opposite role for the works was identified by its supporters. "Imbued with the intoxicating serum of life," these paintings and sculptures could "infuse new life" into an art robbed by academic tradition of its creative spirit (du Bois, 1913: 152). Hapgood (1913c) suggested that a "vital, restless attempt" was being made to "bring art back to life" (p. 9). Stieglitz (1913) argued that an art "deader than Ramses" could only be revitalized with much help from the post-impressionists and cubists: "They are breathing life into an art that is long since dead, but won't believe it" (p. 5). If an artwork is conceived as a physical being, death is its ultimate dismissal. Incapable of regenerating or of providing nourishment, the work becomes a threat to the continued existence of art and must be avoided and marginalized.

Metaphors of illness and disease placed the artworks into the subordinate position of a patient, again to be marginalized. These metaphors also introduced into the criticism a pseudo-clinical vocabulary and a seeming objectivity. Included in this category were any references to the work as diseased, which encompassed physical illness, deformation or decay, and diagnoses of mental illness. Its opposites were identified as indications of the work's "health," its capacity for growth, and its diagnosis as mentally sound. References to physical illness or health were found in 37 percent of the texts.

In a column contributed to the *American* by an author who was identified as the secretary of the Royal Mexican Veterinary Society, paintings were discussed as diagnostic aids that might provide clues as to the illness of the artist: "Some of the pictures show quite clearly what is the matter with the painter, but in looking at others you sort of wish to ask them a few questions about their symptoms" (Levy, 1913: 20). The coloring of a subject in a painting by Marguerite Zorach is identified as being brought on by a day's shopping, after which the "digestive organs are not functioning properly" and for which the author prescribes "salicylate of quinine in small doses" (Levy, 1913: 20). (Digestive problems were believed to be a popular source of modern art.) The author continued, saying there should be a law against artists "getting into such a state" as that exhibited by the cubists (Levy, 1913: 20).

A few critics identified cases of particular diseases. Frank Jewett Mather (1913b) saw in Matisse's paintings "an art essentially epileptic" and in futurism the "effect of a fever delirium" (p. 241). The veterinarian Aloysius Levy (1913) first mistook three of Prendergast's paintings for "Measles, German Measles and Mexican Measles" (p. 20). A letter to the editor of *The Nation* (Morris, 1913) suggested that the problem might not be a disease but "ocular aberrations and hallucinatory obsessions" on the part of the artist (p. 281). Other critics were uncertain as to the exact nature of the illness, choosing to point out conditions or symptoms. Adeline Adams (1913) warned of the "antique corroding neurasthenias [being] spewed out of European capitals" (p. 929).

The advocates of modernism saw in the works not an embodiment of illness but a prescription for the continued health of art. In an *International Studio* column it is argued that were it not for "vehement outbreaks" like that of modernism, art "would settle down into a condition of stupid somnolence" ("The Lay Figure: On Art Crazes and Their Meanings," 1913: 350). Modernism could rouse art from an increasing tendency toward becoming "torpid." William Glackens suggested reviving an ill American art with an "inoculation" of the energy to be found elsewhere in U.S. endeavor (cited in Gregg, 1913b: 162).

Similarly, metaphors of physical decay or deformation and those of growth are employed as if the artwork were as much a biological entity as its creator; they appeared in 35 percent of the texts. Glackens, W. D. MacColl, and Stieglitz all referred to academic art as already decayed. Glackens wrote that American art was "arid and bloodless [and] like nothing so much as dry bones" (cited in Gregg, 1913: 160). MacColl (1913) put forward that the work of Matisse retrieved art, "its bones dried and desiccated, and slumbering," in order to reconstruct it "like a scientist in a laboratory" (p. 34). Stieglitz (1913) referred to the "decaying corpse of art" to be rejuvenated by the Armory Show exhibitors (p. 5). Images of the artworks as somehow deformed are numerous. "Freakish," "hideous," "grotesque," and "monstrous"—all adjectives found repeatedly in the texts—condemned these works as abnormal and to be visually shunned.

In contrast, the same works were also discussed as growing and developing, with parallels made to plant and animal life. Hapgood (1913a) identified in the "unrest," which was evident not only in art but in all aspects of modern life, "the conditions of vital growth" (p. 10). The goal of this vitality was to loosen up the old forms and traditions, to "dynamite the baked and hardened earth so that fresh flowers can grow" (Hapgood, 1913a: 10). Du Bois (1913) likened art to a gardener who tames the wild plant of life. Fertilized by the realistic gardener, the plant "may become a fine symbol of the power of life"; trained by the classicist, it "may become a fine symbol of the rhythm of life"; taught by the romantic gardener, it might "become a fine symbol of the sensuous delight of life" (p. 152). Caffin (1913b) chose the parallel of an animal, writing that the movement of the lines in Brancusi's *Mlle. Pogany* suggested "living, changing growth, as one may see the muscles along the flanks and down the legs of a fine trotting horse" (p. 8).

Finally, there were many diagnoses of the mental health of the artists and of artworks; they appeared in 44 percent of the texts. An exhibition of art by the inmates of an English insane asylum had been held at the same time as the 1912 London Grafton Exhibition of post-impressionism and cubism. These events sparked debate on the connection between insanity and modern art. In an article published in *Nineteenth Century,* T. B. Hyslop (1911) stated that the "gradual retrogression of the mental and physical functions results ultimately in a pathological return to the crude and rudimentary conditions of barbarism" (p. 273). By reason of their mental disease, he argued, insane artists "ignore all contemporary ideals as to what is beautiful, significant and worthy to be portrayed and it is thus that free play is given to the workings of their defective minds, and whereby they evolve their absurd crudities [and] stupid distortions of natural objects" (1911: 273).

In an article published the same month the Armory Show opened, Yoshio Markino (1913) wrote that for those suffering from certain diseases of the brain, "everything looks to them in the straight lines and cubic shapes" (p. 319). Although these authors and editors insisted that "it would be going too far . . . to say that these pictures are any proof that the Post-Impressionists owe their peculiarities to disordered minds" ("Art and Insanity in the Light of an Exhibition of Pictures by Lunatics," 1913: 340), the descriptions of technique and subject matter strongly resemble contemporary critical response to the modernist works. In discussing two of the works exhibited by inmates of London's Bloomingdale Asylum, a writer in the *British Medical Journal* noted of one that "the limbs are out of proportion and do not join up properly with the body" and of the other that it "is executed in squares, and is absolutely a 'Cubist' drawing, though much more intelligible than many of those which recently found a place on the walls of Grafton Gallery" ("Art and Insanity in the Light of an Exhibition of Pictures by Lunatics," 1913: 340). *International Studio* discussed the "connection between the general increase of insanity and the irresponsible character of modern art developments" ("The Lay Figure: On Art Crazes and Their Meanings," 1913: 350). A legitimate effort to discover new forms of expression had demanded a "degeneration" into madness.

Two of the show's critics drew parallels between the Armory and insane asylums. One referred to the rooms of the Armory as "wards" and to the artists as "mentally awry" ("Lawlessness in Art: The Exploitation of Whimsicality as a Principle", 1913: 150). Mather (1913b) felt that although the exhibited works were "very living and interesting . . . something like that might be one's feeling on first visiting a lunatic asylum" (p. 241). Cox (1913a) thought the Armory felt like a "pathological museum where the layman has no right to go. . . . One feels that one has seen not an exhibition, but an exposure" (p. 10). Adams (1913) agreed with these associations, suggesting that "such paintings are to be found in the consultation collections of asylums" (p. 928).

The modernist works were, Cox (1913b) wrote, "mere freaks of a diseased intellect" (p. 43). James Townsend (1913) asked if it "would not appear that the said expression is one of disordered stomachs or deranged minds" (p. 9). *Review of Reviews* described futurism as "an art gone mad" ("Art Revolutionists on Exhibition in America," 1913: 444), and the diagnosis of the paintings as "pathological" was found in numerous texts. A letter to the editor of *Art News* described the modernist works as products of "brilliant brains with mental and moral lesions, resultant from excesses physical, mental, moral, the product of brains absinthe soaked, erotically crazed or jaded—the epileptics of art." The author asks, "Is there no subcutaneous injection to moderate these convulsions of aesthetically deranged nervous systems" (Vezin, 1913: 4). Mather (1913a) advised his readers to "dismiss on moral grounds an art that lives in the miasma of morbid hallucination or sterile representation" (p. 512). B. Stephenson (1913) argued that many of the "faults" of American art could be pardoned because whatever its problems, it had always been "characterized by sanity" (p. 8).

A few defenders of modernism attempted to rescue the artists and their works from this diagnosis. Brinton (1913) advised his readers that "you will find Cézanne, ever sane and balanced, calmly extracting from nature and natural appearances their organic unity" (p. 30). *Review of Reviews* professed that Cézanne "remained sane" in his respect for design ("Art Revolutionists on Exhibition in America," 1913: 444), and Gregg (1913a) argued that "a deep sanity" was to be discovered in Van Gogh's letters to his brother, Theo (p. 21). In a 1913 editorial, Spingarn argued that art had always possessed an "essential madness," without which it could not breathe, and that academic tradition had only been working to suffocate its presence. He insisted that in every civilization "madness and courage are the very life of all art" and are to be encouraged rather than repressed (cited in "Editorial," April 1913: 316).

In their assignment of the role of patient to the artwork and the artist, critics assumed the role of diagnostician, a recovery of power perceived as lost. Decay and deformation further mark a work as incomplete, damaged, or incapacitated and thereby unable to be regenerated as, or undesirable for the regeneration of, a "whole," healthy subject. The crippled and the ill are regularly isolated from the well and, are confined to prevent the transfer of disease or defect. The literature that discusses the works of insane artists emphasized these solutions. T. B. Hyslop (1911) suggested that insane artists do not pose a threat to the artistic world "so long as they are in asylums and recognized as insane" (p. 271). Here they are prevented from influencing the "borderlanders": those who live somewhere between sanity and insanity and who could easily be impressed by these works. Even a sane and unsuspecting member of the public might be vulnerable to these "illusions." Markino (1913) told of his encounter with the post-impressionists: "I felt as if I myself was getting lunatic, so I ran away from the picture." He advised that "we, the sane people, ought to take all the precautions and it is [a] most serious and urgent matter. We must not be unkind to them, but we ought to treat them in the proper way to treat the lunatics" (p. 320).

These texts designate the critic not only as diagnostician but also as a "public guardian" who, with a strong but kind hand, separates the socially acceptable from the unacceptable. Establishing the identity of the artist or artwork as that of a subordinate patient hands control over their welfare and decisions about their fate to another: the critic. Treatment of disease and the promotion of growth remove the patient from the "care" of another, making that patient independent of the "institution" and able to enter the healthy mainstream of society. So situated, the artist and artwork would be able to engender further developments in the art world and influence the future of the dominant discourse.

There is an alternative, and I believe complementary, interpretation of the abundance of illness and decay metaphors found in the texts, one that incorporates the strong xenophobic strain that runs through much of the criticism. It is the idea that the critics identified modernism as something existing *outside* the contemporary social order. Modernism takes on the identity of something alien, constructed on the basis of unidentified values and concerns, that invades the known social and aesthetic order. To return momentarily to the metaphors of illness and decay, the subject of the invasion becomes the "body" art. Modernism is an invasive germ or disease that penetrates and afflicts the healthy organism, disabling or destroying it. Again, the artwork assumes the position of patient to be institutionalized and, if possible, treated.

A similar tactic appeared again in the texts when the critics utilized xenophobia as a category in both actual and metaphorical terms. Ten years after the show, Royal Cortissoz (1923) wrote of his impression of this "immigration" of art: "The United States is invaded by aliens, thousands of whom constitute so many acute perils to the health of the body politic. Modernism is of precisely the same heterogeneous alien origin and is imperilling the republic of art in the same way" (p. 18).

Flint (1983) wrote that the "introduction of politics as a criterion in art criticism is closely linked to the theme of nationalism and patriotism" (p. 61). In their promotion of American art, many of the critics made derogatory comments about the "other." Cox (1913a) wrote that nothing in art can compare with the "depths of badness attainable by the Frenchmen and Germans" (p. 10). An apparent negative stereotype was employed in an *Outlook* editorial that described a work by Goya as "a little incisive cynical Spanish note" (March 1, 1913: 467).

The artists and their works were also paralleled to those who would undermine the social order. Cortissoz (1913a) referred to the artists as "terrorists" and to modernism as the "so-called revolutionary camp" (p. 6). In a *New York Evening Post* editorial, the author wrote that the "rebels have been clamoring" for change ("Artists of the Unintelligible," 1913: 8). To this end, the most popular parallel made was to the "anarchist." Cox (1913a) referred to the painters as "artistic anarchists" (p. 10), and Mather (1913a) argued that "Post-Impressionism is merely the harbinger of universal anarchy" (p. 510). Phillips (1913) denounced the modernists' attempt to "overthrow" traditional rules of art; meanwhile, he continued, American art appears "safe and sane" (p. 79).

In the identification of modernism as an alien movement eating away at the social structure, the detractors of modernism were able to avoid the acknowledgment that this art was a product of the changing order in their own world. T. J. Clark (1973) noted a similar phenomenon in the criticism of Courbet's work: "What the critics feared most was precisely the irruption of a new public not amenable to their own civilized (and one could add civilizing) and responsible instruction" (p. 135). Many critics did not want to acknowledge that modernism emerged from *within* the social order as a response to the shifting values of the public and as a potential influence on future American art. What was feared was both the sentiment the critics recognized in modern art and the public to which it might possibly speak.

In half of the texts, Armory Show critics gave the exhibited works personality traits in addition to mental and physical states of being; most often the works were paralleled to a child or a "primitive." Critics debated the issue of how the essential "spirit" might be captured. "We work only by the sense now, seeking, savage-like, the rage and vitality of vibrations that make no world of beauty as the Academy of Art would see it, but a world none the less" (Willcocks, 1913: 403). The positive reviews of modernism identified in the "primitive" works a return to a simplicity that would save art from the "stupidity and stagnation [of a] debased illusionism" (Brinton, 1913: 28). Brinton (1913) argued that it was the primitives' "rudimentary command of technique" that freed them to picture things "synthetically" (p. 28). Caffin (1913b) concurred, stating that a return "to the primitive, to the simple, to the directly material" permits the artist to once again contact nature. This renewal of contact demanded the breaking of rules and regulations so that fundamental, "natural laws" could again be identified (Caffin, 1913b: 8). *Review of Reviews* applauded the potential effects of the "child's point of view" and the return of the "vitality of primitive, savage decoration" ("New Tendencies in Art," 1913: 245). A renewal of the primitive, as with progress, implies a break with previous structure. The primitive, or child, has yet to assume roles and structure and functions in reply to emotion and instinct.

The ability to return to the primitive state of mind was questioned, however, by a few of modernism's supporters. Caffin (1913b) was concerned that the modernists might be compromised by the conflict between the "crude, rude instinct of the child" and the "highly refined intellectuality of the man" (p. 8). It was a conflict increased by the fact that the childlike was necessarily assumed and was not natural. The modernist, he argued, could *not* be a "creature of pure instinct." It was only through a highly intellectualized process "that he can make the spectator conscious of instinctive and abstract sensations" (1913b: 8). Only with the mastery of the intellectualization of sensation could the artist successfully communicate an instinctive attitude toward life. *Review of Reviews* agreed with this reservation, stating that although Matisse "aims at the child's point of view," the compromise between the naïvéte of childhood and the sophistication of maturity would shock with "its crudity and disregard of values" ("Art Revolutionists on Exhibition in America," 1913: 447). The *New York Times* observed, "M. Matisse gets back some of the decorative value of the work done by savage races, but he presents it with a sophistication that mitigates its effects" ("History of Modern Art at the International Exhibition Illustrated by Paintings and Sculpture," 1913: 15).

Brown (1963) noted that the "conservative critics were hard put to understand how a sophisticated artist could turn his back on tradition and try to see like a primitive or child" (p. 143). Adeline Adams (1913) was outraged by the "overdose of Childlike Attitude" she perceived in the work and labeled it "retrogressive" (p. 925). Theodore Roosevelt (1913) agreed, saying, "Forty thousand years later, when entered into artificially and deliberately, it represents only a smirking pose of retrogression, and is not praiseworthy" (p. 719). The *New York Times* identified the "sudden backward jump" in the work of Matisse and the cubists as "the turning of humanity back toward its brutish beginnings" ("History of Modern Art at the International Exhibition Illustrated by Paintings and Sculptures," 1913: 15). It was ridiculous, Davidson felt, "to try to produce things as if they never had been done before. . . . The thing for sophisticated people to do is, on the contrary, to use the spirit of their age and produce art out of sophistication" (cited in Gregg, 1913c: 180). Cox (1913a) also emphasized the relationship of complex art to advanced civilization, declaring, "The most important question is what is proposed to substitute for this art of painting which the world has cherished since there were men definitely differentiated from beasts" (p. 10). The assumption of the "Childlike Attitude" was simply, it was charged, "one more way of lying" (Adams, 1913: 925). Cortissoz (1913b) agreed that the art did not express the "naivete of a child" but that of an "adult playing a trick" and that it thereby negated "all that true art implies" (p. 6). "Matisse," Phillips (1913) felt, "creates patterns unworthy of children and benighted savages, patterns not only crude but deliberately false, and insanely, repulsively depraved" (p. 78).

The condemnation of simplicity attacked the unrefined and brutish nature of the works and their creators. Phillips (1913) and Mather (1913a) both referred to the modernist artists as "boys" who inflicted "nasty smudges" on canvases. Julian Street is even more severe in his judgment, announcing that a post-impressionist work had been created by "an evil minded child of ten, who had been reared on absinthe" (1913: 815). A medical doctor insisted that these works suffered from a case of "arrested development" (Morris, 1913: 281).

The works were further characterized by their aggressiveness. Mather (1913a) envisioned modern art as "staggering boisterously" in search of an alternative to the traditional and as "intolerably dull" (p. 504). Merrick (1913) accused the modernists of torturing the eyes and minds of the public (p. 2). The modernists were conceived by Cortissoz (1913b) as "foolish Terrorists" (p. 6). Britton (1913) referred to the works as "vicious" and "capable of bringing the people quickly to perdition" (p. 3). Mather (1913b) described Gauguin's paintings as "brutally imposing," and Cortissoz (1913b) described Cézanne's works as "rough to the point of brutality." Adams (1913) wrote that the modernists were "wry souls" who sought "a sinister satisfaction for their maladjustments" by hurtling themselves, in "blasphemous defiance," against an entity more powerful than themselves (p. 928). Leila Meichlen (1913) likened the modernist to a "madman who desecrates the House of God" (p. 940).

Reference to the brutality and aggressiveness of the moderns does not at first appear to correspond to the detractors' earlier treatment of the work as artist or patient. This language creates an image of power and strength rather than weakness. It is, however, an exercise of strength that is aggressive in a socially unacceptable sense. In fact, Merrick (1913) referred to the "torturers" as "art criminals," and Street (1913) insists, in describing a post-impressionist painting, that to "call it a crime in pigment is to praise it" (p. 815). The depiction of the modernist as a criminal occurs again in Meichlen's (1913) review of the show: The "profligate" should be "debarred from society . . . for the protection of the many who might be harmed" (p. 940). Adams (1913) referred to the modernist works as "art crimes," and *Century* (1913) labeled the Armory Show an exhibit of the "lawlessness in art." The artworks' presence is characterized as offensive and potentially dangerous. Although not subordinate in the same sense that the unhealthy patient was, these, too, are potential subjects of incarceration. Their disruptive influence and brutish nature must be removed from the mainstream to preserve its future.

Aggressive behavior was also identified as a positive attribute by two of the show's supporters. MacColl (1913) felt Cézanne's paintings took "possession" of him, drawing him into a reverie of dreams (p. 27). Wright (1913) discussed Courbet's painting *Burial at Ornans* as a "cataclysmic blow to those chlorotic persons accustomed to the pink flesh and wine-colored Greek draperies of the school in power" (p. 757). If necessary, Quinn (1913) proposed, "we must turn to work that is 'brutal,' 'crude,' or 'hideous'" in order to be saved from the "prettiness" and "sweetness" of academic art: "Better crude life than sickly or sentimental decay" (p. 176).

## CONCLUSION

The metaphors and language adopted by the Armory Show critics drew careful boundaries around the aesthetic and social spheres in which art was to function. The personification of art enabled the critics to deal with art as if it were another participating citizen in that social sphere and thereby suggested particular solutions to the emergence of modernism. For modernism's supporters, illness and decay were identified *within* academic tradition. Modernism was described much like a cure to be taken so art might survive and be promised new life. Continued existence was dependent upon the "virility" of the artworks. Sanity, social grace, and a pursuit of the spiritual marked modernism as a "model" citizen.

The detractors of the Armory Show identified modernism as dangerous, if not life threatening, to the aesthetic "body." Its illness, deformation, and antisocial behavior required that the work be institutionalized outside the mainstream culture where its influence could be controlled. Identified as outsider or patient, the work was subject to the regulation of institutions designed to maintain order. The hospital, prison, or asylum was each implied as the appropriate parallel regulator in the critical language of the texts. As the author of that language, the critic assumed the responsibility for identifying potential threats or benefits to the aesthetic order that support his or her claim to critical authority. It is central to this argument that the battle for critical authority that was instigated by the Armory Show was not fought from isolated polar positions and was not dominated solely by negative forces. To reconstruct the show on the basis of its negative reviews, as earlier histories have, creates a skewed history of modernism. As already mentioned, study of these reviews made clear the common discourse inherited by the critics and their continued manipulation of shared evaluative criteria. This was, in every sense, a *debate* over the boundaries of an art world.

As the intervening years have shown, there was no sudden acceptance of the views of modernism's supporters, and much evaluative activity lay between the polarities of acceptance and rejection. If we recognize the distance between the poles as the dynamic site of critical debate over the shifting parameters of art, a closer understanding of the changing "value" of art might be possible. By reversing the process that creates the artistic canon (that is, by examining first the functions deemed fulfilled to *then* determine how the category "art" is constructed), a methodology for appreciating the mechanics of the "transparent" text might emerge. A concentration on the value system adopted in the contexts of production and reception enables the isolation of those historical conditions that have provided the basis for deciding what kind of experience art *ought* to represent. I posit that the relocation of the critic into the "history of taste" will produce a commentary or narrative that comes closer to a recognition of how art and art texts function inside their producing and receiving contexts and of the dynamic nature of their interaction.

The challenge to the objective nature of the historical or critical art text must begin with the healing of the break between function and classification. The discipline of art history must recover its historicity in order to study how art and the critic work within a culture. In the case of the Armory Show, it was the critics who provided the audience with the vocabulary and evaluations that then formed the basis of the audience's reception. Critical control over the subject "art," lost when known evaluative criteria could not accommodate modernism, was being actively renegotiated, and with that renegotiation the conditions of its engagement were being redefined.

## NOTES

1. The following were included in the sample. Art periodicals: *Art News, Arts and Decoration, Art & Progress,* and *International Studio;* Review magazines: *Century, Current Opinion, Forum, Harper's Weekly, Independent, Literary Digest, Nation, Outlook,* and *Review of Reviews;* Newspapers: *New York American, New York Evening Post, New York Globe and Commercial Advertiser, New York Times,* and *New York Tribune.*

## REFERENCES

Adams, A. (1913, April) The Secret of Life. *Art and Progress* 4, pp. 925–933.

Art and Insanity in the Light of an Exhibition of Pictures by Lunatics. (1913, November) *Current Opinion* 55, p. 340.

Art Revolutionists on Exhibition in America. (1913, April) *Review of Reviews* 47, pp. 441–448.

Artists of the Unintelligible. (1913, March 15) *New York Evening Post,* p. 8.

Baldwin, M., C. Harrison, & M. Ramsden. (1981) Art History, Art Criticism and Explanation. *Art History* 4 (4), pp. 432–456.

Bloor, A. J. (1913, March 19) Letter. *New York Evening Post,* p. 8.

Bourdieu, P. (1968) Outline of a Sociological Theory of Art Perception. *International Social Science Journal* 20 (4), pp. 589–616.

Brinton, C. (1913, April) Evolution Not Revolution in Art. *International Studio* 69, pp. 27–35.

Britton, J. (1913, March 8) The "Open Eye": International Circus in Paint. *American Art News,* p. 3.

Brown, M. (1963) *The Story of the Armory Show.* New York: Joseph H. Hirshorn Foundation.

Cabot, W. M. (1913, November) The Paradox of Art. *Forum,* pp. 588–596.

Caffin, C. (1913a, March 3) The International—Yes—But Matisse and Picabia? *New York American,* p. 8.

————. (1913b, March 24) Picabia's Work Represents Further Abstraction in Art. *New York American,* p. 8.

Clark, T. J. (1973) *Images of the People: Gustave Courbet and the Second French Republic.* New York: Graphic Society.

Cortissoz, R. (1913a, February 23) The Post-Impressionist and Cubist Vagaries. *New York American,* Part 2, p. 6.

————. (1913b, March 2) American Work in the Independent Salon. *New York Tribune,* Part 2, p. 6.

————. (1923) Ellis Island Art. In R. Cortissoz, *American Artists.* New York: Charles Scribner's Sons.

Cox, K. (1913a, March 15) The "Modern" Spirit in Art. *Harper's Weekly* 57, p. 10.

————. (1913b, May) The Illusion of Progress. *Century,* 86, pp. 39–43.

deDragon, C. G. (1913, March 2) The Causes of the Modern Revolution. *New York American,* p. 12.

du Bois, G. P. (1913) The Spirit and the Chronology of the Modern Movement. *Arts and Decoration* 3, pp. 151–154, 178.

Editorial. (1913, March 1) *Outlook,* pp. 466–467.

Editorial. (1913, April) *Current Opinion* 55, pp. 316–317.

Flint, K. (1983) Moral Judgement and the Language of English Art Criticism. *Oxford Art Journal* 6 (2), pp. 59–65.

Gregg, F. J. (1913a, February 15) A Remarkable Art Show. *Harper's Weekly* 57, pp. 13–16.

————. (1913b, March) The Attitude of the Americans. *Arts and Decoration* 3, pp. 155–167.

————. (1913c, March) The Extremists: An Interview with Jo Davidson. *Arts and Decoration* 3, pp. 170–171, 180.

Gross, L. (1974) Modes of Communication and the Acquisition of Symbolic Competence. In D. K. Olson (ed.), *Media Symbols.* Chicago: University of Chicago Press.

Hapgood, H. (1913a, January 27) Art and Unrest. *New York Globe and Commercial Advertiser,* p. 10.

————. (1913b, February 17) Life at the Armory. *New York Globe and Commercial Advertiser,* p. 8.

————. (1913c, March 17) The Picture Show. *New York Globe and Commercial Advertiser,* p. 9.

Hauser. A. (1982) *The Sociology of Art.* London: Routledge and Kegan Paul.

History of Modern Art at the International Exhibition Illustrated by Paintings and Sculpture. (1913, February 23) *New York Times,* p. 15.

Hyslop, T. B. (1911, February) Post-Illusionism and Art in the Insane. *The Nineteenth Century* 69, pp. 270–281.

Kuhn, W. (1972) Story of the Armory Show. In W. Kuhn (ed.), *The Armory Show, International Exhibition of Modern Art, 1913.* New York: Arno Press.

Lawlessness in Art: The Exploitation of Whimsicality as a Principle. (1913, May) *Century* 86, p. 150.

The Lay Figure: On Art Crazes and Their Meanings. (1913, February) *International Studio,* p. 350.

Levy, A. (1913, February 22) The International Exhibition of Modern Art. *New York American,* p. 20.

MacColl, W. D. (1913, July) The International Exhibition of Modern Art. *Forum* 50, pp. 24–36.

Markino, Y. (1913, February) The Post-Impressionist and Others. *The Nineteenth Century* 73, pp. 317–327.

Mather, F. J. (1913a, March 6) Newest Tendencies in Art. *Independent* 74, pp. 504–512.

———. (1913b, March 16) Old and New Art. *Nation* 96, pp. 240–243.

Meichlen, L. (1913, April) Lawless Art. *Art and Progress*, p. 940.

Merrick, L. (1913, March 1) The Armory Show. *American Art News*, p. 2.

Morris, R. T. (1913, March 20) A Doctor on Post-Impressionism. Letter. *Nation* 96, p. 281.

New Tendencies in Art. (1913, August) *Review of Reviews* 48, p. 245.

Pach, W. (1914, April) The Point of View of the Moderns. *Century* 87, pp. 851–864.

Phillips, D. (1913, December) Revolutions and Reactions in Painting. *International Studio* 51, pp. 73–79.

Quinn, J. (1913, March) Modern Art from a Layman's Point of View. *Arts and Decoration* 3, pp. 155–158, 176.

Roosevelt, T. (1913, March 29) A Layman's Views of an Art Exhibition. *Outlook* 103, pp. 718–720.

Smith, B. H. (1978) *On the Margins of Discourse.* Chicago: University of Chicago Press.

———. (1988) *Contingencies of Value.* Cambridge: Harvard University Press.

Steinberg, L. (1972) Other Criteria. In L. Steinberg, *Other Criteria: Confrontations with 20th Century Art.* London: Oxford University Press.

———. (1973) Contemporary Art and the Plight of Its Public. In G. Battock (ed.), *The New Art.* New York: E. P. Dutton.

Stephenson, B. (1913, February 24) Editorial. *New York Evening Post*, p. 8.

Stieglitz, A. (1913, January 26) The First Great "Clinic to Revitalize Art." *New York American*, p. 5.

Street, J. (1913, June) Why I Became a Cubist. *Everybody's Magazine*, pp. 814–825.

Townsend, J. B. (1913, February 22) A Bomb from the Blue. *American Art News*, p. 9.

Vezin, C. (1913, March 29) Letter. *Art News*, p. 4.

Willcocks, M. P. (1913, April) The New Fear. *Forum*, pp. 401–405.

Wright, W. H. (1913, December) Impressionism to Synchronism. *Forum* 50, pp. 757–770.

## ❦ 3 ❧

# Public Art and
# Cultural Authority

### RUTH SLAVIN

WRITING THAT SUPPORTS PUBLIC ART stresses two different but complementary ideas. One is the proposal that art in public stands in a direct, unmediated relationship with the audience—as one writer put it, "without the restraining authority" of art world institutions and actors (Beardsley, 1981b: 43). The second is the idea that public art is an exercise in cultural democracy. According to this view, art's ability to transcend and liberate will engage the widest possible audience if only such audiences can have access to it. In this view, the placement of art outside the normal venues of the gallery and the museum becomes an important tool for enlarging the possibilities for participation in the fine arts.[1]

As these liberal good intentions were put into practice over several decades, a few articles published in the arts press and elsewhere suggested that fundamental problems faced the then-emerging field of public art. In one such article, Amy Goldin examined some inherent contradictions of public art, arguing that in general, contemporary art existed in an "aesthetic ghetto" as a result of both art world norms and practices and a more general disintegration in the institutions of public life. The inevitable result was that art as a form of public communication would be highly problematic, if not impossible. Public indifference and public controversy demonstrated that "public art" was merely the most visible example of a breakdown in the communicative system of art (Goldin, 1974). Other writers raised questions about the relationship between public art and its audiences in less inclusive, and often less fatalistic, terms. Lawrence Alloway (1975), Gina Franz (1980), Grace Glueck (1982), Don Hawthorne (1982), Kate Linker (1981), and Lucy Lippard (1973, 1984) all contributed to the debate in the 1970s and early 1980s.[2]

Brian O'Dougherty, the director of the Visual Arts Program of the National Endowment for the Arts (NEA) in the mid-1970s, shared Goldin's concern that problems with public reception of contemporary art were seemingly inevitable, given the realities of contemporary artistic practice. He was particularly con-

39

cerned about the continued hostility of general audiences toward modernist sculpture. Describing public art as above all "a social situation," he wrote:

> The collision of high art coming from the tradition of the privileged space (gallery and museum) and vernacular wisdom often lends an air of comedy to public art projects wrapped in nothing more than their good intentions. The tinker-toy minnow in the shadow of the International-Style leviathan is an image that, for good reason, comes to even sophisticated minds when the words "public art" are spoken. And this image is as much the public art cliché of our age as the 19th century's general on a horse.
>
> It has been the Endowment's concern to avoid not only such clichés, but the imposition of taste that subverts the dialogue between artists and the community through which the role of public art can be clarified. Perhaps the single key to community acceptance of art works is the avoidance of the argument based on privileged understanding, i.e. "I know more than you do and you should accept this." (1974: 45–46)

During the 1970s and 1980s, the "good intentions" of even the most thoughtful promoters of public art wore thin in the face of public incomprehension and hostility toward many public art projects. The dialogue envisioned between the artwork and the people seemed little evident. In a few particularly visible newspaper trials of public art, many art world members who had proposed public art as a tool for increased cultural participation found themselves defending both art and their own cultural authority on what could only be construed as highly elitist principles—essentially confronting opponents with the argument O'Dougherty had cautioned against: "I know more about art than you do and you should accept this" and this particular artwork in your park, town square, or office block plaza.

This chapter deals with three such confrontations. I begin by briefly outlining the economic and social context for the origins of public art after 1960. Subsequently, I describe the events surrounding three works of public art in the modernist tradition: Mark DiSuvero's *Mother Peace*, George Sugarman's *Baltimore Federal*, and Richard Serra's *Tilted Arc*. Each work was the center of an extended controversy, generating substantial coverage in the press, which served as my source of information for the rhetoric of these controversies and their outcomes. Finally, I deal with the *Tilted Arc* controversy as a watershed event in public art practice and put into question the (often implicit) definitions of public art that are emerging in the wake of this particular conflict.

## THE EMERGENCE OF PUBLIC ART

During the past three decades a wide variety of works—funded by individuals, corporations, and city, state, and federal governments—have become known collectively as *public art*. Over this period, a significant number of modernist artworks have been placed in public or semipublic locations. Many were funded by large-scale federal programs such as the General Services Administration's Art-in-Architecture program and a series of National Endowment for the Arts programs for art in public places. These programs originated (along with the NEA itself) in the mid-1960s. At the local level, many cities followed suit, passing "1 percent for art" legislation that mandated that this fraction of the budget for new buildings be set aside for art. Corporate support for public art also increased during this period as corporations responded to new tax incentives for philanthropy as well as to the perception that support of the arts could provide what one corporate executive called "social grease." And powerful and influential real-estate developers stressed the inclusion of artworks as part of the luxury amenities available in their buildings.

Although some scholars have claimed that the arts have long been viewed as important within U.S. society, most agree that ongoing support for the arts is a twentieth-century phenomenon (Senie and Webster, 1989: 287). Changing governmental policy in the period immediately following World War II undoubtedly played an important role in creating the institutional and ideological bases for modernist public art (DeHart-Mathews, 1976; Larson, 1983; Netzer, 1978; and Wetenhall, 1989). The new doctrine stressed the role of culture in progressing toward a better, more enlightened society. In contrast to previous conservative arguments that modernism was an attack on the American way of life, the new cultural policy lauded modernism as a vindication of the individualism at the heart of American culture. President Kennedy's 1963 speech at Amherst, considered the public announcement of the new cultural policy, stressed the value of the artist's individual vision to the nation, tacitly opposing this individualism to the suppression of individual rights under communism: "The artist, however, faithful to his personal vision of reality, becomes the last champion of the individual mind and sensibility against an intrusive society and an officious state . . . [in a democratic society] the highest duty of the writer, the composer, the artist is to remain true to himself. . . . In serving his vision of the truth, the artist best serves the nation" (quoted in Wetenhall, 1989: 306–307).

In this interesting reformulation Kennedy recast the experimentation and novelty of contemporary art into an act of ideological self-definition, not just for the artist but for the nation. Cultural "progress" was rhetorically allied with progress in other fields, and cultural advisers urged government officials to consider cultural welfare to be equally as important as the more traditional health and education areas. At the same time, continuing postwar economic prosperity fueled an unprecedented expansion of cultural and educational institutions (Crane, 1987). Just as corporate patrons had become interested in the potential of arts support as social grease, governments became interested in the arts as "social glue"—a means to social integration (Balfe and Wyszomirski, 1988: 273). It was in this social and cultural environment that many public art programs were founded. Given this, it is not surprising that early proponents of public art had an extremely idealistic view of its role in society.

A new, more ambitious view of the artist's role in society also facilitated the development of public art programs. Harold Rosenberg described the impatience of artists in the early 1960s with the constraints of creating for the existing art world—its dealers, patrons, collectors, galleries, and museums: "The artist has become too big, as it were, for art. His proper medium is working on the world: Ecology, Transforming the Landscape—Changing the Conditions of Life" (1972: 12). Rosenberg posited such 1960s developments as earthworks, happenings, art-povera, and other apparently anticommodity art forms as evidence of the increasing aggrandizement of the artist since the beginning of the twentieth century. He characterized these art forms as statements of the artist's freedom to declare, with Andy Warhol, that "art is what we say it is."

Although some developments within the art world were conducive to the development of public art, in other respects the boom was oddly timed, occurring at a time when the reception of contemporary art was increasingly viewed as problematic—even by art world insiders (see, for example, Rosenberg, 1972; Steinberg, 1977). Public art that embodied a contemporary aesthetic was, therefore, unlikely to be easily understood and even less likely to be appreciated by the uninitiated. When proponents of public art describe its mission as engaging with an audience that is not normally interested in art, by definition these people are not normally participants in the cooperative activities that produce art (Becker, 1982).

The fact that the three works of art discussed here were modernist, abstract sculptures would be expected to contribute additional obstacles to their appreciation by non–art world audiences. Although conservative art critic Hilton Kramer was speaking about *Tilted Arc*, a particularly difficult work even within the modernist tradition, when he wrote "there is no tradition, no training, and virtually no appropriate precedent" for this type of art in our society (1988: 113), this remark could apply to DiSuvero's *Mother Peace* and Sugarman's *Baltimore Federal* as well. Within the art world, interpretive criticism of abstract sculpture often focuses on the physical characteristics of the work and its meaning with regard to problems in visual perception, philosophy, or the art historical understanding of modernism itself. Art criticism of such works is not easily accessible to nonspecialists. In the absence of social references or "content," other avenues for relating the work to the audience's experience are not readily available. Within the orbit of art world institutions, audiences for such work, familiar with the norms of interpretation for abstract sculpture, are able to cooperate to produce art, in Howard Becker's sense. Art world members—critics, curators, dealers, and audiences—are similarly motivated to accept the artwork as meaningful and valuable. These motivations and habitual practices are not invoked for general audiences when artworks suddenly appear on the plaza in front of their place of employment or on their route to a favorite restaurant.

Faced with less than enthusiastic responses, art world supporters might have intervened in the publicly conducted debates to provide interpretations as to how and why the works might be appreciated. In the cases presented here this did not take place. Confronted with hostile public response, art world participants, with very few exceptions, responded to the conflict as a group of specialists defending their professional prerogatives.

## CONTROVERSIES OVER PUBLIC ART

### *Mark DiSuvero's* Mother Peace

In 1974, a large, abstract sculpture by Mark DiSuvero was installed in front of the Alameda County Courthouse in Oakland, California. Constructed from steel I beams, the sculpture was bright orange and stood forty feet high and twenty-five feet across. Known as *Mother Peace,* a reference to the small peace-sign–shaped opening at the end of one of the huge I beams, the sculpture was installed at the Oakland site as part of an ambitious exhibition project by the Oakland Museum. At the time of its installation, *Mother Peace* was on extended loan from the artist to the museum, which had a five-year option to purchase the work for its permanent collection (press release, Oakland Museum).

The Oakland Museum Art Guild's publication, *ART,* for September 1974 described the exhibition—"Public Sculpture/Urban Environment"—as important for the museum and the community. Drawing on the museum's permanent collection, as well as works on loan from other institutions and artists, most of the exhibition was to run from September 1974 through December 1974; *Mother Peace* was to be exhibited until the end of the following year. The exhibit would feature the work of forty-seven contemporary Californian sculptors; artworks were to be exhibited in the gardens and courtyards of the museum and in public locations throughout Oakland. The decision to install sculptures in a variety of locations appears to have been both philosophical and practical. Some of the works were simply too large and unwieldy to exhibit in the fairly small courts and garden spaces of the museum. The planned exhibition was also to include several "environmental pieces" ranging from a "colored smoke environment" (planned for a lakeside site not far from the DiSuvero installation) to projected images on blank billboards in public locations. The museum's intentions of "colonizing" space beyond the museum walls were announced in the guild newsletter's discussion of the exhibition's scope and goals: "Most important, we intend to turn the downtown area of Oakland into a unique exhibition space for contemporary sculpture. By extending art beyond the museum walls and putting the artist within the daily environment, we hope to stimulate new awareness and interest that will not only benefit the citizens of Oakland but the Bay Area art community as well."

The same newsletter also proposed criteria for the works exhibited, among which it identified "physical scale, in most cases larger than human scale; and . . . the philosophical attitude of the artist and his work, i.e. public in nature." As was fairly customary during this period, the use of the word *public* signaled primarily what was described as a "philosophical" attitude on the part of the artist that the work was intended as public art. This intention was typically manifested in a physical scale (too large for "normal" exhibition spaces) or other physical aspects (participation events demanding an audience or participants) that removed the work from the normal routines and spaces of art world exhibition practices. Thus physical location and intention weigh heavily in this concept of public art. In mounting and publicizing the exhibit, those responsible, specifically Art Curator George Neubart, did not appear concerned with other aspects of publicness such as the works' intellectual or aesthetic accessibility to the intended audience of "the city of Oakland." Subsequent actions and statements made it apparent that regardless of whether Neubart took this seriously, he still felt it was legitimate to occupy public space with works unlikely to be accessible to much of Oakland's largely blue-collar or, often, unemployed population.

By mid-August the DiSuvero sculpture was installed in its lakeside location across from the Alameda County courthouse. On August 16 three articles about the sculpture were published in the *Oakland Tribune*. One was a short, factual news piece with a picture of the sculpture. In the arts section, the newspaper published a column by art critic Tom Albright intended to publicize the exhibit. Albright praised the idea of the exhibit, calling the DiSuvero piece "a new Oakland landmark." Albright noted the "value to Oakland" of the exhibit and explained that the city hoped to buy a lot of the works. He characterized the meaning of the exhibit as symbolizing "the hope of Bay area artists that their work will provide the spark to help revitalize the inner city." Albright also quoted from interviews with George Neubart, who made similar statements: "The hope is that this exhibition can help revitalize the whole inner city, and inspire other cities to follow its example."

These and subsequent statements and actions by art world figures involved in this controversy make clear that the exhibition was at least in part a bid for attention and status within the national art world. This was to have been accomplished through the mounting and successful completion of an ambitious multisite exhibition as well as the promotion of "emerging" California artists side by side with such internationally prominent artists as DiSuvero, Richard Serra, and Judy Chicago. This intention was in keeping with art world practices wherein major exhibits help create and maintain the reputation of artists, and museums, in turn, expand their reputations by mounting exhibitions that feature "important" artists. The exhibition also represented an attempt to enhance the prestige of art within the local community. The exhibition, which was quite ambitious for the Oakland Museum, was undoubtedly related to Neubart's career ambitions because such exhibitions, especially if well reviewed by critics, advance the careers of curators. This is especially true in public institutions but is increasingly true for all institutions in the current era of emphasis on exhibition rather than scholarship.

In contrast to Albright and Neubart's enthusiastic promotion of the exhibit, reporter Don Martinez's article, also published in the *Oakland Tribune* on August 16, ran under the headline "Art That a Steel Rigger Could Dig." The article's opening line credited *Mother Peace* with setting off "a full scale cultural war." Martinez reported that Superior Court Judge Lewis Lercara intended to fight the sculpture's installation. Lercara was quoted as calling the work "a disgrace" and a "hangman's gallows." Although most of the article was devoted to describing Lercara's opposition to the sculpture, Martinez also included the comments of Oakland Museum Deputy Art Curator Harvey Jones, who appears to have coped with the unforeseen opposition by quoting from the organization's official press releases. He is quoted as saying, "This exhibit, which is a first in California, will give us a chance to reach outside the walls of the museum and into the total community." Martinez reprinted the statement by Jones, nonsensical in this context, that the exhibit would be "dominated by a sense of monumentality." With respect to the possibility that the work would be or was controversial, Jones is quoted as responding, "We didn't anticipate this kind of reaction. But art has always been controversial."

Subsequent reports noted that Judge Lercara had initiated press coverage of the "controversy," as it soon became known, by inviting reporters to a press conference in his chambers (*San Francisco Chronicle*, August 17, 1974). Articles published in the *San Francisco Chronicle* on August 17 and 21 recapitulated the statements of Lercara and Jones, adding statements by Lercara contesting the museum's use of civic space. He was quoted as saying, "Just because someone gets a grant doesn't mean they can deface the city." The judge was later quoted as arguing that "people should not have this kind of art forced on them. . . . It should be inside the museum. If they want to go and see it there, fine" (*San Francisco Chronicle*, December 21, 1974).

## George Sugarman's Baltimore Federal

On May 1, 1976, under the title "Chief Judge Doesn't Like It," the *Baltimore Sun* carried an article about an abstract sculpture planned for the forecourt of the new federal building in downtown Baltimore. The article briefly discussed the credentials of the art selection panel and the artist, George Sugarman, and described how federal judges, whose offices were in the new building, had objected to the planned sculpture on the basis of claims that it posed a threat to public "safety and security." About the sculpture itself, the article stated—quoting from some promotional material on the piece provided by the project architect—"*Baltimore Federal* is an example of so-called environmental art that fills and occupies space and invites the spectator to participate in the experience of perceiving space, form and color." According to the article, all work on the sculpture had stopped because of the judges' protests.

*Baltimore Federal* had been commissioned under the Art-in-Architecture Program of the U.S. General Services Administration (GSA). Under this program, a

*Baltimore Federal,* George Sugarman. Photo courtesy Art-in-Architecture Program, General Services Administration.

certain amount of the total funds allocated to new construction of federal buildings was set aside for art. At the time of the Sugarman controversy, this amount was one-half of 1 percent. The commissioning process for *Baltimore Federal* had followed the normal GSA procedures: The General Services Administration had worked with the National Endowment for the Arts to assemble an initial "expert panel." The NEA-nominated panel, after being approved by the GSA, made an initial recommendation of three artists for each work to be commissioned. GSA Administrator Arthur Sampson reviewed the choices and in November 1974 selected George Sugarman as the artist to be commissioned for the Baltimore project; in December 1974 Sugarman was awarded a $98,000 contract.

By August 1975 Sugarman had delivered a moquette of the proposed *Baltimore Federal* to the design review panel appointed by the GSA, which in this case was composed of the project architects from Baltimore architecture firm RTKL, administrators from the "Art-in-Architecture" Program, a representative of the mayor's office, and "citizens" interested in the development of Baltimore's Inner Harbor where the new courthouse and federal building was located. This somewhat cumbersome review procedure seems to have been designed to provide a kind of quality control that would ensure that art world evaluations played a strong role in the initial selections and that final choices would remain under the control of GSA administrators.

In this case, a group of federal judges who were to occupy the new courthouse asked for and received permission to review the plans for the sculpture. The early stages of the conflict, which took place between December 1975 and May 1976, were never reported in the newspaper but are briefly recounted in a GSA publication, *The Place of Art in the World of Architecture* (Thalacker, 1980). The judges' involvement began when Edward Northrop, chief judge of the U.S. District Court, having heard of the design, wrote a letter of protest to GSA Administrator Sampson and to Maryland's congressional representatives. Sampson arranged for Karel Yasko, the GSA's lawyer for fine arts, to meet with Judge Northrop and some of his colleagues and, subsequently, for Yasko and the judges to meet with George Sugarman.

Despite the judges' objections, Thalacker described these meetings as amicable. When the GSA received a letter of concern from one of the members of Congress to whom the judges had written, it responded that "both meetings were considered fruitful and the judges have been assured that the final work will not be executed without their concurrence" (Thalacker, 1980: 9). This wording was subsequently interpreted by the judges as a promise by the GSA that any objection by them would be sufficient to block or cancel the project. Indeed, on April 1, the judges wrote asking that the GSA take steps to cancel the contract with Sugarman "in accordance" with the GSA's earlier letter. Several members of Congress also wrote the GSA administrator in support of the judges' position. Jack Eckerd, who had replaced Sampson as administrator, ordered Sugarman to stop work on the sculpture. It was this decision that prompted the *Baltimore Sun* report on May 1. The judges claimed their objections were based on the conviction that those "bent on mischief or harm" could conceal themselves in the metal folds of the sculpture, which incorporated a bench and some cavelike areas, and that children and pedestrians might be injured by its edges (*Baltimore Sun*, May 16, 1976; Thalacker, 1980: 8).

A long article by critic Phoebe Stanton in the *Baltimore Sun* on May 16 defended art as a domain of connoisseurship. Focusing on the credentials of the artist and the judge, the article strove to establish a context for Sugarman's work within the national art world: "Knowledgeable visitors to the Whitney Museum annual shows, to the Monumenta exhibit in Newport, to the American Sculpture of the Sixties show learned to seek out his work for it invariably was suggestive of fresh possibilities for its creator and the art." Stanton attacked the right of the federal judges to evaluate the sculpture directly: "The fact of the matter seems to be that the judges do not understand and so do not like the sculpture, and, if such is indeed the case, then their preferences and judgement must be set against the informed choice of two panels of responsible authorities on modern art. The people of Baltimore have been offered a significant work of art by an important American sculptor. . . . These are the essentials against which the opinion of the judges must be appraised."

Accompanying this article under the title "Experts' Views on Sugarman's

Work" were excerpts from six letters by art world figures who had written in defense of the sculpture and the artist. This group included a curator from New
York City's Museum of Modern Art, the director of the Whitney Museum, the
deputy director of Washington, D.C.'s Hirshhorn Museum, a critic and a contributing editor to *Art in America*, and the dean of the art school at Yale University.
Sugarman had shown the moquette for the sculpture to these and other art world
members during the period of conflict with the judges, perhaps anticipating the
need for public support (Thalacker, 1980: 9). Not surprisingly, the letters were
uniformly positive toward the sculpture and supported the position that expert
views should prevail. These people and many others affiliated with the local and
national art world, the mayor's office, and local colleges and universities also
wrote letters to the GSA protesting the idea that the usual selection processes of
the Art-in-Architecture Program could be stopped by an "unfair" veto of a small
group of people (Thalacker, 1980: 9). Art world organizations and individuals
seem to have acted in accordance with the adage that the best defense is a good
offense. A surprising number of national-level art world figures became involved
in this controversy from the beginning. This was probably facilitated by Sugarman's residence in New York City and by Baltimore's proximity to Washington,
D.C., where GSA and NEA officials were located.

During the following week the *Baltimore Sun* published other letters about the
controversy, the majority of which came from those with formal affiliations with
the Baltimore arts community. These letters echoed the sentiment that the judgment of art was best left to experts. A local sculptor wrote, "Sir, one thing more
amusing than having judges decide what is acceptable sculpture would be having
sculptors decide what is acceptable jurisprudence" (May 21, 1976). The president
of a local professional association for artists, John Blair Mitchell, acknowledged
in his May 23 letter that "tastes do vary and all that" but supported relying on
expert panels of judges in selecting art. He cautioned, "Obviously if a small group
of non-experts can bring political pressure to bear at a very late date in the construction of the building, the concept of 'art in architecture' is destroyed."

As in other such conflicts, we confront the paradox that art world defenders
saw no contradiction between the elitist notion of expertise and the conception
of a "public art."

### Richard Serra's Tilted Arc

New York City is commonly considered the U.S. cultural capital. Accordingly, in
several of the conflicts I have studied (Slavin, 1991), New York, along with Europe,
was envisioned as the place where people would appreciate the artwork locals
considered rejecting. Indeed, New York media reports on conflicts over public art
elsewhere in the nation often implied "it couldn't happen here." On March 6,
1981, just six months before the *Tilted Arc* controversy began in New York, the
*New York Times* ran an article on a controversial Richard Serra sculpture in, "of all
places," Peoria. The article, written by art critic and commentator Grace Glueck,
began: "No one could ever accuse Peoria, Illinois, of being an avant-garde out-

*Tilted Arc,* Richard Serra. Photo courtesy Art-In-Architecture Program, General Services Administration.

post. Last month a proposed $100,000 work by minimalist sculptor Richard Serra for Peoria's new civic center was unanimously rejected by the civic center authority, after weeks of public outcry that brought more letters to the *Peoria Journal Star* than any other event within memory."

The sculpture, which was composed of two forty-foot-high slabs of corten steel, had been commissioned by the Junior League of Peoria, which had raised the $50,000 needed to match a $50,000 NEA grant to buy the sculpture. Obviously enjoying herself, Glueck continued: "Some citizens proposed some more appropriate monuments—a pink flamingo two and a half stories high, a tractor on a pole (Peoria is headquarters of the Caterpillar tractor company), a statue of an Indian, or a huge carp. Oh, there were calmer heads that decried Peoria provincialism, but they were in the minority. 'I think Peoria doesn't like anything unless it's second rate and out-of date,' commented Adelaide Cooley, a local leader, who was on the sculpture-selection committee."

Describing Serra as "one of the most sought after public sculptors in the country," Glueck noted that although St. Louis had also recently rejected a Serra work, the artist was "elsewhere doing all right," including commissions for the cities of Madrid and Barcelona, shows at the Museum of Modern Art and the Pompidou Centre, and a commission for Federal Plaza in New York City—the commission that was to be *Tilted Arc.* Having described what Peoria "thought" of Serra, Glueck closed with what the artist thought of the city: "What did he think of Peoria? Mr Serra said he tried not to think of it at all. 'It's like negative energy, and I don't want to be bothered with that. In Peoria, a contemporary mode of [an] equestrian statue would be Ronald Reagan on a bronze horse.'"

On September 23 of the same year, a short front-page news story in the *New York Times* reported that the General Services Administration had commissioned Richard Serra to create a sculpture for the plaza in front of the federal complex in lower Manhattan. The photograph showed a large wall-like steel sculpture identified as *Tilted Arc*, with the caption "Yes, It Tilts." On September 25 the paper ran a long article by Grace Glueck about a protest developing against the sculpture. One thousand Housing and Urban Development (HUD) employees and three hundred workers at the Environmental Protection Agency (EPA), housed in the buildings opposite the plaza where *Tilted Arc* had been erected, had signed a petition requesting that the work be removed. Avoiding the question of the aesthetics of *Tilted Arc*, the petitions focused on the use of the plaza, claiming that the work "destroyed vistas," "blocked access to the buildings," and generally reduced the workers' ability to use and enjoy the plaza. One of the people who had helped to write the petition, identified as Herman Phillips, an information specialist with the EPA, admitted that the people who had organized the petition "didn't like it aesthetically [but] didn't want to complain on that basis because art appreciation is such a subjective thing."

Donald Thalacker, director of the Art-in-Architecture Program under which *Tilted Arc* was funded, defended the work in the *New York Times* on September 25, 1981, with the argument that such an "initial reaction to a new visual expression is as old as recorded history." Thalacker also invoked the positive judgment of experts, saying, "We have received expert opinion from museums in New York, and the city's Department of Cultural Affairs endorsed the work and the Art-in-Architecture Program's objectives. We hope that those who object to it will give the work an opportunity over a period of time before making their final evaluation." As for Serra's contribution, he was quoted as saying that his aim for *Tilted Arc* was to "dislocate the decorative function of the plaza," thus "actively bringing people into a sculptural context." Although the reaction of HUD and EPA employees recently "brought into a sculptural context" arguably reflected an "understanding" of the work not so far from Serra'a own aims, he disavowed any interest in the controversy. The possibility that the audience would wish to dislocate the sculpture rather than be dislocated by it was clearly not part of the communicative encounter for Serra.

## PUBLIC ART AND CULTURAL AUTHORITY:
### THE AESTHETIC DISCOURSE

In an article on the failure of Marxism to generate a viable aesthetic theory, Tony Bennett defined and discussed two discourses pertaining to the evaluation of cultural products. He called these the *discourse of value* and the *discourse of aesthetics*

(1987: 42–44). Bennett defined discourses of value quite broadly as those expressions and activities that constitute evaluation within any valuing community. The aesthetic discourse is one type of discourse of value that in its attempts to establish a universal value is inevitably hegemonic in its intentions. In addition, the aesthetic discourse is directed exclusively toward those practices it nominates as artistic and privileges those practices above other social practices. In simple terms, discourses of value are concerned with why a given practice or object is or is not valued by a designated social group, whereas aesthetic discourses are concerned with why some objects or practices should be universally valued (see also Smith, 1983).

In the conflicts described, the views of the art world participants are not automatically treated as dominant or correct. To underline the obvious, prolonged conflicts occur precisely because the cultural authority of art world selectors and supporters of public art is contested. Despite general recognition of art as a specialized sphere of activity, the perceived intrusion of the art world into space not normally reserved for its activities opens the door to other claims. In response, the strategy of art world participants in defending these works is (1) to establish the central issue as "who can legitimately judge art," (2) to suggest that this issue can be considered and decided only within an aesthetic discourse, and (3) to reject the discourse of value as perhaps worthy of sympathy but irrelevant to the issue at hand.

On their side, opponents attempt to establish other contexts for evaluation besides the aesthetic, thus not so much challenging art world expertise directly as attempting to shift the debate from the aesthetic ground. In these conflicts the discourse of value is present in the form of statements such as the one by the office worker in New York during the Serra controversy, cited previously, that lots of people thought the sculpture was ugly, but they had decided not to pursue that as a rationale for its removal "since art is so subjective." Rather, the opposition argued that the sculpture deprived workers of the full use of the plaza and interfered with their legitimate needs for space to relax, eat lunch, and so forth (*New York Times*, September 25, 1981). Although the discourse of value sometimes attempts to speak for a poorly defined constituency ("the people"), it is normally couched in terms of the individual, his or her group, or a specified community—judges, office workers, occupants of the neighborhood, people of Oakland, people who work or live in lower Manhattan. Even statements during the Serra case such as "the removal of this work will be a triumph for thousands of people who live and work in New York" (*New York Times*, June 1, 1985) remain within the discourse of value in that their orientation is toward a named valuing community and not toward the value and transcendence of art.

It is important to state that the difference between the aesthetic discourse and discourses of value is not that the discourse of value is naive or unstrategic. Discourses of value are also used by people who wish their own view to prevail and are deployed in reference to an enduring American doctrine of pluralism and tolerance for difference. Thus, for example, although emphasizing their own values as "individual," "subjective," or just some among many, speakers characterize the art world as "imposing" the work on people who just want to live and let live as long as the art world will "keep that stuff inside the museum where it belongs." However, because its essential appeal is to pluralism of tastes, the discourse of value cannot openly aspire to win but only to coexist. In situations in which decisionmaking rather than the multiplication of coexisting tastes and values is the order of the day, the crucial issue becomes which discourse is most effective in constructing a legitimate expertise as the basis for power. And it is here that the discourse of value is at a disadvantage.

One indication of what Bennett (1987) calls the "hegemonic intentions" of the aesthetic discourse is the tendency of speakers using this discourse to position themselves as speaking for everyone. An example is seen in the following statement about the sculptor of *Mother Peace*: "We need to see . . .what makes DiSuvero so compelling a spokesman for his time. There is room here for his interpretation of our society, for his sculptural statement of its values" (*Oakland Tribune*, February 27, 1977). Clearly, this obscures the fact that DiSuvero is only a compelling spokesperson for a very small number of people inhabiting his time. Under the heading "Why It's Important," critic Thomas Albright wrote about the DiSuvero work and the exhibit within which it was to have been featured: "For the basic message of the exhibit is that art matters and can have a profound and constructive effect on the lives of everyone it touches" (*San Francisco Chronicle/ Examiner*, September 1, 1974). About *Baltimore Federal*, critic Phoebe Stanton stated, "It should be a matter of great pride in this country that the federal government is trying to seek out the very best artists in the land and give them the opportunity and the challenge to make some sort of meaningful artistic sculpture" (*Baltimore Sun*, July 18, 1976). These critics do not acknowledge particular subjects for whom "art matters"; nowhere is it explained or demonstrated how the sculptures might be meaningful and what they symbolize or for whom. As mentioned previously, an interesting aspect of the role of art world participants in these controversies is their near-total abandonment of any interpretive critical activity directed toward increasing understanding of the work itself. Such criticism belongs to their role within the interpretive community of the art world but not to the hegemonic aesthetic discourse they propose in attempting to resolve controversy about public art.

The construction of the persona of the artist also plays a role in the aesthetic discourse, as can be seen in an example from the New York public hearing the GSA eventually held on *Tilted Arc*: "Art requires freedom for the artist to make his statement about the life and times we live in. It is an expression of the deepest values of our society" (Senator Jacob Javits, quoted in Jordan, 1987: 122–124). Here it is the artist who has the ability to speak for and to everyone. The artist's personal vision and personal freedom become the expression of "the deepest values of our society." Complementing this emphasis on individual expression are the frequent characterizations of the artist as a lone figure in the social landscape of these controversies. In New York, where art world participation in the conflict was strong and ongoing, the controversy was nevertheless continually described as being a disagreement between "Serra and the people of New York."

Because the aesthetic discourse is deeply rooted in the idea that art has universal and transcendent meaning and value, those who recognize its value do so as "stand-ins" for a universal or ideal subject. The proposition that art world speakers only stand in for this ideal, speaking not for themselves or their community, is a key aspect of the hegemonic ambitions of this discourse, as it both establishes their authority and obscures their own real interest in the debate. The ideal subject for whom they speak can also be be displaced in time or in space—for example, in the form of a "hypothetical posterity" who will recognize the true value of the work (Bennett, 1987). The construction of the past, of the future, and of ideal cultural places is a popular theme in these conflicts.

As many observers have noted, histories inevitably reflect the needs and uses of the present. Many participants in debates over controversial public art constructed a past in which great "art has always been controversial" (*Oakland Tribune*, August 16, 1974). Some speakers placed the origin point for this "normal" state of affairs as the Renaissance, some the eighteenth or nineteenth century, whereas some intrepid souls boldly set it "at the beginning of time." But whatever starting point was named, part of the purpose is to establish that art has always existed in the same relation to society. Similarly, the thrust of some testimony in support of public art is that all controversies revolve around the same issues. Thus George Sugarman, testifying not for his own *Baltimore Federal* but on behalf of *Tilted Arc* in New York, described Pope Julius II as finally agreeing to leave Michelangelo alone while he was "on the scaffold" (*New York Times*, March 7, 1985). In general, proponents of public art construct a past in which great art was not always recognized as such. Ironically, these descriptions of a past era in which no one understood art have a particularly illogical relationship to their construction of a future in which everyone will understand it.

With regard to the future, the basic contention is that art takes a long time to be appreciated, and the best art often takes the longest time. The alchemy by which present controversy implies future greatness is at times so powerful that presumably intelligent people make ridiculous remarks. The director of the Brooklyn Museum said, "The more controversy there is at the time it [the work of art] is created by a tried and true artist, the more chance there is that it is a significant statement. Therefore I see this as the destruction of a masterpiece" (*New York Times*, June 6, 1985). The further implication here—that even the expert is unable to judge the eventual significance of the work for posterity—is common although not typical, and creates a curious double and contradictory logic in the critic's construction of his or her own relationship to the hypothetical posterity. The work may be a masterpiece, but even the critic isn't sure. At the end of a May 19, 1985, *New York Times* article about *Tilted Arc*, another critic rhetorically left the speaker's podium and rejoined the (he or she hoped awestruck) audience: "One thing that emerged from the hearing is that we have not yet begun to explore the meanings and possibilities of *Tilted Arc*. Another is that we are not even remotely in a position to make an irrevocable decision about a work of this complexity and imagination."

The displacement of the ideal valuing subjects in space rather than in time is evidenced in the discourse about cities. The prestige of the city is linked rhetorically with its citizens' ability to emulate the taste of the truly cultured people who live elsewhere and who would never be so Philistine as to reject the artwork under consideration. So, for example, a member of the board of the Oakland Museum defended DiSuvero's *Mother Peace* by saying "the museum is more respected outside Oakland than it is here" and suggesting that the sculpture program would focus national attention on Oakland. At the public hearing regarding the work, a professor of art said, "There are pieces like this in other cities and this is the only place where people are saying 'take it away' rather than trying to look at it, trying to understand it" (*Oakland Tribune*, September 25, 1974). An amusing example of a kind of uncomprehending acquiescence to this idea is the statement of support for DiSuvero by an Oakland Museum board member who said, "It's not my favorite kind of sculpture, but it's the kind of thing I see in New York, London and other great art centers" (*Oakland Tribune*, September 23, 1974).

Whereas the cultured "elsewhere" is sometimes general, as in the vague "other cities," for Oakland and Baltimore it is most often New York. In the Baltimore controversy a New York museum director wrote, "My only regret is that . . . [*Baltimore Federal*] . . . will not be in New York" (*Baltimore Evening Sun*, May 16, 1976). For New York writers, the standard was, interestingly, often an idealized conception of their own city, but in the *Tilted Arc* controversy, Europe, especially Paris, often stood in as the place where people truly understood art. These arguments are particularly interesting when seen in contest with the arguments about local space and local control over that space by the works' opponents. Art's defenders situate themselves, as well as the artworks, within a national or even an international culture whose interests, in the name of art, they defend against the merely local or regional interests of art's opponents.

In a variety of ways, the aesthetic discourse as used by art world participants in these controversies posits itself as speaking for all: transcending merely local conditions and values, understanding the message of the past, and seeing farther into the future. It is from this discourse that art world participants construct their own expertise and from this expertise their right to judge and to overrule the discourse of value as irrelevant, composed, as it is, of the interests of specific valuing subjects in present time and local space. The aesthetic discourse is oriented toward establishing art as a matter only experts can judge, a judgment they make for an ideal valuing community displaced in time and space. Opponents attempt to counter these claims with claims based on other kinds of rights such as public safety, "use" rights of public spaces, and other values and needs related to specific communities or groups. Despite occasional grandiose claims about representing "the people," in these three controversies, opponents generally were unable to link their arguments to any overarching principles that would allow them to make hegemonic claims or to effectively counter the claims of the aesthetic discourse. And at least in terms of the recounting of the controversies in news and editorial reports, more and more ground has been lost to the aesthetic.

To the extent that even their opponents in these conflicts gradually concede more and more terrain to the expertise of art world "judges," the aesthetic discourse and its real-world speakers do succeed in establishing their authority. When the Federal Court judges in Baltimore received word that the decision of the GSA hearing was in favor of retaining *Baltimore Federal* and that the argument that the sculpture was unsafe had not been seriously regarded, they responded angrily in the *Baltimore Sun* on August 12, 1976, "We don't think it's silly. . . . It's absolutely essential [that we judge] and we can judge and we did judge and we expressed our opinion." In the paper the next day the editorial comment on the judges' opinion concluded, "The judges' intrusion is not silly but shameful and should be viewed as such by the public, which may not know much about art but has more respect than the judges for those who do."

I would emphasize that the judges' response is almost the only assertion in these three controversies that opponents do indeed have "the right to judge," and this transgression is nearly unanimously vetoed. The sentiments of the editorial are, however, frequently voiced in all three controversies, even by people who oppose the works and seek their removal. This is not to say that people easily abandon their position that the works should go. Rather, they intentionally focus the debate on issues constructed as being outside the aesthetic (where they readily admit they are not competent to judge). Even hearing officers upheld this idea by insisting they were not judging the work on aesthetic grounds. In Oakland, a city council member said, "Should we even get into this [art selection]. . . . I question whether we should sit here as an art jury or even if we are qualified" (*Oakland Tribune*, September 22, 1974). And the chair of the public portion of the council's deliberations announced to those about to testify, "We're not here as art critics, but as concerned citizens" (*Oakland Tribune*, September 25, 1974).

It is possible to question the sincerity or transparency of these statements, given that the council was in fact empowered precisely to make a judgment and was also well aware that the audience included professional art critics. Such apparently counterfactual statements can best be understood as both appeals to the discourse of value and openings that eventually undermine it. This is the sense in which, at least at the rhetorical level, I have referred to the discourse of value as essentially pluralistic rather than hegemonic. As I have described, opponents attempt to continue the fight on the basis of personal or community tastes and values, but as the conflicts continue—in slightly different ways in each case—increasing ground is lost to the aesthetic, a specialized realm in which the expertise of the art world rules. Because the discourse of value (we don't like it here, it doesn't meet our needs) also identifies specific subjects whose tastes or needs can be denied as too idiosyncratic to be valid standards for judgment, it remains vulnerable to the larger claims proposed by the aesthetic discourse. Does the rhetorical dominance of the aesthetic discourse equal the ability of the art world to dictate the outcomes of these controversies? It would seem that the answer is no, for the outcomes indicate mixed results.

In Baltimore, the judges never gained popular support, and the sculpture was installed essentially as planned. Minor modifications (for example, the installation of additional lights on the plaza) were made in acknowledgment of the judges' claims about safety. In Oakland, the conflict ended in a sort of draw. Despite the city council's assertions that in theory it and the other non-experts had no right to judge, in practice this is exactly what the city council did. The DiSuvero sculpture remained in place for a large part of the year but was taken down five months early. Both sides declared victory. Perhaps most significant, as part of its deliberations the Oakland City Council passed a city ordinance that required prior council approval for any temporary or permanent display of art on public land. Everything Oakland advocates had feared came to pass on the national cultural scene, as NEA Chairperson Nancy Hanks began to refer to Oakland as "the West-coast city where they like art so much they take it down and put it in a closet" (*San Francisco Chronicle/Examiner*, June 20, 1976).

The *Tilted Arc* controversy was exceptionally long and complicated, and events at several crucial points suggest that the aesthetic arguments of supporters played a substantial role in prolonging the controversy. Initially, things looked promising for *Tilted Arc*'s opponents, as William Diamond, the local GSA administrator, promised a hearing based on the anti-*Arc* forces' carefully worked out contentions that the sculpture prevented them from using and enjoying the plaza. It appeared that these arguments would successfully shift the terms from the aesthetic to the needs of the "local community," as Diamond announced a hearing specifically based on "the issue of the site" as opposed to the piece's aesthetic value.

After launching several trial balloon arguments (including statements by Serra's lawyer that the plaza was never intended as a service, "like a cafeteria," for the federal employees who opposed *Tilted Arc* but instead was like a courtroom in symbolizing the people's search for justice), the art world also focused on the issue of the site. Participants argued that the work was synonymous with the site and that to remove *Tilted Arc* was to destroy a work of art (*New York Times*, May 31, 1985, December 16, 1985, December 18, 1987). This became the central argument in support of keeping the work in Federal Plaza. It is also an exceptionally clear example of attempted "aestheticization" of the debate. Although *Tilted Arc* *was* designed for that particular site, this argument only surfaced at the point at which the opposition had seemingly found an effective way to undermine the claims of art by focusing on arguments about the site and its use by federal employees and local residents.

The outcome of the 1985 GSA hearing was a ruling that another site should be found for the sculpture and that, provided an appropriate site could be found, *Tilted Arc* would be moved. Although the victory was a muted one, it was indeed considered a victory at the time by the sculpture's opponents. When the committee appointed to study the problem of an "appropriate site" was named over one year later, it consisted of seven people nominated by the National Endowment for the Arts, whose mandate had shifted slightly in keeping with the argument that the work was the site. After a short deliberation that commenced with a meeting with Serra, the committee concluded that, as supporters had argued, to remove the work was to destroy it (*New York Times*, December 18, 1987). The arguments about the site-specific nature of the artwork were central to the committee's decision. In invoking such a specialized concept as an artwork that depends for its "artness" on remaining at a certain site, this outcome is a good example of the instrumental nature of the arguments of the aesthetic discourse in the legitimation of art world interests over the interests of other groups. Despite the finding by this GSA-appointed committee that the sculpture could not be moved, the GSA did decide to remove *Tilted Arc*, thus demonstrating that whereas power often finds ideology handy, it is not indispensable.

The question of the relationship of ideology to power is generally relevant to these debates. Although the art world does not always prevail in these controversies, its rhetoric dominates the representation of the three conflicts considered here. Since ideology clearly does not always dictate the outcome, of what importance is the central position accorded the aesthetic discourse? The progress of these controversies illustrates the continued inaccessibility of the modernist aesthetic for many people and particularly highlights the problems posed by the absence of social reference points in art. Further, in Harold Rosenberg's terms, art world participants disdain even to try to "make the fetish potent outside the cult" by attempting to convey the meaning of these works within the artistic tradition in the West (1972: 38). Failing this, the social import of art world arguments about expertise seems to be to confirm opponents' sense of these encounters as autocratic attempts to colonize public space for artworks that were never intended to have significance for much of the audience.

The lasting impression given by these arguments is that art, like so many other realms in our society, is a technical area best understood by experts. What does this mean for the idea of a public art if the public turns out to be largely irrelevant? Whether opponents or supporters prevail is interesting with regard to the issue of who controls decisionmaking in a particular instance. But arguments about art as just one more technical problem best left to experts reveal more about the general position of art in society. The issue of who has a legitimate interest in art is less central to our long-term survival than other social issues, yet it reveals characteristic problems of our society. Inasmuch as these arguments are oriented toward silencing illegitimate (non-expert) speakers, they are a rhetorical attack on the idea of a public and seem to bode ill for the possibility of using cultural products to constitute a public or even multiple publics. This is an issue to which I return in concluding this chapter.

I have argued that the claims of the aesthetic discourse dominated the debate in these three controversies and even shaped the way in which alternate claims might legitimately be advanced. This can be seen in everything from the Oakland City Council's statements that it can't really judge art to the extreme reluctance of the *Tilted Arc* opponents to state the rather obvious fact that they found the work physically ugly and aesthetically unappealing. Art world participants managed to shape the terms of the debate in these three cases, to reaestheticize issues that seem to escape the confines of the aesthetic discourse. They also succeeded in establishing their expertise. Yet they could not always convert this authority into the power to effect the ends they chose. In addition, a central irony of these conflicts is that in successfully constructing a public "who doesn't know what art is but knows that he or she can't judge it," art world defenses of public art naturalize the current marginalization of art and may ultimately help to shrink rather than expand the space available for it. Rather then making a contribution to cultural democracy, encounters over public art in these cases seem to have reproduced and even heightened existing social divisions produced by differences in education, socialization, and the distribution of wealth.

## PUBLIC ART AFTER *TILTED ARC*

The long and bitter debate over *Tilted Arc* appears to have been a watershed event in the field of public art. In the late 1980s and beyond, an informal consensus emerged that the Serra debacle marked the end of the era of innocence in public art and, perhaps most particularly, of the acceptability of a common-sense notion of the goals and methods of public art.[3] In the wake of controversies over public art and the loss of tacit consensus on what public art should look like and do, artists and critics have sought to articulate new definitions and directions for public art. Among many otherwise diverse responses, a common theme stresses a renewed emphasis on audience reception and community participation. Yet exactly what proponents mean by such terms as *audience, public,* and *participation* varies widely. And, indeed, the use of these terms as implied in new public art policies and practices emerging in the late 1980s and the early 1990s suggests both a new idealism and a new cynicism about the possibilities of public art.

In considering art world responses to the perceived need for a reconsideration of public art, it is important to note that an expanded and expanding infrastructure for such art is a factor in shaping these responses. Indeed, despite controversies over public art and well-publicized political attacks on art institutions in general, the field of public art is still perceived as a "growth industry" within the artistic field. (See the 1989 issue of the *Art Journal*, vol. 48, no. 4, pp. 287, 289, for articles about the "public art boom.") As of 1988, there were 135 annually funded public art programs at the state and local levels. In addition, the NEA, which to

that date had funded 518 works in forty-seven states, planned to continue its public art programs, as did the GSA (with new restrictions on "political and/or ob-
scene art"). A small but significant number of artists, architects, planners, art administrators, and even lawyers across the country now consider themselves to be
public art professionals. *Going Public: A Field Guide to Developments in Art in
Public Places* (Cruikshank and Korza, 1988), published with NEA support and intended as a resource guide to shape policy and practice for public art in the 1990s,
attests to the size and health of this infrastructure on nearly every page. In short,
despite questions, compromises, and decommissioning policies, increasing
numbers of people find their self-defined personal and professional interests intertwined with public art.

I have tried to show in the three cases discussed here that public art's supporters have rarely acted as disinterested actors for the public good. However, I do not
wish to leave the impression that they are malevolent elitists out to dupe the public. Many people involved in public art projects appear sincere in their intention
to make contemporary art more widely available and accessible. In order to bring
public art projects to fruition, they most often fight those who feel such projects
are a waste of time and money. Such opposition may increase their conviction
that public art is, as Janet Kardon (1980: 8) termed it, a "social service" that, like
other valuable social programs, lives with the constant threat of elimination in
economic and social "hard times."

Well-intentioned as such efforts may be, they are often characterized by a poor
grasp of the communicational and experiential bases for understanding and appreciating art, as well as by a failure to analyze accurately the contemporary social
context for art. Commissions of public art are rife with misunderstandings between art world participants and "the public," which may result in increased hostility toward art world institutions and toward art. This breakdown in communication has been, and may continue to be, a significant unintended consequence
of public art practices. Further, whereas the majority of Americans would presumably not sponsor or actively endorse the attacks of recent years on various
artistic and literary works, a growing sense of incomprehension of, or exclusion
from, entire realms of culture is likely to lead to indifference about the outcomes
of such assaults.

Recent literature displays four main approaches to the practice of public art,
each of which grapples in a slightly different way with the problematic matrix of
audience, reception, interpretive activities, and meaning. A common thread
among the four approaches is an emphasis on reception and participation. The
emphasis on dialogue refers back to the most idealistic early formulations of
public art as a tool of wider cultural participation and, in the broadest terms, of
"cultural democracy." However, exactly what proponents of public art mean
when they discuss audience participation varies widely. Not only the audiences
implicated by the term *public* but also the modes and media of communication
through which art reaches the public are likely to be significant issues in the next

decade. Therefore, I now focus on the implicit definition of public art and its audiences as suggested by each of the four emerging approaches.

## The Chat-Them-Up Approach

Arlene Raven's introduction to a recent collection of critical essays on public art noted that the original aims of such public art programs as the NEA's Art in Public Places have of necessity been modified:

> Commissioning a sculpture for a city's public square now seems, even to the Endowment, artistically and politically naive as well as possibly imperious. The "plunk" art theory—a site is secured and a sculpture installed, thereby making it accessible to the masses—according to Suzanne Lacy, has given way to the more recent "chat them up" procedure: artists try their models out on the community, work with architects and city planners, and are somewhat receptive to public feedback, as long as artistic expression is not compromised. (1989: 11)

In Suzanne Lacy's own words, "Public art of this ilk attempts to interface traditional sculptural forms with the existing environment so that the audience 'buys into' the work" (1989: 297). "Community involvement" is the order of the day in the revised version of mainstream public art. In *Going Public*, Kathy Halbreich wrote that "the recent practice of and critical discourse on public art suggest that equal stress be placed on the words *public* and *art*" (1988: 9). The many public art policy statements on community involvement are undoubtedly both sincere and well-intentioned. However, they tend to emphasize persuasion rather than participation. In practice, all too often "community representation" still means only the addition of a community member to the selection committee (see examples in Cruikshank and Korza, 1988: 9, 66, 103, 171). Although there are some examples of dialogue, unfortunately most are token efforts that seem primarily oriented toward public relations. Inevitably, public art administrators are advised to count on media relations, events, and special programs "to win support for the project" (Cruikshank and Korza, 1988: 105).

Public statements about controversy as a form of dialogue give way in this approach to the perception of social conflict over art as something to be managed and, in today's parlance, contained. To a great extent, this is the logical outcome of remaining committed to a public art that reflects current art world tastes and standards. The underlying assumption is still that public art means bringing culture, hatched elsewhere, to the masses (Kathy Halbreich talks about artists "injecting meaning [into] public spaces" in 1988: 10). With this orientation, it seems somewhat inevitable that the focus of "educational efforts" will be on promoting and rendering acceptable works that are approved by art world members. Community involvement or public relations campaigns, brass bands, or balloons—each may serve as a tool in gaining public acceptance. Thus, for example, Judith Balfe and Margaret Wyszomirski wrote that the "threshold of acceptability [of a work of public art] varies according to how the commissioning process is carried out" (1988: 275). Again, new policies addressing the "public" in public art seem primarily directed toward upholding the kinds of prerogatives of art world judgment I have described in other sections of this chapter.

## Art as Amenity

The art-as-amenity approach emphasizes the role of art in making the human-built environment more beautiful and useful through art and design. Proponents often trace the heritage of this kind of public art to architecture and landscape design, as well as to the traditional uses of the fine arts. Amenity art differs in philosophy from the chat-them-up approach in that proponents express a willingness to discover and meet "social needs" (see, for example, Cruikshank and Korza, 1988: 17; and Elsen, 1989: 293). Another concept often identified with this approach is that of "place making," the idea that public art may be used to impart a civic or neighborhood identity (Cruikshank and Korza, 1988: 17; Elsen, 1989: 292; and Fleming and von Tscharner, 1987). Artists such as Scott Burton have explicitly recognized the way class and education structure the audience for art and have turned to this approach as a way of rendering art more accessible. Other artists have designed parks or other green spaces on unused or reclaimed urban or rural sites.

Artists and others working within this approach recognize that a general audience for (or users of, as they might prefer to put it) public art will not necessarily appreciate the fine-art objects, writ large, valued by the art world. But in its search for social utility and beauty, this movement has created some surprisingly banal and ugly objects, installations, and even parks. Mary Miss's very spare green space with industrial materials near Washington, D.C., is a case in point (for the artist's own perspective, see Miss, 1984). Many of these artists are still conceptually indebted to modernist, minimalist, and avant-garde aesthetics even as they reject many organizational aspects of the contemporary art world. Even when they do not express contemporary art world taste, many, if not most, products of this approach have no discernible social content. Despite the political and ethical self-image of many practitioners, many art-as-amenity projects would prove absolutely unobjectionable to corporate and government sponsors. The idea of place making and civic identity is particularly appealing to corporations that wish to appear to be "part of the community" rather than national or international entities that may take decisions very much counter to the interests of the community.

Art world members who believe public art should continue to present the "best" the art world has to offer have been critical of the neutral, crowd-pleasing aspects of the art-as-amenity approach. For example, Harriet Senie spoke of such art as a "civic or corporate logo" (1989: 288). Other critics have spoken disparagingly about so-called art furniture (such as Scott Burton's oversize "easy chairs" in stone arranged in a public location).

Neither the "chat-them-up" nor the amenity approach is likely to produce art objects or experiences that are oriented toward the formation of a discourse-oriented public. In the first case, art world members seek better control over public perception and want to continue to use public venues as a showcase for art valued by the art world. In the second case, practitioners recognize the vexed nature of public art and try to surmount it by producing objects that will be perceived as unobjectionable at worst and pleasing at best.

## Gallery Leftism

Lucy Lippard, an important participant in and propagandizer for social activist art, has suggested that the venue for public art is not as important as its social-political intentions. In a recent article she stated, "As the eighties end, a crosscultural, crossdisciplinary trend that began on the mainstream margins a decade ago seems to be gaining momentum. The relationship between art and environment, art and context, artist and audience remains at the heart of any public art that's worth its turf" (1989: 210).

She clarified, "The real challenge lies outside conventional venues—not only outside museum gardens, but outside of bank plazas and civic spaces." She also noted that "sometimes the exchanges take place in (gasp) a gallery or even a museum" (Lippard, 1989: 210). Critic Patricia Phillips (1988) also emphasized that public art could not derive its "publicness" from its location. Location as irrelevant is taken to the extreme—intentionally—by Phillips, as she concludes with a description of two recent installations she considers to be exemplary public art. One is a suburban lawn—half of which was tended and mowed and half of which was overgrown—that bore the label *Half Slave, Half Free*. The second she described as follows: "For this project, the collaborative team of Kate Ericson and Mel Ziegler, with a work entitled *Picture out of Doors*, methodically removed all the doors in Pat and David Farmer's home, including doors from closets, cupboards, and cabinets, even from bedrooms and bathrooms. The tangible evidence of sanctioned voyeurism was stacked in the living room. In a sense, the teams's project publicized intimacy by denying privacy" (Phillips, 1988: 96).

Phillips characterizes these works as being about the relationship of public obligation and private freedom (*Half Slave, Half Free*) and of private (personal intimacy) and public life. Both of these examples occur in or on the private space of suburban homeowners, illustrating Phillips's contention that it is content and orientation that construct the public.

The major problem with the kind of art Phillips describes as public art essentially concerns the audiences it may hope to address. However deeply the two art installations discussed here may probe the public-private relationship, it seems highly unlikely that they will attract the attention of people outside the art world. This is consistent with the romantic position, espoused by Phillips, that artists are the advance scouts of society, also known as the avant-garde. In this view, art legitimately addresses a small elite who is prepared to grapple with the unfamiliar and contentious. Such art seems primarily addressed to the left-leaning contingent of the art world itself. Donald Kuspit made this point when he coined the phrase "gallery leftism," defined as art concerned with "the establishment of a political identity in the art world that has ambiguous significance in the larger world" (1989: 264). This is not to say that the establishment of such political identities is not in itself a valid activity but is simply to point out that any aspirations of achieving a wider social effect seem to be abandoned. The forms and locations of such activist avant-garde art seem to confirm this point.

Implicit in proponents' arguments about the "publicness" of this art is the intention to oppose the "business-as-usual" aspect of art as a commodity and instead to use art to instigate more awareness of and action on (often specific) social issues. Yet much of the work within this stream, although not the mainstream, retains strong ties to the norms and practices of the contemporary art world. In addition, locations such as college campuses or suburban homes seem unlikely to entice general audiences not already interested in experimental forms of socially engaged art. Finally, if activist artists eschew mass media as vehicles for discussion or presentation of artwork, they will again essentially limit the audience for such work. Ultimately, despite the sophisticated political goals of this work, the title *gallery leftism* seems an accurate description of the likely social impact. As is discussed later, to the extent that artists are willing to explore means and modes that may allow such work to reach more popular audiences, this approach to public art may address the goal of cultural participation through art. Sites that are perceived as physically and, perhaps more important, socially accessible are also important.

### Artists and Communities: Community-Based Activism

The sense of art as not only political but also moral-ethical action is common among contemporary artists who work with communities. Some artists within this group refer to themselves as community artists rather than public artists and note that content takes on prime importance when working with specific social groups (Gude, 1989: 321; see also Cockcroft, 1989; for antecedents to this movement, see Cockcroft, Weber, and Cockcroft, 1977). Although the idea of activating or collaborating with specific groups of people is at the heart of much artist activism, community has a wide variety of meanings. Some "community-based" efforts are broadly defined (and only marginally aesthetically oriented) such as Greenpeace's attention-getting strategies (see Durland, 1989). The work of Mierle Ukeles with and about the Department of Sanitation in New York is frequently mentioned as an example of such community-oriented art. Ukeles's work is an example of a project that addresses multiple communities: She has worked closely with administrators and workers in the Department of Sanitation; her work has been widely written about within the art world; and the artist considers it relevant to all New Yorkers, as well as, presumably, to all consumers (Raven, 1989: 201–202). Linda Frye Burnham (1989) has detailed the work of various artists who work within more narrowly defined communities. Many of the projects described involved artists working in institutions including hospitals, schools, homeless shelters, hospices, refugee asylums, health centers, and retirement communities, on Skid Row, and with environmental groups. In general, environmental and feminist agendas seem to have been particularly influential, although homelessness, gay rights, and AIDS have also been important topics and motivators (Marter, 1989; and Weinstein, 1989).

As these few examples can only suggest, there are many ways in which artists have attempted to establish dialogue with different constituencies through art. Sometimes their work is viewed and evaluated positively within art world contexts; in other cases this is more problematic. Artists who work with institutionalized populations or disadvantaged groups have been accused of performing social work, a label that may interfere with their identity as artists and thus with their ability to gain recognition and income as artists. Working collaboratively with nonartists and often creating "products" that are not easily assimilable into the commercial art world may mean that economic support must be obtained from alternative means. Thus artists who choose to work with a community-based or activist orientation may face many social and economic challenges.

From the vantage point of art as communication, one of the interesting dilemmas of this approach to public art is that in following what might be called a direct democracy approach to public art, artist activists often choose of necessity to work with small, well-defined social groups that are not the educational and social elites typically comprising the audience for art. In addition, when artists and administrators involved in these projects speak of "collaboration," it typically means something more than token representation on a selection committee. Thus this approach may come the closest to realizing the cultural participation ideals of public art. Yet one price for this may be the sacrifice of efforts to create a cultural realm invoking a general public, leaving this to advertising and popular culture. Many proponents of this approach implicitly or explicitly reject social dependence on mass media and view mediated communication as inevitably manipulative or as being in service to the status quo. Face-to-face relationships and communication seem intimately related to the egalitarian ideals of such projects and perhaps also to their relative success in realizing such ideals. Yet one may legitimately ask how such efforts (as with other direct democracy projects) may interact with and affect the structures of the larger society. Can they be used as a model for projects on a larger scale, or, like a mythical republic, are they unrealizable beyond a certain scale? (See Calhoun, 1988, for a related discussion.)

Some artists have sought alternative ways to reach a mass audience. The Greenpeace demonstrations that exploit the controversial visual marking of sites in order to obtain mass-media coverage are one such example. Intentionally highly visual and dramatic, these protests rely on the support of an organized community (Greenpeace activists and other environmentalists) while attempting to activate the general public. Actions by ACT UP and by animal rights activists have employed similar strategies. Other strategies include that of Sue Coe, who works as a fine artist but also as what she calls a visual journalist: Coe's drawings (with accompanying captions, slogans, or commentaries) concerning feminism, human rights, and the animal rights movement are often reprinted in newspapers. New York's Gorilla Girls feminist art collective has "taken over" various New York City billboards to protest the discrimination against women by New York art world institutions. A final, recent example was described by Lucy Lippard (1989). Lippard recounts how artists David Avalos, Louis Hock, and Elizabeth Sisco surreptitiously made additions to a San Diego tourist poster (displayed on the city's fleet of buses during the Super Bowl). The altered posters commented visually and verbally ("Welcome to America's Finest Tourist Plantation") on San Diego's dependence upon and exploitation of illegal alien labor. This project was seen by an estimated 80 percent of the population of San Diego, the seventh-largest U.S. city, and launched a debate about the ethics and aesthetics of the project that lasted several months (Lippard, 1989: 219–223). These artists, with the exception of Sue Coe, operate at the edge of socially acceptable (and legal) action to engage a mass audience.

## CONCLUSION

Both the norms of contemporary artistic production and evaluation and the social role of the artist in contemporary society contribute to the current predicament of public art. As has been discussed throughout, large, modernist sculptures without apparent social reference seem particularly opaque to non–art world audiences. The prototypical art criticism of such art objects, often focusing on the visual-perceptual and existential characteristics of the work, even if it were attempted as explanation would likely do little to enhance understanding or appreciation of these works. In addition, although there have been significant alternative undercurrents in recent years, the dominant attitude of contemporary artists with regard to their social role is still heavily influenced by ideas of nineteenth-century romanticism and the overriding importance of individualism, novelty, and self-expression.

The creation of a near-autonomous sphere for art may have been an important concomitant of its increasing commodification in a previous historical era. As the production of art became divorced from the patronage of the church on the one hand and an aristocratic class on the other, it is easy to imagine the doctrine of art's social autonomy as both necessary and useful. Moreover, this ideology appears to have won for art a certain freedom of movement, embodied both in law and in practice (e.g., special treatment in obscenity cases), that is viewed as an important aspect of civil liberties in a democratic society. However, the development and existence of a highly specialized art world has also led to a situation in which art is increasingly perceived as an isolated activity of dubious social value. In turn, this very isolation has rendered increasingly vulnerable art's special status and concomitant special protections.

The claim that the artist's commitment is primarily or only to self-expression merges easily into the assertion that artists bear no social responsibility for their actions, including the artworks they produce. This makes for some very strange politics. For example, the social autonomy of the artist was perceived as a key stake in the controversy over a portrait of the late mayor of Chicago, Harold Washington, by David Nelson, an art student at the Chicago Art Institute. In a thoughtful essay, the Graduate Division chair at the school, Carol Becker, pointed out that the liberal faculty and staff were put in the position of defending, on the basis of artistic freedom, a portrait many viewed as racist, sexist, and homophobic (see Becker, 1989). Similar ironies abounded in the Serra controversy. An avowed socialist, Serra expressed on many occasions his utter contempt for "the people" even as columnists wrote about Serra's working-class background and his years working in a steel factory.

I have taken up the idealized view of public art of the past several decades, or what one might call the ideology of public art, in the interest of using those ideals to explore art's potential for communication and, specifically, its role—both actual and potential—in public life. I have tried to show that far from fulfilling these ideals, many of the consequences of public art's current practices run directly counter to them. Much intervenes in the supposedly direct relationship between art and public, and public art is often anything but an opportunity for cultural democracy. In the wake of the kinds of controversies I have documented and discussed, there has emerged among art world members both a new cynicism and a new idealism about public art. In the meantime, changes in the general social environment and, specifically, what some have called the cultural wars (Bolton, 1992) provide a different background against which to evaluate even the most elitist claims about the need to protect the autonomy and integrity of art. Nevertheless, to the extent that public art's proponents continue to invoke the highest ideals of democratic culture, it would seem both desirable and important to weigh carefully the ways and means of reaching those ideals. As with efforts to democratize many social institutions, change is likely to be only incremental, as well as frustratingly slow and imperfect. Cynical use of the public domain in any field frustrates this ambition. It is only through concrete practices in all areas of life that we might achieve not just the symbols and ideology but the reality of a democratic culture.

## NOTES

1. For general works on public art that express the liberal hopes for public art in the early years, see Beardsley, 1981a; Fleming and von Tscharner, 1987; Karden, 1980; Perlman, 1973; Redstone and Redstone, 1981; Robinette, 1976; and Thalacker, 1981. For historical or critical perspectives on controversies over public art, see Nordland's exibit catalog, 1984: Elsen, 1985: 114–137; Merryman and Elsen, 1987: 281–374; and the chapter "You Mean It's Going to Be Up There All the Time?" in Park and Markowicz, 1984. Also of interest are

Senie, 1992; Doezma and Hargrove, 1977; and Reidy, 1981 (especially pages 183–184 and the chapter on the nineteenth-century movement for public sculpture).

2. For a minority viewpoint that is extremely hostile to public art and that provoked substantial response, see Stalker and Glymour, 1982, and "Dissent and Reply" by von Eckhardt, Beardsley, Fleming, and Levine, 1982.

3. See, in addition to specific works already cited, Danto, 1987; Deutsch, 1988; Elsen, 1989; Glowen, 1990; Hall, 1989; Kangas, 1989; and Tacha, 1989, as well as the special issue of *Art Journal* (Winter of 1989), which was republished, with additional contributions, as Senie and Webster, 1992. On *Tilted Arc* itself, see Jordan et al., 1987; and articles by Hoffman, 1987 and 1991; Senie, 1989; and Storr, 1985. For the artist's perspective, see Serra (1989 and 1991). Harriet Senie, who has written on this and related topics, has a book forthcoming on the *Tilted Arc* controversy.

## REFERENCES

Alloway, Lawrence. *Topics in American Art Since 1945.* New York: W. W. Norton, 1975.

Balfe, Judith H., and Margaret J. Wyszomirski. "Public Art and Public Policy." Originally published in the *Journal of Arts Management and Law* 15, Winter 1986; reprinted in *Going Public: A Field Guide to Developments in Art in Public Places* (Jeffrey Cruikshank and Pam Korza, editors). Amherst: Art Extension Service Division of Continuing Education, University of Massachusetts, 1988.

Beardsley, John. *Art in Public Places: A Survey of Community Sponsored Projects by the National Endowment for the Arts.* Washington, D.C.: Partners for Livable Spaces, 1981a.

————. "Personal Sensibilities in Public Places." *Artforum,* Summer 1981b.

Becker, Carol. "Private Fantasies Shape Public Events: And Public Events Invade and Shape Our Dreams." In *Art in the Public Interest* (Arlene Raven, editor). Ann Arbor: UMI Research Press: 1989.

Becker, Howard. *Art Worlds.* Berkeley: University of California Press, 1982.

Bennett, Tony. "Really Useless 'Knowledge': A Political Critique of Aesthetics." *Literature and History: Education Issue* 13:1, Spring 1987 (published by the Thames Polytechnic, London, England).

Bolton, Richard (editor). *Culture Wars.* New York: New Press, 1992.

Burnham, Linda Frye. "Monuments in the Heart: Performance and Video Experiment in Community Art." In *Art in the Public Interest* (Arlene Raven, editor). Ann Arbor: UMI Research Press, 1989.

Calhoun, Craig. "Populist Politics, Communications Media and Large-Scale Social Integration." *Sociological Theory* 6, Fall 1988.

Cockcroft, Eva. "The La Lucha Murals: Making a Political Art Park." In *Art in the Public Interest* (Arlene Raven, editor). Ann Arbor: UMI Research Press, 1989.

Cockcroft, Eva, John Weber, and Jim Cockcroft. *Towards a People's Art.* New York: Dutton, 1977.

Crane, Diana. *The Transformation of the Avant-Garde: The New York Art World, 1940–1985.* Chicago: University of Chicago Press, 1987.

Cruikshank, Jeffrey, and Pam Korza (editors). *Going Public: A Field Guide to Developments in Art in Public Places.* Amherst: Art Extension Service Division of Continuing Education, University of Massachusetts, 1988.

Danto, Arthur. "On Public Art and the Public Interest." *ARTnews* 86, October 1987.

DeHart-Mathews, Jane. "Art and Politics in Cold War America." *American Historical Review* 81: 4, October 1976.

Deutsch, R. "Uneven Development: Public Art in New York City." *October*, Winter 1988.

Doezma, Marianne, and June Hargrove. *The Public Monument and Its Audience.* Cleveland: Cleveland Museum of Art, in cooperation with the Ohio Program in the Humanities and Kent State University Press, 1977.

Durland, Steven. "Witness, The Guerrilla Theater of Greenpeace." In *Art in the Public Interest* (Arlene Raven, editor). Ann Arbor: UMI Research Press, Ann Arbor, 1989.

Elsen, Albert. *Rodin's Thinker and the Dilemma of Modern Public Sculpture.* New Haven: Yale University Press, 1985.

————. "What We Have Learned About Modern Public Sculpture: Ten Propositions." *Art Journal* 48:4, Winter 1989.

Fleming, Ronald, and Renata von Tscharner. *Placemakers: Public Art That Tells You Where You Are.* Cambridge, Mass.: Townscape Institute and Hastings House Publishers, 1981; republished as *Placemakers: Creating Public Art That Tells You Where You Are.* Boston: Harcourt Brace Jovanovich, 1987.

Franz, Gina. "How Public Is Public Sculpture?" *New Art Examiner,* February 1980.

Glowen, Ron. "The Triumph of the Public Artist." *Artweek,* January 11, 1990.

Glueck, Grace. "Is Public Art Really in the Public Interest?" *San Francisco Chronicle,* June 12, 1982.

Goldin, Amy. "The Esthetic Ghetto: Some Thoughts About Public Art." *Art in America,* May/June 1974.

Gude, Olivia. "An Aesthetics of Collaboration." *Art Journal* 48:4, Winter 1989.

Halbreich, Kathy. "Stretching the Terrain: Sketching Twenty Years of Public Art." In *Going Public: A Field Guide to Developments in Art in Public Places* (Jeffrey Cruikshank and Pam Korza, editors). Amherst: Art Extension Service Division of Continuing Education, University of Massachusetts, 1988.

Hall, Michael. "Forward in an Aftermath: Public Art Goes Kitsch." In *Art in the Public Interest* (Arlene Raven, editor). Ann Arbor: UMI Research Press, Ann Arbor, 1989.

Hawthorne, Don. "Does the Public Want Public Sculpture?" *ARTnews,* May 1982.

Hoffman, Barbara. "Tilted Arc: Legal Aspects." In *Public Art, Public Controversy: The Tilted Arc on Trial* (Sherill Jordan et al., editors). New York: American Council for the Arts, 1987.

————. "Law for Art's Sake in the Public Realm." *Critical Inquiry* 17:3, 1991.

Jordan, Sherill, Lisa Parr, Robert Porter, and Gwen Storey (editors). *Public Art, Public Controversy: The Tilted Arc on Trial.* New York: American Council for the Arts, 1987.

Kangas, Matthew. "Art in Public Places: Seattle." In *Art in the Public Interest* (Arlene Raven, editor). Ann Arbor: UMI Research Press, 1989.

Kardon, Janet. *Urban Encounters: A Map of Public Art in Philadelphia, 1959–1979.* Philadelphia: Falcon Press, 1980.

Kramer, Hilton. "Visual Noise: Isn't Public Sculpture Better Thought of as Litter on a Large Scale?" *Art and Antiques,* May 1988.

Kuspit, Donald. "Crowding the Picture: Notes on American Activist Art Today." In *Art in the Public Interest* (Arlene Raven, editor). Ann Arbor: UMI Research Press, 1989.

Lacy, Suzanne. "Fractured Space." In *Art in the Public Interest* (Arlene Raven, editor). Ann Arbor: UMI Research Press, 1989.

Larson, Gary O. *The Reluctant Patron: The United States Government and the Arts, 1943–1965.* Philadelphia: University of Pennsylvania Press, 1983.

Linker, Kate. "Public Sculpture: The Pursuit of the Pleasurable and Profitable Paradise," Parts 1 and 2. *Artforum,* March 1981 and Summer 1981.

Lippard, Lucy. *Six Years: Dematerialization of the Art Object.* New York: Praeger, 1973.

———. "Art Outdoors in and out of the Public Domain." *Studio International* 193:986, March–April 1977.

———. *Get the Message? A Decade of Art for Social Change.* New York: Dutton, 1984.

———. "Moving Targets, Moving Out." In *Art in the Public Interest* (Arlene Raven, editor). Ann Arbor: UMI Research Press, 1989.

Marter, Joan. "Collaborations: Artists and Architects on Public Sites." *Art Journal* 48:4, Winter 1989.

Merryman, John, and Albert Elsen. *Law, Ethics and the Visual Arts.* Philadelphia: University of Pennsylvania Press, 1987.

Miss, Mary. "On a Redefinition of Public Sculpture." *Perspecta* 21, 1984.

Netzer, Dick. *The Subsidized Muse: Public Support for the Arts in the United States.* Cambridge: Cambridge University Press, 1978.

Nordland, Gerald. *Controversial Public Art: From Rodin to DiSuvero* (exhibit catalog). Milwaukee Museum of Art, 1984.

O'Dougherty, Brian. "Public Art and the Government: A Progress Report." *Art in America,* May/June 1974.

Park, Marlene, and Gerald Markowicz. *Democratic Vistas: Post Offices and Public Art in the New Deal.* Philadelphia: Temple University Press, 1984.

Perlman, Bernard, and RTKL, Inc., Architects and Planners. *1% Art in Civic Architecture.* Baltimore: Maryland Arts Council, 1972.

Phillips, Patricia. "Out of Order, The Public Art Machine." *Artforum,* December 1988.

Raven, Arlene (editor). *Art in the Public Interest.* Ann Arbor: UMI Research Press, 1989.

Redstone, Louis G., and Ruth Redstone. *Public Art/New Directions.* New York: McGraw Hill, 1981.

Reidy, James. *Chicago Sculpture.* Urbana: University of Illinois Press, 1981.

Robinette, Margaret. *Outdoor Sculpture: Object and Environment.* New York: Whitney Library of Design and Watson-Guptil Publications, 1976.

Rosenberg, Harold. *The De-Definition of Art.* New York: Collier Books, 1972.

Senie, Harriet. "Richard Serra's Tilted Arc: Art and Non-Art Issues." *Art Journal* 48:4, Winter 1989.

———. *Contemporary Public Sculpture: Tradition, Transformation, Controversy.* New York: Oxford University Press, 1992.

Senie, Harriet, and Sally Webster. "Editors' Statement." *Art Journal* 48:4, Winter 1989.

——— (editors). *Critical Issues in Public Art: Content, Context and Controversy.* New York: Icon Editions, 1992.

Serra, Richard. *Tilted Arc.* 1981.

———. "Tilted Arc Destroyed." *Art in America,* May 1989.

———. "Art and Censorship." *Critical Inquiry* 17:3, 1991.

Slavin, Ruth. "Controversial Public Art: A Communications Approach." Unpublished M.A. thesis, Annenberg School for Communication, University of Pennsylvania, 1991.

Smith, Barbara Herrnstein. "Contingencies of Value." *Critical Inquiry* 10, September 1983.

Stalker, Douglas, and Clark Glymour. "The Malignant Object: Thoughts on Public Sculpture." *Public Interest*, No. 66, Winter 1982.

Steinberg, Leo. "Art and the Plight of Its Public." In *The New Art* (G. Battock, editor). New York: Dutton, 1977.

Storr, Robert. "Tilted Arc: Enemy of the People?" *Art in America* 73, September 1985. Reprinted in Arlene Raven (editor). *Art in the Public Interest.* Ann Arbor: UMI Research Press, 1989.

Sugarman, George. *Baltimore Federal.* 1978.

Tacha, Athena. "From the Other Side, Public Artists on Public Art." *Art Journal* 48:4, Winter 1989.

Thalacker, Donald. *The Place of Art in the World of Architecture.* New York: Chelsea House Publishers and R. R. Bowker, 1980.

von Eckhardt, Wolf, John Beardsley, Ronald Lee Fleming, and Edward Levine, "Dissent and Reply," *Public Interest,* No. 66, Winter 1982.

Weinstein, Jeff. "Names Carried into the Future: An Aids Quilt Unfolds." In *Art in the Public Interest* (Arlene Raven, editor). Ann Arbor: UMI Research Press, 1989.

Wetenhall, John. "Camelot's Legacy to Public Art: Aesthetic Ideology in the New Frontier." *Art Journal* 48:4, Winter 1989.

# ❦ 4 ❧

# Artists Entering the Marketplace: Pricing New Art

### KRYSTYNA WARCHOL

THE 1980S WITNESSED AN UNPRECEDENTED BOOM in contemporary art. More galleries than ever before were exhibiting and selling contemporary art (in New York alone there were about five hundred); more magazines were reporting on it; more museums were exhibiting and collecting it; and more people were buying it. Private and corporate demand raised prices not only for blue-chip contemporary artists, but for some young artists as well, many of whom were hardly known before the 1980s.

The commercial success of these young artists was highly publicized by the media, and it contributed to the construction of an image of the successful artist-businessperson. To the outside observer, it seemed that Allan Kaprow's observation that "the best of vanguard artists today are famous, usually prolific, financially comfortable" was still true (1964). However, the reality of being an artist in the 1980s indicated that Kaprow's idealistic vision had failed, since success and prosperity were achieved only by a minority of artists, whereas the vast majority struggled financially, supporting themselves with miscellaneous jobs, teaching, and grants.[1]

Despite the disparity between the socioeconomic reality in which most artists lived and the success of a chosen few, this very success—perhaps in combination with the dominant values of the Reagan-Bush decade—contributed to a shift in artists' attitudes toward the marketplace. Following the early example of Andy Warhol, in the 1980s artists eagerly moved away from the "starving artist" image rooted in traditional romantic ideology and in the process were accused of embracing the marketplace. Peter Halley, who built a career on the pretense of a contestation between art and the market, commented on the phenomenon: "A lot of people say younger artists embrace the market. I have not seen that to be the case. However, the attitude of disdain and hostility towards the mechanism by which the arts support system in the modern area functions has begun to seem ridiculous" (in Heartney, 1987: 29).

Artists' acceptance of the market was a logical consequence of a shift of power in the art world of the 1980s—it was a survival mechanism. During the decade, among all of the art world players who are fundamental in defining artists' careers and producing value for art—dealers, critics, museums, and collectors—the leading collectors of contemporary art achieved a great deal of power in terms of how artists' careers develop, because those careers were very much tied into and judged by the price for which works sold.

Purchases by influential collectors served as a stamp of approval of artworks' economic, as well as cultural, value. Although the domain of the market has traditionally been separate from the aesthetic domain, economic and aesthetic evaluations of artwork are interrelated: The purchase of work by collectors confirms the work's cultural value, and this act, as Pierre Bourdieu pointed out, in addition to giving the artist economic and intellectual independence, "is not entirely lacking in cultural legitimacy" (1969: 164). In a system where the market functions as an arbiter of value, it would be naive to expect artists to stay "pure"—as the outdated romantic myth expects—and to distance themselves from commerce, which has the power to influence their lives and careers.

A work by a new artist enters the marketplace through the gallery-dealer system, which is the primary distribution mechanism for contemporary painting. As Howard Becker explained, distribution has a crucial effect on reputations: "What is not distributed is not known and thus cannot be well thought of or have a historical importance" (1982: 95). In the 1980s, the development of artists' careers and reputations was increasingly tied to dealers' complex promotion and marketing schemes, and it was difficult for artists to establish themselves outside of the dealer-gallery system. Within this system, artworks function primarily as commodities offered for sale, and art publics, including artists themselves, are often bewildered and confused by the issue of pricing. Those artists who choose to become professionals by selling their art—within or outside the gallery system—are faced with the problem of how to price their art; therefore, they have to learn the pricing conventions.

The research reported here discusses how emerging artists priced their art and how prices for fine art by emerging contemporary artists were determined in commercial galleries in the 1980s. The discussion is divided into two parts. The first focuses on the development of artists' (primarily painters) attitudes toward pricing art; the second considers how prices for fine art by emerging contemporary artists were determined in the art world of the 1980s. The research consisted of in-depth, open-ended interviews with over fifty art students from the Pennsylvania Academy of Fine Arts (PAFA) in Philadelphia and emerging artists from New York City and Philadelphia and with over thirty art dealers from these art worlds, all conducted during the 1980s (Warchol, 1992).[2]

## LEARNING ABOUT PRICING:

## THE SOCIALIZATION OF ART STUDENTS

All of the artists I interviewed attach a variety of positive meanings to the sale of their work. Not only do they realize that selling art gives them the economic independence and freedom to do further artistic work, but the majority of the artists also see sales as legitimation of their work's value and as a special form of appreciation by the public. This evaluation is integrally tied to an artist's sense of worth and self-esteem. An emerging artist from New York said, "If someone buys your work, it is the highest commitment and flattery. It shows their belief in your value, your worth as an artist." One art student said, "What it means to sell work—it is an affirmation. If someone thinks enough of the work to pay money for it, then it is an affirmation of myself. I am thoroughly tied up with my self-esteem. If people hate my work I am in trouble, I begin to doubt myself."

Artists do want to sell their art, but most experience difficulties in pricing it. For most beginning artists—who tend to view making art as a personal matter—pricing art is a difficult issue directly linked to both their sense of self and their artistic identity. One student said, "Art is very personal. It is as if you put yourself up for sale, your own ego." Another remarked, "The painting is a part of me. And that's so hard to separate. How much is my art worth? That's almost what it's like. It's like an extension of myself." Yet another said, "How much do you price your arm or your leg?" And another: "I am putting a price on my own beliefs, on part of myself. I am putting a price on them for people."

Pricing is also difficult because of an attachment to the romantic ideology and an anticommodity notion of art, which creates uneasiness about financial issues. One student said, "Also, it is hard because I don't like the idea of pricing things. I feel embarrassed about selling my work. I am getting better. It is almost something I feel I should give away. I don't like the idea of being money-oriented, but that's the fact."

How do beginning artists learn to price their work? As noted, a large part of my research on how artists develop their knowledge of art pricing was conducted at the Pennsylvania Academy of Fine Arts, one of the most distinguished artistic institutions in the nation. Although the school stresses the notion of art as a vocation rather than a career, it does offer students some opportunities to learn about the business aspects of art. Most important, however, are the student art shows, in the context of which the majority of students get their first socialization experiences to the market.

During the academic year the faculty selects student work that is exhibited and offered for sale in a student gallery. The most important event is an annual spring show that takes place at the school's museum. All third-year and fourth-year students are invited to participate, as well as first- and second-year students selected by the faculty. Prior to the opening of the exhibition, student work is judged by the faculty, and numerous awards are given. The most prestigious is the Cresson Memorial Travelling Scholarship, which allows the chosen student to spend a year in Europe and return to school for an additional year. In honor of this fellowship the show is commonly referred to as "the Cresson show." This show gives students a unique opportunity to sell work and is a fundamental part of their professional training and experience. One student commented on the Cresson show, "It's very important. It is the only show in the city that gives that kind of exposure. It teaches you how to be an artist—not so much how to make art, it teaches students how to get a piece hanging for the show, how it looks next to something else in terms of selecting works for the show, getting up an installation, and so forth. Even the opportunity to sell the work. It is a very unique experience."

The majority of students are aware of some basic pricing rules—for example, oils cost more than watercolors, watercolors costs more than drawings, prints should be priced lower than unique works of art. However, regardless of their awareness of the rules, most experience difficulty in translating them into real numbers when it comes to a particular work. At PAFA, students have a great deal of autonomy regarding prices and can post any price they wish. The only formal involvement on the part of the school is a 10 percent commission on all student work sold, which is much lower than the standard 50 percent galleries charge.

Students commonly seek advice inside and outside the school. Faculty members are often asked for an opinion, especially those who exhibit and sell their own work. (At PAFA—much like other art schools in the country—many teachers themselves are struggling to establish their careers and are not affiliated with a gallery.) One student said, "I went to a faculty member I really trusted. I respect him. And he exhibits, so I know he won't be out of line." Within the student body, students who have experience with selling are also turned to for guidance. A student said, "X—we both do printing. She sells her work on a regular basis, so she is a good person to talk to." Students also look for guidance outside the school, not only from other artists and people who deal with art but also from friends, family members, romantic partners, and others.

Despite all the sources students consult, they often feel they get little help. The faculty, although willing to help, seldom suggests actual prices. The prevailing message is that there are no rules and that students have to find their own way. One student said, "I asked some faculty for advice, but what can they say? They didn't say anything." Another student recalled, "And when I got my piece in the show I went to see a friend who is an artist, and I asked, 'How do you figure out what you are asking?' or 'How do you make a price?' The friend said, 'That's a problem; you have to figure that out.' 'Well, how?' 'I am not going to tell you because it is hard to figure out. You have to decide for yourself.'" Another student said, "In the last three years I have been talking to lots of people, and everybody gives a different opinion." In fact, students gave numerous examples of getting different advice from different people, which only contributes to their confusion. One said, "I can remember having talked with faculty members about pricing work, and I have also listened to some advice some students got from their faculty. In most cases, I don't think what they get is really fixed. A student may have talked to one [faculty member] and talk with another and get a totally different answer."

Some students find that rather than asking for a general opinion, they have a better chance of getting an opinion regarding a specific price. One explained,

"When I ask people I would say, 'If I were to ask $100 for that, would you consider it a lot? Or is it a good price?' If you say '$100 for this?' you get answers. They say, 'Well, that would be high' or 'Well, that's reasonable, it is good, you framed it nicely.'"

Searching for clues, most students watch closely the prices of students who actually sell their work—especially those who do work comparable to theirs in terms of medium, technique, size, and other factors. As one second-year student said, "I think I look more at the third- and fourth-year students. They have a better idea what they want in price. I really never looked at the first- and second-year students because they are usually in the same frame of mind as I was, they didn't know what to think about pricing. Third- and fourth-year students knew what they wanted. Either they priced too much or too little, and I just balanced myself between that." Generally they try to make their own prices comparable to those of their peers. One student said, "I look at what other people are doing, and if I see something comparable about the price and I think whether it makes sense to me. . . . I noticed from looking at what other students sold and what prices they sold at that one guy I know has a piece he sold for $1,200. It's free-standing, but it is about the same size as mine, about the same level or whatever."

Students are concerned about not pricing lower than their peers for fear of sending the message that their work is not as good. They are aware early on of the communicative meaning of the price and the tendency on the part of the public to view it as indicative of the work's quality. The students feel strongly that the idea of "art as gift" doesn't function well in the market economy, since many found their art was not appreciated when it was given freely. Many students agreed with one who said, "If I sell too cheaply, it won't be appreciated—it would be treated too cheaply." One student gave this example, "I used to give my sculptures away to my family. I'd go into people's houses to find out where they were, and I would be really unhappy to see where they put them. I remember going to New York once, and one of my pieces was stuck in a bookshelf, sideways; it was meant to be set on a table or something. I think if they paid something for it they would display it differently."

Yet just paying "something" is often not enough to ensure proper appreciation. Horror stories about how the work ended up on the refrigerator door or behind the sofa because it was sold too cheaply are a vivid part of student folklore. One student said, "There is a certain minimum. I am not going to charge less than probably $50 for any of my drawings because that's enough money that you are going to appreciate what you get. If I charge $5 for a drawing, you might hang it behind your sofa when you get home. And I am not interested in that. If I charge you $50 for something, chances are you are going to have it framed and find a place for it."

All students are struggling to find the right price that strikes a balance between pricing the work so high that it won't sell and so low that it won't be appreciated. In this search, they go through various stages.

Although prices for art are clearly not determined by production costs, as Marx would have it (although his labor theory recognized the special status of artistic production), it is common for students to start by pricing their work according to the time they spent on it and the cost of the materials. They often write down all the hours they have spent working on the piece and pay themselves an hourly wage (usually between $7 and $15). Then they add the cost of supplies and framing. Although students sometimes managed to get bargain prices (e.g., for framing or supplies) and sometimes used found materials, many said that in figuring the price they did not take into account what the materials actually cost them but used their retail price. One sculpture student said, "I figured out the hours I put into it. I figured out the steel at the cost they could get it at, not at a bargain price, not the cheapest I could possibly get. What's reasonable. What the steel is priced now." A painter gave a similar explanation, "I framed that piece. I try to judge how much that framed work would have cost if they [buyers] walked in and ordered it. Not in my prices, not what I get, because I buy the frame chops and put it together myself."

Most students soon find pricing according to labor and cost of materials unsatisfactory, because it tends to result in prices that are too high. Students whose work is time-consuming or who use expensive materials (as in sculpture) find they cannot even pay themselves a minimum wage if they want to make their prices realistic and competitive. One student said, "Even if I paid myself minimum wage, my price would be thousands of dollars. I just don't feel I could do that . . . it would make my prices so high that no one would look at my work." And another, "One of the teachers said, write down your materials. I don't think that's right, because you end up with some exorbitant price that doesn't make sense to me. I would end up making it less expensive anyway."

A faculty member said about her own beginnings, "I did that originally. How to make that initial decision about the price. This is the first step." When asked if she still prices this way, she said, "No, it is too depressing. If you start doing it too much it doesn't help you. You realize that you are not always getting a good hourly wage for what you do. At other times the opposite is true. Later on it really doesn't matter. You base pricing on your previous track record, on your credentials. Different things matter."

Students also find this approach to be of little help in the case of pricing works that take little time to do since it leads to underevaluation. A faculty member elaborated, "It is not the time and materials and frame that you put into the piece. It is all those failures you have had, all those successes you have had, all that time getting to this point in this piece, whether it takes you an hour or years to do it."

As students become dissatisfied with these objective criteria, they begin to base their decisions on subjective criteria. Consider the following examples: "Once I figure that out [materials and labor] I look at the piece and see how much I like it, how much I really like it," said one. Another commented, "So I write that down [materials and labor] and I add 10 percent commission. And I say, 'This piece is this big and how much time did it take me to do.' And I try to figure out what I would need, how much money you would have to give me to make me feel good to let you have this piece. And that's how I come up with the price."

As these statements indicate, students consider what the work is worth to them, how much they like it, how important it is to them, and how good they feel it is. Thus at the beginning of their careers, young artists combine a pre-Renaissance craftsmanship attitude toward pricing (in which labor, materials, and size are the chief criteria) with a post-Renaissance addition of how they personally feel about the value of their work.

Among the criteria students consider, the perceived quality of the work is the most pronounced. In figuring out the price, students calculate how good they feel their work is not only compared with other students' work but also with that of artists seen in Philadelphia and New York galleries. One student who prices works at over $1,000 said, "You see in New York works much higher than that." Another, who sells medium to large paintings for around $3,000, explained, "I wasn't going to go above the prices I see in the galleries around here. I saw works in New York that have the maturity of my work that can be selling for anything over $25,000. I don't feel that some of these paintings are any more complex or creative than some of my best. I do feel my prices should be higher if I were an established artist, but I am not, I am a student."

Many students revealed a line of reasoning consistent with a story described by Lillian Bregman, who wrote, "An amusing story making the rounds of the galleries is about a young artist, a recent graduate of an art school, who came to see a leading dealer, painting in hand. He had priced it $4,000. Though interested, the dealer was astonished by the price tag. She opened negotiations by showing the novice a painting the same size by an established artist who had been one of his teachers—tagged at $3,000. 'How can you ask more?' she demanded. The fledgling artist did not hesitate. 'Mine is better'" (1987: 181). This approach leads to overpricing. One student said, "Most students tend to overprice. There is a tendency to forget they are students, because they feel their work is so good." A faculty member explained, "Unfortunately, lots of people price their work in comparison to people who are successful. Let's say Rauschenberg gets $100,000 for a painting, so a student says $6,000 is reasonable." A recent graduate who is working at the school said, "I think a lot of people who put higher prices on things are just unrealistic, inexperienced, or young and they just don't know."

The tendency to base prices on the perceived quality of the work reveals a lack of experience that leads students to disregard the commercial history of artists and their track records, on which prices are based in professional art worlds. Even if students understand that as students they can't charge as much as established artists, they still tend to overprice. To illustrate, prices for emerging local Philadelphia artists are between $1,000 and $5,000, with a starting level of $1,000 or less.[3] In comparison, one often sees paintings at the Cresson show priced between $1,000 and $3,000 and even higher. I was told about a student who priced her paintings at $10,000 a few years ago. The works did not sell.

In commercial galleries, how well the artist's work has sold in the past is the primary criterion for price increases, and students tend to disregard this factor also. Instead, they increase their prices according to their own assessment of how well they are developing artistically. One student said, "Right now I am becoming better at such a rapid pace that there is no way my price can stay the same. The amount of work, time, thought, everything that goes into my pieces is doubling and tripling within the month. You can't just keep selling for the same price with that going on." Another student, whose prices jumped from $1,800 to $2,300 within a year, explained, "This was a jump, but I felt the quality of the work really jumped."

There is another fundamental reason students tend to price their works too high—they have seen examples of high-priced work that sold at school, especially at the Cresson show. The Cresson show is a very popular event in the artistic life of Philadelphia, with a long-established tradition and strong support from the local community. The show, which, as one student put it, "opens people's pockets," attracts a lot of people who buy student work in order to support the school. Students are well aware of this and price their works with the Cresson public in mind: Prices are generally higher at the Cresson show than at the less prestigious monthly shows held during the year.

The problem is that students who sell for high prices at the Cresson show do not always realize that this is a false market on which it would be difficult to build a track record. For most students who sell works for $2,000 or $3,000 or more at the show, it will be difficult to obtain the same prices once they leave school, especially since galleries take a 50 percent commission. One teacher said, "The Cresson has a reputation for sales. Students expect to sell, and most of them do. It doesn't mean it is going to be that way. It is a tradition, people would buy. It is a false thing, it's part of the reputation of the school. Some people would give a student $2,000 or more. It is too much. It is like giving the child too many toys." Another commented, "If you are in an environment like this, it is hard to realize that it will change, and it is hard to realize that the cliché [of the starving artist] is true. . . . Don't expect that for the rest of your lives, because you're going to fall really hard."

This problem might refer especially to the Cresson winners, since their work sells the best. As in any other market, buyers like a guarantee when buying new art; at PAFA the prizes students win serve as a stamp of approval. "Prized work sells, unless there is something 'wrong' with the picture—too big, too whatever," a faculty member said ironically. Another commented, "It is a matter of a subjective appraisal on the judges' part. But to the public it looks different. If a student wins the Cresson, the public looks at it and it is just like having a piece in the museum. Not a true value, unfortunately—well, maybe fortunately; it makes them secure in paying a higher price."

Not only does faculty validation encourage buyers to purchase the works of winners; faculty opinion about students might also influence the price of the works. A student's own sense of worth and self-image as an artist evolve in the process of repeated interaction with the art community, including faculty. Positive feedback students receive from faculty through criticism, awards, and prizes contributes to how they feel about themselves as artists. One faculty member observed, "Students who have gotten a lot of good criticism from faculty usually have the courage to price higher. They have greater self-confidence, greater self-esteem."

All of these various forms of approval validate students' talent. As Henry Kingsbury observed in a music conservatory, "An authoritatively stated attribution of talent transforms a succession of special events into a manifestation of interpersonal traits of an individual person" (1988: 71). In an art school, faculty appraisal is one of the fundamental elements on the basis of which the definition of talent rests. This definition, in turn, carries consequences for the students' assessments of the economic value of their work. In contrast to students who are valued by faculty, those who have not received recognition may tend to price their work lower as a reflection of their unformed belief in their worth as artists. In addition, those who price lower also seem to see themselves more in student than in professional terms. One student said, "You can always go up with prices later. In a way we are still learning. It is kind of like you are in medical school—it is not quite the same, but you wouldn't expect a medical student to charge as much as a doctor." In comparison, one student who priced his paintings for over $3,000 said simply, in response to a question about why he prices this way, "Because I am a professional artist, not only a student."

One of the fundamental lessons students learn is that when their prices are too high their work won't sell. One student described how she gained this knowledge, "I had this piece priced at $1,000 last year. It didn't sell. I think it is a decent piece, and I was surprised that it didn't sell. Then I started thinking, maybe it is because it is too expensive . . . and then the teacher said student work is overpriced. I guess I don't have a sense of what the market will bear for my work as a student, so when I don't sell things my first reaction is to lower the price." In fact, the majority of students attributed the lack of sales not to the quality of the work but to the price being too high.

The process of becoming a professional artist through selling one's work requires that students, as well as other emerging artists, learn to suspend their own feelings toward the work and consider the perspectives of others. This means acknowledging that what it is worth to them is not necessarily what the work is worth to others. One student who priced his painting for $500 seemed to have acquired this ability when he said about his work, "It means a lot to me, but I didn't think it would mean a lot to other people." Since he wanted to sell the work, he said he tried "to price it at the point so it would sell, not [at] what it is worth."

For most students, learning to evaluate their art the way others do is not easy. Although PAFA provides an unusual socializing experience to the market through student shows, most students feel unprepared for the market and wish they had a better understanding of the business aspects of art when leaving school. This need is easy to understand, given that all students see themselves as being a part of the marketplace in some way in the future: The majority believe they will be able to support themselves from their art; those less optimistic feel they may have to supplement their income from selling art with other work. None of the students, however, see themselves functioning as professional artists outside the marketplace.

There is a belief among art dealers that art schools do not adequately prepare students for the market. One of the reasons may be a lack of authority resulting from insufficient faculty experience in market matters. The well-known New York dealer Ivan Karp has commented on this problem: "Just as there are no formal educational opportunities for dealers to learn their trade, the art schools hardly prepare their graduates for the harsh reality of the contemporary art scene since most fine arts instructors are artists themselves, usually without gallery affiliations, and they generally possess little knowledge of commercial aspects of the arts" (1989: 53).

The New York and Philadelphia dealers I interviewed feel the majority of artists entering the marketplace have unrealistic notions about the market value of their work. Like the students discussed here, they frequently compare the quality of their work to that of other artists and make quality-based price determinations. Emerging artists tend to compare themselves specifically to their colleagues and to artists of a similar age, and they adjust their own prices to match those of their peers. Yet while doing so, they often disregard the other artists' commercial histories and track records, which often results in unrealistic expectations and pricing the work too high, further hindering the building of demand for their work. One long-time New York dealer commented about emerging artists' lack of knowledge of market mechanisms: "They are not aware for the most part. I have some artists who have exhibited before, and they have some notion of what the prices should be. Some artists come with prices on their work, they have friends suggest what the price should be, they get information from auction catalogs. Artists are often confused. I said to someone $6,000, he said no, it should be $10,000, although $6,000 was a good price. They take it as a personal insult."

The development of inflated expectations is related to and strengthened by the 1980s market boom and its myth of the successful artist. A well-known New York dealer commented on the high expectations of artists and the danger fast realization of such expectations carries.

I have artists who wish prices could be more aggressive, and I have artists who want to take it slow because they never trust the art world. Some for good reasons, that the art world does not represent tremendous security. So if you are going to be a real jerk and think you are God's gift to the world and that everything you do is worth millions of dollars, that's fine, you are welcome to do that. But it just isn't going to work. And maybe you should go back to school, or maybe you have to learn the hard way. The scary thing in the art world is that there is an opportunity for such mistakes.

Another dealer said, "They want prices to be really high, and they don't understand that they should be kept low. That's always a problem."

## ART PRICING IN THE COMMERCIAL ART WORLD

### Pricing Low

If students and emerging artists have unrealistic ideas about how art should be priced, how are prices actually determined in commercial galleries? The pricing of contemporary art, as with older art, is based on the general principle of supply and demand. However, there is a crucial difference between prices for contemporary and established art, described well by Raymonde Moulin: "The price paid for an established work of art is meaningful—it is the amount actually paid by a buyer competing with other buyers to win the work. Since works of comparable quality fetch comparable prices, these prices are valid at different points of sale, with minor variations. By contrast, the price of contemporary art is largely unpredictable. . . . At a larger stage, gallery prices are often arbitrarily set with no relation to actual demand" (1987: 173).

In the beginning of an artist's career, prices are often set in anticipation of demand that has yet to be created. One of the fundamental ways by which the demand for the work is built is by pricing low. In fact, as suggested previously, pricing low is the most fundamental convention for emerging artists. As Picasso once said, "For paintings to be worth lots of money, they must, at some point, be sold cheaply." The purpose of pricing low is to introduce the work to collectors and to encourage them to buy the work so it can be seen by others in these collectors' homes and, therefore, build demand. A low price is meant to help the work leave the artist's studio. One dealer said, "Having prices so high that people won't buy it would do nobody any good. It would not do the artist good if his work goes back to the studio; it's not good for the gallery business. The best approach is to have the prices incredibly low." Another dealer said, "I tell almost all of the artists that have shown here that it is to your own best interest to have prices as low as you can because the work is actually sold and gets out of your studio and out of my gallery and into somebody's collection, where it may be seen alongside other famous artists, where it will be reviewed in certain social strata who are financially able to afford more pieces. That his name would be mentioned in circles that otherwise he would never reach."

Annina Nosei, Jean Michel Basquait's dealer, describes how she built demand for the artist by selling at low prices:

I saw Jean Michel Basquait as an exciting addition to my gallery, and for his first exhibition I priced the work very low, selling to the most intellectual collectors, those who got excited immediately. . . . I told them that they should have a work by Jean Michel Basquait also, for $1,000, or $1,500 more on the bill of $25,000 they had already run up. This worked quite well: these collectors gained an early commitment, told their friends, and all of a sudden Basquait's paintings were found in collections besides more well-known artists, as the youngest of all. (quoted in Coppet and Jones, 1984: 287–288)

The concept of pricing new artists low is linked to, and results from, a fundamental art historical evaluative principle, according to which individual artworks can only be evaluated adequately within the context of an artist's entire oeuvre. The total reputation of the artist—which reflects the general consensus of opinion at any given time—is a basic factor that determines the possible price range. Young artists in the beginning stage of artistic development do not have established reputations, and, unlike their older colleagues, they have yet to prove their worth. Unknown artists can't charge lots of money precisely because they are unknown—meaning they do not have a following among critics, curators, and collectors: They lack a reputation. One dealer commented, "Prices of emerging artists have to be lower than experienced artists. One can say firmly that those artists who have been in the field longer have paid their dues and in many cases have broken the ground for the younger artists to be able to do their work. A young artist has to grow, and part of this growth is that they are able to charge more for their work." Another dealer said, "My philosophy has been, you underprice in the beginning and you make up for it later, because once you get the demand going, you can dictate the price." And yet another, "People would say, 'I like his work and I think he is really good, but he is not well-known.' There is a point where people want the price to match publicity . . . there is a point where people say, 'Well, this person is not that known, I don't think the work should be that expensive.'"

Low prices also minimize the risk that the artist's career won't progress (which would make the investment a failure). One dealer commented, "He may develop and he may not, he may decide it is too difficult, or after one or two successful shows he may have a nervous breakdown and never do anything. I have seen it happen often in my gallery." Another dealer explained why he prices low: "This way when the person buys the art and takes it home it is no big risk. They don't see it as a big deal, they are not spending a fortune to buy it. It has almost a playful quality about it."

Although the dealers' primary objective is to attract collectors who will contribute to the artists' careers and to place the work in important collections, they also want to attract collectors of lesser stature since they, too, build an artist's track record. Low pricing frequently attracts less important and even beginning buyers. One dealer explained, "He [the artist] has got something that appeals to a lot of different collectors and a lot of different types of people, and one thing is that some people who buy his work are not real professional collectors. Some of the people have never bought any artwork before, and it would be nice that the work is inexpensive enough that [it] attracts them. I have made a number of sales [to buyers] who have never bought anything before."

Although guided by the convention of pricing low, dealers usually negotiate the price of the work with the artist. As already mentioned, the basic factor that determines the price is the artist's track record—whether the artist has sold work before and for how much. When an artist is starting in a new gallery, he or she may have established a track record by selling works from the studio, in a non-commercial gallery, or in another setting, or the artist may have previously been associated with another commercial gallery where a certain price level was established. One dealer who said she always asks the artist "How much do you want, and how much will you be happy with?" commented, "I asked him if he sold any pieces when I looked at the studio. That's a question I ask everybody. Most artists are very honorable and trustful. . . . I ask what range they have sold in—thinking about it, I will see if he is realistic."

Negotiation with the artist establishes a shared understanding about the price level, and during the process the dealer often explains to the artist the basis of his or her pricing philosophy. The following is an example.

> I say, I think this little sculpture you made, $1,500 is a reasonable price. They may say, terrific, I thought it would only sell for $800. Or they may say, I am disappointed, I thought it would sell for $3,000, and you are saying only half as much as I thought. And you start talking back and forth, and they say $3,000. I would say maybe in the next year I could sell one of them. But we start at $1,500, I think people will be very excited. Would you rather sell four for $1,500 or one at $3,000? Isn't it better to get four of these into people's homes where people will be enjoying them and talking about them? I always say to artists, choose prices where you don't feel you are being cheated, get the work out into the world. Let it be talked about—and then people start coming, and it is a supply and demand thing.

Although the dealer tries to achieve a compromise with the artist on the price, at the beginning of the artist's career the bargaining power belongs almost totally to the dealer, since emerging artists depend heavily on dealers to promote their careers. The dealer who, as Bourdieu pointed out, is the one who "creates the creator" plays an important role in producing value for art in all stages of an artist's career. The dealer's role, however, is the most crucial in the very beginning of the career because other forms of validation—from museums, critics, and collectors—are lacking. One dealer, when asked how many times he prevails with a new artist, said simply, "Always." Another described consequences when he and the artist were not able to share a common ground regarding price:

> There were a couple of artists whose work I really liked and wanted to show, but we were worlds apart on the price. And I knew not only that I can't get anything approaching the price they wanted for the work, but also by having it in the show next

to another piece of work the same size and having that person's work be ten times more I am making a statement implicitly that this artist is ten times better even though nobody knows about him, nobody has heard of him. Price does make a statement about what I consider to be the value of the work. And I couldn't allow that.

## Starting Price Level

During the 1980s, a large painting by an unknown artist in most New York galleries was priced between $2,500–$3,000 and $5,000–$7,000, with $3,000 being the most common price. One renowned New York dealer explained, "It is a kind of consensus . . . that's where you start. Nobody knows the artist. You want to encourage people to buy. It can be little more than $3,000, but that's what you need to get for a picture these days. It is sort of what the emerging artist is worth."

This starting level also relates to sculpture, unless production costs are high. However, the price of sculpture of an unknown artist may not even cover the cost of materials. One dealer said, "In the very beginning we tried to price according to the reputation of the artist, which may be very minimal, as to how many works we have available of the artist in the gallery, and how much effort went into making the work—how much materials went into it. What's the cost of this work? Many times you can't even price to the amount of the cost, you have to sell it for less. The intention in the beginning is to get it sold."

As these quotations suggest, rather than being determined by the quality of a specific work, prices for works by unknown artists are determined according to a shared understanding in the art community of what unknown artists are worth. In the 1980s, a work by a new artist was worth around $3,000.

This standard $3,000 price level was related to the overall economy and to the economics of running a gallery. At the time of my interviews in the late 1980s, the average cost of running one of the less expensive galleries in New York was $20,000 to $25,000 per month; this figure went up to $100,000 or more for the most established galleries, which spend a great deal on promotion and advertising. In contrast, costs were much lower in the earlier days of the art world and so were starting prices. "In 1967 a large painting cost $750, but now with inflation, you must charge $3,000 to cover the basic costs," observed one dealer. Additionally, prices in local art worlds are lower than those in New York City, partly because rents and the costs of running a gallery are lower. Noncommercial galleries have low publicity costs, and they do not take the usual commission.

## Price Increases

The commercial career of the artist is based on gradual increases in price, a practice that is rooted in a belief in the artist's continual growth and development. Even when works do not sell during or after a show (in fact, a great deal of selling occurs after an exhibit and between shows), most dealers nevertheless raise prices when the artist exhibits again, usually 5 to 10 percent, to convey a sense that the artist has developed and the work has improved. These regular token increases suggest to collectors that the artist's work is becoming better and more valuable over time. One dealer commented on the need to always raise prices: "Just because otherwise someone bought something not as valuable, if it wasn't 10 percent more valuable the next year, they are not going to feel so good about dropping three or four thousand. It is keeping pace with inflation, or whatever you call it, but you have to increase prices each year."

The price is always raised when the artist has a new show and sometimes between shows. The amount of increase depends on how well the artist is doing between the shows in terms of interest from critics, curators, and, above all, collectors. With each increase the dealer bases his or her decision—as was true at the beginning of the artist's career—on the anticipated demand for the work. There are two methods for raising prices: the gradual, slow increase (e.g., when the artist is "doing well," both in terms of interest and actual sales; a common increase in price is 15 to 25 percent) and the "stock market" method, which is to increase the price each time a work sells to as high an amount as the market will bear. Although the latter method was not uncommon in the 1980s, most dealers are, in fact cautious and are not in favor of fast, large increases because raising prices too quickly might result in an artist being priced out of his or her market. As one dealer put it, "At one point, the demand always stops . . . there is always a point at which people stop buying." Another said, "You have to meet the prices with an understanding that you didn't find the last individual to pay the high price."

Whether they raise prices dramatically or gradually, dealers must decide what kind of collectors they want to target. Moulin observed, "To the extent that a dealer is able to control the price, he must determine whether he prefers a broader market or a higher price" (1987: 159). There is a small group of collectors who support an artist at very low prices before he or she has any reputation, and there is a small group of collectors who buy at big prices at the top. The biggest group of collectors is in the middle, and dealers are careful not to lose them. There are many more collectors who can afford work at $20,000, for example, than at $50,000. One dealer said, "If you have fifty people that can afford the painting at five thousand, but only ten who can afford it at ten, and maybe only one at fifteen, you're not going to jump to fifteen."

Most dealers want the security provided by a broader market; they agree that radical price jumps alienate collectors but admit, as one put it, that "the temptation is there . . . it is hard not to raise prices when there is a demand." The temptation seems to have been especially strong in the 1980s, when so many careers were built on rapid price escalation.

The amount of increase also depends on the type of work that is being offered for sale at the next show. Frequently, artists move into a higher price bracket simply by making bigger works. Big works are generally harder to sell, especially in the beginning of a career. One dealer commented, "Often until you get established you don't show really big things. It is hard to sell them. You want things to go out into collections, so you don't want really huge work. I don't want to give specific examples. If you start out at $2,000, $3,000, then the prices not only go up, but they also make bigger works. So in the second show there is more like a $4,000 to $5,000 range, because the work is usually bigger."

## Never Lower

Why don't dealers raise prices to the level of resistance and then, if demand stops, simply lower the price until it meets demand? Because another dominant convention holds that prices for works of art should never be lowered. Since the artist's reputation is based on an assumption of increasing growth and development, the artist's work is always supposed to increase in value. Lowering the price reveals not only that the artist's work is not growing in value but that, in fact, it is losing value. It shatters the myth on which the commercial careers of artists are based. Publicly lowering the price also alienates the collectors who bought the artist's work earlier for higher prices. A drop in price is considered a serious breach of confidence and a betrayal of the collector's trust. If the dealer sells work with the understanding that the artist is good and promising, then how does he or she explain to collectors that the work they bought two years ago for $5,000 is now worth only $3,000?

When prices reach too high a level or demand for an artist's work stops because of collectors' lack of interest, "the price never goes down, the work just doesn't sell," as one dealer put it. In fact, in many situations it would be better for business if the dealer lowered the price instead of maintaining the pretense that the artist is still in demand. Many dealers agree with one who said, "The idea that work has to increase in value has cost lots of artists their careers and has cost lots of gallery business." The "never lower" convention is destructive to midcareer artists, who have established a certain price level and for whom demand has lessened. It also causes difficulties for some artists who establish careers in local markets, which they leave once there is no more demand for their work and try to establish themselves in New York. This is not easy, since often the prices these artists receive locally are higher than what New York collectors might be willing to pay because the artist is unknown to them. Although in some cases dealers have no other option than to publicly lower the price, they often try to correct the situation by giving discounts.

## Discounts

In fact, discounting prices is a widespread convention. Artwork is seldom sold at the asking price and is commonly negotiated down during interactions between the dealer and the buyer. Discounts are given to encourage the sale of the work, and they symbolize a special privilege and courtesy extended to an important buyer. They also function as a sign of the dealer's recognition of the risk-taking collector. "If there is a discount, it makes it special," said one dealer.

Discounts are not a new phenomenon. Many renowned collectors, such as

Peggy Guggenheim, Joseph Hirshhorn, or Robert Scull, were known for striking hard bargains when it came to art. For them, as for today's collectors, discounts were a necessary part of the game of art buying.

The truth is that this "special privilege" is extended to almost everyone who buys art: private and corporate collectors, private dealers, private and corporate advisers, museums, and so on. As one dealer said, "It is sort of a farce, because everyone gets 10 percent." Because the practice is so widespread, some dealers build anticipated discounts into the asking price, raising it to the point where they can freely offer discounts. One dealer recalled, "We had two pieces of an artist who is in demand. I couldn't decide whether it should be $9,000 or $10,000. Then I thought, who am I going to sell the pieces to, and I knew they will want 10 percent, so I decided to do it [at] $10,000."

The amount of discount given depends primarily on the demand for the work. As one dealer put it, "If you are in a seller's position, you can be hard. If this is a buyer's market, and you are dying to sell the work, you say, OK, I will make you a deal." Another summarized his approach: "If the artist is not doing well, we are trying to do anything to make the sale so the artist feels encouraged." Although the courtesy discount of 10 to 15 percent is almost automatic, dealers often give larger discounts, the amount of which depends on—in addition to the demand for the work—how much the gallery needs the money, how much the artist needs the money, the volume and quantity of the collector's purchases, and how important and, above all, loyal the collector is. In contrast to loyal clients, on whom the gallery business rests, many dealers say they never give discounts to first-time buyers since, as one dealer put it, "one acquisition does not make you a good customer." Although first-time buyers have the most difficulty getting discounts, when the dealer needs a sale such a buyer may have as good a chance of obtaining one as a faithful client. Such discounts might make the first-time buyers feel special and encourage them to return to the gallery, as one never knows what "collecting potential" a newcomer may have.

Instead of or combined with discounts, dealers sometimes offer a loyal collector a payment plan. Cash or the collector's ability to pay for the work soon also tend to lower the price. Discounts may be offered not in terms of a percentage of the price but as an actual amount of money, usually for more expensive works. As one dealer noted, "At a certain point, the dollars are more important than percentages. So we say, 'I will give you $10,000 off, but I can't do more.'"

Most dealers split the discount with the artist. Others feel it is not necessary to discuss the matter with artists and absorb the discount themselves. There are many types of arrangements in between these extremes; for example, one dealer splits discounts of up to 15 percent with the artist but absorbs anything higher than that.

Most dealers consider discounts to be necessary business practices and accept them as a "fact of life" in the art world, which helps to fulfill their responsibility to sell art. Others, however, criticize them as unfair to both artists and dealers.

One dealer said, "[Discounting] is a problem in the art world. I have a real ax to grind about that. I think that if you have a very fair price, the price should be the price." Charles Cowles, a well-known New York dealer, revealed a similar sentiment: "One of the biggest problems that art dealers have is discounts. Recently a lot of young collectors have come to expect discounts and don't want to buy unless they receive one. I price my artists as fairly as possible. If a collector asks me for a discount, he is asking me to take money out of my pocket, or, even worse, out of the artist's pocket. It is dishonest ultimately to the artist" (quoted in Coppet and Jones, 1984: 249).

Many emerging artists have problems with discounts and view discounting not as a courtesy or an incentive to sell art but as demeaning to artists and art—as something appropriate for regular commodities but not for art. As one student put it, "This is not Macy's basement." Another student who was asked to lower prices described her reaction: "I said, look, this is not some kind of supermarket. You don't bargain on prices like that. I said, sorry, if you like it buy it, if you don't like it don't buy it. Because this is not only a matter of money but also a matter of pride. This is not selling goods and vegetables."

Most emerging artists express this attitude out of a lack of experience with real discounting, because most buyers purchase student work without bargaining. Students—like most artists—are, however, willing to discount work when they feel the potential buyer can't pay the full price but truly appreciates the work. In this case, they feel lowering the price is justified by the fact that the work is really wanted. In fact, it is not uncommon for artists to lower the price for their fellow artists, who are viewed as the most appreciative of all audiences.

### Size—A Calculus of Value

Another convention that exists early in an artist's career is pricing according to the size of the work (e.g., all paintings of the same size by the same artist are priced similarly). This convention appears to conflict with the evaluative principle that holds for established art, in which work is priced according to aesthetic quality. Pricing new art by size is motivated by a belief that when an artist begins his or her career, it is too early to reflect judgments of quality in the price—the "judges are still out." New York dealer Miani Johnson explained, "I feel that new work can be priced only by size in the beginning because there is no way to know what will be most coveted" (quoted in Coppet and Jones, 1984: 270). This convention has roots in the French system, in which canvases were given a number of points according to their dimensions and were priced accordingly (Moulin, 1987).

Pricing by size is not only an evaluative practice but is also a fundamental business strategy that allows the dealer to sell the myth that all of the works of the same size that are offered for sale are of equal quality. The dealer can therefore promote them equally, and the myth of consistent quality gives all work the same chance of being sold. By pricing one work lower than another, a dealer implies that less expensive work is less valuable, which would be devastating for business. As one dealer put it, "If the person likes the other work more, are you going to tell the person, 'your judgment is worse than mine?' If you do that, you will never see the person again." Another dealer gave this example: "It may be the last work in the show that's available and the dealers with a better sense of humor, perhaps, will say, 'Isn't it the best work in the show? I have always loved that.' It makes a very nice line. . . . On the other hand, there is someone who is going to look at the work, and how would they feel to know that the other work the same size sold for $5,000 more. I know my first question would be, 'Why? Isn't it a good enough work?'"

Unlike the dealers, emerging artists prefer to reflect their own value judgments in price and largely resent the price-by-size convention. A second-year student who priced only a few works and didn't sell any said, "It all depends on how much more I feel. If the smaller piece, to me, represents more of my time, more of my work and effort, I charge more for it. If the larger piece didn't represent that, I would probably charge less. I want to make it fair. . . . I want to price it for the quality." A third-year student who won a prize at the Cresson show said, "When I have pieces of work I tend to look in terms of how much art appeals to me. A number of us tend to think that when a painting is large it should be really expensive. . . . What I look at in particular is how the work has come to itself. So sometimes I have a small piece that is more expensive than a larger piece. Smaller pieces were most expensive, the difference was something in the hundreds." Many artists who are affiliated with galleries and who have accepted the convention for business reasons still feel pricing by size is demeaning and insulting to the artist and leads to unnecessary commodification of art. An art teacher who has been showing in New York said, "It is offensive. Every artist would say that pricing by size isn't good, that there is something offensive about it, like you are buying cloth. It is just ludicrous to think about painting in these terms."

If galleries followed the artists' point of view on pricing by size, it would have rather detrimental consequences for business. A dealer commented, "Can I say to collectors with good taste and a wonderful collection, 'The artist thinks this isn't as good a work'?" This is precisely the type of question and situation pricing by size allows the dealer to avoid.

## Productivity

One of the most important factors that determines the actual price of the work, within a general consensus of what people are willing to pay for the work of an unknown artist, is the productivity of the artist. As in any area of consumption, scarcity implies high prices. In established art, the rarity and scarcity of the work are key elements affecting its value. Similarly, in contemporary art, works by less productive artists customarily have higher market values. When more works are available, the dealer can sell more. One dealer explained, "If there are a lot of them around, you would sell for $2,200 or $2,500, something like that. If there are very few around, you would think of $2,700 or $2,800 or even $3,000." Other dealers feel they would price closer to the $5,000 range.

Putting higher prices on works by less productive artists is also an attempt to assure the artist's income. One dealer commented, "In your mind somewhere, there is an aspect that if this artist is only producing ten paintings a year, possibly you should try to get more for those paintings because that artist has to live on the money they get from producing the work." Most dealers believe an artist who produces only a few works a year should be rewarded for the time and energy that went into the production of the work, which will be reflected in the work itself. Collectors are always told about the artist's productivity and are expected to understand that labor and time investment are reflected in the price. "If they [collectors] have any degree of humanity, they will recognize it," said one dealer. Also, in the case of less productive artists, less work is available to choose from, and all works are therefore expected to be of high quality. One dealer said, "Being less productive, each work must be almost perfect. . . . You try to make them appear terribly precious to your audience . . . and it is visible and it is something that you ought to tell your clients."

In the case of less productive artists, the increase in price might be larger than that of prolific artists. One dealer said, "So that fewer people are able to buy the work at specific price increments, and slowly it works its way up—this is more business than art, but that concept of scarcity causes people to understand price hikes."

It is well-known that some dealers pressure artists to produce less work in order to create a false sense of scarcity and manipulate demand. Even without influencing the artists, the dealer is always in a position to control the supply of work to some extent by choosing only certain works to sell from the artist's available supply. Sometimes artists limit their own productivity to keep prices up. Yet the dealer must make sure enough work is available on the market to maintain public interest. Maurice Rheims wrote that "for something to fetch a good price, it must be rare, very rare . . . but not too rare" (1959: 216), meaning that the work must first become widely known before it can be financially valuable. Therefore, if artists produce too little work early on, it may be much harder for them to emerge than is true for prolific artists, since they won't have enough collectors to support their careers. One dealer said, "At the level of a new artist, [scarcity] only affects price if there is demand. If they are selling. To mention to a new artist that he would be smarter to do very little work . . . could kill his career. It is not a sure bet."

## Gallery Reputation

Another important factor that determines prices is the context within which the artist is showing and the reputation of the gallery. Galleries with established reputations are generally able to charge higher prices than are their less known counterparts. Seldom will one see works priced in the $3,000 to $5,000 range in renowned galleries. One of the reasons is that these galleries seldom accept totally unknown artists. When they do, they often try to build the demand for the work before giving the artist his or her first individual show. The example noted earlier of the method by which interest in the work of Jean Michel Basquait was built illustrates this point.

The gallery with a successful track record has legitimacy that supports higher prices and serves as a guarantor of the value of the artists and works exhibited. Collectors trust dealers who have proved their authority, and the dealer's reputation is, in fact, his or her most important asset in creating demand for the artist's work. The role dealers' reputations play cannot be fully understood in strictly rational terms, however. Moulin wrote, "A subjective theory of value governs the market as a whole. Demand—a subjective affair, unstable and manipulable— plays a decisive role; thus irrational factors are important in determining art prices, and it would be an irrational attempt to eliminate them" (1987: 178).

## CONCLUSION

Because of the unknowns inherent in the demand for art, dealers stress that a great deal of pricing is instinctual and is done "by gut feeling" rather than according to calculated strategies. One dealer said, "It is an impulse, it is art." Another commented, "There are so many variables, there has to be a feeling of the pulse of the moment. You can have all the theories you want, and if you have no instinct, something gut, what they call the pulse, you are going to be wrong. It is a little bit of the grease in the cogs of the machine."

A subjective theory of demand for artwork, which is always affected by complex socioeconomic and political, as well as individual, factors, undermines the neoclassical theory of value recognized by institutional economists (e.g., Grampp, 1989). Neoclassical theorists apply general principles of the creation of value in fixed-priced markets to the art market and view buyers as fully informed, making perfectly rational choices. However, as Charles Smith showed, even the auction—the most critical element in neoclassical theory—is not a "socially uncontaminated mechanism for matching the individual preferences of buyers and sellers" (1989: 163). Crucial to the neoclassical model is an assumption of perfect information, which is especially hard to sustain in a contemporary market where the uncertainty of value is inherent. This uncertainty is caused not only by the essential uniqueness of the work but also by the absence of an artist's entire career, which would provide a proper context for interpretation.

This uncertainty is lessened by a shared consensus among members of the art world as to the value of work and artists. A fundamental fact about works of art is that their cultural and economic value is collectively produced in the process of interactions among the members of the art world (Becker, 1982). Although individual and institutional art world members employ explicit and implicit means of legitimation of work, value can only be constructed through the entire net-

work of relationships among all of the members of the intellectual field (Bourdieu, 1969).

Today, market evaluations are increasingly interrelated to and interdependent
on other evaluative structures. The demand by collectors for work is affected by
and, in turn, affects the evaluations and judgments of other art world members:
dealers, critics, curators, as well as artists. In fact, known artists who promote
their colleagues exert a great deal of influence on careers, and established artists
are also the most uncredited "discoverers" of new art and artists (despite, as
Bourdieu pointed out, the fact that the discoverer never really discovers anything
that has not already been discovered by at least a few). All art world members
customarily rely on the opinion of artists they trust as to who is worth seeing,
exhibiting, writing about, and buying. Dealers always rely on the opinions of the
artists they respect, and the easiest way for a young artist to get into a gallery is
through the recommendation of a more established colleague.

Artists entering the marketplace, as well as commercially unsuccessful artists,
often view the art world as a closed system in which a few people have the power
to make or break careers. There is little doubt that those members of the art
world who are in positions of authority do have the tastemaking power to influence others. However, because of the fundamentally interactive nature of the
contemporary art field, no member or group within the art world—no matter
how much authority they wield—has the power to singlehandedly create an artistic reputation and impose their judgment on the rest of the art world. Reputation conferral occurs within so many channels that despite some (usually short)
success in constructing manipulated careers, no lasting reputation can be created
without general consensus among artists, dealers, critics, curators, and collectors
about the value and historical significance of the artist.

## NOTES

1. An article by Robert Storr (1988) brought Kaprow's work to my attention. A number
of studies published in the 1980s showed that despite the art boom, in the 1970s and 1980s
most artists earned little from their art. A survey of 4,146 visual, literary, and performing
artists conducted by Columbia University's Research Center for Arts and Culture found
that more than half of the artists who responded earned less than $3,000 from their art in
1988. Gross income for 85 percent of those surveyed was $30,000 or less. Only 27 percent—
including painters, sculptors, musicians, and dancers—earned their primary income as
artists. Of the 83 percent who said they earned some money from their art, only half
earned enough to cover expenses (Swaim, 1989). According to another study conducted
by the American Council for the Arts (reported in Robinson, 1990), artists' earnings de-
clined about 37 percent during the 1970s, and the earnings of painters and sculptors
dropped by 62 percent. Experts predicted that as the population of working artists increases, individual earnings are likely to decline further.

2. For the purposes of this discussion, students are viewed as representing emerging
artists, as they are in the beginning stages of artistic careers. Since art schools constitute a

primary socializing agent in the artists' professional role (e.g., Griff, 1970; Strauss, 1970), the development of artists' attitudes toward pricing art was studied within this context.

3. It should be noted that artists in Philadelphia who sell at the $1,000 level are seldom just out of school. In fact, dealers rarely take on recent graduates, preferring those who have been working on their own for at least five years. They feel this is the amount of time necessary for artists to prove they are serious about their commitment to artistic work and to shed the often too-visible influence of their teachers.

## REFERENCES

Becker, Howard. *Art Worlds.* Berkeley: University of California Press, 1982.

Bourdieu, Pierre. "Intellectual Field and Creative Project." *Social Science Information,* 1969, 8(2):89–119.

Bregman, Lillian. "What Price Art." *Philadelphia Magazine,* March 1987:181–187.

Coppet, Laura, and Alan Jones. *The Art Dealers.* New York: Clarkson N. Potter Publishers, 1984.

Grampp, William D. *Pricing the Priceless: Art, Artists, and Economics.* New York: Basic Books, 1989.

Griff, Mason. "The Recruitment and Socialization of the Artist." In Milton C. Albrecht, James H. Barnett, and Mason Griff, editors, *The Sociology Of Art and Literature.* New York: Praeger, 1970.

Heartley, Eleanor. "Artists Versus the Market." *Art in America,* July 1987:27–33.

Kaprow, Allan. "Should the Artist Become a Man of the World?" *ARTnews,* 1964, 63(6):34–37.

Karp, Ivan. "A Curious Relationship." *Art in America,* October 1989, 77(3):51–53.

Kingsbury, Henry. *Music, Talent and Performance: A Conservatory Cultural System.* Philadelphia: Temple University Press, 1988.

Moulin, Raymonde. *The French Art Market: A Sociological View.* Translated by Arthur Goldhammer. New Brunswick: Rutgers University Press, 1987. Originally published in French as *Le marche de la peinture en France,* Editions de Minuit, 1967.

Rheims, Maurice. *Art on the Market.* Philadelphia:Weidenfeld and Nicolson, 1959.

Robinson, Walter. "Art Careers Still Pay Poorly, Surveys Find." *Art in America,* February 1990:35.

Smith, Charles. *Auctions: The Social Construction of Value.* Berkeley: University of California Press, 1989.

Storr, Robert. Statement in "Critics and the Marketplace." *Art in America,* July 1988, 76(7):106–107.

Strauss, Anselm. "The Art School and Its Students: A Study and an Interpretation." In Milton C. Albrecht, James H. Barnett, and Mason Griff, editors, *The Sociology of Art and Literature.* New York: Praeger, 1970, pp. 159–177.

Swaim, C. Richard. *The Modern Muse: The Support and Condition of Artists.* New York: American Council on the Arts, 1989.

Warchol, Krystyna. "The Market System of the Art World and New Art: Prices, Roles and Careers in the 1980s." Unpublished Ph.D. dissertation, University of Pennsylvania, 1992.

# 5

# "Woman Artist": Between Myth and Stereotype

BETTE J. KAUFFMAN

THE CONTEMPORARY WESTERN VERSION of the role of "artist" emerged from the Renaissance and achieved modern form in the romantic movement of the nineteenth century (Gimpel, 1968; Becker, 1982). It is a male role, which is to say the conditions of producing art and the relations of power that have institutionalized art as a category of valued cultural products have historically favored men as performers of the role.

This tradition of male performance of "artist" is not without consequence. In social systems dedicated to the ongoing construction of gender as dichotomous, such that there are only two acceptable gender categories, each having its own attributes and social tasks to perform (cf. Kessler and McKenna, 1978), the distinction between social roles and typical incumbents tends to blur. The activities and persona that constitute a given role are conflated with gender categories and attributes. Gender groups achieve "natural" ownership of role skills and activities; roles achieve normative gender expectations and gendered personas. Thus when Jackson Pollock told Säri Dienes that she could not paint because she had no balls (Edelheit, c. 1980), he was expressing both male ownership of "artist" and its activities and the role's acquisition of attributes socially defined as masculine; for example, daring, aggressiveness. In addition, the artist is independent, highly individuated, and dedicated to his work above all else—all attributes constitutive of masculinity in Western society.

The presumed lack of these attributes is an issue for women artists, for they are caught between two cultural constructs: the mythic "artist as male hero" on the one hand and the stereotypical dabbling lady painter on the other (Garfunkel, 1984). The woman artist as dabbler or "lady painter" descends from Victorian notions that well-brought-up women should be generalists, proficient in a number of useful, refined, but not too intellectually demanding activities, rather than excelling in one (Nochlin, 1971). According to one popular nineteenth century book of etiquette, painting (usually watercolor) and drawing were particularly appropriate "feminine accomplishments [that] keep the mind from brooding upon self" and fit well with the domestic priorities of women: They were quiet (disturbed no one) and could be dropped and resumed as needed (in response to wifely and motherly duties) "without any serious loss" (Nochlin, 1971: 28, citing Mrs. Ellis, 1844). Beyond overt reinforcement of the patriarchal notion of self-effacement as a feminine virtue, the more insidious damage done by such texts is that the aesthetic production of women was a priori defined as amateur and functional, a pastime with the benefit of producing useful or decorative objects—all that "fine art" could not be.[1]

In this chapter, I examine the social models of "artist" and "woman artist" and draw upon interviews with members of women's cooperative art galleries in Philadelphia and New York City to discuss how women artists position themselves in relation to these models.[2] I argue that women's stories about becoming artists reproduce the "artist" myth in significant ways, even as they conflict with and diverge from it. Further, the stories of the women artists in this study diverge along two distinct paths that are related to the Philadelphia versus New York contrast, neither of which coincides with available models of "woman artist." Essentially, Phila Group women tended to integrate their artist identities and career paths with traditional family structures and feminine concepts of self, whereas NYC Group women tended to acknowledge or celebrate—and thereby politicize—the dual and often conflicting arenas of career and family.

## SOCIAL MODELS OF "ARTIST"

At the core of the modern conception of art and the artist is the belief in genius as a "gift" unique and rare persons are born with and that is revealed in great works of art (Pollock, 1980; Becker, 1982). From this core, defining aspects of the artist role emerge: To be an artist is a "calling," a destiny compelled by innate characteristics; the artist is different from ordinary mortals, in some sense a social deviant whose difference is the source of, and is evidenced in, not only profound artworks but eccentric lifestyle and behavior.

### Manifest Destiny

"I've often questioned my need to make art but knew there was never a choice."

"The artist in you will eventually come out. It has to."

The first of these statements was written by Eleanor Allen for her women's cooperative gallery's tenth anniversary exhibition catalog (Muse Gallery, 1988). The second statement was made by a Phila Group member in the context of explaining her pursuit of an art career after taking time out to raise a family. Like virtually all artists, she painted and drew constantly as a child. She was "encouraged a lot" by upper-middle-class parents who "helped Dr. Spock write that book" and provided "unlimited paint and paper." Her grandmother was a painter; from kindergarten on she was the class artist. Yet "as much as [family and teachers] put energy into creativity," an art career "wasn't what everybody had in mind," so she married after high school and raised three children. She spoke of being frustrated and "angry at the whole world" as her mothering career appeared to be ending, of being compelled by an inner need, and of sometimes being fearful of what would happen if she could not make art; she felt her mental health depended on it (Ph9).[3]

These women artists are expressing the typical belief in "artist" as manifest destiny. The artist is different from birth by virtue of certain innate talents and inclinations. He or she might resist in various ways, perhaps by acquiring skills and trying a more ordinary occupation, but eventually will be compelled to acknowledge and claim the artist identity. A variety of social-contextual factors might encourage or discourage different people, but the artist is "in you." Although it can be suppressed for a time, it must eventually be let out.

In a society that requires artists to be born rather than made, to be different because of innate talents and traits, one of the ways of presenting oneself convincingly as an artist is to tell a story of having always been one. Artists characteristically report that they "knew" they were artists at a very early age (Simpson, 1981). Typical childhood activities of making things, painting, drawing, copying, sewing, building, and the like, are viewed by artists as different from the usual childhood pursuits and are reported as the earliest manifestations of the artist identity: *"How did you become an artist?* Oh, I've always been. I remember going into kindergarten and seeing pots of paint, brushes, blank sheets of paper—and freaking out. I know I was drawing before that, always. I was an only child, I had a sandbox and a teepee and two imaginary friends. I just played all the time . . . and made things. . . . I did that when other kids would read. I would always draw" (NY5). Further evidence of the artist identity is found in the reinforcement by elementary and high school teachers, who, along with classmates, interacted with the child as the class artist (Griff, 1964) and involved the budding artist in creative projects: "I was always the one chosen to decorate the bulletin board" (Ph6).

Although they are role models or mentors and sometimes the first people to notice "talent," early art teachers are often retrospectively defined as limited, ones the artist child "jumped past . . . real quick" (Ph13). In some cases, their greatest perceived value was that they simply left the artist child alone. Art class was "just . . . a nice time to do whatever you wanted," the role of the teacher to "just let you draw" (Ph10) or to recognize and reward "what you see in my work [that] has been there all along" (Ph13).

The art educational philosophy evidenced in such comments is described by Larry Gross (1983: 74) as "not erect[ing] any . . . barriers that might stifle . . . talent in its rare appearances," an approach compatible with a cultural belief that artistic competence is the province of the naturally gifted "chosen few." Indeed, the exceptional cases in which a high school art teacher and a future artist did not get along are viewed as resulting from overly didactic and conventional teaching methods in the face of advanced artistic sensibility and an already firm conviction of one's destiny: "In high school, the [art] teacher detested me. . . . She . . . called my parents and tried to persuade them not to send me to art school; thought it would be a waste of their money and my time. She believed in watercolor, liked to make drawings of doorways and stuff. I hated watercolor. I just couldn't do any of the things she thought I should do, and I guess I didn't have much respect for her work" (NY8).

The "genetic theory of artistic ability" gains credence from familial tendencies (Gross, 1983: 75). Most artists identify parents and other family members as "'doers' and 'makers'" (Cogan, 1985: 1)—mothers who do needlework, fathers who make things from wood or leather, perhaps even a parent or relative who is an artist. These role models are viewed as part of a supportive environment for the child's early artistic efforts but not as modifying in any way the innate nature of creative genius and the compulsion to be an artist. In other words, rather than seeing such families as social contexts "in which everyone engages in a symbolic mode, and it is . . . conveyed to children that they too are expected to join in" (Gross, 1983: 75), the creative parent is viewed as the "hearty individual who . . . for many . . . artists was an early . . . reinforcement for their own innocent urge" (Cogan, 1985: 13).

The artist's innate difference, although laudable or at least benign in the child, becomes cause for concern when the child decides to go to art school. Family support turns to family crisis over economic and social deviancy issues.[4] Women artists report family resistance as often distinctly gendered.

> My first love was art, but I couldn't sell my parents on the idea that I should go to art school. It's an old story. It wasn't clear how one would make a living at that. Unless I wanted to be an art teacher, and I didn't. . . . They were delighted to send me off for two years to become a [nurse's aide][5] because that is what I would fall back on if, quote, unquote, something ever happened to my husband. (Ph6)
> *Your parents rewarded you as a child, but didn't think you could do art as a career?*
> Absolutely not. In fact, they were enormously discouraging. To them it was all right to be a lady watercolorist, but it was nothing that a woman should do. (NY7)

At this point the stories of NYC Group and Phila Group members diverge, both from each other and, particularly for Phila Group members, from the social model of artist. NYC Group members went to art school anyway but may have compromised: "I . . . majored in art education as a sop to my parents" (NY8). Many also married and raised families as they pursued an art career or after they had established themselves as artists. Most Phila Group members married and raised a family before pursuing an art career, which leaves them with a wife-mother interlude to account for in the construction of a continuous sense of self as an artist. Before I discuss the consequences of these divergent paths and the strategies for dealing with them, I turn to the ideology of artistic "difference," for the traditional familial roles of women are particularly problematic in a social context that valorizes eccentric individualism.

## Individuation and Social Marginality

The idea that certain persons are born to be artists is central to the set of beliefs Howard Becker (1982: 352) described as "a particular, intensely individualistic theory of art and how it is made." This theory states, in part, that specially gifted people create artworks having special qualities that testify to the maker's gifts, as the already known gifts of the maker testify to the special qualities of the art-works. In a similar vein, Griselda Pollock (1980) argued that art history, in its preoccupation with individual artists, is not really "history" at all. Rather, it is "psychobiography," an essentially circular process of constructing the artist (per-sonality, psyche, biography) from the artworks, then defining meaning in art-works as "solely . . . the 'expression' of the creative personality of the artist" (pp. 58–59). This historical practice effectively isolates art from the public, political, and social contexts of art making in the (presumed to be) "ideologically pure" space of the artistic personality.

In short, the modern art world is a highly individualized context, at the center of which stands the paradigmatic Individual whose idiosyncrasy, expressed not only in artworks but in lifestyle, dress, and behavior, locates him on the margin of "normal," conventional society. It is here that women artists' stories diverge from the social model. Acculturated to be specialists in human relationships, women tend to reject the "monolithic individuation" (Garfunkel, 1984) and so-cial marginality of the artistic persona. Thus I turn to a twentieth-century proto-type for these aspects of "artist."

In the opening sequence of Henri-Georges Clouzot's film *The Mystery of Pic-asso* (1982), widely spaced paintings on easels stand in pools of light on a black-ened set. The camera tracks Picasso as he walks slowly from one to another, his features sculpted by the light as he pauses briefly before each painting then disap-pears into the darkness. He reappears to gaze intensely at the next painting. A husky male voice solemnly intones:

> One would give anything to know what was going on in the mind of Rimbaud . . . and Mozart. . . . To know the secret mechanism that guides the creator in his peril-ous adventure. Thank God, what is impossible in poetry and music is possible in painting. To know the mind of the painter, just follow the hand. He walks, he glides . . . he walks a tightrope. One slip and everything could be lost. The painter gropes on hopelessly like a blind man in the darkness of a white canvas. The light that comes to life little by little is the painter who, paradoxically, creates by adding black. For the first time, this confidential daily drama of the blind genius is pre-sented in public, since Pablo Picasso has accepted to live today for you and in front of you. (Clouzot, 1982; English subtitles)

In this formulation, artistic production is from the individual mind of the poet, the composer, the painter. It is a mind that is different by virtue of a "secret mechanism." In the case of the painter, the mind can be constructed from the paintings and the process of making them. The painter at an easel in a pool of light set against blackness is clearly the sole author of the paintings. He is god-like, appearing and disappearing at will to admire his own works. He is not merely a hero but a wounded warrior—a "blind genius" daily engaged in a life-and-death struggle; with each canvas, either all is lost or life begins anew.[6]

Aspects of the artistic persona missing from Clouzot's portrayal are provided by Edward Quinn's films for television, *Picasso: The Man and His Work, Parts I and II* (1986). Picasso's early hardships are evidence of a justly earned reputation: He contracted scarlet fever from living in an unheated garret in Madrid; in Paris, he "lived in squalor" and painted at night by the light of a candle. His lifelong series of overlapping liaisons with various women testify to the extraordinary sensuality, emotional needs, and temperament of the artist. After the dissolution of one of his marriages, he spent a "long, lonely winter" drawing women (mostly as models for and with himself, the Artist), his art and life "nourished by the fountain of suffering." His last wife is particularly cast as Picasso's muse, model, and manager. She is praised at length in glowing terms for her physical beauty, adaptability to his moods, ability to "absorb" his angry outbursts, and finesse in maintaining household order without fettering the extravagantly messy, cluttered, spontaneous working style of the genius.

In tracing "the birth of the modern artist," Jean Gimpel (1968) argued that under patronage systems, as in early fifteenth-century Italy and seventeenth-century France, the artist was integrated into society by virtue of serving the church or the state and produced socially useful, pedagogical works.[7] When patronage was superseded by artistic freedom and market competition based on personal reputation, the artist's social utility and economic security were undermined. Subject to an unreliable market flooded by unsolicited artworks having no particular social purpose, artists lost "their psychological and social bearings" (Gimpel, 1968: 43). Excepting the few who become famous and rich, artists found themselves living on the fringes of society, doing menial labor for room and board while peddling their overabundant paintings. Isolated, indigent, and insecure, artists resorted to the bohemian life, flouting norm and convention by arrogant excess in dress and behavior. Those who fared well on the market used the power of their reputations to challenge church and state authority, claiming, as did Veronese, "the licence that poets and madmen claim" (Gimpel, 1968: 59).

Gimpel further argued that the romantic movement of the nineteenth century put the finishing touches on the artistic personality: glorification of the irrational, detachment from everyday reality, and—excepting the adherents of social art—indifference to the needs and problems of ordinary humanity, including the need for art that can be understood by other than the elite few who devote their lives to it. The artist is a social misfit, and any therapeutically aided adjustment to real life is viewed as a detriment to the creative impulse.[8] Gimpel names Gauguin, Cézanne to a lesser degree, and the writers Zola, Baudelaire, and Mallarmé as prototypes of the modern artist: demigods, solitary, unstable, eccentric, and depressed.

Belief in neurosis as the source or catalyst of artistic genius is exemplified by the ongoing commentary on Van Gogh. The title of Jane Addams Allen's review (1986) of a Van Gogh exhibit is revealing: "A Portrait of the Artist as a Disturbed Man." In the review Allen often referred to the exhibition catalog's correlations among Van Gogh's life, work, and state of mind through his correspondence, and she interpreted the paintings as showing an alternation between the "highest consistent level" of achievement and the diminution of powers "of a man who senses approaching death" (1986: 66–67). Both Allen and Robert Pickvance, curator of the exhibit and catalog editor, are contributing to the art historical production of the artist through the tracing of a life "within the narrow limits of only that which serves to render all that is narrated as signifiers of artistness," a process enhanced by "the assimilation of VG [Van Gogh] to . . . the myth of the mad genius" (Pollock, 1980: 63–64). "All aspects of VG's life story and the stylistic features of the work culminating in VG's self-mutilation and suicide have provided material to be reworked into a complex but familiar image of the madness of the artist— 'sensitive, tormented, yet incredibly brilliant'" (Pollock, 1980: 64). These beliefs about the relationship between madness and art, argued Pollock, have less to do with medical diagnoses (as Clouzot's characterization of Picasso as "blind man" has less to do with physical blindness) than with "categories of difference, otherness, excess . . . those special and distinct modes of being which set the artist ineffably apart" (Pollock, 1980: 65).

June Wayne (1979) has labeled the artist "stereotypical female" and argued that the "demonic myth" of the artist bears striking resemblance to the feminine mystique described by Betty Freidan. Both woman and artist are biologically determined, one by virtue of physical attributes and the other by innate talent or creative genius. Both reside on a pedestal of helplessness and moral superiority, for the feminine and artistic temperaments are ill equipped to deal with business and politics and are easily seduced by power and money. Both are mediums through which procreative and creative miracles are manifest without the exercise of will or intellect. Women make babies as the natural course of things. Artists make art in a moment of inspiration, an upwelling of "mysterious forces . . . inchoate in source . . . [that] may be vitiated or even destroyed" by analysis or control (Wayne, 1979: 130–131).

Many women artists readily embrace the attributes of sensitivity and intuitiveness and participate in the continuity of the social model of the artist in ways already discussed. In so constructing themselves according to the model, women artists are using and regenerating social knowledge about what is required to be viewed as a "serious" artist. But, as Wayne's analysis suggests, the cultural myth of the artist includes elements contemporary women artists find incompatible, if not ideologically oppressive. Thus they select, refine, and equivocate as they talk about their identities as women and artists. Freud's argument that the artist "belongs to a special category of introverts who avoid neurosis by expressing their fantasies in art" (Gimpel, 1968: 128) is echoed by the woman artist who feared the loss of her mental health if she couldn't make art. She is expressing a variation on the stereotypical relationship between art making and madness, yet in the context of her entire interview it is clear that she is not totally adopting the model of the neurotic artist. Rather, she is using an art career as a way out of an oppressive social situation and as a way of expanding her identity beyond the traditional roles of wife and mother. But she is talking about it in terms that signify artistness.

## SOCIAL MODELS OF "WOMAN ARTIST"

### Women Passing as Artists

The image of women artists as less serious and dedicated than men artists was reinforced by the critical discussion of women of earlier times. Anna Jameson, nineteenth-century feminist organizer and champion of women in the arts, praised women artists in a manner that expresses dominant social definitions of "woman."

> In general the . . . habits of attention and manual industry, the application of our feminine superfluity of sensibility and imagination to a tangible result—have produced fine characters. The daughter of Tintoretto, when invited to the courts of Maximilian and Philip II, refused to leave her father. Violante Siries of Florence gave a similar proof of filial affection; and when the grand duke commanded her to paint her own portrait for the Florentine gallery . . . she introduced the portrait of her father, because he had been her first instructor in art. (Jameson [1834], quoted in Holcomb, 1987: 19)

Jameson continued in a similar vein to recognize Dutch painter Henrietta Walters for declining "magnificent promises of favour and patronage" in foreign courts because she was "contented with her lot" and devoted to her homeland; she praises Italian painter Sofonisba Angusciola for preserving "the most delightful sisterly union" by taking her sisters with her when invited to the court of Spain (quoted in Holcomb, 1987: 19).

The image of women artists as less dedicated and serious than men artists by virtue of the "higher calling" of family maintenance has persisted. In her sociological analysis of the St. Louis art world, Michal McCall found women artists to be a "unique instance of professional marginality" (1978: 290). Citing Becker, she defined "artist" as one who not only produces works that conform sufficiently to appropriate conventions to be "capable of being treated as art" (McCall, 1978: 291) but who also asserts enough control over his or her products to ensure that they are treated as art. In order to exert such control, the producer must be perceived as both serious and dedicated, the former defined as intending that products be considered art, signaled by making them look like art and presenting them as art is presented, and the latter as committed to "continued productivity . . . as the primary life activity" (McCall, 1978: 292). A group McCall labels "BFA mothers" were thus perceived as having proved their lack of dedication by getting married and having children.

As students, these women learned that a choice between art and motherhood was expected of them. However, they all believed they could have avoided that choice if others in the art world had not perceived their marriages and pregnancies as choices already made. In other words, these women felt they had not given up art so much as they had been given up on. . . . One BFA mother said, " . . . I think [teachers] forgave me my first child, but when I was pregnant with the second . . . I felt them marking me off." (McCall, 1978: 295)

McCall's BFA mother described being "marked off" as encountering teachers who refused to advise her about graduate school and responded to her attempts to discuss her paintings with questions about her family. Another of McCall's groups, the "semi-picture painters," were viewed as not serious because of the "decorative qualities" of their work and their willingness to show and sell in local art fairs, even though many of them also sold through mainstream galleries. The experiences of women artists like those McCall interviewed were aptly characterized by June Wayne:

[The woman artist] is an instant Mrs. So-and-so living in a tract house with hubby and the babies. She is thought to dabble in oils in the family den, which only she refers to seriously as her studio. And her art is assumed to be a matter of tight little landscapes and flower arrangements or decorative, derivative abstractions displayed over the couch. . . . To be a wife, a mother, and forty is to suffer a fatal syndrome; no matter what the truth or how large the talent or accomplishment, she is only a woman trying "to pass" as an artist. (Wayne, 1979: 132–133)

Such is one of the available models of woman artist. She is the "lady watercolorist" who would have been acceptable to one NYC Group artist's parents and the "suburban housewife Sunday painter" image a number of the Phila Group struggled to cast off.

## Women Artists as Honorary Men

In her transition from artist's model to painter of the nude, Suzanne Valadon "took on and lived out the male Bohemian stereotype: a succession of lovers, a scorn for money and a wild lifestyle," thereby creating great tensions in her relationships with her mother and son (Betterton, 1987: 226). Rosa Bonheur cropped her hair and adopted men's clothing but denied the symbolism of these gestures and sharply criticized other women painters who followed suit "in the desire to make themselves pass for men" (quoted in Nochlin, 1971: 35).

One way to combat the lady painter stereotype has been to embrace the social model of the male artist. Becoming an "honorary man" involves defining oneself as an exception to gender norms, distancing oneself from the gender group and feminism, and somehow cultivating an unnatural yet female image. Women writers of the nineteenth century used these strategies to combat both the lady novelist stereotype (like the lady painter, not serious) and the bluestocking label (shrill, aggressive women). Seeking to be taken seriously, they took masculine or androgynous pen names and fiercely resisted the gentlemanly condescension of critics. Seeking to affirm their own femininity, they criticized the audacity of women writers as a group. When *Jane Eyre* was received as "a radical feminist document," Charlotte Brontë was offended; George Eliot and Elizabeth Barrett Browning paid lip service to feminism but could not believe that Victorian women were ready to assume the responsibilities of equality (Showalter, 1971).

The price of honorary male status is at times made explicit by media and art world institutions. In the catalog of a Georgia O'Keeffe exhibit, Patterson Sims linked O'Keeffe's laudable "independence and singularity of purpose" specifically to an interpretation of her relational life: "Her dependence on others is strictly contained. When an alliance became too confining, it was broken off or put at a distance—as when, within five years of her marriage to [Alfred] Stieglitz, she began to spend her summers alone in the Southwest. The price of this existence— though the artist might call it the pleasure—has been a profound and enduring solitude" (Sims, 1981: 3).

Sims interpreted O'Keeffe's childhood on a farm in Wisconsin with her parents, four sisters, and two brothers as an example of having been "raised in a geography of isolation" (1981: 3). O'Keeffe's biographer described instead a childhood of extended family and the security of a farm community in which the activities of the "visible and prominent" O'Keeffe family, including Georgia's ninth birthday celebration, were reported in the social column of the local newspaper (Lisle, 1980: 18).

Georgia O'Keeffe is a particularly relevant example of the honorary man phenomenon. Nearly every woman artist interviewed named her as a role model or as an actual or a potential great woman artist. Her life is often interpreted in terms of the strategies described previously (defining self as exception to gender norms, distancing from gender group, demonizing image), and her death in 1986 inspired yet another critical debate over the importance of her work, causing some concern that she is already being written out of art history (cf. Salisbury, 1987).

How O'Keeffe demonized her image is so familiar as to scarcely require mention. Her "black, loose-fitting . . . shapeless" (Asbury, 1986: A17), "intentionally out of fashion" (Drohojowska, 1986: 16) attire; severe hairstyle (Wooster, 1987); and "solitary, ascetic" (Sozanski, 1987: 16-G), "reclusive" (Asbury, 1986: A1), "desert Buddha" (Wooster, 1987: 8) lifestyle have long been grist for the media mill. However, whereas Picasso's eccentricities and excessive behaviors are interpreted as signs of artistness, O'Keeffe's are viewed as "a conscious attempt at media manipulation" (Wooster, 1987: 10), "promot[ing] her own mystique" (Drohojowska, 1986: 19), and "sentimental hogwash" that must be separated from critical evaluation of her paintings (Sozanski, 1987: 16-G). Picasso was a temperamental genius, O'Keeffe "as much an actress as an artist" (Yau, 1988: 114).

When feminist Gloria Steinem pilgrimaged to Abiquiu, New Mexico, with a bouquet of red roses, O'Keeffe refused to see her. This rebuff of an act of homage and an attempt to claim her for contemporary feminism has come to symbolize O'Keeffe's repudiation of womankind and the women's movement. According to Laurie Lisle (1980), it was not always so. As a young woman, O'Keeffe read the radical feminist writers of her day and was a long-time member of, and occasional speaker before, the National Woman's Party. But O'Keeffe's answer to the sting of art world reluctance to take a woman seriously had been unrelenting work, at the sacrifice—with Stieglitz's urging—of her desire to have a child. By the time Steinem appeared on her doorstep, she had "boxes of establishment honors neatly stacked on shelves in her Abiquiu house" (Lisle, 1980: 334) and was well aware that men had helped her: Stieglitz, his band of loyal men artists and patrons, critic Henry McBride. O'Keeffe felt the new feminists were "undignified" in behavior and repeatedly stated that if they "worked more and complained less" they would have a chance to get their art into museums and galleries (Lisle, 1980: 334).

Lisle also reported a usually overlooked change in O'Keeffe's view of her own art. In a letter to friend Anita Pollitzer, O'Keeffe wrote that her charcoal drawings, which scandalized the art world when Stieglitz later exhibited them, expressed "essentially a woman's feeling" (Lisle, 1980, quoting O'Keeffe [1916: 67]). Critics, however, wished to dismiss the work on this account. "All these pictures say is 'I want to have a baby,'" said one (Lisle, 1980, quoting Evans [1945: 75]). Measured by the dominant art world ideology of universality, she was "being a woman and only secondarily an artist," her work viewed as "the personal statement of a woman rather than the universal statement of an artist" (Lisle, 1980: 139). O'Keeffe felt invaded and trivialized by these interpretations and came to be embarrassed by "the ladies" who flocked to her exhibitions. Taking a cue from a journalist in 1921, for the rest of her life she shielded herself by saying that people who saw a woman's eroticism in her paintings were "talking about themselves, not about me" (Lisle quoting O'Keeffe, 1980: 134). Said one Phila Group artist who named her as an influence, "It's the only thing I never understood about you, Georgia" (Ph9).

For all her fame and establishment awards, O'Keeffe's hold on a place in art history is tenuous. Writing in 1985, Kenneth Baker wished to forestall the "almost certain . . . avalanche of uncritical praise" he predicted would be triggered by O'Keeffe's (surely imminent) death (p. 57). Charging that her reputation has been "inflated" to meet "the need of both critics and the art market for a modern American woman artist to make it into the ranks of the 'major'" (1985: 56, 58), he dismissed her oil paintings and argued that her true accomplishment was in the area of watercolor. Since O'Keeffe's death, both John Yau (1988) and Edward Sozanski (1987) have repeated Baker's analysis, including O'Keeffe's early charcoal drawings with her watercolors in the category of "important" work. Not coincidentally, watercolor and drawing are traditional "feminine accomplishments" and are subordinate to oil painting in the art world hierarchy of mediums.[9]

## BETWEEN MYTH AND STEREOTYPE

Over the years, women artists have positioned themselves and been positioned by media, critics, and art world institutions along a continuum ranging from McCall's BFA mothers who have been "marked off" to the relatively successful but still marginal honorary men. Where does "woman artist" fall? It is a designation about which women artists disagree. Some reject it as a ghettoizing label and, when asked to respond to the term, call themselves an "artist who happens to be a woman." At the opposite extreme, a few claim "woman artist" as a title, a political stand, and an expression of an aesthetic philosophy and goal. Others accept or tolerate "woman artist" as a transitional term, the goal being "artist" with no gender component.

In this disagreement and ambivalence, women artists are acknowledging the stigmatizing capacity of an identity that challenges social norms. According to Erving Goffman, ambivalence is inevitable when "the stigmatized individual acquires identity standards which he applies to himself in spite of failing to conform to them" (1963: 106). In the case of "woman artist," the stigma is double-edged. On the one hand, women artists visibly and by social definition fail the tacit standard of maleness and certain aspects of the social model "artist" even as they know and strive to meet social criteria for being taken seriously as artists. On the other, they reject the stereotype of the lady painter with which they are most immediately and visibly identified and that is undeniably part of their social history. "Woman artist" draws attention to both that which they fall short of and that which they strive to leave behind.

For women artists, social identity is thus a problem of tension management. The honorary man strategy is a form of "covering," an attempt to draw attention away from "those failings most centrally identified with the stigma" (Goffman, 1963: 102–103). In contrast, claiming "woman artist" as an aesthetic philosophy and political stand is an attempt to build group cohesion around the very attribute for which women artists are stigmatized. Like "black is beautiful" and "gay pride," it is a militancy intended to defy social norm by displaying that which social norm defines as a liability and claiming "special values and contributions" for those who share it (Goffman, 1963: 113). It is a strategy that draws attention to difference, "in some respects consolidating a public image of . . . differentness as a real thing and of [the] stigmatized as constituting a real group" (Goffman, 1963: 114). Claiming "woman artist" thus makes visible and challenges the tacit gender boundary of the social role "artist." But it also foregrounds the lack of qualification of women artists, with the possible consequence of constituting them as a ghetto.

Media and art world institutions provide the sort of ghettoizing criticism that validates women artists' fear and ambivalence. Not all sexist criticism is necessarily ghettoizing criticism; I reserve the latter term for commentary that isolates women artists, emphasizing their otherness in a manner that reinforces their marginal status. One form this takes is defining women's art as not that of some great male artist. An example is provided by Robert Hughes (1983) in a review intended to bring Lee Krasner "out of the shadows" of her late husband, Jackson Pollock. In addition to situating the review within the marital relationship, Hughes described Krasner's work, albeit glowingly, as concerned with some of the same aesthetic problems Pollock had addressed but "without impromptu drip" (1983: 92). In other words, both she and her work are, in the first instance, not Pollock. Such "rescues" of the women artist wives of famous men artists tend to occur after the husband's death and are usually couched in terms that not only emphasize the otherness of the widow but that do as much to preserve the superior standing of the late husband as to advance the cause of the widow. Robert Hobbs (1987) made this agenda quite clear in the title of an article in which he discusses his discovery of Sally Michel, the widow of Milton Avery: She is "The Other Avery."

This form of criticism is not limited to women artist wives. Sozanski (1988) introduced a review of Diane Burko's paintings by noting that they "make you think immediately of Monet." He then spends three paragraphs—a third of the review—discussing how Burko's paintings are "not Monet" before noting that "it would be misleading to belabor this comparison, because Burko is neither imitating Monet nor competing with him" (1988: 3D). Having thus protected Monet from the possibility that Burko's paintings are as good or better, Sozanski offered mostly praise in the remaining two-thirds of the review.

Perhaps the most common form of ghettoizing criticism is the ongoing effort to name the first great woman artist. This practice specifically protects the status quo by containing women artists' success on the margin of mainstream competition while offering the "first great" designation as a consolation prize. Baker's concern (1985) about the inflation of O'Keeffe's reputation to meet the need for a first major woman artist is an example, although Henry McBride named O'Keeffe the "top . . . woman artist" as early as 1946 (quoted in Lisle, 1980: 266). The O'Keeffe debate has not, however, prevented speculation along similar lines about Nevelson, Frankenthaler, and other successful women artists. Conceding that the exhibit of works on paper he is reviewing may not be an adequate test, Valentin Tatransky (1985: 14) nevertheless posed the "pressing" question, "Is Helen Frankenthaler the first major woman painter in recorded art?" He concluded that she is in spite of the "slips" in her work, but, "the question is whether she will simply remain a pioneer among many major painters. . . . There has arisen in recent years a body of very fine and ambitious women painters . . . some of the strongest of [whom] have been influenced by Frankenthaler, and they are not inferior to her in rank" (Tatransky, 1985: 14). In other words, not only must a "first great" be named in every field (painting, sculpture, and so on) and time period (all recorded art, the twentiethth century, and similar eras), but there is always the possibility that a first great will be matched or even surpassed by a proliferation of "not inferior" women artists and then the process can begin anew.

Unlike the search for origins and innovators that typifies art history (and history at large), the search for first great women artists in various fields effectively isolates them from mainstream competition, for it construes women as competing primarily with other women for honors delimited by gender but not based on considered analysis of the social, historical, and aesthetic relationships between gender and art making. It constitutes women artists and women's art as real categories without addressing what makes them categories, what their particular contributions and qualities might be. It argues that there have not yet been great or major women artists and further implies that there will be none until so named by a mainstream art historian or critic. The cultural capital to be gained by naming a first great woman is surely the larger part of what is at stake, for the woman so named has not displaced or even achieved equal standing with a first great (man) artist.

## NYC Group: Taking on the Myth

How do social experiences position contemporary women artists in relation to myth, stereotype, and woman artist? I have discussed how both Phila and NYC Group members tell similar stories of being artists by birth and destiny, how many were the class artist at school, and how, when the young artist became interested in art school, parental support often turned to discouragement. At this point, the stories of the two groups diverge: Many Phila Group members became suburban housewives. Their NYC counterparts went to art school anyway. It was a validating experience. "I took art history, then my first studio course and after that . . . just never stopped. I took one studio course, then another and another. But of course I painted and drew all along, it was just nothing I ever thought I could grow up to be. I suddenly realized my parents were wrong about everything" (NY7).

For some, art school affirmed not only their defiance of parental discouragement but their rejection of traditional social norms as well. "It was great. Wonderful. For the first time in my life I had people I could talk to, that I had something in common with. In [hometown] everybody wanted to go to stenotype school or get married. . . . Nobody had any aspirations. They never knew what I was talking about, being an artist" (NY8).

Most important, as this example suggests, art school was a homecoming that confirmed resoundingly the artist identity, including the sense of one's difference: "I got into [art school] and I felt like . . . I was home. A pig in shit, right? I was so-o-o happy" (NY5). "I'd always felt like such a changeling. . . . For me it was the most delicious thing that had happened. I'd found something that confirmed who I was in a way I'd had no inkling existed" (NY7).

NYC Group members were enrolled in art schools or departments in and near New York City in the 1960s and early 1970s. Concurrently, the art market was expanding rapidly, and the New York City art center was moving from Madison Avenue and 57th Street to the bohemian artists' community of Soho. Toward the end of the period, the 1960s counterculture, aided perhaps by the memory of successful activism that transformed Soho from a decaying industrial district to a living, working art community and market, spawned an artists' revolt first formalized as the Art Worker's Coalition (AWC) (Lippard, 1984).[10] In 1969 members of AWC formed a cooperative art gallery (Lippard, 1984), and a group of disaffected women broke from AWC to form Women Artists in Revolution (Chiarmonte, 1982). In 1971 several women artists combined a countercultural strategy with feminist politics, took for a name the initials early 1960s squatter artists had stenciled on Soho buildings to alert fire departments and forewarn demolition crews, and founded the first women's cooperative art gallery, A.I.R. (Artist in Residence).

The point of this capsule history is twofold. First, most NYC Group members entered art school before the contemporary women's movement had touched them personally, much less reached into the art academy. Second, many had graduated from art school or were attempting to launch their careers in a highly charged social scene of apparently expanding opportunities, an essentially sexist but fading counterculture, and the first fires of the women's movement. In between, they had personally experienced the patriarchal structure of the academy and its role in social control: "I had one female teacher the whole time I was in college. And the whole time *until* college, I had had all women teachers. And all of a sudden . . . ! *Did you notice that then?* Yeah, because I had always been around these strong female types. . . . I was a little intimidated, and I thought, how do you talk to these people? But I got used to it. . . . There were mostly women in the class. I'm sure a million people have said this, but art faculties are mostly men" (NY1). As this example suggests, art school experiences did not immediately turn women artists into activists: "When I graduated I didn't know what to do with myself so I went to the placement office. . . . They said, learn how to type. I said, no, thank you, applied to graduate school, and got my degree in painting and art history. . . . When I was at [graduate school] it was completely male dominated and sexist. . . . I definitely noticed that. And that was . . . in the 60s. In fact, we used to grumble about it, the women. But no one did anything about it. I mean, when you're a student and young . . ." (NY2).

For another NYC Group member, the identity confirmation bestowed by her undergraduate experience contributed to her delayed politicization. Her classmates were mostly women and the faculty all men, but she didn't notice. She was "naive about women's politics" and, equally important, "very happy, too. I'd found what I wanted to do, it was good, I loved it. I was *flourishing*" (NY7). For this woman and others, it was graduate school that provided the experience of overt sexism.

> One of my male teachers said to me, "Ramona, if you love art the way I think you do, then you'd better marry . . . a male artist." And I remember just thinking [draws a deep, sharp breath], meaning, if you want your life to be about . . . [art, do] like my wife did. That way you'll always be next to art. *Why not be next to your own?* Women have short attention spans. Women aren't really serious. If you had to choose between a man and your work, you'd choose a man. You don't know it now, but you're gonna get involved with children, and then . . . *Your male teachers say this?* Yup. They wouldn't do that now. (NY5)

Indeed, by the time Phila Group members attended art school in the early 1980s, male art teachers did not say these things. But they did say them to NYC Group members, and it was a politicizing factor: "When you get to grad school it's like the world turned upside down: All [faculty] are men. . . . There weren't any women teachers, I *finally* realized. It was so overtly sexist that even I caught on. Because [artist teacher] actually said to me, 'What does it matter to you, you're only going to get married and have babies.' . . . But I must say my consciousness was raised, and I didn't play the game" (NY7). Playing the game was "painting to please, trying to be a *good girl* . . . make paintings like the boys, then people liked my paintings."

At the end of her first year, Doris (NY7) flunked her jury with the action that she could return, and she might have if her parents had been willing to pay another year's tuition, "but I was sort of glad to be out." Instead, she quit painting altogether and didn't make art for about five years. When she resumed, her work quickly became feminist in its conceptual base and in the use of techniques and materials "associated with women." Doris mentioned in passing that during her five-year hiatus she broke an engagement to one man and married another. Judging by the age of her oldest child, she also gave birth during that time.[11] But in constructing herself as woman artist she spoke of this period as not working and made no attempt, as Phila Group members did, to recoup her wife-mother activities as somehow an expression of her artist identity. Perhaps the lesson learned from overt art school sexism was that to be taken seriously it was better to have a period of not working than to get married and have babies.

By and large, NYC Group members told the story of how they became artists in terms of the quantity and intensity of art making, with times of low productivity or disruption defined as the reduction or absence of working as opposed to *doing* something else. This contrasts with Phila Group members, who told stories of starts and false starts, interrelated but consecutive careers, and the balancing of commitments. Pam illustrates the NYC Group pattern. She migrated first to Philadelphia for her B.F.A., then "came to New York, went to [museum art school] for a year, worked on my own, shared a storefront studio with two people . . . Got married, continued to work, had two children, continued to work, but it was more sporadic and less ambitious. Then suddenly I got really desperate and depressed. I was thirty-three, felt like nothing's ever going to happen unless I buckle down and start getting really serious and working hard" (NY8). In other words, even when—perhaps especially when—disruptions were caused by gendered role commitments, the continuity of the narrative was "working." Moreover, the problem to be overcome was not having been sufficiently serious and hardworking rather than, say, having been busy with babies.

NYC Group members thus constructed a continuous artist identity by downplaying gendered role commitments and defining the various times and events of their lives in terms of working. I attribute this to the identity-affirming experience of art school *before* they married and had children and to the lesson provided by art school that for women, marriage and family are immediate threats to seriousness. This is not to say that these women are any less committed to their gendered roles than are Phila Group members. Rather, it is to say that they "know better" than to attempt to integrate them into their artist stories.

In other words, NYC Group members more fully internalized the social model "artist" and reproduced a more socially correct and nuanced version of that model in their own stories. They benefited from a proximity to the artist model that was not enjoyed by their Philadelphia counterparts, for they came of age in or near New York City at a time when "more and more middle-class youths set out on an artistic trek which led them inevitably to New York City, the nation's center for art education, museums, and art sales" (Simpson, 1981: 2). They grew up in a milieu in which being an artist, although a troublesome prospect for many of their parents, was hardly an oddity.

Their ease with the social model "artist" enabled NYC Group members to resist its totality as a political and an aesthetic stand—which, in turn, testified to their confidence in their artist identities. They had never been suburban housewives. Their artist stories display the signs of seriousness and dedication: art as an individualized calling, art school out of high school in the face of parental resistance, lives cast in terms of working, gendered and professional roles segregated. With artist credentials well in hand, they can take on the myth in a sort of hand-to-hand combat in which the combatants are sometimes difficult to distinguish from each other. "I didn't like the idea of being an artist. I've never been in love with that mythology," said one group member who gravitated to the art department after beginning college as a history and government major. She was "eminently unsuited for" those fields because "my mind really doesn't work that way—it leaks all over the place" (NY7). In the space of four sentences, she distanced herself from the myth and reaffirmed her artist identity in a sublime expression of the irrepressibility of the creative temperament.

## Phila Group: Shedding the Stereotype

In general, Phila Group members held a less overtly critical view of the myth as they strove toward it. Their problem was proximity to the stereotype. Not only were many of them suburban housewives, but their journey back to art school was often circuitous and included the very sort of training that threatens seriousness in art world eyes.

> I had my second child and I raised them until they . . . were in elementary school full time. Then I just began doing the local art center . . . a painting course here, a painting course there. . . . I did a series of those little watercolor instructions, and then I realized that I really was more serious than that. I really wanted to *be* more serious than that. So I thought, I'll take some college courses and see how that works. I took some at [university suburban campus] . . . and they went well. And then I thought, maybe I really oughta be in an art school. At the time [art school] was the only one in Philadelphia where they would take part-time students in the daytime. I enrolled, took all the basic art classes. The kids were in school; I tried to get my courses in the morning. It was a hassle. (Ph6)

Phila Group members took their art instruction where they could get it in a manner that accommodated their gendered role priorities. This included neighborhood art centers, whose clientele are stereotypically hobbyists; suburban colleges or branch campuses, whose faculties tend to be career teachers and less well-known as artists than those who teach in major art schools; studio courses run by local artists; and self-teaching, with the work occasionally critiqued by a local artist. These kinds of instruction have consequences beyond their marginality as artist credentials. Neighborhood art centers tend to emphasize mediums low on the art world hierarchy, such as watercolor. And choosing a school around the contingencies of motherhood shapes, in turn, one's artistic choices.

> We were living out at [distant suburb] and I went to [x liberal arts college] and took all the courses they had in art and art history, til there wasn't anything more to take. When we moved here, I looked into going back to [x art school], I looked into [y art school], and [y liberal arts college] was the most supportive for continuing ed students, in that they accepted my college credits from when I was eighteen, nineteen. I could go part-time, which I would not have been able to do at [y art school], so it really fit in with the tail end of raising my children. . . . I majored in printmaking because I didn't like the head of the painting department . . . and started working in fibers and weaving. (Ph5)

This woman had always painted and had had studio instruction in painting. The default choice of printmaking as a major turned her work toward media that bear the stigma of being craftlike in art world eyes.

Another woman, compelled to justify the expenditure of family resources on an education that seemed "so self-indulgent," first majored in fashion illustration to ensure there would be a "payoff." She could get a job, and, although the family was already financially secure, that would make it "okay to be an artist." When she switched to painting, being unhappy with the "vacuous nature" of fashion illustration, the drafting skills she had acquired were "a terrible handicap . . . too narrative . . . too illustrative." Worse yet in the eyes of the faculty, she eventually turned to the watercolor skills gained from "all these years in these dumpy little art centers."

> I realized that . . . my heart was not in oil painting. That was considered the classical mode, and everybody should be in oil painting. But in my heart I knew I didn't have a feel for the medium. That's the only way I can describe it. . . . I had watercolor skills, and I said, I want to do my senior thesis in watercolor. I tell you, they were horrified. They didn't want me to do it. The implication was that it was an old woman's medium, that it was a suburban Sunday painter medium. It just wasn't valid. And I said, no. I had at that point grown up enough—it's strange to say, because I was thirty-nine years old—but I hung in there and I said, no. It will be good, but this is the way I'm going to do it. (Ph6)

She did the watercolor thesis, yielding only to concern that it wouldn't be "monumental enough" by painting on oversized paper. She also won an award for it, although "wherever [the faculty] perceived that the paintings might be dropping back into . . . Sunday painting, they were very quick to point that out." In short, under certain conditions the presumption of "seriousness" is not granted but must be earned anew by each artwork.

Unlike the youthful NYC Group members, Phila Group members came to art school as mature women with other identities already established. For some, art school was a search for a new or broadened identity and a return to an artist identity that was not confirmed in adolescence.

> I . . . had so submerged myself in these kids that them leaving [home] seemed to be a total loss of any identity. It was easy to find identity at eighteen, as a mother, and I understood that, knew about that. And I *did* that, my whole life was that. And that seemed like a . . . worthy thing to be doing. But it came to an end. I felt like I was out of a job. So I sort of up and went to art school. . . . I decided I just had to find a me . . . and who I had the most education in was being a painter. I've given that most of my life; in one form or another, I've been practicing. So I said, go with your strong point. (Ph9)

In the midst of talk about loss of one identity and the search for a new one, this woman nevertheless constructed a continuous sense of self as an artist. But rather than downplay gendered roles, Phila Group members integrated roles and identities in various ways—in this case, first, by casting a major shift in gendered role commitments as the impetus to active development of the artist identity and, second, by incorporating the wife-mother period as in some way "practicing" even as she was *doing* something else wholeheartedly.

A further consequence of attending art school as mature women with established identities is that Phila Group members did not always experience the unreservedly positive feelings of validation and homecoming reported by NYC Group members. For some this was specific to gendered role commitments: "So going back to school was variously tough, because I felt guilty about not being fully available for my family, and glorious, because for the first time I was getting to do something I really wanted" (Ph6).

Perhaps Phila Group members' reluctance to subordinate their gendered roles contributed to their struggle with self-image. Certainly, those who reported the most positive experience were those who attended schools with programs specifically designed to serve the large influx of women continuing education students spawned by the contemporary women's movement. Most, however, encountered implicit ageism and sexism. In the late 1970s and early 1980s, art faculties were (and are today) still composed largely of men, and although those faculties rarely made the overtly sexist comments reported by NYC Group members, the patriarchal structure of the academy played into the fears and anxieties of Phila Group members.

> For a long time when I was in school, I was dealing with the whole . . . image I carried in myself of being just a suburban housewife who went back to school, who

did what was at that time the "in thing." That at any moment, someone—and it was going to be one of these male teachers—was going to take me aside and tell me that I had no talent. And that I really should probably just go back to the suburbs and paint bowls of fruit or something innocuous where I wouldn't hurt anybody. . . . I think a lot of the seeds of that I carried within myself, but there was also a sort of patriarchal system at work that made me always tuned in to who my audience was and who I was pleasing. (Ph6)

For another woman, the experience was overwhelmingly negative, although she separates herself from the self-image problem.

I would like to burn [the art school] down. And hang up all the men who are in it by their balls. Horrendous place for a woman to go. Women like myself coming back to school who might not have looked quite as colorful. . . . Nobody could pigeonhole me by the way I looked; I didn't look like a housewife from the suburbs, but I was in a real way. I'd see these women coming in who . . . weren't as gutsy but wanted to develop their art and who looked like intimidated housewives. So the message was out there very clearly, and I'd see these people attacked and belittled. And there was an element of truth to it, because if you don't take yourself seriously nobody else is going to. . . . On one hand I wanted to strangle the men for treating them that way, on the other I wanted to strangle the women for allowing that to happen. (Ph13)

As both of these examples indicate, Phila Group members were as quick to locate the problem within themselves or within women as a group as they were to situate it within the patriarchal structure of the art world and the art academy. Many, in fact, felt their preferred mediums were denigrated, their art misunderstood, or their talent a threat to faculty, but they were reluctant to politicize those feelings. One displayed paintings in her home that were about, and had helped her to deal with, her husband's recent death. Yet she had taken to heart faculty criticism that the images—small, calm, pastel in color, incorporating marital momentos—couldn't possibly be about death. Another's story covers the issue so well I quote it at length.

I'll show you [a piece] that I did. . . . I thought I was being just as bold and as abstract as I could get. And I was really criticized on it as being . . . sort of a wild and hysterical piece. . . . And I had a friend in the class who is a master [of] semantics, and she said [to the faculty], "You know, I don't know if you understand the meaning of the word 'hysterical,' but it has its roots in 'womb-like.'" And the piece was a very implosive, womb-centered piece. And she said, "I think you're right. I think it is hysterical, but I don't like the word the way you're using it, which is kind of 'off-the-wall, self-indulgent, illogical woman's piece.'" . . .

I went into this thinking these men are wonderful, they're artists, and I need to accept everything they say. And it's always, if there's something that's not right or I don't agree, it's probably me, my lack of talent, whatever. By the time I'd gotten to my senior year, I'd teamed up with a couple of other women . . . [and] had begun to become politicized. And some of this was this anger and frustration that I wasn't really being heard and a sense that maybe it's not really all me. Maybe they aren't tuned in to where I am. . . .

But I don't think it was ever intentional from anybody. It just was. It was kind of a patronizing attitude that existed, like . . . we know and she doesn't. And maybe we can teach her what we know and then she'll be a better person. It was never any concept that maybe we can learn something about what she's trying to say from her situation. (Ph6)

As with NYC Group members, growing awareness of the patriarchal structure of the academy did not immediately make activists of Phila Group members. Unlike NYC Group members, Phila Group women persisted in their reluctance to interpret and to act in explicitly political ways. The difference has to do, in part, with ideas about what it means to be political. Doris (NY7) [all names have been changed] views her work as political and feminist largely because she uses techniques and materials "associated with women." Joan (Ph6) makes watercolors of subjects associated with women and views her work as feminine but as neither political nor feminist. Doris's response to art school sexism was to refuse to play the game and flunk out. Joan's response was to take a firm stand on doing her senior thesis in watercolor, make her point, and define herself as not being political.

*Do you consider yourself to be a feminist?* [pause] I think the question that's more to the point is, Am I political? And I think not. I mean, I think I'm aware of the injustices, and it angers me sometimes. For me sending money to this [National Museum of Women in the Arts] in Washington, that's a political move on my part. *Your stand at [art school] about your senior thesis, did that feel political?* No, it didn't. Now as I talk about it, I see that it was. But . . . I'm a subtle person. I think I was raised not to rock the boat. So . . . what I do will never be confrontational. (Ph6)

In comparable fashion, Marie (Ph13), who wanted to burn the art school down for its ill treatment of other women, had her own complaint. She had won important awards in her junior year but felt that as a senior she had "made enormous jumps" in her painting, was producing "very sophisticated stuff," and was a model of what the school purported to be about: "a dedicated artist . . . so prolific there was nobody else that could touch me in years." The faculty was very threatened by this, began to ignore her work, wouldn't hang it in student shows, and gave her "one little token prize . . . an obscure little thing" at the end of the year. Nevertheless, in discussing women's political organizing, she is not convinced of the need for it, does not feel discrimination against women has affected her "except maybe at [art school]," and thinks many women's complaints are "easy grumbling because someone doesn't want to take on what you have to do as an artist."

To be sure, there are differences between Joan and Marie. Each must shed the suburban housewife, lady painter stereotype, but Joan wishes to preserve and express her gender and gendered role identities through her artist identity, whereas

Marie seeks to subordinate her gender and gendered role identities to her artist identity. Joan's strategy is to try harder and to stand firm on the most important issues but avoid overt politics by defining the problems she encountered as unintentional and herself as not political. Marie's strategy is the honorary man strategy previously described: She disavows her suburban housewife identity, criticizes other women who can't or don't wish to play the "boys' game," and lionizes the masculine aspects of her personality and work. Joan struggles to call herself "artist" and is able to do so only after joining the women's cooperative; having a gallery makes it legitimate and official. Marie makes a point of calling herself "artist" and distances herself from other women artists' struggles. Neither can afford to ignore her social proximity to the stereotype or to distance herself from the myth.

Phila Group members have, thus, more fully internalized the stereotype of the lady painter than the myth of the heroic male artist. Two patterns of response emerge: The more common is Joan's struggle to take herself seriously and to convey her seriousness to a skeptical art world while expressing gender identity in ways defined as not political. A few, like Marie, convey seriousness not by downplaying gendered role activities while making a political point of claiming gender identity, as do NYC Group members, but by subordinating gender identity. Both Phila Group patterns involve incorporating or accounting for the wife-mother interlude in the construction of a continuous artist identity, whereas the NYC Group pattern involves maintaining separateness and sometimes celebrating conflict between gender and professional identities.

### Time as a Moral Issue

There is, however, a level of agreement between the two groups that was best introduced by Doris, who had "never been in love with [the artist] mythology." The mythology, she said, is "that the single male under thirty makes the greatest art. That somebody who has any sense of social responsibility or responsiveness to other people . . . I mean, it's good art, lousy life; good life, lousy art. That's it in a nutshell." And responsiveness to others is "we all have these *lives*, these other roles," "children demand you," "I have a husband," "if you're out shopping for clothes for the kids, you think, 'I should be in the studio.' You should always be doing something else" (NY7).

For women artists, time is a moral issue. Responsiveness to others is felt to occur at the expense of some other aspect of self—in this case professional identity, goals, and potential for being seen as successful (cf. Gilligan, 1982). The aspect of "woman" that women artists are least willing to concede to "artist" is their connectedness to others, particularly gendered role others. They are caught between the myth of the heroic (male) artist as dedicated to the lifelong production of works of art at the expense of all else and the stereotype of the lady painter who cannot be a serious artist because she is committed in gendered roles. Ultimately, they reject both. Perhaps most important, they reject the forced choice, that is, the social pressures that say women can *either* be committed artists with some chance of success *or* committed wives and lovers and mothers but not both; the social consensus on definitions of "woman" and "artist" that say "woman artist" is a contradiction in terms.

## NOTES

1. Mainstream critics and institutions have accused feminists of wanting a second set of standards by which to evaluate women's cultural products, affirmative action standards that would "allow for" their historical disadvantage. Historically there have, in fact, been two sets of standards, in the sense that women's cultural products have not been considered to be in the same category as men's. That is, they were defined in advance as not constituting art; thus they never entered the competition for social recognition as art (cf. Showalter, 1971). What follows in part is that the aesthetic qualities and principles of art forms elaborated by women are not necessarily part of mainstream aesthetic norms and values.

2. The research from which this chapter derives was a twelve-month field study of two women's cooperative art galleries, one in Philadelphia and one in New York City, chosen for similarity in group size, age, and program. Near the end of the observation period, in-depth interviews with all Phila Group members (the primary group) and half of the NYC Group members were conducted, in their studios, at the gallery, or at another site of their choosing. Nearly 75 percent of those interviewed were or had been married, and all of that group had children, with Phila Group members tending to have two or three children and NYC Group members one or two. In age, the women ranged for twenty-six to sixty-two, with most being in their late thirties to late forties.

3. Interviews were assigned numbers for citation purposes only. Thus: "Ph9" is Philadelphia interview #9. "NY5" is New York interview #5.

4. In Chicago in 1964, Mason Griff found parental concern over economic issues (how the artist would make a living) and social deviancy. Having an artist in the family was viewed as a social disgrace because people would assume the family member was neurotic and immoral. In Soho in 1981, Charles Simpson found only materialism; that is, bourgeois parents concerned about downward mobility.

5. Certain potentially identifying facts in interview excerpts have been changed to comparable or generic terms and enclosed in brackets in order to protect the anonymity of those interviewed.

6. Jean Gimpel (1968) quoted written testimonies to Picasso's heroic and godlike image. Claude Lévi-Strauss sought "nothing less than a metaphysical perception" from Picasso's pictures (p. 6). Pierre Cabanne called Picasso "this being outside time . . . this providential man . . . this incarnation of his century with his implacable gospel" (p. 6). Roger Garaudy rhapsodized that "he bears the world in himself . . . he has harnessed dreams to serve the future . . . he carries within himself the cultural history of mankind, he participates in the total movement of the universe" (p. 7). According to Robert Hughes (1984), since Picasso's death in 1973 the hyperbole has escalated in keeping with the general inflation of artists' reputations: "[He] has to be deified and never mind the language" (p. 76).

7. Gimpel (1968) identified the writings of neo-platonic humanist Marsiglio Ficino in 1576 as the first statement of the notions of both man as "universal artificer" of godlike

genius and the artwork as mirror of the soul of the artist. This literary coup d'état culminated a century-long crusade to move painting and sculpture from the mechanical to the liberal arts.

8. Simpson (1981) found the romantic view especially predominant among unsuccessful Soho artists and used by them to justify behaviors ranging from excessive drinking to the inability to make money. In a study that largely ignored distinctions between the experiences of women and men artists, Simpson indicated that the artists who behave in this fashion tend to be men who "set up [their] wives as the bourgeois upon whom [they] rely and . . . seek to scandalize." These wives are often artists who have put their own careers on hold or resorted to some form of commercial art, an option vehemently disdained by the husbands, in order to perform the supporting role.

9. Both Yau and Sozanski also made much of O'Keeffe's relationship with Alfred Stieglitz. Yau suggested that "Stieglitz's legacy of more than 500 photographs of O'Keeffe constitutes not only his greatest statement, but perhaps also hers" (1988: 116). In an obituary, Sozanski repeatedly related the trajectory of O'Keeffe's career to Stieglitz's beneficence, eventually concluding that "she owed her success to Stieglitz" (1986: 176).

Sozanski's obituary was met with indignation by women artists in Philadelphia. At a Phila Group exhibition opening shortly after it was published, clusters of women spoke heatedly of Sozanski's disrespect and planned a collective letter to the editor in response. Several noted that whereas many men artists—for example, Mark Rothko—owed a great deal to the loyal support of a gallery owner, it would never be said that their success resulted from such relationships. One saw Sozanski's mention of the fact that O'Keeffe sometimes painted in the nude as representative of the voyeuristic license and power of the male gaze. The letter was written and mailed but never published, although one written by a woman voicing similar criticisms was (Mabey, 1986). However, it speaks to the dilemma of women artists that at a Phila Group meeting a few weeks hence, regrets about sending the letter were expressed. Even as they were concerned that O'Keeffe was already being written out of art history, the women feared it had been too political a move and that Sozanski—who rarely visited the gallery—would never darken their doorway again.

10. Among their targets and causes were the Vietnam War, admission prices to public museums, the control of museum boards by wealthy capitalists, the spending habits of public museums, and the right of artists to control the exhibition and treatment of their work (Lippard, 1984).

11. This information was confirmed by another NYC Group member who volunteered, in discussing various group members' career trajectories, that Doris had given birth to both her children during the period of not working and thus had "come out" somewhat later than other members who had only one child or who had postponed having children.

## REFERENCES

Adato, Perry Miller. 1977. *Portrait of an Artist: Georgia O'Keeffe.* Educational Broadcasting Corp.

Allen, Jane Addams. 1986. "A Portrait of the Artist as a Disturbed Man." *Insight,* December 22, pp. 66–68.

Asbury, Edith Evans. 1986. "Georgia O'Keeffe Dead at 98: Shaper of Modern Art in U.S." *New York Times,* March 7, pp. A1, A17.

Baker, Kenneth. 1985. "The World in a Drop of Water." *Artforum* 24, no. 4, pp. 56–59.

Becker, Howard S. 1982. *Art Worlds*, Berkeley: University of California Press.

Betterton, Rosemary. 1987. "How Do Women Look? The Female Nude in the Work of Suzanne Valadon." In *Looking On: Images of Femininity in the Visual Arts and Media*, Rosemary Betterton, ed. London: Pandora Press.

Chiarmonte, Paula L., ed. 1982. "Women Artists: A Resource and Research Guide." *Art Documentation* 1, no. 5.

Clouzot, Henri-Georges. 1982. *The Mystery of Picasso*. Vestron Video.

Cogan, Katherine Stiles. 1985. "In the Beginning . . ." *Art Matters*, December 1985/January 1986, pp. 1, 13.

Drohojowska, Hunter. 1986. "The Western Canvas of Georgia O'Keeffe." *Applause*, September, pp. 16–19.

Edelheit, Martha. c. 1980. *Hats, Bottles and Bones*. 16mm film screened by the New York City Chapter of the Women's Caucus for Art, March 18, 1986.

Garfunkel, Gloria. 1984. "The Improvised Self: Sex Differences in Artistic Identity." Ph.D. dissertation, Psychology Department, Harvard University.

Gilligan, Carol. 1982. *In a Different Voice*. Cambridge, Mass: Harvard University Press.

Gimpel, Jean. 1968. *The Cult of Art*. Translated by Jean Gimpel. London: Weidenfeld and Nicolson.

Goffman, Erving. 1963. *Stigma*. Englewood Cliffs, N.J.: Prentice-Hall.

Griff, Mason. 1964. "The Recruitment of the Artist." In *The Arts in Society*, Robert N. Wilson, ed. Englewood Cliffs, N.J.: Prentice-Hall.

Gross, Larry. 1983. "Why Johnny Can't Draw." *Art Education*, March, pp. 74–77.

Hobbs, Robert. 1987. "Sally Michel: The Other Avery." *Woman's Art Journal* 8, no. 2, pp. 3–14.

Holcomb, Adele M. 1987. "Anna Jameson on Women Artists." *Woman's Art Journal* 8, no. 2, pp. 15–24.

Hughes, Robert. 1983. "Bursting out of the Shadows." *Time*, November 14, pp. 92–93.

————. 1984. "Picasso: The Last Picture Show." *Time*, March 19, pp. 76–77.

Kessler, Suzanne J., and Wendy McKenna. 1978. *Gender: An Ethnomethodological Approach*. Chicago: University of Chicago Press.

Lippard, Lucy. 1984. *Get the Message?* New York: E. P. Dutton.

Lisle, Laurie. 1980. *Portrait of an Artist: A Biography of Georgia O'Keeffe*. New York: Seaview Books.

Mabey, Sarah E. 1986. "Georgia O'Keeffe." *Philadelphia Inquirer*, March 23, p. 6G.

McCall, Michal M. 1978. "The Sociology of Female Artists." In *Studies in Symbolic Interaction, Vol. 1*, Norman K. Denzin, ed. Greenwich, Conn.: Jai Press.

Muse Gallery. 1988. *Muse/10*. Philadelphia: Muse Gallery, exhibition catalog.

Nochlin, Linda. 1971. "Why Have There Been No Great Women Artists?" In *Art and Sexual Politics*, Thomas B. Hess and Elizabeth C. Baker, eds. New York: Macmillan.

Pollock, Griselda. 1980. "Artists Mythologies and Media Genius, Madness and Art History." *Screen* 21, no. 3, pp. 57–96.

Quinn, Edward. 1986. *Picasso: The Man and His Work, Parts 1 and II*. Paris: Teleproductions Gaumot; View Video.

Salisbury, Stephen. 1987. "The Changing American Landscape." *Philadelphia Inquirer*, December 27, pp. 1G, 6G.

Showalter, Elaine. 1971. "Women Writers and the Double Standard." In *Woman in Sexist Society*, Vivian Gornick and Barbara K. Moran, eds. New York: Basic Books.

Simpson, Charles R. 1981. *Soho: The Artist in the City*. Chicago: University of Chicago Press.

Sims, Patterson. 1981. *Georgia O'Keeffe*. New York: Whitney Museum of American Art, exhibition catalog.

————. 1988. "On Galleries." *Philadelphia Inquirer*, April 7, p. 3D.

————. 1987. "A National Gallery Celebration of Georgia O'Keeffe." *Philadelphia Inquirer*, November 1, p. 16G.

Sozanski, Edward J. 1986. "Georgia O'Keeffe, at 98, a Pioneer in American Art." *Philadelphia Inquirer*, March 7, pp. 1A, 17C.

Tatransky, Valentin. 1985. "Helen Frankenthaler." *ARTS Magazine* 59, no. 10, p. 14.

Wayne, June. 1979. "The Male Artist as a Stereotypical Female." In *Feminist Collage*, Judy Loeb, ed. New York: Teachers College Press.

Wooster, Ann-Sargent. 1987. "A New Beauty in New Places." *Amtrak Express*, October/November, pp. 8–12, 32.

Yau, John. 1988. "O'Keeffe's Misfocus." *ARTnews* 87, no. 2, pp. 114–119.

## ❦ 6 ❧

# From East
# to West: Polish Artists
# in the New York Art World

### KRYSTYNA WARCHOL

IN THIS CHAPTER I EXAMINE how Polish émigré artists adapted to the New York world of commercial and fine art in the 1970s and 1980s.[1] The research discussed here is divided into three parts. In the first I describe the social organization of the Polish art world as it existed under communism—primarily the post-Stalinist 1960s and 1970s—until the government's suppression of the Solidarity movement on December 13, 1981. In the second I focus on Polish graphic and fine artists' adaptation to the New York art world. Finally, I look at the changing environment of the art world in Poland after the fall of communism and explore the consequences these changes might have for artists and artistic life.

## THE POLISH ART WORLD UNDER COMMUNISM

### Recruitment and Training

The art world in Poland under communism was quite distinct from that in the West. As in other communist countries, culture and the arts in Poland were controlled by the state and the party, which created a monolithic, centralized art system that affected the social existence of artists in profound ways—by deciding who became artists, how they were able to practice and distribute their art, and how they could make a living.

First, the system of recruiting and training artists in Communist Poland was highly structured and rigid. An aspiring artist would go through five or six years of graduate art education in one of the seven university-level art academies. The competition for acceptance into a graduate art school was stiff, and the criteria for acceptance were high. Only a few—the most skillful applicants—were granted admission, which strengthened the belief that only the chosen, the exceptionally gifted, could be artists. Art schools in Poland gave artists excellent professional training; the education was both deep and broad, as there was no demand for narrow specialization. Artists in Poland were used to performing a number of different tasks, and they did not limit themselves to a single artistic medium or role.

Art schools in Poland performed the primary gatekeeping function that is handled by the marketplace in the West. They not only trained artists but also defined who would get to become artists and how they would practice their art. An art school diploma was a prerequisite for being a professional artist in Poland and greatly defined the artist's future. It allowed the artist to join the Union of Polish Artists, which was difficult to do without an art school diploma.

Although membership in the party-controlled union was not a precondition for working as an artist, practicing and distributing art without belonging to the union were barely possible. Membership in the union was often necessary for obtaining employment as an artist, for selling work, for receiving grants and commissions, for obtaining (largely subsidized) studios, and even for procuring art supplies, which were not generally available on the open market. The union was also the major organized distributor of art in Poland. The Union of Polish Artists maintained a great deal of freedom from political control, but it was suspended in 1983 by the Jaruzelski regime, which established a new Union of Visual Artists that was heavily boycotted by the artists. At this time the government also suspended publication of the Polish art magazines *Sztuka* (Art) and *Projekt.*

## Distribution and Reputation

The organization of the cultural system in Poland made it easy to reach the audience, which, as Jeffrey Goldfarb (1982: 30) pointed out, was administered through subsidization of exhibits and performances and various forms of cultural promotion and education. Exhibiting art without an organizational affiliation was almost impossible. The dealer-gallery system did not exist in Poland—galleries were state sponsored, and a few semiprivate galleries were run by artists and subsidized by the ministry, the union, art schools, and similar organizations. Artists could easily exhibit in various galleries that belonged to the state, the union, or the Ministry of Culture. Placing a show in the most prestigious venues was often only a matter of time, and artists could put little effort into showing their work because they were frequently invited to exhibit. One artist said, "There were many shows organized: in the galleries, in the union's clubs, even in the factories or who knows where else. You had to put your name on the list in the union and wait for your turn. Often you were asked to take part in a show. It was not a problem to show your work."

Artistic careers in Poland generally proceeded according to a prescribed pattern. One of the artists explained, "After school everything goes automatically. You have contacts from school, you are a member of the union. You do not have to look hard for a job. Many things are taken for granted."

Especially taken for granted was the belief that if one were a good artist, a reputation and career would follow. This belief is more understandable if we realize that the art world in Poland was and is very small. Information about what went on was easily available, in part because there was little division of labor. As one artist explained, "In Poland, everybody knows everybody. Besides, there are the same people everywhere: The professors from the academy judge art competitions, make decisions about stipends, grants, shows, and so on. After school, if you are good you do not have to compete hard because your reputation has already been established."

The theory of reputation assumes as an ideal a condition of perfect information in which "everyone whose opinion affects the formation of reputation has access to and knowledge of all the work relevant to his judgments . . . and can make truly informed judgments" (Becker 1982: 363). The centralized distribution system in Poland approached this condition of almost perfect information, which, as Howard Becker pointed out, is both unreasonable and unrealistic to expect in the large U.S. art world. One artist answered my question about competition in the Polish art world with amazement: "Competition in Poland? Is it a joke? Who do you want to compete with? If you are good, you do not have to compete, at least not like [in the United States]."

## Making a Living Making Art

In order to fully understand the Polish artists' social existence under communism, it is necessary to realize that artists in Poland were thought of as intellectuals and were a highly regarded and respected group. One of the artists explained, "If you are an artist in Poland, your status is automatically very high. People admire artists in Poland, probably because art constitutes the last foothold of freedom. Here, because you have freedom everywhere, being an artist does not mean too much. There was strong artistic egocentrism in Poland. It was not difficult to have a good self-image."

The esteem experienced by artists in Poland is rooted in the European tradition of social prestige, based on a humanist notion of cultural rather than economic values (Deinhard, 1970). Artists in Poland, like other Eastern European artists, possessed prestige but not necessarily money. The absence of a free-market economy in Communist Poland, together with the organization of the art system at the time, was not conducive to making a profit from art. The dealer-gallery system did not exist in Poland, and most galleries did not make a profit from exhibiting art. The state-owned commercial chains *Desa* (joined later by *Sztuka Polska*), which sold art largely to foreigners visiting the country, offered limited possibilities for sales. Museums bought art, but their budgets were very limited.

Unlike in the United States, there was no middle class to buy art. Rather than relying on the limited local market, some artists sold their art from their studios or at street fairs to visiting foreigners, particularly private dealers, interior decorators, Polish Americans, and similar groups. In fact, for foreign buyers Poland was a lucrative market where lots of good art was available at prices much lower than those in the West (e.g., in the 1970s it was not uncommon to find a large painting by a good Polish artist selling for $100 to $200). This situation was good for both the artists and the buyer—the buyer could purchase art cheaply, but the artists were getting good money (in Polish terms), which often allowed them to live well for some time from the sale of a few paintings for foreign currency. Sales to foreigners, however, were neither stable nor reliable.

Given the nonexistence of the Polish market and the instability of foreign sales, how did artists support themselves? A small minority of artists who established reputations abroad lived from the sales of their work in foreign galleries. Some artists taught in art schools, which was viewed as a prestigious vocation; unlike the situation in the United States, many of the best artists in Poland also taught.

Most artists in Poland did not live from their art but from *chaltura*. *Chaltura* is an untranslatable Polish word that designates different kinds of jobs periodically made available to artists. These ranged from designing a window display to making decorations for a Polish-Russian friendship day to creating a stage design for the theater. What distinguished *chaltura* from a sideline job was that *chaltura* was always artistic in nature and, as such, never threatened the artist's primary identity. A situation common in Western society, in which an artist becomes a cab driver or a waiter to make a living, would have been inconceivable in Poland in this period. One of the interviewees asked me, "Have you ever heard of an artist who would wash dishes in a restaurant to support himself? I had not."

*Chaltura* varied in relationship to the artist's own art—some jobs were purely mechanical work done for money; others, such as stage design, allowed an expression of the artist's creativity and were closer to his or her artistic identity. *Chaltura* jobs were often distributed by the union and produced a livable, yet far from luxurious, income. Good *chaltura* arrangements were envied by other artists.

It was often hard for the artists I interviewed to explain how they made their living in Poland. They often said, "You know how it is in Poland." Many, in answer to the direct question "How did you make your living in Poland?" said, "I don't know." Given the realities and absurdities of life in Communist Poland—where customarily people spent more than they made and got by somehow—it was not easy to answer this seemingly simple question. It was characteristic for an artist in Poland to do many different things: One artist who currently works as an illustrator in New York was a consultant for feature films, a radio producer, a stage designer, a writer and illustrator of children's books, a producer of animated films, and a celebrated cartoonist.

The fact that there was no Western-style market for art in Poland had crucial consequences for the notion of artistic success, which was understood in terms of critical, rather than economic, recognition. Its signifiers included participating in important group shows and having individual shows in renowned galleries, taking part in art competitions, getting awards, being in museum collections, and being reviewed in art magazines.

The construction of artistic reputations in Poland was divorced from the economic signifiers of value. One artist said "You could be the best artist in Poland and never sell a work." Another commented, "Of course, it is better if you sell your work, but basically it does not matter. You don't have to sell to feel you are a good artist in Poland. In America, if you are good, you must sell. If you do not sell, it means you are not good enough." Artists in Poland were free from market constraints and, unlike their Western counterparts, never worked with the market in mind. One artist explained, "There is an absolutely sterile situation in the arts in Poland because there is no market for it. Art in Poland is for its own sake. When you make art in Poland, you do not think about whether somebody will buy it."

## Graphic Arts

It is important to realize that the previous discussion refers not only to fine artists but to graphic artists as well. In Poland there was no clear dividing line between painting and the graphic arts; the two fields were merged. Graphic art was recognized as a fine art. The best-known form of Polish graphic art—the cultural poster—was collected by museums, displayed in art galleries, and reviewed in art magazines. Similarly, there was no difference in status between fine and graphic artists. Their training and career patterns were similar. Polish graphic art was divorced from advertising, since commercial advertising and competition were practically nonexistent. One artist explained, "A poster in Poland is not commercial art. A film poster does not try to sell a film. In a country where there is a shortage of everything, people will go and see the film regardless of what is on a poster." The purpose of the poster was not only to encourage people to attend cultural performances but also to supply a creative interpretation of the event.

The style of Polish graphic art, best exemplified by the Polish cultural poster, gained worldwide recognition as a poster tradition derived from an Eastern European sensibility. Its vocabulary was based on poetic and individualistic use of metaphor, allusion, humor, and condensed messages. "In contrast to the severe geometrical precision to much American graphic design at the time," wrote Steven Heller—an art director at the *New York Times*—about Polish posters of the late 1960s and early 1970s, "the Polish poster was unfettered by formal (or 'international style') tenets of art and design. The images were raw, sometimes grotesque, yet extremely effective" (1986).

Graphic artists appreciated the room allowed for artistic freedom not only in the design of cultural posters but in other areas of graphic art as well. Because of the absence of a specialized division of labor, artists themselves (rather than an art director, as in the United States) often made decisions regarding typography, design, and illustration. A Polish art director might not even have been a professional, as these positions were sometimes filled by bureaucratic assignment. In this context, graphic artists were not told specifically how they should illustrate an article or make a poster. A Polish graphic artist who has had success in the United States commented:

> My most fruitful and creative years were the late '70s, Solidarity's heyday. There was real freedom then, perhaps even more than in America. This is not to say that America has censorship, and certainly there are many outlets that afford unhampered freedom; but for the poster artist there are commercial restrictions. Not so in the Polish cultural arena, when any graphic artist could produce daring, controversial images for the theater, dance and cinema without fear that they would fail to sell the product. (quoted in Heller, 1984: 76)

## Political Censorship of the Arts in Communist Poland

Artists in Poland, free from market constraints, also managed to retain a relative autonomy that contrasted with the concurrent political control of artistic expression in other Eastern European countries. Visual art in Poland always enjoyed more freedom than it did in any other communist country. The period of social realism lasted only from 1949 to 1956, and artistic production was never controlled as it was in the Soviet Union.

As Goldfarb (1982) has shown, Poland realized cultural freedom in the face of political control by subverting the system of bureaucratic and political constraints distinctive to Communist Polish society. Poland exemplified Goldfarb's assertion about the nature of the relative autonomy of cultural freedom in the East: "Systematic constraints arise when cultural ends are not reached because of political interferences. But this is by no means a general rule. Numerous occasions arise when culture dominates politics or at the very least circumvents politics. Herein lies cultural freedom" (p. 31).

The true nature of artistic freedom in Poland can only be properly understood within the wider context of the clash between cultural freedom and the state's control of cultural life. The political power exercised in Poland by the Communist Party was continually challenged. The upheavals of 1956, 1968, 1970, 1976, and 1980 led to the total delegitimization of party rule in the eyes of the public. In spite of official ideology, Poland managed to develop an independent cultural life. In theater, film, and literature, gaining control of cultural life proved to be more difficult than the authorities had anticipated. In many arenas, but especially in theater, culture not only survived but flourished under communism, despite censorship.

Censorship was one of the commonly practiced methods of maintaining state control in Communist Poland, and it was intended to suppress works viewed as sabotaging the values of state and party. The mechanisms of censorship in the arts, as well as censorship's consequences for production and distribution, were fairly complex; despite the state's intentions the institution of censorship seldom functioned efficiently. As Goldfarb (1982) pointed out, it is easy to decide what topics or personalities are forbidden, but it is much more difficult to screen cultural objects that may imply complex and multifaceted interpretations. Often censors themselves were not politically astute enough to discover a hidden meaning, and at other times they decided to publicly ignore those meanings. Their decisions were triggered by numerous political, social, bureaucratic, and even personal factors. The following example was given by a well-known artist:

> I was invited to take part in the show "Art Now." I presented a work there entitled *The Integration into Consciousness*. The work consisted of twenty-four graphics presenting some kind of landscape, with blue sky, green grass, and a green tree. Gradually, everything becomes red—the tree fights the longest, but finally it becomes red too. And suddenly, again the sky is blue, the grass is green, but the tree stays red. The Soviet vice minister of culture came to see the show and understood the allusion immediately. The work was taken down the following day. The thing is that this work, in spite of its meaning, was shown in some other galleries, and it was okay until the Russian came.

On the one hand, censorship limited the freedom of artistic creation, but on the other it often forced artists to find more subtle forms of expression. One artist described the "benefits" of censorship as follows: "The continuous play with the censor enemy often brought wonderful results. More dangerous ideas had to be hidden. It forced you to a greater intellectual effort, to more subtle interpretations. Censorship was not such a bad thing after all. It taught you a special way of thinking. There was a continuous problem of how to outsmart censorship."

This battle with censorship showed up clearly in the style of Polish graphic art, in which the aesthetic vocabulary was based on individualistic use of metaphor, allusion, and condensed messages. Although censorship might positively affect creativity by forcing an artist to use unconventional forms of expression, there was a danger that in the long run it would undermine the communicative potential of art. Oppositional writer Tadeusz Konwicki described the mechanism well in the case of literature: "Initially it [the impact of censorship] may be positive because it forces an author to find subtle forms of expression to evade the censor's ban." He warned, however, that "these forms soon become conventions, the secret language becomes public, and the censor will ban it, too. So new, more subtle forms are devised. And so it goes, on and on, the literature becoming increasingly obscure, eventually losing all traces of life" (quoted in Goldfarb, 1982: 31).

The other negative influence of censorship on artists was widespread self-censorship as an adaptive mechanism to the political situation. The artists learned to anticipate the reactions of the censor and to avoid the forbidden. One artist explained, "We knew what was and what was not allowed. Many subjects were taboo. Nobody would draw a hammer and sickle dripping with blood. If I had known that something would not get through, I would not have even tried. What for? I did not even bother." Most artists internalized censorship to the extent that they no longer even experienced it as a constraint, which contributed to the illusion of their artistic freedom.

The audience in Poland under communism was often politically more astute than were the censors. In fact, one of the most characteristic features of the public's perception of art was the tendency to look for hidden meaning. "You cannot draw a hand in Poland without people thinking it has a meaning beyond," complained one graphic artist. Artists I interviewed gave many examples of how their work was read as being politically motivated, even when they had no such intentions.

By giving artwork political meaning that may or may not have been intended by the artist, the state, often unintentionally, promoted the status of artwork in Poland. One of the interviewees recalled that the closing of his show caused a strong protest by the Artists Union, which then displayed the censored works in the local Union Club. "Twice as many people came to see the show [as would have] if the show had been in the gallery," commented the artist.

Although censors and the public in Poland were searching for political references, the majority of those who immigrated to the United States strongly denied any intention to create political art. Most of the interviewees characterized their art as apolitical and related it to general human, rather than political, conditions. Only two artists interviewed were engaged in political art. One of these was the leading political cartoonist in Poland; the other was a graphic designer of Solidarity literature. Both artists were imprisoned on December 13, 1981, when the Jaruzelski regime imposed martial law. However, these artists felt they were prosecuted mainly because of their political activity in the Solidarity movement rather than because of the political dimension of their art. Most of the other artists, who, as noted, had no intention of invoking political references in their art, seldom personally encountered censorship. This comment by one fine artist was typical: "Everybody knew there was censorship in Poland. Every single show, publication, and so on, had been censored. Fortunately, I did not feel it personally. The censors were not interested in the kind of art I was doing. My art was not political."

Most artists chose to separate their art from politics and found refuge in themes that were "bigger than politics." One can argue, however, that the suspension of the political—and the refusal to engage in political art—was, in fact, part of a carefully calculated and clever strategy of the Communist government that made artists believe a lack of involvement in political art was their own choice and an appropriate response to a politically repressive environment.

## Why They Left

As noted, artists in Communist Poland enjoyed social prestige and security that might be envied by their Western counterparts (although it could be taken away at any moment), a livable income, and relative artistic freedom. Why, then, did they leave? The motive for emigration can only be understood within the broader context of the institutional structures of the Polish art world and its political determinants. Two of the artists I interviewed left Poland because of political persecution. One, Andrzej Czeczot, explained in an interview with the *New York Times*, "After martial law in Poland you had only two choices, to be a dissident or to be a pig. But I am an artist, not a professional dissident" (quoted in McGill, 1984).

Most of the artists I interviewed did not make the decision to emigrate before they left the country. Some were taking extended vacations when martial law was declared in Poland, which prompted their decision to stay. Many agreed with one artist who said, "I never emigrated to the United States; I just never returned."

Some emigrated for economic reasons, but the majority left primarily for artistic reasons. Without exception all claimed the problem was not so much political control as the lack of artistic stimulation and hope brought on by the system. This feeling was expressed by younger and older artists, by those who were highly regarded and successful in Poland and those who were not yet successful, by those who were and were not politically involved. One of the artists described the problem graphically.

> The major difference between the two countries lies in the hopes and aspirations one may have. In Poland, even if something important happened it stays within the knowledge of the country. An artist in Poland is in a way a national artist. Here, when you make art it is more like "a man for a man," not so much like "a Pole for a Pole." There are many limits in Poland, and you know that no matter what, you will not go beyond them. For example, some disciplines of art are inconceivable in Poland. I do not even speak about censorship and this kind of stuff. If Christo had wanted to do his works in Poland, thousands of bureaucratic regulations would have made it impossible. Here you can be free in your human dreams. In Poland lack of hope was a slavery.

These artists suffered from their inability to respond freely to their artistic dreams, expectations, and ideas. They felt the small art world, the lack of competition, and the prescribed pattern of artistic career and reputation did not stimulate artistic development and that once they had achieved a given level of reputation within the Polish art world, the artistic merits of their work no longer mattered. Many expressed a similar opinion: "Once you reached the top of the Polish art world, it was very unlikely that you would get a bad review or that you would not be invited to show. You did not have to prove all the time that you were still good. It did not influence your artistic development." None of the artists saw a chance for artistic development and success if they stayed in Poland.

Living in Poland, with limited access to the international arts press, many felt isolated, worrying that the art they made had been done before somewhere else. For those who had achieved artistic success, success on Polish terms was not real. One artist said, "Poland is a superficial country. Money is superficial, all life is in a way superficial. So is artistic success." The stagnation and hopelessness characteristic of many other areas of social life in Poland in this period were not missing from the realm of art. Having searched in vain for inspiration for their artistic development in Poland and wanting to prove themselves as artists beyond the borders of the Polish art world, these artists came to New York to compete with the best artists in the world and to fulfill their artistic dreams in the challenging new environment.

## ADAPTATION TO THE NEW YORK ART
## WORLD: GRAPHIC ARTISTS

### Market Adaptation

The Polish graphic artists who emigrated to New York in the 1970s and 1980s encountered problems. One of the most basic was the loss of the social prestige they had enjoyed in Poland as they confronted the relatively low social status associated with graphic arts in the United States. One artist commented, "When we left Poland, we thought a graphic artist is an important social position, like an actor, a painter, or a writer. This is not so here. In the United States the graphic artist is hardly expected to be an intellectual. That is why many Polish graphic artists are disappointed here."

Most artists found themselves in a situation of anonymity, regardless of their past achievements in Poland. They were faced with the difficult task of finding a job in the highly competitive world of commercial art in New York. This problem was strengthened by the fact that most were truly looking for a job for the first time in their lives. Finding a job—and, consequently, surviving—took time, energy, and persistence. There were multiple reasons for initial difficulties in getting a job. The most basic were connected to a lack of understanding of how the graphic art system worked and a lack of knowledge of market mechanisms and marketing tools. All of the artists reported how they discovered the portfolio, for example. One artist said, "When I came here I was completely mystified by the way the system works. One of the first discoveries was the portfolio." An established illustrator who has been in New York for over twenty years remembered the following anecdote from his past: "I did not know that such a thing as a portfolio existed. I will never forget my first portfolio. I had a couple of works, and I put them into a brown bag—the kind they give you in a supermarket. The art director almost fainted when she saw it. She gave me her old portfolio and said, 'Mr. X, this is the way we do it here.'"

The artists felt the competitive nature of the graphic arts market in New York required that they know how to sell themselves, an ability they had not acquired in Poland. Learning marketing skills was neither easy nor fast. One of the graphic artists explained, "It took me two years to realize that the more money other people make on me the better it is for me. It was a matter of psychological change and adjustment. Graphic art in the United States, like all American art, is a business. You make art here to make money. So you must know how to run the business. I am learning all of it." Another commented, "The competition forces you not to be shy. My handicap, like [that] of all of us from Poland, was that I didn't know how to sell myself. I understand now that if I go to the same person ten times, this is considered to be businesslike, not a pest."

Most Polish artists felt they were disadvantaged relative to their U.S. counterparts in understanding the business of the graphic arts in the United States. One artist explained, "The Americans learn from their childhood about money, how to handle business, how to deal with people professionally. Somebody from Poland does not have the slightest idea how to do all these things. I remember from my experience in the very beginning how many mistakes I made, how much I trusted people, simply because someone was nice to me. Generally, I operated as if I was in Poland."

Even though illustration is a silent profession, lack of English language fluency was often a serious obstacle in landing a job. Said one artist, "An art director may like [your] style and so on, but he may not give you a job assignment simply because of the possibility that you will not understand the assignment." The art director of the *New York Times* described the importance of English language fluency: "The only problem I have with Polish artists is lack of language. True, the work sells itself, and all this talk does not do any good if the work is bad, but the artist must be able to express himself in relation to the work that is being offered. He should be able to explain his work."

Another major problem Polish artists faced was created by the market demand for specialization, which came as a surprise to them. The majority felt their lack of specialization served as a handicap rather than a virtue in the New York graphic arts world. They learned that if one was looking for a job, it was better to present oneself as being narrowly (rather than broadly) educated. One artist said, "If you are looking for a job and say that you can do many different things, they are very suspicious, and they do not know what to do with you. They do not believe you can do many different things well. I have always thought that the more you know the better it is. It is not the case here. It really is better to say you do one thing." Another said, "In Poland, if you are a graphic artist you can do posters, illustrations, graphic design, typography. Here, theoretically, you can do it as well, but you have to have a separate portfolio for everything. If you are looking for a job as a typographer, you can't say you are an illustrator as well, because they do not believe you can do two things well." Although most of the artists initially resented the demand for specialization, with time many accepted the value of the narrow U.S. approach. They started to believe, as one artist put it, that "in the end it is better for you if you can specialize really well in one thing [since,] after all, you cannot be really good at everything."

## Stylistic Adaptation

The major difficulties in getting a job as a graphic artist related to the aesthetic style of the work. Generally, the work of Polish artists did not conform to prevailing conventions of U.S. graphic design. The Polish work was not commercial enough and was perceived by art directors as fine art rather than commercial illustration—some artists were advised to try their luck in galleries rather than in the applied arts. The work embodied too much private commentary by the artist, and it was judged to be too strong, too depressing and gloomy, too loose, and generally not light and colorful enough. Also, it did not meet the standards of technical excellence expected of U.S. artists. One artist explained, "Americans pay more attention to the technical than creative conception. Everything must be well done, in art as well [as] in other fields. This was the first shock, because in Poland, it is the opposite."

The views of the New York graphic art world expressed by Polish artists are reminiscent of historically recognized stereotypes and differences between European and U.S. advertising. Victoria de Grazia wrote about the 1920s, "The European-American exchange was marked by mutual mistrust and misunderstanding. In stereotypes that both sides fostered, the Europeans were thought to be too devoted to the poster and to the idea of arty, but ineffective imagery; while the Americans, more given to editorial-style text in their ads, were thought, for better or worse, the masters of market research and campaign" (quoted in Varnedoe and Gopnik, 1990: 297). All of those who adapted successfully as graphic artists in the United States believed that in order to establish themselves professionally within the U.S. context, they had to transform their styles. Generally, changes had to be made in the direction of more precise, tighter drawing and a lighter style in the sense of color and expression. One of the artists explained, "My works in Poland were heavier in style and more personal. But I had to adapt to the subject matter here, and I had to change my style. I think it is cheerier and more colorful now." All of the artists felt strongly that changes in their artistic code were necessary adjustments to the U.S. system. Many expressed the opinion that "one must change. If you do not change, they do not buy. This is almost a physical necessity."

How much were they able and willing to change in order to work as illustrators in New York? Most artists tried to find a compromise between the U.S. and the Eastern European traditions, seeking to retain the idea that the graphic artist is a fine artist while accommodating the requirements of the system. A well-known illustrator said, "I was always against that dreadful separation that exists in commercial work, the idea that illustration cannot employ free imagination. I always thought it was possible to be an illustrator and at the same time remain a fine artist."

Mason Griff (1970) identified three roles assumed by commercial artists in the United States: the traditional, the commercial, and the compromise roles. The *traditional* role is represented by artists who work as commercial artists but remain symbolically attached to the role of the fine artist. They work in the commercial field for economic reasons, unable to live from the sale of their paintings. Artists who assume the *commercial* role conceive of themselves as instruments for the fulfillment of their clients' demands. They accept the norm that the customer is always right and create illustrations in the cheapest and quickest way possible. The *compromise* role combines the traditional and commercial roles. Artists who adopt this role believe they are instruments of their clients but conceive of themselves as active, rather than passive, agents. They translate the demands of the client but at the same time attempt to persuade the client to accept innovations.

The Polish graphic artists I interviewed fell into only two of Griff's three categories: traditional types and compromise types. There were a few painters who, unable to make a living as painters, moved into graphic arts to support themselves (I return to this group later). The majority of the artists, however, although not identifying themselves as painters, tried to achieve a compromise between the traditional and commercial roles. No one accepted the rules that "the customer is always right" and that they must make illustrations in the "quickest and cheapest fashion" (Griff, 1970: 156). They tried to sell both their skill and their creativity, not just their skill. The following comments were typical: "My artistic credo was always to be the best. This is what it was in Poland, and the same holds true here. It is not always successful, but basically it works." Another said, "I decided from the beginning that I am not going to produce inferior work." Another observed, "It is true of all of us: We are trying to do things better than they want from us."

Although adapting to and working within U.S. conventions, the artists all struggled to maintain their individuality. One recalled, "Since illustration has to solve the problem, I had to do two things: I had to rework my form. I had to find the form that would be mine but at the same time [be] different from those [forms] of 80,000 other artists. Second, I had to work on the anecdote itself, which would be recognizable for Americans but still mine. In other words, I had to force the American iconography to sell a non-American anecdote." Finding acceptance for one's style was not easy. As Heller has observed, "Despite the apparent stylistic internationalism of the applied arts, the average buyer of design and illustration in New York needs time to adapt to what rightly must be called 'foreign' approaches" (1986).

All of the artists strongly felt the pressures of market requirements and perceived them as limitations on their artistic freedom. Since the conventions of U.S. advertising were translated to them in the form of art directors' demands, it is not surprising that their frustrations were directed toward the art directors. All of the interviewees who chafed at the restrictions on their creativity blamed the art directors, not the U.S. public, for the situation. In the artists' opinions the art directors were responsible for "commercial censorship," as one artist put it, expressing a view shared by many: "Censorship, which theoretically does not exist here, is even bigger than in Poland. The market dictates this censorship—not even the market but art directors who don't have the courage to present something new and important. Art directors are part of the business machine, and they fear they would get in trouble if they accept something unconventional. They create censorship; often they are conservative in their views of what good art is."

The effort to retain the freedom of expression experienced by graphic artists in

Communist Poland within the new context of the U.S. art world emerged as a fundamental problem for Polish émigré artists. Some, a minority, were not willing or able to adapt at the expense of their artistic freedom. Said one, "I tried to find a compromise, which in fact was not a compromise, because I changed more the way I wanted than the way they wanted. . . . I am trying to escape from graphics now. I hope that in video I will have more freedom. When I came here, graphic art was the only thing I wanted to do. I believed I could succeed here. Now I do not want to find it anymore. So much energy is expended to get these jobs. It is not worth it given the kind of work you have to do here."

The majority of artists, even the most successful, were not totally satisfied with the type of work they do. For example, of the five successful Polish graphic artists I interviewed who had achieved international recognition, three moved from graphic arts into painting (although only one identified himself at the time of the interviews as primarily a painter) and began to exhibit in Soho and other galleries in New York. One said, "I do painting for myself. . . . When you do illustration, it always involves the client's intervention. It is great to do your own ideas. You know, the appetite grows as you eat. . . . One always wants to do something more." In addition to painting, graphic artists also tried to do independent work over which they could have more control, such as video, film, and illustrating their own books.

Although all of the artists felt the market constraints, most admitted that in the end working within the system had a positive effect on their artistic development. They criticized the U.S. method but not the final result. They believed, for example, that the need to improve their technique led to a balance between idea and execution that their work often lacked in Poland. One artist said about learning to prepare camera-ready art, "I was not prepared to do it and did not want to do it. I thought it was boring. I felt humiliated. From today's perspective, I think my objections were wrong. This is a good approach and allows you more control of your work." Another commented, "In Poland I used to place all stress on the value, not on the form. The combination of both elements is more appropriate and honest. One should not allow oneself to exaggerate one at the expense of the other. Balance of these two elements has a positive effect on the seriousness of your work." Some of those who achieved this balance achieved recognition in the U.S. world of graphic arts.

The majority of the graphic artists felt their art had improved and that they had developed in valuable new directions. They encountered a variety and richness of styles here, a variety of clients they had to learn to respect, competition that never allowed them to rest and that always exerted pressure on them to do a better job—all factors that contributed to their artistic development.

The vast majority of Polish graphic artists successfully adapted to the field of graphic art in the United States and are making a living as graphic artists. A few have achieved international success and have won major awards, received critical recognition, and had their work included in well-known collections. Most Polish artists, however, work as freelance illustrators and designers for major publishers of magazines, books, and recordings. Some work in graphic studios and advertising agencies. One specializes in computer graphics, and another uses graphics in video production. Some concentrate on one activity, whereas others combine several activities within the applied arts. A few, the least successful, supplement their income from commercial work with nonart jobs.

In summary, the orientation to the graphic arts formed in the art world of Communist Poland and the European aesthetic traditions affected the artists' integration into the applied arts in the United States. On the one hand, the artists' background handicapped them in comparison to their U.S. counterparts in such areas as knowledge of market mechanisms and the workings of the commercial world. On the other hand, their unique background was also responsible for much of their success.

The experience of living in Communist Poland taught them, among other things, how to avoid the norms, how to be open, how to find a compromise between their own ethical values and those imposed by the regime. The adaptive success of these artists can be explained by their life experiences, the kind of art education they received in Poland, and the flexibility with which they approach social reality. Polish graphic artists took much from the United States in terms of the development of their own aesthetic possibilities, but they also have a lot to offer.

## ADAPTATION TO THE NEW YORK
## ART WORLD: FINE ARTISTS

Unlike the graphic artists, who overall became well integrated into the applied arts in New York, the majority of Polish émigré painters remained on the margins of the New York art world. For almost all of the Polish artists, gaining entry into the New York art world proved more difficult than they had expected. The highly competitive arena lacked the institutional underpinnings and organizational structures that existed in the applied arts, where jobs—although difficult to get— were more clearly defined. Also, within the commercial world networking proved to be an effective way to get work, and the network of Polish graphic artists grew strong. Polish émigré graphic artists were able to recommend others for jobs in the field or at least to direct newcomers to places where they could find work.

The Polish painters who arrived in New York in the 1970s and 1980s lacked this institutional and social support. The majority of artists, despite their achievements in Poland, found themselves in a situation of professional anonymity in New York. Neither Polish nor wider European careers helped much in gaining entry to the U.S. art world. Most of the Polish émigré artists had few or no initial contacts in the U.S. art world, although some had contact with Americans or Poles who lived in the U.S. and had bought works from the artists before they emigrated. A few well-known artists were welcomed by the Polish immigrant community and were invited to show their work in Polish organizations, where they would even sell a work or two, but in general the interest did not last long. Further, exhibitions within the Polish community in New York did not help artists to enter the U.S. art world.

Since the artists were not being invited to show in New York galleries, they were left on their own to rebuild their careers from scratch. Most did not even try to join galleries when they first arrived, as they were discouraged by other Polish artists who told them how difficult it was to make it in New York. Many of the émigrés felt intimidated and decided to wait and see how things would develop. From the perspective of several years later, they believed it might have been a mistake to not have tried to get into galleries sooner, when they still had energy and faith and before the demands of everyday reality and the struggle for survival settled in.

In contrast to this majority, a few did try to get into galleries when they first arrived. These artists tended to be fairly young, recent graduates who were full of faith in, as one put it, "the power of their paintings" and determined to make it in New York. They went from one gallery to another, only to find, like their American counterparts, that making the rounds of galleries was useless because one seldom finds a dealer that way. One artist said, "I tried for two years, and no one ever looked at my work." The difficulty in attracting the dealers' interest was compounded in the case of Polish artists by the fact that many had not brought their work with them, only slides. On a few occasions dealers did express interest in a young Polish artist and told the artist to come back when he or she had a body of work developed.

An artist who said "I went to eighty galleries in New York and was rejected by all of them" displayed an exceptionally creative attitude in approaching the U.S. art world. He came to the realization that "the problem lies not in my art but in my methods and tactics." Instead of continuing to go to galleries, he decided to look for stipends and grants that would support him. He spent several weeks in a library searching for possibilities. Even though few grants were available for immigrant artists, his attempts paid off. He received a residency and as a result took part in a group show in the Soho Center for the Visual Arts, where two dealers became interested in his work. He was even offered a contract with a Soho gallery, which gave him a stipend for a year. Unfortunately, this relationship ended, and the artist's career languished for five years until he had another show in a well-known Soho gallery.

## Making a Living and Maintaining an Artistic Identity

Regardless of differences in approach to the U.S. art world in the initial immigration period, and despite some initial luck for a few, all of the artists eventually faced the problem of how to make a living in the new environment. Polish artists did a variety of things to support themselves in New York at first, but over time a few distinct patterns emerged. As I have suggested, some artists went into the applied arts and found work as graphic artists. Others made a living from various art-related jobs such as renovating old paintings, painting copies of pictures in a "picture factory" (a shop that reproduces copies of decorative pictures), painting portraits, doing interior design, making decorative pictures to sell through a dealer, and similar work. A third group did primarily nonart-related work, such as painting houses, doing construction work, driving cabs, or working as messengers.

Although they worked different types of jobs in order to support themselves, Polish artists—like their U.S. counterparts—experienced a threat to their fine-arts identity since, as Charles Simpson pointed out, "while these jobs pay the rent, the more substantial they become, the more likely it is that they will swallow up the fine arts identity. The more menial jobs leave little time for painting" (1981: 58).

The choice of sideline careers Polish émigré artists made was motivated by their primary identity as artists and had consequences for this identity. All of the painters who went into graphic arts said they did so only to survive. One artist described in detail what drove him to graphic arts: "I was suffering for two years. I was afraid I would go crazy. It was exhaustion, depression, lack of money, loneliness. How long can you live like that? Everybody has his own romantic dream that regardless of the circumstances, regardless of how much you suffer, you will do what you want to do. This is impossible here. Here nobody pays attention when you are dying. In a situation like this your dream must be changed. You are alone here, and if you are alone you will not be dying in order to paint."

The majority of artists felt they could have worked in graphic arts but refused to do so for fear (not unknown to U.S. artists either, according to Simpson, 1981) such work would contaminate their creativity. Polish painters who did go into graphic arts recognized this problem, but most felt commercial work had a positive effect on their painting and saw this effect in terms of a transformation from one medium to another rather than as a contamination. One artist said, "I could not believe it myself, but as a result of doing illustration, ideas emerged that I transformed into painting—it was a sort of continuation." Another commented, "Graphics helped my painting. . . . I find lots of problems working as a graphic artist, I am learning from them."

The major problem experienced by painters who adopted a full-time career in graphic arts was a lack of time left to do their own art. Most of the painters who did commercial work let their primary identity slip away. They said they would like to go back to painting sometime in the future, but these are unspecified hopes rather than active and realistic career plans. The artists who gave up painting for the foreseeable future did find satisfaction in their new careers, however, or at least rationalized their failure in fine arts with the success in a new career. One artist who has his own computer graphics business said, "I am actively involved in computer graphics. I am getting patents, I have done gigantic projects, many people have worked for me. I am recognized in the field. I have achievements."

Compare these comments with one from a successful graphic artist who remained faithful to his original identity: "For someone else it would have been a success; for me it is just a survival. To do illustration for me is like for a poet to write for a newspaper. One has ambitions. . . . I believe that [making it as an artist] will happen—whether in one or five years. I can't be satisfied with illustration, because I would not sleep at night if I would admit to myself that I would stop there." Another said, "I know I can be rich working as an illustrator, but this is not what I came for. I am afraid I will go in this direction and forget what is most important in my life: painting."

The artists who chose not to go into graphic arts in order to maintain their fine-arts identity and who made a living in art-related jobs instead found this work threatening in a different way. Artists who did work involving painting often found that after working eight hours with a brush they were reluctant to pick up their own brush at home. One artist who later moved into graphic arts recalled, in an interview with the *New York Times*, an effect of working in a painting copy shop: "I walked into an art store on Madison Avenue and got a job making six paintings a day. But I would just paint the sky, and another guy painted the buildings, and another person did the people. Then someone would sign a phony name, took it out front and sold it for $300. After six months I gave back my brushes and did not paint for four years" (McGill, 1984: 1).

In order to avoid the contamination of the artistic identity by art-related jobs, some chose to do side work that was separate from the art world. These menial jobs also had the advantage that artists could do them intensely for some time, make some money, and then be free to do their own work. As Simpson observed, U.S. artists resist the erosion of their artistic identity "by alternately cultivating the secondary career and then dropping it" (1981: 59). Not having a steady job gives the artist freedom a full-time job does not. However, the freedom the artist strives for is often just an illusion, as getting these jobs takes a great deal of time and energy, which again leaves little time or concentration for painting. A painter for whom a career in graphic art was fairly profitable commented, "I have friends who are painters and who do not have steady jobs. They unload trucks. Many people live with the illusion that they are painters, but they paint two hours a week. From this point of view, I decided that it is much better to stand on your feet and not to sell yourself."

The majority of Polish émigré artists found it difficult to reconcile their secondary careers and the necessity of making a living with their fine-arts identity. They all suffered from a lack of time and energy to do art when faced with the task of surviving in the new environment. Many gave up painting altogether. As one artist put it, "Making a living, one can easily forget that one is an artist." They all spoke of "the bleak reality of living" that entered their artistic lives with force.

Although the reconciliation of two careers is not easy for U.S. artists either, the difficulty experienced by Polish artists stemmed in part from their past orientation, where no pronounced dichotomy existed between making a living and making art.

The majority of Polish artists in New York were less actively involved in making art when I interviewed them than they had been in Communist Poland, where artistic activity was more central to their lives. This is of consequence not only for the artists' self-image and sense of worth but also for their professsional careers. The problem is that the majority of Polish artists, even years after immigration, still did not have enough work to form a show, which is a prerequisite for getting into a gallery. No dealer in New York would commit to an artist who had no proven ability to produce work. Many Polish artists were aware of this, which is one reason they didn't even try to get into galleries.

## New World, New Art World

Many Polish émigré artists not only had difficulties staying concentrated in painting but also lost faith in their art and confidence in themselves as artists. Even those who had accumulated a body of work frequently talked about not being satisfied with their art and not being ready to show in U.S. galleries. The following comment was typical: "I haven't tried yet, because I did not feel 'that's it.' I did not have that feeling that I walk in the gallery and I know they could not possibly refuse me."

A fundamental reason Polish artists have difficulty making it in the U.S. art world is that they lack an understanding of market mechanisms. The majority of Polish artists showed a rather passive attitude toward approaching the market and did not know how to market themselves. One artist said, "When I was rejected by a gallery I was too proud to go back." Another artist, who was told by a gallery that they might call him, waited a couple of months for the call then finally returned and said "more strongly that he wished to make an appointment." Older artists who were well-known in Poland found it especially difficult to actively look for exhibition and sales opportunities. These painters, who "never really tried to be successful in Poland" but nevertheless were, felt humiliated at asking someone to show their work, at going from gallery to gallery. Overall they invested little energy in attempting to enter the U.S. art world; they waited, as in Poland, for success to come to them. A well-known Polish painter, who only occasionally showed his work in the United States said, "In order to sell outside the gallery system you must continuously work on it; you must meet people, make appointments, think about it all the time. Since I did not do this, the result was total financial failure."

The majority of unsuccessful Polish artists revealed a lack of understanding of the importance of the dealer-gallery system in the establishment of artistic careers in the United States. They were reluctant to affiliate with a gallery, afraid the commercial gallery would constrain their creative freedom—a sentiment not unknown to successful U.S. artists as well. In order to stay free from any constraints the gallery might impose, the Polish artists often demonized the dealer and exaggerated his or her influence. One artist said, "Any contact with a gallery terrifies me. It limits your freedom. If you achieve success, you are kept by one gallery. I can't forget about it. I think that the better it will be, the worse it will be in this respect." Another put it similarly: "Until now no one asked me to join the gallery, but I prefer to be independent. Once you get into the gallery there are constraints. They want you to do what sells. I don't see myself in that situation."

Only a few artists recognized the importance of the dealer. A successful Polish painter commented on his experience: "The dealer is absolutely necessary in the United States. The situation is different in Europe, but in New York number one is dealers, number two is dealers, and number three is dealers." Developing an understanding that art is business was one of the most difficult tasks that faced the émigré artists. One artist commented, "I did not think it would be such a hard road. When we came from Poland, we were very romantic. We were waiting for something great to happen instead of thinking about business."

One artist who displayed a realistic attitude warned against clinging to remnants of the pejorative meanings "business" and "commercial" had in Communist Poland: "You must do business here. You must understand at once that what you do is your business. You must deny the negative meaning of business, which does not exist in the United States. If you are an artist, your art is your business, because you do not have anything else. And you must do everything for it."

Although many U.S. artists also feel they are not prepared for the market, Polish émigré artists are especially disadvantaged in this respect, given that they lack the general experience of living in a capitalist society. They also lack the networks and professional contacts many U.S. artists have from school and previous jobs that help them to become a part of the system. Émigré artists have to learn everything from scratch and have little help in doing so. One artist told me that after eight years he "discovered" that it was useful to send a gallery an artist's statement together with a résumé (although in reality neither matters much) and that he was just learning to write grant applications; understandably, these skills are learned more easily by U.S. artists. Lack of language fluency is another major obstacle that prevents many émigré artists from engaging in dialogue with their American colleagues. One artist, who has not been able to master the language, said, "The language is my biggest tragedy in America."

In addition to the special difficulties experienced by the émigré artists, they also encounter the career struggles, failures, and accomplishments faced by their American counterparts. In fact, the career patterns of most Polish émigré artists are characteristic of those of unsuccessful U.S. artists. Polish artists in New York participate in various group shows in commercial and noncommercial galleries and occasionally have individual exhibitions, sell their work, and receive some reviews; but this recognition is unsystematic and uncoordinated, and the careers of the majority of these artists lack momentum and steady progression. They appear on the New York art scene occasionally—even in places that count—but are not regularly visible. The majority are not represented by a gallery. Only three of the artists I interviewed were affiliated with a Soho gallery in some form at the time of the research update (1990). Only one artist has achieved success in the New York art world. He is represented by a Soho dealer and has exhibited world-wide, and his works are included in private and museum collections (including the Museum of Modern Art). Although he achieved a level of visibility inconceiv-able to most Polish painters, his success is moderate in New York art world terms.

## Polish Network

Having difficulties making it in the New York art world, many artists turned for support to other Polish artists who live and work in New York, especially to the Polish American Art Salon (PAAS)—an organization of about thirty Polish im-migrant artists established in 1986 to popularize and support its members' artis-tic activities. The organization owns a small gallery space where the artists ex-hibit. Before PAAS was created, and before the political situation in Poland changed, most Polish artists avoided exhibiting in U.S.-based Polish institutions such as the Kosciuszko Foundation or the Polish Institute of Science for fear of being perceived as "ethnic artists." Said one artist, "I did not want to be identified as a painter of Polonia. I would rather be identified as a painter of the Poles."

In the beginning, many purposefully avoided contact with other Poles, afraid of getting stuck in the Polish ghetto and not assimilating. One artist said, "I do not intend to confine myself to the Polish ghetto. We do not live in Poland; we live in the United States."

It seems, though, that over time many Polish artists, painfully aware of a lack of recognition from the U.S. art world and experiencing difficulties with distribu-tion, turned to their Polish colleagues for support and welcomed the opportunity to exhibit in PAAS. Although they realized PAAS was in no position to foster their careers in the U.S. market (although some hoped this would eventually change) and that it would function best as a social rather than a professional network, they valued the support and stimulus to do artistic work that it offered. Although as a group Polish artists lacked esprit de corps, many believed more organization would help them to achieve greater visibility in the New York art scene.

## Artistic Development

All of the artists felt immigration had had a positive effect on their artistic devel-opment. Most of the artists asserted that their basic artistic attitudes and values had not changed but that their visual codes had been transformed. "The melody stays the same, but the performance is different," observed one artist. The major-ity of artists interviewed perceived the changes more in terms of evolution and improvement than of radical departure. Most changed within the conventions of an old style; rarely did artists react so strongly to the new environment that their new style showed little affinity to the old one. One artist explained:

New York has had an incredible impact on me. It would have been inconceivable for me to do things like I am doing here in Poland. I would have never done things like this, simply because there is no Broadway there, no East Village, no graffiti. My art is more aggressive, the color is more aggressive, and I use more light. I used light in Poland, too, but altogether differently. I use graffiti and captions written with a brush, written fast, without precision, without concentration. I saw here that the art schools are different. There are no rules, and this inspired me.

A performing artist and painter elaborated on the degree and direction of changes.

There are changes, but at the same time there is a continuation of my own style. Being in New York affects your art—sometimes it is difficult to verbalize how. When I look at my work, I see the changes in its aggressiveness, because everything here is more intense, loud, dramatic, drastic. Some of my works seem to me to be too quiet. Without changing the basic values of my art, I see the changes as a rein- forcement of the means of expression. For example, in terms of space there is an increase in the number of elements, in density, in the application of rhythm. This city has its own rhythm; one must use more rhythmic composition. The colors are different as well—more aggressive. When you make art here, you must remember that the artist next to you will make a very strong thing.

Even though the majority of Polish émigré artists stayed professionally mar- ginalized in the New York art world, they felt the experience of living in New York gave then unsurpassed stimulation and challenges and enriched their human ex- perience in ways that made immigration worthwhile, even though they could not call themselves successful. An artist who was driving a cab said, "It was absolutely worth it. I did not come here to make money. It was important to leave Poland, to see a different world—it is important for your image as a person." There are few regrets, even though many artists believed that had they stayed in Poland they would probably have been more actively involved in making art and had the psy- chological comfort, concentration, and balance they were striving for in New York. Years after immigration, many Polish artists still felt alienated from U.S. culture. One said, "In a way we should work where we were born. Childhood is quintessential to all our understanding. I will always feel like a foreigner here. In Poland, I would always have my childhood memories to fall back on in my art."

Only a few artists considered going back to Poland after the fall of commu- nism. They expressed disappointment with opportunities in New York and nos- talgia for the culture and lifestyle of Europe. The majority, however, did not in- tend to return. Most felt that after years in the United States it would be difficult to find a place in Poland. Many had nostalgic feelings for the Poland they had known and for the artistic life they had led there, but they felt their "real" life was now in the United States. One artist said, "Poland has gone very far in a psycho- logical sense—it is always something beautiful, something close, but at the same time quite improper for my needs." Another commented, "I am too old to immi- grate again. This period ended, and it is okay." Although most did not want to return, many said that in light of the changing political situation they would want not only to visit Poland more frequently but to work there as well—perhaps have a summer house or spend half the year there.

Most important, however, is the fact that all the artists wanted to become visible in the new Polish art world—to "become known again," as one put it. Because of the fall of communism and the artists' lack of success in the United States, Poland was reevaluated by émigré artists and had become a valuable and desirable place to exhibit and build a career. Many said they would like to represent Poland internationally and enter European galleries in that way. In September 1990, two curators from Poland organized a large show of work of the émigré artists, in the prestigious Warsaw *Zacheta* gallery, called "We Are Here." Many of the artists I interviewed were invited to participate, and all saw it as an important artistic event and were proud to be involved; some traveled to Poland for the opening of the exhibition.

## THE NEW POLISH ART WORLD

The Poland in which these artists want to build an artistic career has undergone complex political, social, economic, and cultural changes since the fall of communism. Questions arise as to how changing conditions, including the transition to a free-market economy, will affect the social existence of artists in the new Poland and how native artists will adapt. Will they find a place in a system that is gradually moving toward the West? In what ways will their patterns of adaptation to the new environment, as well as the nature of the cultural and economic challenges they face, be similar to those experienced by émigré artists who moved from Communist Poland to New York?

The art system in Poland is at the beginning of a transformation from a state-sponsored system to a market-driven one. This era presents special difficulties for artists and artistic organizations. When Polish émigré artists moved to the West, they moved into—although foreign to them—a well-defined and well-established environment with rules and norms that could be learned (albeit with difficulty). In contrast, the artists in Poland will have to reinvent themselves, as the reality they live in is reinventing itself. Goldfarb referred to this special problem encountered by the artists and scholars of the old, political East: "In the Western democracies, the market is strong and alternatives to the market have developed, or have always existed: state and foundation support, private and corporate patronage. In the democratizing East, neither of these conditions exists, although they are being fought for" (1992: 236).

The art system in today's post-Communist Poland combines state control with a market economy. The system of art is still largely subsidized by the state, although all of the arts are suffering from severe budget cuts and artists' organizations must find ways to adjust to the cuts. The Ministry of Culture still owns museums and major galleries, but the state-owned commercial chains such as *Desa* and *Sztuka Polska* are slated to be privatized.

The beginnings of a Western-style art market are evident. In 1989 Poland had its first contemporary art auction, and private commercial galleries are emerging in major cities. As in the former Soviet Union, the distinction between commercial and noncommercial galleries is not clear, because many private galleries are still subsidized in some way by government—and sometimes business—sponsors; few can support themselves on sales. Getting funds from various public, municipal, and state organizations is not easy, given the economic situation in Poland, but with ingenuity and inventiveness some gallery directors have managed to "scrounge and lie to get the money for exhibitions," as did Leszek Jampolski, who directs Warsaw's *Brama* gallery and supplements its budget from his own pocket (Dornberg, 1990: 164).

The majority of new private galleries, which vary greatly in seriousness—some resemble boutiques and shops more than art galleries—are supported from the sale of crafts (such as jewelry and clothing) made by artists rather than from the sale of art. Although selling clothes in galleries might raise questions about the seriousness of the venue, jewelry sales are often seen as a valid way of supporting a gallery, because artistic jewelry is well regarded—a recognition that results from the previous era, when the distinction between arts and crafts was blurred. In the Polish art world under communism, jewelry was sold by certified artists at many state-sponsored galleries. As artists sell their works in new commercial galleries in the present era, however, many fear that jewelry, along with other crafts, will become increasingly commercialized.

The galleries, many of which are run by artists, art historians, or art critics, are selling to foreigners who can obtain bargains because of the exchange rate (although the rate is not as good as it was under communism). Moreover, the cost of living in Poland has risen; therefore, artists are not doing as well as they once did. To catch up with the inflation rate, artists need to sell more work than they did before, which is not easy, partly because there are still no native Polish buyers of contemporary art. The middle class in Poland is emerging slowly, and the middle-class art buyer still belongs to the future. The few existing Polish collectors are reported to be interested in more established art, and the *nouveau riche* class of Polish entrepreneurs is looking for antiques and kitsch (Dornberg, 1990: 167). Its members also prefer to decorate their homes with copies of old pictures rather than contemporary art, which does not yet signify status.

In light of the gradual loss of state subsidies, artists in Poland are now faced with the problem of making a living—including maintaining a studio, since rents are quite expensive. With the fall of communism, artists have lost many *chaltura*, but the new democracy is bringing other possibilities. Book and magazine publishing is increasing, an abundance of new political parties need visual propaganda, and new Polish and foreign business interests need advertising to sell products and services. However, marketization poses threats to Polish graphic arts: "These firms want to do typical commercial posters like in the West. There is no coming back to the Polish poster—no one subsidizes for films and supports that now," said one artist.

Although the line between fine and commercial art is still blurred in Poland, it seems that with the increasing move toward commercial advertising the division may become more clear. Subsidies for theater and film have been severely cut, which decreases the demand for the cultural poster and, above all, causes serious problems for filmmakers. Leading Polish film director Krzysztof Kieslowski commented, "The truth is, we have no money. Filmmakers have to find other work. Some will try to make commercials. Co-production? 80% of them are rubbish. And we are too proud to produce rubbish" (quoted in Attias, 1992: 30).

Thus, Polish artists are beginning to experience some of the problems faced by their colleagues who emigrated to the West. Like those now in New York, artists in Poland must put greater effort into finding and organizing work than they used to, and for the first time they are experiencing threats to their artistic identities because secondary careers are taking more of their time and energy. A recent immigrant from Poland who supported himself by designing and selling clothes to galleries and boutiques said, "I was taking a lot of time to do that, and there was little time to do creative work."

Artists in Poland are struggling to survive on their own; they need to support themselves with different kinds of commercially oriented work (e.g., church art, portraits, copies of old paintings, decorative art), but they haven't yet considered working as waiters or taxi drivers. As one artist said, this "won't happen for a long time." This difference between Polish artists and their New York counterparts is a result not only of the artists' social position in Poland but also of the fact that these jobs are not readily available to artists, since they pay well and are monopolized by powerful people who control access to them. One artist said, "How could an artist afford to buy a taxi to drive it?" Another commented ironically, "It is not so easy to become a worker in Poland."

Artists in Poland still enjoy a high social position, but there are indications that this may change as well. Kieslowski commented on the privileged position artists enjoyed under communism: "It is changing. I am afraid one day we will have no position at all" (quoted in Attias, 1992: 30). Although that day is still in the distant future, artists now find themselves in an environment in which money is becoming increasingly important as a signifier of social status as the society becomes stratified along economic lines. "It won't be fashionable any more to be an artist in Poland," one artist observed.

Polish artists will have to reinvent themselves to survive and even to succeed in a new reality in which they are losing privileges and security they took for granted under communism. Changing old expectations and attitudes might be difficult. An artist who recently came to the United States from Poland commented, "Artists in Poland expect things all the time. They expect to get work, to get a studio, to get an apartment. Now you have to learn that you are on your own. This mentality, which is a result of communism, is the worst." As the Polish art world becomes Westernized, artists in Poland might find their expectations that the world owes them a living not only unrealistic but, as Robert Storr said in the U.S. context, reactionary (1988: 106).

The process of democratization poses serious challenges to artists and cultural life in general, the most obvious (and the most commented upon) being the danger of commercialization of culture. "As Poland struggles to make a transition from Marxist utopia to modern market economy, one might well be tempted to recall Tadeusz Kantor: 'It is hard to tell which is worse: political terror or terror of the market,'" wrote Halina Filipowicz (1992: 71). Filipowicz argued that with the loss of a common enemy, the arts in post-Communist societies might confront not the danger of commercialization but "rather, a more perfidious enemy: irrelevance and oblivion" (Filipowicz, 1992: 85). The example of theater, which played a central role in Poland's cultural and political life and that in post-Communist Poland has been increasingly abandoned by audiences, exemplifies the problem.

For visual artists, in order to avoid marginality it may be necessary to reclaim and reinvent political art, from which many visual artists withdrew under communism. What Richard Bolton has argued in the context of recent attacks on freedom of expression in the United States might serve as a lesson in democracy for Polish artists and arts administrators: "Cultural institutions could more deliberately promote a renewal of public life; a shared public culture might be created that encourages a large number of people to examine society in detail. If artists protect themselves, but can't circumvent the marginalization of their practice—if artists can't link themselves with larger social practices and struggles—then the free speech of artists will fall on deaf ears" (1992: 20).

Under communism, artists in Poland learned how to protect themselves and to stay free of political constraints. Now, with the enemy gone, they face an even greater challenge—not only how to maintain freedom of expression in the face of growing market constraints but, more important, how to use this freedom to promote and preserve the newly emerging diversities and complexities of democratic life in Poland.

## NOTES

1. The discussion is based on extensive interviews with about twenty-five Polish fine and graphic artists who immigrated to the United States between 1972 and 1981 and who were living and working in New York City in the 1970s and 1980s. The primary research was conducted in 1985, and the majority of the artists interviewed initially were interviewed again in 1990. Some newly arrived artists were also interviewed in 1990, as well as several artists who live permanently in Poland but were visiting New York at the time. The art directors of *Time* magazine and the *New York Times* were also interviewed. All but two of the artists who participated in the study were men, and they ranged in age from mid-twenties to late fifties. All but three held graduate art degrees from schools in Poland; two graduated from the Polytechnic Institute, and one was an art history graduate of a university. The sample includes a range of artists who were very well-known in Poland to recent graduates who were just beginning their careers when they left.

## REFERENCES

Attias, Elaine. "A Free Market Which Is Costing Artists Dear." *The Guardian*, January 7, 1992, p. 30.
Becker, Howard. *Art Worlds.* Berkeley: University of California Press, 1982.

Bolton, Richard, ed. *Culture Wars: Documents in the Recent Controversies in the Arts.* New York: New Press, 1992.

Deinhard, Hanna. *Meaning and Expression: Toward a Sociology of Art.* Boston: Beacon Press, 1970.

Dornberg, John. "Waiting for Solidarity." *ARTnews,* May 1990, pp. 164–167.

Filipowicz, Halina. "Polish Theatre After Solidarity: A Challenging Test." *Drama Review* 36, Spring 1992, pp. 70–89.

Goldfarb, Jeffrey C. *On Cultural Freedom: An Exploration of Public Life in Poland and America.* Chicago: University of Chicago Press, 1982.

———. *After the Fall: The Pursuit of Democracy in Central Europe.* New York: Basic Books, 1992.

Griff, Mason. "The Recruitment and Socialization of Artists." In Milton C. Albrecht, James H. Barnett, and Mason Griff, eds., *The Sociology of Art and Literature.* New York: Praeger, 1970, pp. 370–385.

Heller, Steven. "Rafal Olbinski." *Graphics* 40: 230, March–April 1984, p. 76.

———. "Man Bites Man." *Upper and Lower Case* 21:1, May 1985.

———. Polish American Artists Society Members' Annual Exhibition, Exhibition Catalog. Organized by the Polish American Art Salon. Arsenal Gallery, New York City, November 12–December 5, 1986.

McGill, Douglas. "Polish Artists Struggle, Thrive in New York." *New York Times,* August 26, 1984.

Simpson, Charles R. *SoHo: The Artist in the City.* Chicago: University of Chicago Press, 1981.

Storr, Robert. "Critics and the Marketplace: 10 Statements." *Art in America,* July 1988, pp. 104–111.

Varnedoe, Kirk, and Adam Gopnik. *High and Low: Modern Art and Popular Culture.* New York: Museum of Modern Art, 1990.

# 7

# Directorial Intention
# and Persona in Film School

LISA HENDERSON

IN 1985–1986 I SPENT A YEAR as ethnographer-guest at Graduate Film and Television, a Master of Fine Arts program in narrative film- and videomaking in New York City. I had gone to Grad Film to study the culture and practice of film school—how students learned to make films, the kinds of films they made, the relationships they developed with each other and with their teachers, and how they saw themselves as aspiring artists. In the wake of a rising profile for university filmmaking programs in the U.S. film industry, and in the scholarly tradition of studies in cultural production, I was interested in what is taught and what is learned in film school.

Like many programs, Grad Film offers instruction in script writing and adaptation, casting and directing actors, cinematography and videography, editing, sound recording, and production management. Although many students become accomplished technicians, the program is designed to train writer-directors, a position virtually all Grad Film students aspire to. And although advanced students can also study related subjects outside the department (for example, film theory or theater set design), few do, instead building close networks of student colleagues within Grad Film. In the first through third years of a three-year program, roughly 150 students put in long class hours and spend exhausting weeks on each other's productions. They engage in demanding class reviews of work in progress, meet frequently with faculty for intensive advisement, and in many cases sustain themselves with thirty hours a week of "part-time" employment in restaurants, retail stores, film supply outlets, day care, or occasional freelance production, among other trades. Popular caricatures aside, film school life is not glamorous, although the lure of film directing is.

During my fieldwork, it came as no surprise to discover that students were deeply concerned about whether and when their film school investment would pay off. Despite the many advantages of school training in filmmaking, Grad Film tuition was high, and students could still expect skepticism about film school "types" (even film school "brats") in some industry sectors. Their degree, moreover, was neither necessary nor sufficient for success in filmmaking or related professions. Like their counterparts in art academies and music conservatories, they were being trained for a vocational commitment, if not licensed for employment (particularly since only a handful expected to teach). And unlike placement track records in other elite professional schools—for example, in medicine, business, or law—neither film schools nor film industries could project what proportion of graduates might still be making movies or otherwise working in the film business within a few years of leaving the program.

Cast against such uncertainties, however, were the experiences of several school-trained directors who had "made it," usually meaning they had directed an independent, feature-length fiction film, often from a script they had written; that the movie had attracted attention and a distributor on the festival circuit; and that it had garnered decent box office returns and at least modest encouragement from the critics. While I was at Grad Film, Susan Seidelman's *Smithereens* (1983) and later her *Desperately Seeking Susan* (1985), Amy Heckerling's *Fast Times at Ridgemont High* (1982), Jim Jarmusch's *Stranger Than Paradise* (1985), and Spike Lee's *She's Gotta Have It* (1986) were among the success stories; these directors were preceded by a still more illustrious group of film school alumni in the "new" Hollywood, including George Lucas, Francis Ford Coppola, Martin Scorsese, Steven Spielberg, and Oliver Stone. In Grad Film, the living testimony of successful school-trained directors, often encountered in the program's weekly Visiting Directors Series, reaffirmed the faith not that all students *would* become writer-directors but that with the right combination of talent and other qualities, some students *could*. No one in the department ever claimed that most graduates would make films beyond film school (and most were familiar with the dreary statistic that barely 10 percent of Directors Guild of America members work with any regularity [Litwak, 1986: 204]). Only one student among those I interviewed or surveyed, however, acknowledged that she might never get the chance. Others conceded that the select group would be small, but each believed that eventually he or she would be among the chosen.

Although such a belief might appear to reflect bravado or simple naïveté, I see it instead as a strategy for surviving the very odds it denies. In a graduate program that rewards a student's work and development as writer-director, to claim from the outset that one does not expect to direct becomes a preemptive admission of failure or marginality, however modest or even realistic the claim may be.[1]

Neither the anecdote nor the survival strategy (of distancing oneself from unfavorable odds) is peculiar to student filmmakers; indeed, such a strategy is likely to prevail in any formation structured by intense competition and meritocratic individualism (Newman, 1988: 75–80). But at Grad Film, it was a strategy engaged amid specific institutional conditions—of school life and professional filmmaking—that can be understood through the lens of marginality and its transformation. In this chapter, I use an ethnographic account of social interaction in the school to examine three critical points at which relations of marginality are articulated: between students and teachers, between film school and film industry, and between film as a popular medium and the cultural precinct of "art."

First, like students elsewhere, those at Grad Film are neophytes in an enduring and uncertain rite of passage. Ritually and officially subordinated, they enfranchise themselves through the process and discourse of filmmaking and film viewing. Until 1988, the experience of subordination was strongest for first-year students (in a three-year program), about 20 percent of whom would be dropped at the end of the second semester regardless of the overall performance of the first-year class. It was a harrowing practice (one since disbanded) known among students and faculty as "the cut."

Second, although the box-office and critical successes of school-trained directors have challenged industry skepticism, there are few long-term industrial investments in academic film training. Despite popular declarations about the most prominent narrative schools (usually meaning USC, UCLA, NYU, and Columbia) as the major source of directorial talent in the United States since the early 1970s, and despite such concrete forms of assistance as equipment donations, occasional internship programs, corporate-sponsored student film festivals, and student awards from both the Academy of Motion Picture Arts and Sciences and the Academy of Television Arts and Sciences, the institutional relationship between film school and the commercial industries is fairly short and fairly underdeveloped.

Some industry observers venture that with the advent of cable and home video, Hollywood's "insatiable need for more product" (Goldberg, 1987: 48) will continue to transform industrial neglect into breathless speculation about who will be (and who will manage) the next Lucas or Spielberg. Talent agencies, studios, and independent distributors do scout, for example, among film students and student films for potential winners who can be contracted for fairly small investments, adapting the strategy of American International Pictures' founder and producer Roger Corman in the early 1970s. But relative to established professional schools and to more traditional academies of fine art, narrative filmmaking programs still vie for professional legitimacy. In the commercial marketplace of popular cinema, film schools are only as good as their most recent famous graduates. Some programs, notably those in California and New York, can use their proximity to the centers of production to claim a lion's share of available industry resources and attention. The marginal relationship of school to industry may change, moreover, if an increasing number of successful, school-trained producers and directors reinvest in their alma maters.[2] But although filmmaking programs are widely established in U.S. colleges and universities, outside the academy (in the professional milieus to which students and faculty appeal) the campaign continues.

Third, in Grad Film the dynamics of marginality and its transformation are inflected by long-standing cultural tensions among art, industry, and the "popular." Where elite art worlds are organized around the singular artist, critics, curators, collectors, and other specialized audiences attribute uniqueness, originality, and innovation to his or her (usually his) talent and artworks. Popular film, in contrast, suffers from its history and conditions of production as profit driven, highly industrialized, labor divided, and formulaically oriented toward mass audiences (cf. Steiner, 1983: 1; Powdermaker, 1950). Although many cultural producers and critics (myself among them) debunk or at least resist such an absolute valuation of art over pop as the defensive response of cultural elites, investigating the politics of such a position and observing that corporate impulses long attributed exclusively to mass culture also prevail in the world of fine art (e.g., Gans, 1974) have not resolved the art-pop and art-industry oppositions for other producers and critics. Such oppositions, I would argue, are particularly rife in schools, which are charged with the contradictory tasks of cultural democratization and canonical preservation.

For Grad Film faculty and students—most of whom appeal to the independent feature sector of commercial filmmaking—art, pop, and industry are partially reconciled through cinematic *auteurism*, although few would use that term. In school parlance, the phrase is *personal vision*, referring to a writer-director's construction of what a film should look and sound like and, more important, what it should say about the "human condition." However essential the art of the deal and the profitable audience may be in contemporary feature production, in the school filmmaking is the work of artists, not deal makers, corporate functionaries, or the technicians of commercial formulas. "Juilliard," commented one faculty member, "doesn't give you a degree for writing jingles." His alignment with the conservatory tradition expressed a recurring bid for the aesthetic and institutional legitimacy of a popular form inside the rarefied walls of the academy.

From the perspective of these marginal positions—of students contending with rites of passage and the threat of dismissal, of film schools contending with industry volatility and recognition, and of popular culture contending with the traditional exclusions of art qua art—the striking confidence with which Grad Film students imagine their eventual success loses some of its bravado and becomes a more nuanced means of negotiating contradiction, of working the system. In the following account, I turn to the practical routines of school filmmaking and evaluation to consider *how* such negotiations are accomplished, particularly through appeals to the valorized figure of the writer-director. As student films are produced and discussed, aesthetic intention becomes the key to a student director's authority and enfranchisement and, in turn, to the school's institutional position in the art world of professional filmmaking.

## DIRECTORIAL INTENTION AND
## NARRATIVE COMPETENCE: *THE RAIL*

One of the attractions of Grad Film as a site for field research was its robustly public and collective approach to the processes of filmmaking and film viewing. Unlike programs in which students pursue filmmaking as independently as possible ("untrammeled" by others' interventions) and where a departmental viewing of student work occurs once a semester, all Grad Film students present their scripts and, later, their edited films for class review at several stages in the course of each project.

The multiple readings and screenings are designed, in theory, to provide a built-in audience whose interpretations are checks to be incorporated as a student works on a film. They are practices informed by an explicit theory of narrative cinema in which a good film evokes identification with "real human feeling" through a clear, if not always linear, story. Characters are developed through conflict (with themselves and with each other), narrative function precedes cinematic form, and narrative information about character and plot is best conveyed through visual rather than narrowly verbal means. It is a manifestly *communicative* theory in which, in the popular sense of the term, the gesture is successful when the intended message is the one received.

The question remains, however, whose intention? Importantly, it is the writer-director who faces the class to pose and answer questions following the screening of a student work. Regardless of the innumerable others involved in its making, the director accounts for the film as a technical, aesthetic, and narrative artifact, a practice that dramatizes the individualism of the directorial role despite the profoundly collective nature of film production in the school.

But however privileged the writer-director's perspective, the communicative standard also demands that he or she remain accountable to the audience. Thus students are impatient, during class commentaries, with unresponsive directors, attributing to them either inability or pretension—the caricature artiste who dismissively implies that "the work speaks for itself" or, maddeningly, that he or she "doesn't care what people get out of it." Throughout the commentary, the student audience solicits the director's accountability by carefully and collectively reconstructing "what happened," who characters are to one another, what the conflict is. About particular scenes and sequences and about the film as a whole, students recapitulate events and relationships, always implying and sometimes stating the question, "Is this what you mean?"

Although textual analysis of a script or film cannot distinguish between "what is meant" and "how it is to be presented," such a distinction emerges quite clearly in class discussions among student directors and student audiences, who share a set of ideas about how narrative films work. Indeed, it is their discourse that poses a narrowly personal directorial intention as the standard, the reason for writing, shooting, and cutting in a specific way, even though aspects of a particular message may not have occurred to the director prior to the articulation of that message in the commentary. In other words, the causal relationship between intention and outcome is partly engendered by the commentary itself (cf. Smith, 1984). An example comes from a rough-cut discussion of a first-year final project called *The Rail*.[3]

*Plot Summary:* George, Caroline, and Roy all inhabit a small, depressed mill town. Caroline and George work in a bar called The Rail, he as bartender, she as waitress. He is a quiet, good-looking, contemplative man in his mid-thirties, and she a pretty but faded woman in her late twenties. Caroline's husband, Roy, is mean, bitter, and spent at the age of forty-five. Although married, Roy and Caroline never had children because, as we come to understand within minutes of the film's opening, Roy is sterile.

The film opens in the bar, pool-playing patrons in the background, Caroline and George talking, she languishing over a cigarette and reflecting on the depressions and broken promises life in the town has brought her and stands to bring others. George listens sympathetically and in the course of conversation asks why she never had a family. Caroline reluctantly alludes to some medical problem of Roy's, then quietly tells George that "we don't never do it, 'cept when he's real tanked, and since the mill cut back . . ."

At this point Roy enters the bar and orders a drink. George asks for cash, reminding Roy that his tab hasn't been paid. With a snarl, Roy tells George to take it out of Caroline's tips and downs the shot in a single swallow. The scene fades to black.

Fading up, Caroline and George are closing the place for the night while Roy, drunk, sleeps at the bar. Caroline tries to rouse him and get him outside to the car. Roy wakes in anger, insisting he'll drive himself, and violently grabs the keys from her hands, muttering something about the "fuckin' doctors." Still drunk, he starts to leave the bar. He and Caroline struggle, Caroline declaring her embarrassment, but Roy has made up his mind. Viciously he asks her if she's embarrassed in front of her "lover boy," referring to George, and threatens her with his fist. George catches Roy's arm and tells him to get out, warning him angrily that "if there's one mark on her tomorrow . . ." Roy staggers out, and Caroline rushes to catch him, but George steps in and tells her to let him go. Again the film fades to black.

We fade up on George and Caroline parked in George's pickup—he has brought her home to the trailer park where she and Roy live. They talk briefly, say goodnight, then find themselves embraced in a passionate kiss, despite George's reluctance at first. The scene fades.

We fade up on Roy seated in the trailer at dawn the following morning. Caroline enters the trailer and is startled to discover Roy awake. He is ferocious, telling her he knows she was out all night with George. He starts to hit Caroline around the trailer, she trying to escape, he trapping and beating her. He ends the beating by handcuffing her to a chair. Roy then calls George to tell him that if he loves Caroline so much, he can come find what's left of her on the tracks.

The film cuts to a daylight exterior scene where Roy drags Caroline, kicking and screaming, to the railroad tracks. He forces her down and cuffs her wrists to the rails, straddling her and putting the shaft of a revolver in his mouth. Together they will die under the steel of an oncoming train—that is, were it not for George, who arrives at the tracks, skidding across the dry, dustry terrain in his pickup with barely enough time to rescue Caroline.

George persuades Roy to drop his gun and give him the keys to the handcuffs by telling Roy that "nothing happened" between himself and Caroline; indeed, nothing could happen because "I don't got nothin' to do it with. Got it shot clean off in 'Nam . . . I can't even pee standin' up." When Roy doesn't believe him, George unbuckles his belt and drops his trousers to prove that indeed he has no penis. Sickened and pathetic, Roy falls away from Caroline as George rushes to her side. Amid the whistle of the train fast approaching, the handcuff key breaks off in the lock. Roy pitches his gun to George, who shoots open the remaining cuff and pulls Caroline to safety. In pathetic misery, on hand and knee by the tracks, Roy apologizes to George. George holds Caroline, who beats hysterically at his chest. The train whooshes by behind them, and the film ends.

After the rough cut was screened, the following commentary ensued among Peter, the student director; Ilona, a writing teacher; Richard, a production teacher; Arthur, the teaching assistant; and Roberta, Irene, Helena, Carol, Vanessa, and Lee, six female students. Although the class appreciated the film overall, several people were taken aback by the "funniness" of the final scene at the tracks, ending an otherwise "dramatic" film.

ROBERTA: I'm sorry, him showing that he doesn't have anything is very funny . . . [*class laughter*] . . . maybe . . .

PETER: It's supposed to be . . .

ROBERTA: Okay, if it's meant to be, yeah. I don't know if it's the pacing part to it, maybe something you can fix in the editing, but, uh, it's pretty funny . . .

PETER: Uh huh . . . what would you suggest?

ROBERTA: I don't know, the fact that he [George] actually does that [lowers his trousers] to show him seems kind of . . . funny.

PETER: Well yeah, that's the whole point, it's like a showdown . . .

IRENE: It really doesn't fit with the mood of the film.

HELENA: And it breaks your suspense.

PETER: It doesn't fit?

IRENE: Well, the whole film isn't funny. I mean, it's definitely B-movie style. It's not, we're not like laughing out loud until you get to that point where it's just . . . ridiculous!

CAROL: What if you just go to the first shot where he's going to make the gesture, like, I'll do this if you want, and stop it there. That shot between the legs of that guy starting to whoah! is just kind of . . .

PETER: I wouldn't drop it for my mother . . . [*class laughter*]

CAROL: You wouldn't?

ARTHUR: I think you absolutely need it. I think it's a black comedy, and that's like where it's comic relief. Without it it's a tacky melodrama, and when you get there you realize what the picture's all been about. I think you absolutely need it.

VANESSA: Oh, this is a comedy?

LEE: This is a comedy, excuse me?

VANESSA: Wait, this is a serious question. Is this intentionally a comedy?

LEE: Peter, did you think of this as a comedy?

VANESSA: Is it supposed to be funny?

PETER: Well, let's face it, I think it's hysterical that the guy has no dick [*class laughter*].

VANESSA: Wait wait wait wait wait . . . is the movie supposed to be funny?

ILONA: No, it's a melodrama, and melodrama is always somehow exaggerated . . .

LEE: Can he answer that please? [*To Ilona, requesting that Peter answer the question*].

ILONA: Yeah, sure.

[*background group: part of it is . . .*]

VANESSA: When are we supposed to be amused, actively amused?

PETER: Well yeah, I mean it's either that or I have them all killed on the tracks.

LEE: No, Peter . . .

VANESSA: When do you as a director want me as an audience member to be laughing and thinking it's funny?

PETER: Well, that's a good point, because I do mix a lot of stuff up. Like the beating scene is certainly not funny . . .

CAROL: But when he comes out of the trailer it's sort of funny. He looks like a gorilla . . .

PETER: Yeah, it is. It is meant to be like a B-movie action picture.

LEE: Action picture is not a comedy.

VANESSA: Because I think that you need to trim a lot of . . .

PETER: To me there's nothing wrong with having a comedy in an action picture . . .

During the screening and the class commentary, I was struck by some students' seemingly guilty response to the film as comedy (to wit, the early comment from Roberta, "I'm *sorry*, but . . . it's funny"). Few films made that spring had so moved or amused the class. As we watched the rough cut together, I was laughing, too—a response I'd anticipated when Peter first recounted the story over the telephone, when I read the script, and again when I was with Peter, the cast, and the crew on location, shooting the final sequence. Perhaps unsympathetically, the scene had struck me at the time as an Oedipal caricature. That had not, however, been my sense of Peter's intention; nor had it been the crew's reaction, all of whom described the scene on location as "intense" and "cool" but never as "funny." Crew members were present but silent during the class discussion.[4]

As the commentary continued, students and faculty explained the final scene's "unintended comedy" in terms of the mood set up earlier in the film. In contrast to the style of the beating sequence, shot handheld with a wide-angle lens in long takes and described as "social realist" and "very disturbing," the final sequence at the railroad tracks appeared "highly stylized" and "comic"—"campy" in the perils-of-Pauline tradition. As Roberta and Carol suggested, this was particularly true when George reveals his injured genitalia to Roy, a low-angle medium shot of Roy through George's legs in the immediate foreground in which George lowers his Levis just enough to suggest the revelation. In other words, the visual style of the first three-quarters of the film was mismatched to the visual style of the final quarter.

According to several class members who spoke up after *The Rail* had been screened, the film's style was "inconsistent" rather than (the more favorable) "unconventional," making the final sequence's effect on the audience seem "unintended." Late in the commentary, Vanessa returned to the issue of intention.

VANESSA: Um . . . maybe I'm crazy, it's possible [*laughter*] . . . I would like permission . . .

RICHARD: Let's take a vote on that! [*laughter*]

VANESSA: [*with humor*] This is a serious request, because I totally misunderstood the movie. . . . When I was snickering and laughing, I was really embarrassed; I thought, oh my god, Peter's going to kill me, I'm going to hurt his feelings. I felt really guilty, I thought . . . I'm reading this movie all wrong. I should be crying and really upset the whole time, and if it's supposed to be funny and it's supposed to be a farce, almost a parody, I want you to give me permission to laugh, so I don't feel guilty when I watch it. Because I really didn't get it, I really felt like such a jerk the whole time.

Here Vanessa (whom other students said was neither "crazy" nor alone in her response) suggests both the fragility and the sacredness of intention. On the one hand, she judged her own response to the film as unintended by the director; on the other, she felt bad about that response, about suggesting to Peter that he had failed to do what he'd set out to do. In such a comment intention is fragile because its expression and interpretation are not entirely controlled by the person thought to possess it; it is sacred in that it ought to account for why audiences respond as they do to an expressive attempt, at least a competent or successful one.

From the perspective of communications theory, *fragility* might be renamed *polysemy*, a term that suggests the variety of meanings different social actors attribute to aesthetic objects or events and that carries less valuative weight than *fragility*. But Grad Film students, especially those facing the cut, are less concerned with illustrating theory than with presenting themselves as competent filmmakers; thus fragility aptly connotes the threat they experience in unstable meanings. As a student commented on location one day, "The perfect Grad Film script is where in your first draft you figure out what you want to say, and in the second you force the audience to think in your terms."

Although most students would concede that there are bound to be unintended meanings attributed to a film, I actually heard a student speak such a notion only once in my year at the school. At the time, other students agreed, although dismissively. True enough, their response implied, but so what? What counted was what the director wanted to say.

Late in the commentary, Ilona, who liked *The Rail* very much, recast the entire film as melodrama and the final scene as absurd, appropriately so, she thought, given the requirements of melodrama as a genre. The problem, Ilona insisted, was the beating sequence.

ILONA: I am very interested listening to this discussion concerning the genre. Melodrama is a very complicated genre, and you try to simplify it, whether it should be a kind of . . . very dark tragedy, or whether it should be a light comedy, and it is definitely the opposite of both and this is the power of the film. It works on the absurd in the sense that it deals with madness. This man [Roy] is really beyond the normal. So therefore to prepare this kind of absurd, this kind of unbelievable violence has to be somehow beyond the normal reaction we have. We have to laugh but not because it is ridiculous in the very simple way but because it is absurd, because it's beyond the very conceivable or very banal . . .

LEE: And do you think that that's happening?

*[much questioning from the class]*

IRENE: But Ilona, I don't think it's working on that level.

LEE: Only intellectually . . .

ILONA: It is working on that level because it is so strong and so aggressive and so violent . . . it has to be built up, where we get into this kind of cool madness, and therefore I believe that the whole beating sequence is wrong because it is too long and kind of realistic . . .

IRENE: Exactly.

ILONA: Psychologically it is not justified, because he prepares something in a kind of cool madness. He has this crazy idea, he knows already, so he has no reason to beat her up so violently, because the real idea is to handcuff her. So, if someone is so much beyond . . . the kind of reasonable, then it cannot be combined with this kind of everyday passionate . . . violence, and therefore I think this has to be shortened. Then if we get into this kind of really inconceivable level of violence, then we go to this kind of hilarious, or ridiculous I don't know what, which is the absurd again.

IRENE: I agree with what Ilona's saying because . . .

ILONA: It has to be . . . somewhere it is a very strange mixture of it . . . and therefore the laughter we all had, it *is* a kind of hysterical relief, and it has to be, and this is the power of the film.

IRENE: But when you spend such a long time on the beating, you're definitely brought away from that whole genre, because, . . . in the beginning I get this feeling of like 1940s, you know, Humphrey Bogart, I don't know, something, and then when you come into the house the shot with the handcuffs is totally ridiculous. I like that, but then the beating is just, it's like from a different movie to me . . .

Although Ilona says the film is powerful, she does not expressly attribute the comedy of the final scene to Peter's intention. Her interpretation does, however, legitimate the audience's response in artistic and directorial terms. What some students saw as failed intention becomes emotional intensity in Ilona's authoritative commentary. She says the film needs some *technical* work; Peter ought to shorten the beating sequence. With this advice, Ilona invokes the familiar premise of style at the service of narrative. Although the final sequence is comic in its stylistic homage to the perils-of-Pauline melodrama, according to Ilona its primary function is thematic and emotional. It conveys Roy's psychosis and the near-mythical quality of his violence. Against this ground, the "social realist" treatment in the first beating sequence contradicts the overall theme, juxtaposing the dramatic finale with an incompatible and somewhat prosaic characterization of Roy as "merely" violent but not crazy. To lift the beating sequence would not only make the film stylistically more coherent, it would sustain what for Ilona is the more compelling characterization of Roy.

Not surprisingly, Peter decided to barely allude to the beating and leave the "comedy" intact. The following comment comes from our conversation a few days later, at which point Peter was exhausted and somewhat tentative.

LISA: You said you were planning to cut down the beating scene?

PETER: Yeah, I'm going to cut that down, and I'm cutting the end way down and keeping strictly with telling the story. I'm having a problem with being very caught up in the visual nature of the film. I just need to simply, straightforwardly tell the story. There were some comments I did really take to heart and . . . at the time felt . . . I came out of the session yesterday feeling very bad. . . . Several people came up to me to tell me they really liked the film, they thought it was really good, but obviously it needs a cut, it needs work. I think that it was controversial in a way because the tone of the film is confusing. It is serious in the beginning and sort of leads you into this drama, even melodrama, but still, it leads you into it, and in fact by the time we get to the tracks the tone changes. I think the tone changes gradually, but there is a . . . disjointed tone between the intense violence of the beginning and the melodramatic violence of the end, that dragging along the tracks and all that stuff. I personally really like the dialogue, "I loved you" [*deadpan*] and everything. To me it is melodramatic, and that was my intent, to make it . . . funny . . . but I mean dramatic but funny, in essence melodramatic. I *was* trying to be melodramatic.

Again, I was struck by Peter's presentation of the last scene as comic after the class discussion, knowing that had not been his declared intention or the effect he anticipated during rehearsal and shooting. But in a communicative environment in which the fit between intention and outcome becomes a principle measure of competence and where students compete among each other for scarce symbolic and material rewards based on their perceived competence, better to recast one's intentions than acknowledge having unintentionally created such a strong comic effect when a highly dramatic one was planned. Particularly since the new effect is regarded as good, accomplished as comedy (or melodrama) if not recognized as tragedy, Peter can say, in effect, "I meant it all along."

For Peter to suggest the comedy was intended is not deceitful, a gesture calculated to lay claim to an achievement not rightly his. (Some students' pushing him to account for his intention, however, suggests they felt he was making just such a claim.) It is, instead, his attempt to resolve the dissonance provoked by the class response and to salvage his position as student director at a particularly vulnerable, public moment.

By realigning intention and outcome, Peter left his competence intact during the commentary. In later appraisals of craft skill, however, he was not quite as successful: An external committee, whose three members evaluate first-year projects, unanimously commented on the semantic confusion between drama and humor. For example:

> About the direction (from reviewer #1): Directing is hard to judge because the intent is so unclear. Is this just parody? If so, it doesn't have the right tone. In terms of setting the shots, the results are mixed.
>
> Also about the direction (from reviewer #2): Needs a style to carry off the vision. Is this a mock movie takeoff on *Perils of Pauline, Sun Also Rises*, etc.? Or a social realist dialogue drama, as it seems to begin? The audience is lost—we can't take it straight, and direction hasn't given us a handle.
>
> About the writing (from reviewer #1): The writing is badly mixed. The first part

seems like a filmed stage play. Then, with the railroad track idea, it seems like an awkward parody.

Also about the writing (from reviewer #3): Moviemaking not bad, but to mix a device from old movies that we cannot take seriously with serious melodrama is a bit difficult to take. All ends up being funny but not amusing.

General evaluation (from reviewer #1): This film has a rather garbled quality, even though there are some forceful moments.

Unlike Peter's teachers and classmates, committee members had only the film to go on, not the appeals to Peter's aesthetic intention produced in the class critique nor other encounters with Peter that might have conveyed his artistic sensibility and seriousness. Importantly, despite the emphasis placed on first-year final projects in assessing a student's standing in the program, Peter was promoted to the second year. In the eyes of his principal instructors (who, indeed, knew Peter *and* the critique, and whose comments stand in marked contrast to those of the three reviewers), the technical errors in *The Rail* couldn't obscure its feeling and expressiveness, which they, in turn, attributed to Peter himself.

ILONA:   Magnificent film, tremendous sensibility, tremendous feeling . . .
RICHARD:   Wonderful film . . . real film talent . . .
JIM:   Real film talent.

The commentary on *The Rail* is an atypically self-conscious example among the dozens of class screenings I attended at Grad Film. But it brings into high relief a dynamic that was everywhere present if not everywhere spoken, which is that intention is both an a priori motive in the creation of film texts and a form of currency traded and banked in the social construction and evaluation of a student's ability and "talent." This is not to say that intention is mere performance: As *The Rail* discussion suggests, students are indeed invested in their ideas, visions, and images of what their work will look like and how audiences will respond to it. As neophyte writer-directors, however, they must also present themselves as being in control of the meaning and significance of their films. Such presentations occur, I would argue, not despite the program's radically collective approach to filmmaking but because of it. Appealing to directorial intention as the centerpiece of meaning and competence infuses the highly labor-divided (and ultimately commercial) enterprise of narrative filmmaking with the romantic discourse of the artist's innate sensibility and integrity. Thus, although there may be no garret directors in Grad Film, there are visionaries.

## FROM MARGINAL TO SINGULAR

In *Music, Talent and Performance* (1988), Henry Kingsbury interprets the ritual significance of the solo recital in an elite conservatory of music. Quoting Erving Goffman (1967: 5), Kingsbury notes that rituals in contemporary, secular society

are enacted to save "face," the sacred, positive value individuals claim for themselves. But although Kingsbury agrees that a recital performance "confirms the
sacredness of the concrete, individual self" (1988: 120), the student performer, he
goes beyond Goffman to suggest that recitals also affirm the abstract and collective notion of individual*ism*, quite apart from the particular recitalist: "A solo recital ritualizes the social distance between the performer and the audience. What
is ritually enacted in all cases is the conceptual split between the individual and
collectivity" (Kingsbury, 1988: 120). Although they are less reverent occasions
than the formal recitals Kingsbury studied, Grad Film screenings also ritualize
both the sacred face of individuals (like Peter) and a social commitment to individualism. Indeed, such commitments define the context within which one can
"save face," in which, to paraphrase Goffman, social actors show they are worthy
of respect.

Social commitments are especially compelling as the institutional stakes rise;
for example, as Peter and his classmates approached the first-year cut. As Kingsbury points out, unlike traditional rites of passage, in schools one can live
through the rite and its rituals, participate in prescribed ways, and still not move
from probation to security; indeed, one can fail to achieve the new state or even
to maintain the current one. Thus for Peter to recuperate the class's interpretation of *The Rail* as his aesthetic intention is to brace himself against the threat of
marginality that comes with knowing some first-year students will eventually be
dismissed.

The commitment to individualism in the figure of the writer-director also rec-
onciles narrative cinema as a popular form to the honorific category of art. As I
suggested earlier, such a reconciliation is accomplished through the language of
auteurism, which, like Grad Film, began in the United States in the mid-1960s
with both critical and industrial purveyors. For critics, auteur theory resolves
certain crises of attribution about who is principally responsible for creative
achievements in commercial film by situating directors, auteurs, at the artistic
crest and treating films as the products of their distinctive aesthetic visions and
abilities. For distributors, as Bordwell, Staiger and Thompson (1985: 372) suggest,
"new" Hollywood fiction film (emerging in the late 1960s and early 1970s) has
been promoted in part as the product of a singular artistic vision among a handful of school-trained directors in the independent production system, directors
whose "versatile" production training reportedly fostered that vision. In both domains—criticism and publicity—the rarefied commodities are artistic intention
and control, glorified in some at the expense of others—that is, other directors
and the many other contributors to any professional motion picture.

To cultivate students as writer-directors is to enable them to compete as inde-
pendents who begin their professional careers by raising comparatively low production budgets, making films, and negotiating distribution contracts. This order of events generally describes both the early path taken by "new" Hollywood
directors and, as I have suggested, by those film school graduates who have made

names for themselves and, in turn, for their alma maters in the independent feature sector. Contrary to publicity claims, it is not quite a matter of equipping students with a knowledge of all areas of production, which Grad Film's emphases on writing and directing hardly cover (although students also acquire technical skills). Rather, it is a matter of developing a persona, an identity that students and others will exploit as an industrial resource.

To the extent that a reliable (if small) number of graduates do "make it," Grad Film consolidates its position as training ground in the professional field and thus as an institutional mediator in the production of popular culture. If a film school can continue to produce successful filmmakers, it hardly matters whether there is consensus about its curriculum or any established route from film school to film industry. Indeed, it is symbolically more compelling for a school to succeed in a speculative environment than in a predictable one, since such success sustains the art world ethos of risk and uncertainty. As a genuinely excited Grad Film instructor once told me, "I don't know what it is, but we're certainly doing something right." His comment articulated the captivating mysticisms of art (the unknown "it") to the more prosaic but still potent experience of industry recognition ("doing something right").

## POPULAR FILM AND ARTISTIC ELITES

When I visited Grad Film around eighteen months after my fieldwork had ended, Judy, a student colleague, took me on a tour of some of the department's new facilities. We stopped at the equipment room, where she pointed out an epigram scribbled inconspicuously on a wall. It read "educating the rich to entertain the poor." According to Judy, the slogan voiced hers and others' impatience with the recent trend toward "only admitting rich students" to the program. I cannot say whether Judy was right, whether there was now a greater proportion of wealthy students than there had been a few years earlier. But the epigram struck me as making sense of the old Grad Film as well as the new. Although it did not adequately describe the department community or the audience for popular cinema (some students, like Judy, are not from elite backgrounds, and many moviegoers are—recall that it was Richard Nixon who opined, "I like my movies made in Hollywood"), from my perspective it articulated a general class critique of the relationship between film form and the figure of writer-director. The contradiction occurs when the populist aesthetic of narrative cinema meets the exclusionary ideal of the auteur. As Peter's screening commentary suggests, narrative film is communicative and honors an audience's desire to participate, to reject the logic of "art for art's sake" and the distancing of life and art that characterize the formalist avant-garde (cf. Bourdieu, 1984: 4, 32–33). On the other hand, students claim their identities as artists, not as cultural functionaries or businesspeople, and they base their claim, however tentatively, on that very rarefied and individualizing quality called vision. Although they long to appeal to a sizable audience, they also long to be recognized for their distinctive aesthetic contributions, their ability to do something not everyone can. In other words, they claim for themselves a cultural position at some remove from precisely the audience their aesthetic seeks to include.

In Pierre Bourdieu's terms (1984: 12), Grad Film students command a form and a degree of cultural capital that most members of their potential audience do not. They are art world trainees pursuing advanced degrees in a prestigious academy, and the majority of their backgrounds are in the professional classes.[5] Thus to different degrees they construct their artistic identities as cultural elites, not necessarily the economic haute bourgeoisie (although some are wealthy) but the artistic petite bourgeoisie, that nondominant, although well-schooled, fraction of the dominant class.

That someone at the school graced the wall with the aphorism of rich and poor (and that others sympathized) makes clear that at least a few people at Grad Film recognize that a schism exists between popular cinematic form and artistic identity within the hierarchy of cultural value. This was also true while I was in the department, although not all students were so critical. On a second-year shoot, for example, crew members debated whether they would be willing to work for Steven Spielberg. That it was a debate came from the group's ambivalence toward Spielberg's films, the sense that they were masterful but "pure Hollywood." One crew member quoted a teacher as saying, "The students who criticize Spielberg the most would probably jump at the chance to work with him." Others scoffed, and for a moment no one was willing to concede the point. But then one lamented, "We might work for him but not because we want to." His comment distinguished between popular cinema (represented by Spielberg's films) and his elite identity as an aspiring artist by suggesting that the commercial feature industry is coercive; it may provide employment but, for him, only at the cost of serious aesthetic compromise.

This student's aesthetic preferences fell to the European art cinema and select films from the repertoire of "new" Hollywood. But even those students who roundly embraced Spielberg and the popular aesthetic upheld their distinctive position as neophyte writer-directors, a reasonable strategy given the professional milieus to which they aspire. Although some were critical of *whose* vision makes it into distribution, most were not fundamentally critical of the reality or significance of vision as a legitimate basis for distinction. As neophyte writer-directors, Grad Film students are not the countercultural resisters of bourgeois individualism who fueled North American and European avant-garde cinema in the late 1960s and early 1970s (Vogel, 1974: 306), although some selectively appropriate avant-garde aesthetics or oppose establishment culture in other domains. On the contrary, most aspired to enter the independent feature sector of contemporary commercial filmmaking, a volatile arena that reduces economic uncertainty in part by awarding "clout" to directors with profitable track records (Hirsch, 1972; Faulkner and Anderson, 1987) but, as I have pointed out, that also commodifies vision and persona and circulates directorial reputations in aesthetic as well as economic terms.

In this domain, like others (I would include academic scholarship), identities and substantive work are critically rooted in the individualizing tendencies and rewards of their material social practice. In other words, what is reproduced in Grad Film is the cultural and economic exchange value of individuation amid collective activity (cf. Faulkner, 1983). Authors are not dead, contrary to polemic in cultural theory. They are alive and well, sustained by the radically social construction of meaning as an individual event.

### NOTES

Research presented in this chapter was partially supported by doctoral fellowships from the Social Sciences and Humanities Research Council of Canada and the Annenberg School for Communication, University of Pennsylvania.

1. Advanced students in the three-year program may also concentrate on cinematography, editing, or production management instead of directing, although a fairly small proportion does so. In 1985–1986, only 10 percent of second-year students and 12 percent of third-year students opted for specialty majors.

2. An industry veteran recently suggested to me, however, that with few exceptions, the high-risk competitiveness of both motion picture and television production does not lend itself to generosity or to long-term investment in "peripheral" activity.

3. I should note that final projects are crucial to a first-year student's final standing. Also, I wrote the plot summary for *The Rail* using a modified Proppian rule of describing the sequence of actions undertaken by the heroes or protagonists (Propp, 1968). My test of adequacy for such summaries was to ask (1) whether the description was detailed enough for readers to understand faculty and student responses to a film (quoted or paraphrased from taped classroom commentaries) and (2) whether characters' actions beyond those I describe challenged my analysis of the film or the response. When I could answer "yes" to the first question and "no" to the second, I considered the summary adequate.

4. The representation of the woman character in *The Rail* did not come up in the class commentary, in part (I expect) because some women students' earlier resistance to images of sexual violence toward women was ultimately dismissed by other students (and some faculty) as feminist moralizing. During production, one of the lead actors asked Peter if women in the class might "get on your case for sexist violence." "A couple," Peter resigned, but he added that "deep in their hearts they'll know this is a good film." Suspense and heightened drama were the standards in Peter's comment, combined (perhaps) with resistance or indifference to feminist critiques of representation. In a conversation several weeks after his screening, however, Peter lamented the intensity of the violence, calling it "gratuitous . . . really not necessary for the drama."

Although I am speculating here, women students may have pursued the question of Peter's intention most vigorously because they were both moved by the treatment of the woman character but uncomfortable, at that point, about explicitly addressing questions of female portrayal. This is not to suggest that intention was not the issue after all but that their sense of urgency arose partly in response to the violence directed toward "Caroline."

5. Eighty percent of student questionnaire respondents are from upper- or upper-middle-income professional families (measured by parents' occupations), and 15 percent are from white- and blue-collar working-class families. (Data are missing for 5 percent of respondents.) Although the questionnaire was administered or mailed to all students, I report the percentages in terms of respondents, since the 57 percent who returned the survey are not necessarily representative.

## REFERENCES

Bordwell, D., J. Staiger, and K. Thompson (1985). *The Classical Hollywood Cinema: Film Style and Mode of Production to 1960*. New York: Columbia University Press.

Bourdieu, P. (1984). *Distinction: A Social Critique of the Judgement of Taste*. Cambridge, Mass.: Harvard University Press.

Faulkner, R. (1983). *Music on Demand: Composers and Careers in the Hollywood Film Industry*. New Brunswick, N.J.: Transaction.

Faulkner, R., and A. Anderson (1987). Short-Term Projects and Emergent Careers: Evidence from Hollywood. *American Journal of Sociology* 92(4): 879–909.

Gans, H. (1974). *Popular Culture and High Culture: An Analysis and Evaluation of Taste*. New York: Basic Books.

Goffman, E. (1967). *Interaction Ritual: Essays on Face-to-Face Behavior*. Garden City, N.J.: Anchor.

Goldberg, R. (1987, November). Hollywood Discovers Film Schools. *Premiere Magazine*, 1(13): 44–51.

Hirsch, P. (1972). Processing Fads and Fashions: An Organization-Set Analysis of Culture Industry Systems. *American Journal of Sociology* 77: 639–659.

Kingsbury, H. (1988). *Music, Talent and Performance: A Conservatory Cultural System*. Philadelphia: Temple University Press.

Litwak, M. (1986). *Reel Power: The Struggle for Influence and Success in the New Hollywood*. New York: William Morrow.

Newman, K. (1988). *Falling from Grace: The Experience of Downward Mobility in the American Middle Class*. New York: Vintage.

Powdermaker, H. (1950). *Hollywood: The Dream Factory*. New York: Little, Brown and Company.

Propp, V. (1968). *Morphology of the Folktale*. Austin: University of Texas Press.

Smith, B. (1984). Narrative Versions, Narrative Theories. *Critical Inquiry* 7(1): 313–316.

Steiner, F. (1983) Foreword. In R. Faulkner, ed., *Music on Demand: Composers and Careers in the Hollywood Film Industry*. New Brunswick, N.J.: Transaction.

Vogel, A. (1974). *Film as a Subversive Art*. New York: Random House.

# 8

# "A Photograph Is Not a Picture": Distinguishing Anarchy from Art in the Late Nineteenth Century

## PAMELA INGLESBY

PHOTOGRAPHY IS A WIDELY AND DIVERSELY practiced medium of communication, which makes it a useful focus of study for scholars who seek to understand the social foundations and implications of human expression. Many narrative histories of photography have been written, and many compelling claims have been made about its social power and effects. Most of this work, however, has focused on small groups of inventors and practitioners and has placed the camera and the photograph at the center of the story. An alternative approach, with which I am more intrigued, examines photography not as an end in itself but as a set of socially and historically situated rules and practices that serve different functions for different groups of people.

In order to stress the diversity and specificity of these practices, John Tagg (1988) wrote of "photographies" rather than photography and argued that the medium can only be understood as it functions within a broader context: "Photography as such has no identity. Its status as a technology varies with the power relations which invest it. Its nature as a practice depends on the institutions and agents which define it and set it to work. Its function as a mode of cultural production is tied to definite conditions of existence and its products are legible and meaningful only within the particular currencies they have. Its history has no unity. It is a flickering across a field of institutional spaces. It is this field we must study, not photography as such" (p. 118).

The historical moment examined in this chapter is the social reconstruction of

An earlier version of this chapter was published as "Button-Pressers Versus Picture-Makers: The Social Reconstruction of Amateur Photography in the Late 19th Century U.S.," *Visual Sociology Review* 5(1), Summer 1990.

amateur photography that occurred in the United States in the late nineteenth century. This phenomenon resulted in the establishment of a distinction between amateur art photography (pictorialism) and snapshot photography, or what has come to be called "home-mode" photography (Chalfen, 1987). The distinction in the amateur world between art and casual photography is marked by differing motives, knowledge, subject matter, audiences, and developing and display practices between the two groups of photographers; these differences are to some extent projected onto and inscribed within the equipment they use, which differs in its technical capability, ease of use, and price. Here, I attempt to illuminate the origins of this distinction, as amateur photography was not always split into two separate worlds.

In order to understand how people use photography for social and political purposes (in conjunction with expressive ones), I have been guided by the work of Pierre Bourdieu and his colleagues (1990). Bourdieu, interested in the variety of photographic meanings and practices that exist among different social classes, wrote, "The relationship between individuals and photographic practice is essentially a mediate relationship, because it always includes the reference to the relationship that the members of other social classes have to photography and hence to the whole structure of relationships between the classes" (p. 9). If he is right, examining the practices and attitudes of amateur photographers in the late nineteenth century is an exercise in social history as much as it is a chapter in the history of photography.

## THE GROWTH OF AMATEUR PHOTOGRAPHY

Until the late 1850s, amateur photographers were a small, homogeneous group of scientifically oriented and trained men, primarily interested in making technical improvements in the medium.[1] The period from the late 1850s through the mid-1860s saw a large growth in the number of amateur photographers, however, because of the transition from daguerreotypes to the wet-plate process. Although photography remained a messy and arduous hobby in the wet-plate period, it became less expensive and could also provide a source of amusement for the photographer's family and friends.

By the early 1860s, amateur camera clubs had been established in Philadelphia and New York (as well as around the world). They served as conduits for disseminating technical information and as forums for debating aesthetics and standards, and their members included leading figures in photographic art and science. These wet-plate photographers took pictures of artistic, sentimental, or historical scenes and of each other, their families, and their friends. During this "first wave" of serious amateur photography, its practice was considered a respectable hobby and was indulged in by a cohesive group of upper-class enthusiasts.

The technical innovation that provided impetus for dramatic change in the amateur world was the introduction in the late 1870s of dry-plate photography. Dry-plate cameras, which became increasingly popular among amateurs in the 1880s, were smaller, less expensive, and much easier to use than wet-plate models. They could also capture action very easily, which led to the creation of the term *snapshot*. Thousands of new amateurs took up photography during the 1880s because of the advantages the new cameras offered: One could now take a number of photos in rapid succession instead of taking one and treating it immediately with chemicals; few adjustments of the camera were necessary in order to obtain clear photos, and movement could easily be captured; processing and developing of photos could be done at home, hours or even days after the plates were exposed; and the decade saw the birth of D & P services, or photographic businesses that would develop and print photos made with dry-plate or film cameras. Dry-plate technology was also popular because photography had already been established as a respectable pastime that could contribute to family and social life.

The new dry-plate amateurs grouped together in photographic clubs and societies, which held exhibitions of amateur work, provided darkrooms, published journals, and served as a social environment for their numerous members—a predominantly middle-class, professional group including physicians, lawyers, artists, merchants, publishers, teachers, and a growing number of women. The equipment they used ranged from large dry-plate cameras useful for panoramic work to small "hand cameras" more appropriate for casual snapshot photography.

As amateur photography became more widespread, amateur photographers became an increasingly diverse group. Some were still serious photographers, making careful photographic studies on large plates with complicated cameras and developing their own prints. At the other extreme were the new "snapshot fiends," using small plates in tiny cameras that required little skill or experience, drawn toward the medium because of its ability to freeze action and capture people in candid poses. Some of these cameras—called detective cameras—were disguised as other objects, which allowed photographers to take surreptitious pictures. Along with the more respectable dry-plate hobbyists, this new group of photographers formed the beginning of a mass market for photographic equipment, supplies, and how-to books. The immense popularity of the hand camera encouraged the development of yet cheaper cameras and eventually the replacement of dry plates with roll film.

The culmination of this trend toward a relative democratization of photography was the introduction of George Eastman's Kodak in 1888. It should be clear that Eastman did not invent either the hand camera or the market for casual photography—he was successful precisely because simple hand cameras were already familiar and the social demand was already in place. Eastman's contributions were to make the equipment even less expensive and easier to use and to successfully expand the market outward from the increasingly casual amateur photographers, who were still affiliated with societies, to a photographically illiterate, middle-class public.

Although similar cameras had been on the market for several years, the fact that the Kodak was marketed to the general public as well as to established amateurs made it a powerful symbol of changes that had been slowly but continually occurring in the world of amateur photography. For several years, amateurs had been experimenting with cameras similar to the Kodak, using them in strange and unfamiliar ways—for example, taking candid shots of friends and strangers rather than artistic views, and using photography to create visual mementos rather than carefully executed studies. One might say they used the camera for social, rather than technical or aesthetic, experimentation. The popularity of the new Kodak highlighted and exacerbated differences that had already become apparent among amateur photographers—differences in motives, preferences, practices, and class background.

The changing nature of photographic practice became an issue of public debate. Many historians have noted that snapshot photography was perceived in some contexts as a social problem during the late nineteenth century (for example, see Jay, 1984; Conniff, 1988). The popular press often presented the growing number of new, untrained amateur photographers as challenging both photographic and social conventions by engaging in practices described as threats to privacy and decorum. Snapshot photography itself was not considered disreputable; in fact, it was often discussed as a healthy middle-class hobby that could accompany other "fads" such as bicycling, tourism, and sketching. Many artists were using the hand camera in their work as well.

In the wrong hands, however, it was argued that a Kodak or a similar hand camera could be used for purposes of humiliation, the degradation of women, and blackmail. Two particular types of practice were usually singled out as "the problem": They can be categorized as surreptitious photography (the taking of a photograph without the subject's knowledge) and unexpected photography (the taking of a photograph with the subject's knowledge but not permission). These activities were supposedly indulged in by the fiendish "snapshot photographer," an inconsiderate (and perhaps criminal) Kodaker who annoyed lovers, stalked attractive women, and tried to make his peers look ridiculous. These fears were first articulated in the popular press in the early 1880s with the introduction of the British detective cameras, and they mushroomed with the introduction of the inexpensive, more technically accessible Kodak.

Although popular discourse about snapshot photography in the late nineteenth century has been documented, the role the photographic press (which primarily catered to amateurs) played in this negative construction of the amateur photographer has been ignored. The image of the new snapshooter presented in the popular press was relatively simple and can be interpreted as a class-based reaction to a perceived threat to control over personal space and visual information. The discourse about snapshot and amateur photographers found in

the photographic press is more puzzling, however. Why would amateurs participate in a cultural construction of amateur photography that challenged its very
validity as an institution? In order to answer this question, the discourse itself
must first be described.

## THE NEW MEANING OF AMATEUR

The late 1800s saw a drastic change in the public image of the amateur photographer. As their ranks swelled with new snapshooters, always on the prowl in the
cities and prone to popping up unexpectedly in remote rural locations, amateurs
began to be described in both the popular and the photographic press as pests as
often as they had formerly been praised for their dedication to "the art-science of
photography." The new amateur was obnoxious, immoral, and perhaps even diseased. Stories abounded in newspapers, magazines, and photographic journals
about their unbelievable behavior and their power to upset daily life: " 'How shall
we move the masses?' cried the Chicago anarchist on Christmas day. Just then an
amateur photographer was seen pointing his camera out of a window—and the
masses moved."[2]

Much of the discourse focused on the photographers' arrogance and lack of
social consideration. Before public photography was banned in Asheville, North
Carolina, the city passed an ordinance "conferring the freedom of the city" on all
amateur photographers in an effort to promote tourism. "Our amateur friends
from all parts of the country promptly availed themselves of the privileges offered, and since then they have acted as if the Asheville people and hotels and
their guests had no rights which they are bound to respect," wrote a contributor
to *Wilson's Photographic.* "I know an amateur who asked permission (and got it)
to make a street view from a gentleman's balcony, and then, when he passed
through the family parlor to return to the thoroughfare, made snap-shots of
every member of the household along the way, and thought he was sharp."[3]

Amateurs were also reported to have little sympathy for human suffering. An
amateur photographer visiting Niagara Falls displayed a lot of "nerve" by taking a
picture of a woman in the act of throwing herself into the river (a suicide); "while
she was being whirled towards the brink of the precipice the ever present camera
was leveled at her."[4] And in an 1894 cartoon, a train conductor asks, "Is there a
physician here? Man in the next car's got a fit." A photographer jumps up and
exclaims, "By Jove! Where's my Kodak?"[5]

In another story, a young amateur on board a steamer became bored with taking traditional views of the ship "and now wanted something in the ghastly line."
He approached a fellow traveler and asked "if he would kindly put a black cloth
over his face and hang by a rope around his neck from a yardarm a moment,
adding, assuringly, that he would use a plate requiring the shortest possible exposure."[6] Perhaps less disturbing to the "victim" was the amateur photographer who
posed a recently deceased train robber in an upright position, eyes open, with

guns in hand. Apparently, the local authorities assisted in the event.[7] Regarding amateur photographers' insensitive behavior toward women, attitudes were succinctly summarized in the following: "'Write me a story that hasn't any moral to it,' said the editor to the author. 'All right,' said the author. 'I'll give you one about a seaside amateur photographer.'"[8]

One explanation for this behavior was that the new amateurs might be deranged. An analogy was often drawn between the practice of snapshot photography and mental illness or addiction. Amateurs were referred to as "insatiable," eager to photograph anything picturesque or odd[9], and one writer declared that "when the mania for photography takes possession of a man it is said to exceed the passion for French cookery. The camera is as constant a companion as tobacco to a smoker."[10] The Eastman Company printed a pamphlet entitled "A Clear Case of Photographic Fever."[11] And, of course, jokes often say what editorialists can't:

VISITOR (at lunatic asylum): "I see you give your patients amateur photographs to amuse them."
SUPERINTENDENT: "No; they bring them with them."[12]

## "BUTTON PRESSERS" AND "PICTURE MAKERS"

Serious amateurs were well aware of the change in public perception suggested by the material I have presented. The death of the old meaning of the word *amateur* was lamented in the photographic journals in pieces such as this: "'Amateur' in its original meaning is 'a lover of,' and as applied to photography would convey that the man to whom it was applied was an enthusiastic lover of, and consequently a skilled adept in, the art. Now the meaning is degraded, and the man who buys a detective, presses the button, and sends his paper or plates to be developed and printed from, is an amateur. He knows no more of the art than does the organ-blower know of music."[13] Other amateurs were not willing to give up the term so easily, however. B. F. McManus, writing for *Wilson's Photographic* in 1890, argued that one group of photographers calling themselves "amateurs" "have as much claim to the title as an Indian organ-grinder has to that of musician. These are the 'press-the-button-we-do-the-rest amateurs.' No matter where you turn, one of these fiends is sure to bob up. In nearly every instance they annoy everybody with whom they come in contact; they are ridiculed by the press, caricatured by the comic papers, despised by the real amateur, and laughed at by everybody."[14] Another writer not only avoided calling "press-the-button" photographers amateurs but wondered "if they can be designated as photographers at all."[15]

Why were the new photographers unworthy of the name "amateur"? As already mentioned, they threatened the status of "real amateurs" by their reputation for being obnoxious or ridiculous. They were also referred to by the photographic press, however, as ignorant and indolent; there is no evidence that these traits disturbed the public, but they were perceived by serious amateurs as a threat to their pride and self-image. These two flaws are attacked in this excerpt.

> There is, unfortunately, a not inconsiderable section of amateur photographers who adopt the lazy and pernicious suggestion involved in the advice, "You press the button; we do the rest." Such persons are, in my judgment, outside the pale of camera civilization altogether, and cannot be recognized in my observations, as they cannot know, and, indeed, do not apparently desire to know, anything of the matter practically. Neither the joys nor the woes that inevitably attend the honest practice of the art can be known to people who "play" at photography, and thus reduce themselves to the level of the inanimate apparatus which they carry and abuse.[16]

One of the ways these amateurs supposedly demonstrated their laziness and ignorance was through their choice of equipment: "The Tom Thumb camera is the latest excitement in our line. It has an arm A, and a catch B, and A strikes B and interferes with the screw C on the catch D which works upon the instantaneous drop, see?"[17]

Another example of the new amateurs' lack of skill was their penchant for promiscuously shooting everything they found interesting, with little regard for technical considerations: "The class which I am bitterly opposed to, and which is increasing rapidly, and must ere long force the profession to retire in disgust, will be found at watering-places and pleasure resorts in the summer time. You see them with their outfits, ranging in value from $10.00 to $125.00, firing away at anything they may fancy, no matter in what position the sun may be."[18] The observation that snapshooters took a great many pictures was usually linked to an assertion that the pictures they *did* take were necessarily inferior. This charge of "quantity over quality" had been made many years earlier in the journals by elite portrait photographers with respect to the "cheap John" portraitists who were stealing much of their trade. It was resurrected by the amateurs to prove that snapshooters were similarly untalented and undiscriminating. A. Lee Snelling, writing for *Wilson's Photographic* in 1890, argued that anyone carrying a Kodak "seems possessed with an insane desire to shoot it off until his hundred exposures have all been made" and that the worthless photographs produced could not be "pictures"; to make a picture takes thought, experience, and artistic training. "There is no danger to the science in the rapidly increasing number of amateurs; or to us," he concluded, "unless we also fall into the error of making exposures at everything and nothing. Quality, not quantity, is now the desideratum of every lover of our delightful art."[19]

Snelling's distinction between photographs and pictures was echoed by other writers who spoke of Kodakers or button-pressers versus true amateurs or picture makers. It probably caught on quickly in the journals because it succinctly invoked the new distinction being created between artists and snapshooters. "We all know that exposing a plate is by no means the same thing as taking a picture," wrote one amateur,[20] and another stated, "We really think some of our camera friends must *think* more when they try to make a *picture*. With a photograph, of course, then it is different—*anything* is allowable for a photograph."[21]

Being able to make a picture required that one know something about art. As early as 1880, an editorialist quipped, "A photographer who is not an artist is like a priest who is not a Christian."[22] This attitude was a handy rallying cry for the serious amateurs in the 1890s. In 1893 the *Photographic News* used it to attack the deficiencies of casual amateurs: "As a rule, the man who purchases a hand camera for the sole reason that it represents a fashionable hobby has no latent ideas whatever with regard to picture-making. He goes through the Academy picture galleries every year as a kind of duty, and marks in his catalogue those works which the newspaper critics tell him are worth looking at."[23] A photographer who must take his aesthetic judgments from the newspaper rather than from within had no right to claim membership in the increasingly demanding world of amateurs. Even worse were those who had no sense of art at all: "Out of the mixed mass of matter that modern photography presents to us, there are some things that would be better suppressed altogether. It is a matter of great regret that considerable numbers of those practicing our beautiful art do not scruple to lower it to absolute quackery, sometimes to revolting indecency, often to the multiplication of 'cheap and nasty' forms of design, and still oftener to silly pastime or childish absurdity."[24]

When amateurs were ridiculed in stories or descriptions, often their clothing, speech, equipment, and ignorance would be singled out for criticism. The most revealing pieces, however, discussed the education, temperament, or social class of the would-be photographer. The fact that European nobility was avidly "taking up" amateur photography was mentioned frequently in the journals, indicating from what class the serious amateurs felt new recruits should appropriately be sought. An early description of the amateur photographer made it clear that merely pushing a button would not gain one membership in serious photography's ranks: "The amateur, as a rule, is a person possessing considerable artistic culture, whose eye is accustomed, by education, to appreciate the beautiful, or whose temperament, the result of education, inclines to the poetic."[25] Robert T. Tramoh argued that it took more than education to make a great amateur: "When they advertise that anybody can make pictures, they advertise that which is false. Everybody can not make pictures. Successful photographers are born; the art is born into them."[26] Clearly, the new criteria for becoming an amateur were almost synonymous for what was traditionally required of artists: education, sensibility, and innate talent. Not surprisingly, these criteria were highly correlated with social status.

These new distinctions between worthy and unworthy amateurs (or between picture makers and button pressers) were succinctly articulated and illustrated in a story told by "H.B.L." in an 1899 issue of the *American Journal of Photography*. The author, a gentlemanly amateur photographer who had been spending the day in the country (presumably photographing something innocent and aesthetic such as cows), told of how he chanced upon the proverbial "youth with a detective camera" surreptitiously snapping a clergyman who was engaged in discussion with a young woman of the author's acquaintance who had recently "suffered the bereavement of a dear friend." ("The traces of deep sorrow were evident upon her countenance, while the face of the clergyman suggested to us Ary Scheffer's wonderful painting of the Consoling Christ.") The young photographer made the mistake of "accosting" the author and gloating over how he had "bagged two cads." The author restrained himself from administering "summary cuffs upon the audacious young offender against decency [in an effort] to think of some plan of frustrating his dastardly purpose." Luckily, however, the young man asked the author to hold his camera while he went a few yards away to examine a rare plant: "The opportunity suddenly suggested the means of frustrating his unmanly intentions. Thought is quick, and in the briefest interval we deliberated with ourselves the casuistry of the choice between a violation of confidence and the prevention of a sacrilege. . . . In a twinkling the slide was drawn and the gracious light ruined that which the ungracious camarist had compelled it to effect."[27]

It was clear to the journal's readers which photographer deserved the title of amateur, and what action it was appropriate for true amateurs to take against the mass of new, ungentlemanly photographers who refused to live up to the standards of the calling. But perhaps in an effort to make sure the point was taken, the photographic press also provided this image of the Kodaker, suggesting resemblance to a murderous anarchist.

> Alone in the heart of the city,
> On the street where the crowd rushes by,
> The crowd of the gay and the witty,
> The crowd of the tear and the sigh,
> Where the people are jamming and pushing,
> Where the strong overpower the weak,
> Where men great and wealthy are rushing
> Along with the lowly and meek,
> There he stands, like a statue of iron,
> In front of a well known hotel.
> In demeanor as bold as a lion,
> With the face of a demon of hell.
> He heeds not the tramp of the people—
> They are taking no notice of him—
> As he stands in the shade of the steeple
> With his hat pulled low at the brim.
> From under its lowering cover

At the door of this palace of wealth
He looks. From one man to another
He glances with quickness and stealth.
He is haggard and worn with waiting,
As a sot is after a spree,
But still on his visage a hating
Grim smile of fiendish glee.
His fingers are clutching convulsive
At a box that hangs by his side,
As he gazes with features repulsive
At the doors, as they swing open wide.
He hears a faint hum in the lobby,
Still nearer it comes. 'Mid the din
and the noise, as the crowd in a body
Are cheering and yelling like sin,
To action he comes. In an instant
Every muscle and fiber awakes.
As tenderly though 'twere an infant
The box in his hands he takes;
It opens, I catch the bright shimmer
Of high polished brass and steel.
Through my body passes a tremor,
My knees are knocking, I feel
That the hour has come for my taking;
That the incarnate devil there
Has a bomb, and with vengeance wreaking
Will blow us all in air.
Now he's holding the box up higher,
Great God! will it ever end?
I reel, my brain's afire,
I wait for the bomb's fierce rend.
A minute seems almost an hour,
I open my eyes in fright,
He has his machine all open,
The darkness has turned to light.
Now I plainly can see its construction
As it points at the entrance there;
As I look, with a feeling of unction
There comes a temptation to swear,
A sigh of relief escapes me
As I look shamefaced at the ground.
He is only a fiend with a kodak,
And Roosevelt's stopping in town.[28]

## CONCLUSION

Many photography historians have chronicled the great changes that occurred within the world of amateur photography in the late nineteenth century. When hand cameras first came on the market in the 1880s, they were enthusiastically embraced by societies of amateur photographers for their compactness and technical capabilities. At the same time, the new cameras led to the expansion of these societies and to the addition to their ranks of many new amateurs who were less "serious" about photography than the traditional amateurs (although just as enthusiastic). These amateurs were often perceived as engaging in photographic practices that were potentially problematic, not only by the public but by serious amateurs themselves.

In an effort to discourage these new photographers from engaging in undignified activity, the photographic journals began to criticize their behavior. The public press was also beginning to criticize this small but colorful group of photographers. With the introduction of the Kodak and other inexpensive cameras in the early 1890s, the situation was exacerbated. To the public press, the new, noncamera club photographers who bought the Kodaks were indistinguishable from the problematic camera club amateurs, and they were all termed amateur photographers. This was intolerable to serious amateurs in the societies, however, who saw their control over amateur photographic practices disintegrating and the meaning of the precious term *amateur* slipping into disrepute.

Their response was to continue criticizing "bad" amateurs and also to create a value-laden discourse that made a clear distinction between "real" amateurs (themselves) and the new, troublesome snapshooters. Their criteria for good and bad amateurs, however, were more complex than the public's. In addition to criticizing practices that were perceived as a social nuisance, they also condemned the new photographers for a variety of other behaviors that had meaning only within the amateur photographic fraternity. The purpose of the criticism was to separate the growing population of amateur photographers into two distinct groups, to set one of the groups (true amateurs) above the snapshooters, or "Kodak fiends," and to recoup for these amateurs some of the dignity their hobby had lost because of the new public image of the amateur photographer.

This dignity was to be regained through reconstructing the community of amateur photographers. The notion of a large, loosely knit fraternity of amateurs interested in a diverse number of facets of the "art-science" was losing its appeal. In its place was envisioned a smaller group of serious, educated amateurs engaged in the pursuit of photography for artistic ends, and we see in the discourse of the 1890s an attempt to consciously construct an elite art world of amateur photography. (This discourse was accompanied by other strategic moves, such as the switch from weekly photographic journals to monthly pictorial magazines.) Howard Becker (1982) defined an art world as the "pattern of collective activity" that surrounds the production, distribution, and consumption of work that is socially accepted as "art." During the initial formation of an art world, one of the primary activities must be deciding what will count as art and what qualifications will dictate who is to be considered an artist. As Becker wrote, "One important facet of a sociological analysis of any social world is to see when, where, and how participants draw the lines that distinguish what they want to be taken as characteristic from what is not to be so taken. Art worlds typically devote considerable attention to trying to decide what is and isn't art, what is and isn't their kind of art, and who is and isn't an artist; by observing how an art world makes those distinctions . . . we can understand much of what goes on in that world" (1982: 36). Understanding the late nineteenth century as a period in which serious amateur photographers were trying to construct an art world for themselves explains much of the discourse found in photographic journals concerning the behavior and character of new, mass amateur photographers. The mass amateurs had to be dismissed not only because they were socially disruptive but also because they would not fit into the amateur art world proposed for the future.

Another way to understand this fragmentation and reconstruction was provided by Bourdieu, who saw all forms of photography as conventional and rule-governed and who argued that values and attitudes held by different types of photographers are socially determined. He stated that part of the sociological study of photography is establishing how "each group or class regulates and organizes the individual practice by conferring upon it functions attuned to its own interests" (1990: 8). The interests of middle-class amateurs are served by legitimizing photography as an art form, thus distinguishing their practice from "ordinary" photography. He wrote that the meaning photography has to the middle class "conveys or betrays" its relationship to culture; "that is, to the upper class (bourgeoisie) who retain the privilege of cultural practices which are held to be superior, and to the working classes from whom they wish to distinguish themselves at all costs by manifesting, through the practices which are accessible to them, their cultural goodwill. It is in this way that members of photographic clubs seek to ennoble themselves culturally by attempting to ennoble photography, a substitute within their range and grasp for the higher arts" (1990: 9).

Bourdieu argued that because of its easy accessibility, photography will never be accepted as a legitimate art form. This fact is suggested by examining the discourse that surrounds it. "Unlike a legitimate practice, a practice in the process of legitimation poses and imposes, to those involved in it, the question of its own legitimacy," he stated (1990: 98). "It is no accident that passionate photographers are always obliged to develop the aesthetic theory of their practice, to justify their existence as photographers by justifying the existence of photography as a true art." Because there can never be a clear distinction between casual and artistic photographic practice, the distinction must be made in discourse instead. "Discourse is the privileged site for the affirmation of differences, because the desire for self-distinction is more easily accomplished by affirmation of principle than by a real practice" (1990: 63).

The first project of a legitimizing discourse is simple criticism, the rejection of another group's norms and values. Without "a body of precepts and principles" to govern practice, Bourdieu felt, "the vituperation of the barbarian is the only way to testify to aesthetic goodwill" (1990: 63). In conforming to the norms of one's own group, one denies the norms of groups from which one wishes to distinguish oneself, "thus depriving their behavior of any meaning" (1990: 69).

Michael Griffin (1987) provided support for Becker's and Bourdieu's approaches, as well as for my interpretation of the amateurs' discourse. He also provided a broader context for understanding the social and technological changes in the photographic world that eventually led amateurs to adopt artistic goals to the exclusion of other pursuits. He described how amateur photography was considered an honorable and elite pastime until the 1880s and how amateurs had achieved a high social status, probably as much because of who they were (mostly middle class and professional) as because of their artistic or technical achievements.

This status was threatened by two phenomena, however: the use of the detective camera for ungentlemanly purposes and the subsequent introduction and spread of the Kodak in the late 1880s and the 1890s. Although the dry-plate revolution had led to a split in the 1880s between serious and casual camera club members, the introduction of the Kodak added a whole new category of amateurs—those who knew very little about photography and had little interest in photographic clubs (and were therefore outside of their influence). Griffin described these new dry-plate and film amateurs as "an ever-growing 'mass' of new amateur photographers, distinguishable from earlier amateurs by their more casual commitment to photography as a hobby, their preoccupation with photographic 'gadgets' designed to minimize training and effort, and their relative lack of concern with technical or artistic issues" (1987: 109–110).

Griffin wrote that by the 1890s three distinct groups of amateur photographers could be identified: the casual mass-market snapshooters, serious camera club amateurs, and educationally and socially elite amateur artists. He argued that photographers in the second group abandoned some of their technical preoccupations and appropriated the aesthetic concerns of the third group in order to distinguish themselves from the Kodakers. Griffin further documented how this was accomplished through the construction of the elaborate pictorialist code for making "artistic" photographs.[29] Ironically, however, the photographers from this period who are generally recognized as artists today are those such as Alfred Stieglitz, who sought to free themselves from the constraining aesthetic codes of the conservative societies and created a new modernist, avant-garde art world of fine-art photography.[30]

The fact that serious amateurs chose to pursue artistic goals is related to a number of historical, social, and technological factors. Activities in which amateurs had previously been active (including technological innovation, scientific discovery, and documentary work) were now being performed by other groups including scientists, inventors, and news reporters. Art photography, however, had not yet been taken away from amateur influence, and because it was associated with prestigious institutions it offered a seductive opportunity for amateurs to rebuild their status. (It was not long, however, before the photo-secessionists claimed credit for establishing photography as a fine art.) The fact that photography has never been completely legitimated as art is hinted at in the work of Robert Castel and Dominique Schnapper, and Jean-Claude Chamboredon (in Bourdieu et al., 1990). Following Bourdieu, they analyze the discourse and practices of contemporary photographic artists—mostly amateurs—who still desperately seek cultural legitimacy by defining their goals, vision, and social position against that of "ordinary" photographers.

The new Kodakers of the 1890s (and the "casual," detective camera amateurs of the 1880s) who were excluded from the increasingly forbidding world of amateur art photography were not successfully discouraged from using the medium, however. As George Eastman had correctly forecast in the 1880s, a large potential market existed for "unserious" photographic pursuits. Photographers who were rejected from the institutional world of amateur photography in the late nineteenth century (an institution in which many new photographers had no interest anyway) became the untrained weekend photographers we are familiar with today, interested in making photographs for quite different reasons than those professed by the serious amateurs. They did not seek special intellectual fulfillment or social status from the pursuit of photography but instead incorporated photographic practices into the pleasures and traditions of everyday life.

## NOTES

1. Useful general histories of photography and photographic equipment in the nineteenth century, from which much of this background material is drawn, include Taft (1938), Welling (1978), and Gernsheim and Gernsheim (1955).

2. *Wilson's Photographic* 27, January 18, 1890, p. 55.

3. A New Contributor, "Sketchy Experiences," *Wilson's Photographic* 27, December 20, 1890, pp. 751–752.

4. In "Notes and News," *Photographic Times* 19, October 4, 1889, p. 499.

5. Quoted in Conniff (1988).

6. "Amateur Photography and the Public Press," *Photographic Times* 19, October 18, 1889, pp. 515–516.

7. "A Ghastly Photograph," from *New York World*, reprinted in *Photographic Times* 20, October 24, 1890, p. 532. Although presented as "ghastly," Jay Ruby informs me that such photographs were actually very common by the turn of the century.

8. *Wilson's Photographic* 29, February 6, 1892, p. 95.

9. "Camera Amateurs," *Philadelphia Photographer* 22, October 1885, p. 338.

10. "Camera Amateurs," *Photographic Times* 22, November 1885, p. 366.

11. In "Editor's Table," *Wilson's Photographic* 27, August 16, 1890, p. 510.

12. From *New York Weekly*, reprinted in *American Journal of Photography* 12, July 1891, p. 319.

13. *Photographic Times* 19, December 6, 1889, p. 608.

14. B. F. McManus, "Amateur Photographers," *Wilson's Photographic* 27, May 17, 1890, pp. 296–298.

15. A. Lee Snelling, "What Life, and Where?" *Wilson's Photographic* 27, April 18, 1890, pp. 225–230.

16. J. S. Hodson, "Photographic Failures and Their Uses," *Wilson's Photographic* 31, February 1894, pp. 89–90.

17. In "Editor's Table," *Philadelphia Photographer* 25, July 21, 1888, p. 448.

18. Robert T. Tramoh, "Thoughts About Amateurs," *Philadelphia Photographer* 21, June 1884, pp. 172–173.

19. Snelling, "What Life," pp. 225–230.

20. "The Use and Abuse of Hand Cameras," from *Photographic News*, reprinted in *American Journal of Photography* 14, March 1893, pp. 131–133.

21. In "On the Ground Glass," *Wilson's Photographic* 31, February 1894, p. 50.

22. E. K. Hough, "Aphorisms, Analogies, and Similitudes," *Philadelphia Photographer* 17, February 1880, p. 42.

23. "The Use and Abuse of Hand Cameras," *Photographic News,* reprinted in *American Journal of Photography,* pp. 131–133.

24. Ellersie Wallace, "Composite Photography," *American Journal of Photography* 8, December 1887, pp. 211–213.

25. E. R. Leyde, "Professionals and Amateurs and Their Relation to Artistic Photography," *Philadelphia Photographer* 20, December 1883, p. 394.

26. Tramoh, "Thoughts About Amateurs," pp. 172–173.

27. H.B.L., "A Question of Casuistry in Photographic Ethics," *American Journal of Photography* 19, 1899, pp. 81–83.

28. Will A. Dahl, "Almost a Tragedy," *Photographic Times* 32, December 1900, p. 557.

29. See his chapter in this volume for elaboration. Also, see Lang and Lang (1990: 43) for discussion of how Sir Francis Seymour Haden, a British surgeon and amateur etcher, sought to establish etching as a fine art in the late nineteenth century by positing it as a "suggestive" rather than an "imitative" mode of representation.

30. Ruby (1985) discussed the status of photography as art at the turn of the century and argued that amateurs who took snapshots and made pictorialist studies can be usefully considered "artists" by photography historians.

## REFERENCES

Becker, Howard. *Art Worlds.* Berkeley: University of California Press, 1982.

Bourdieu, Pierre. "Introduction," "The Social Definition of Photography," and "The Cult of Unity and Cultivated Differences." In Pierre Bourdieu, with Luc Boltanski, Robert Castel, Jean-Claude Chamboredon, and Dominique Schnapper, *Photography: A Middle-Brow Art.* Translated by Shaun Whiteside. Stanford, Calif.: Stanford University Press, 1990, pp. 1–10, 73–98, and 13–72. Originally published in French by Les Editions de Minuit as *Un art moyen,* 1965.

Chalfen, Richard. *Snapshot Versions of Life.* Bowling Green, Ohio: Bowling Green State University Popular Press, 1987.

Conniff, Richard. "When 'Fiends' Pressed the Button, There Was Nowhere to Hide." *Smithsonian* 19, June 1988, pp. 106–117.

Gernsheim, Helmut, and Alison Gernsheim. *The History of Photography*. New York: Oxford University Press, 1955.

Griffin, Michael S. "Amateur Photography and Pictorial Aesthetics: Influences of Organization and Industry on Cultural Production." Unpublished Ph.D. dissertation, University of Pennsylvania, 1987.

Jay, Bill. "The Photographer as Aggressor." In *Observations*, ed. David Featherstone. California: Friends of Photography, 1984, pp. 7–23.

Lang, Gladys Engel, and Kurt Lang. *Etched in Memory: The Building and Survival of Artistic Reputation*. Chapel Hill: University of North Carolina Press, 1990.

Ruby, Jay. "Francis L. Cooper, Spruce Hill Photographer." *Studies in Visual Communication* 11(4), Fall 1985, pp. 12–29.

Taft, Robert. *Photography and the American Scene: A Social History, 1839–1889*. New York: Dover Publications, 1938.

Tagg, John. *The Burden of Representation: Essays on Photographies and Histories*. London: Macmillan, 1988.

Welling, William. *Photography in America: The Formative Years, 1839–1900*. New York: Thomas Y. Crowell Co., 1978.

# ❧ 9 ❧

# Between Art and Industry: Amateur Photography and Middlebrow Culture

## MICHAEL GRIFFIN

ONE COULD ARGUE THAT the entire history of photography has been the history of a medium at the margins of art. Nineteenth-century amateur photographic societies and photography journals were arenas for protracted debates between those committed to photography's status as a scientific recording tool and those determined to establish photography as a fine-art form. The concerted effort of Victorian "pictorial photographers" to legitimate photographic art alongside painting, sculpture, and printmaking and the continuing struggle in the twentieth century to position photography within the institutions of the fine-art world have constituted a central theme for photographic history.[1]

A pivotal juncture in the received history of photography is the photo-secession, the story of a small circle of innovative pictorial photographers led by Alfred Stieglitz, who broke with the traditional amateur clubs and societies in 1902, published their own art-oriented camera magazines, and established their own elite photo salons, exhibitions, and galleries. The photo-secessionists strove to set more rigorous aesthetic standards for pictorial photography, worked to forge closer ties to the established fine-art world, and hoped finally to confirm photography's status as a fine-art medium. The photo-secession in the United States followed similar defections from the venerable photographic societies of Vienna, Paris, Hamburg, and London and was tied to an international circle of secessionists organized through the Linked Ring of London and the Photo-Club de Paris.

But despite the increased intensity within the fine-art movement in photography between 1890 and World War I—including the founding of Stieglitz's art journal *Camera Work*, the establishment of the Little Galleries of the Photo-Secession (later Gallery "291") for the exhibition of the latest modern art,[2] and even Stieglitz's own involvement with organizing the landmark Armory Show in 1913—photography continued to be shunned by mainstream institutions of fine art for decades. It was not until 1940 that the first department of photography was established at the Museum of Modern Art in New York, a milestone that marked only the beginning of a slow, halting process of acceptance by other museums and educational institutions after World War II.

Today, following a twenty-five-year period of steadily growing favor, photography is widely installed (albeit uneasily) in the formal networks and institutions of the fine-art world. But the tensions inherent in the nineteenth-century debates about science versus art still pervade critical discussions and methods of classification as the art establishment carefully delimits the kinds of photographic activity admitted to the gallery. Although a photographic elite, not unlike the elites that formed the photo-secession, has now successfully ensconced itself within the institutions and rhetoric of art, the overwhelming majority of serious photographic work continues to be practiced outside, or at the margins of, the art world (see Schwartz, 1986). Advertising photography, commercial studio and industrial work, professional nature and travel photography, photojournalism, documentary, and skilled amateur photography all constitute parallel worlds of photo production apart from, yet often overlapping with, spheres of photographic art. The unparalleled numbers of people engaged in some form of photographic production, the long struggle to establish photography as a legitimate art form, and the tendency of the art establishment first to exclude and then to narrowly circumscribe the boundaries of admissible photographic art have all contributed to the formation of peripheral spheres of photo activity on the margins of art.

One of these spheres, the world of camera club amateurs, comprises an international network of clubs and societies representing the work of hundreds of thousands of serious, skilled photographers. Sharing historical roots with fine-art photography in turn-of-the-century photographic societies and clubs, amateur clubs have carried on a tradition of pictorial photography whose clearly defined aesthetic formulas have not varied with the fashions of high art.

As a traditional, more craft-oriented arena of activity, the camera club world has been alternately ignored and disdained by artists, critics, and curators. Although the work of club amateurs is regularly shown in photo salons, exhibitions, and workshops (and appears in magazines, photo books, how-to manuals, nature and travel books), it has nearly always been excluded from the museums, galleries, art books, and journals that legitimize and reaffirm high-art status. Because with few exceptions they have been ignored by the official art world, the role and influence of amateur photographers have been unduly minimized by photography historians and theorists. The term *amateur* has come to be associated most commonly with casual snapshot photographers, those masses of so-called button pushers who constitute the largest market for cameras, film stock, and photofinishing. Industry marketing reports contribute to this conception by routinely lumping casual and serious photographers, light film users, and heavy film users together in an aggregate "amateur" category.[3]

The difference between casual or family photographers and serious amateurs may not always be an important distinction for industry sales reports (although it clearly has been an important distinction in many industry marketing strategies over the years). But for studies of cultural production and symbolic practice the distinction is crucial. "Real amateurs," as defined by Robert Stebbins (1979) in his sociology of amateurism, are committed practitioners guided by professional standards. They strive to perfect professional skills and adhere to professional standards, although this is done for the inherent enjoyment and satisfaction of practicing the craft and for the respect and friendship of their amateur peers rather than for occupational gain. They play a unique role in a "professional-amateur-public" social system, often constituting an audience for professional work, intermittently contributing to professional forums, and generally supporting the conventions, standards, and activities of a particular sociocultural world: "They are neither dabblers who approach the activity with little commitment or seriousness, nor professionals who make a living off that activity and spend a major portion of their working hours doing so—for whom it is an occupation. Amateurs, as this chapter has tried to demonstrate, fall between, possessing a constellation of qualities unique to themselves" (Stebbins, 1979: 40).

Robert Castel and Dominique Schnapper, writing in Pierre Bourdieu's *Photography: A Middle-Brow Art* (1990), make similar observations about amateur photographers in Europe, where amateurs cultivate professional skills and standards while perpetuating a taste culture that falls "between" the worlds of popular and art photography.[4] Although their main concern is to identify the different aesthetic emphases of camera clubs associated with different class strata—with working class clubs locating photography "in a different universe from art" (1990: 18) and focusing primarily on photo technology, bourgeois clubs focusing on the traditional aesthetic values that legitimate their activity vis-à-vis upper-class cultural models, and petit bourgeois clubs balanced uneasily between traditional aesthetic values and the "popular" adoptions of photo technology they claim to distance themselves from—Castel and Schnapper recognize that amateur activity as a whole "oscillates between the imitation of painting and an interest in technology" (1990: 104), that it provides a kind of sociocultural scale on which photography's "middlebrow" status is confirmed (1990: 95–98).

An understanding of the amateur tradition not only opens up a hitherto submerged terrain of photographic history but also reveals a great deal about interrelationships among art, craft, and industry and the social factors underlying artistic standards. Over the years amateur pictorial work has contributed to the evolution of commercial and industrial forms of photography at the same time that it has influenced the development and institutionalization of art photography. More than any other realm of photographic practice, the amateur camera club world seems to have occupied a central position, intersecting or influencing nearly all other spheres of photo activity. As Bourdieu and his associates realized thirty years ago, the study of amateur photography can tell us a great deal about the social forces shaping aesthetic conventions of photographic form.

## THE AMATEUR WORLD AND THE HISTORY
## OF PICTORIAL AESTHETICS

Pictorial art photography, institutionalized in nineteenth-century amateur clubs whose members included the founding pioneers of art photography (Henry Peach Robinson, Peter Henry Emerson, George Davison, Alfred Stieglitz, Edward Steichen, Alvin Langdon Coburn, Clarence White, Gertrude Kasebier), has prevailed over time as a relatively static parallel to the changing styles of elite art. Contrary to the impression given by some historical accounts, the pictorial approach to photography was not born with the fine-art movement of turn-of-the-century secessionists, nor did it die with the waning influence of Stieglitz and his circle after 1910. It developed prior to the photo-secession as a conventionalized, middle-class art form, whose carefully preserved aesthetic principles became firmly entrenched in the activities and judging procedures of growing networks of amateur clubs and societies. Both the clubs and the pictorialist approach survived the defection of the secessionists and enjoyed unprecedented growth during the 1920s and 1930s.

The growing centrality of pictorial aesthetics was somewhat ironic. After all, the pictorialist movement began as an attempt to establish more elite and rigorous standards for photographic "art," to separate the serious artistic efforts of experienced amateurs from the photography of both commercial "hacks" and the newly emerging mass of snapshot takers. The secessionists tried to take the pictorialist movement a step further, identifying themselves with the most modern developments in fine art and attempting to make photographs that would conform to "higher standards [of] beauty and truth," to ideals of "individual expression" and "visionary spirit," not through the recording of facts but through "pictorial effect" (see Hartmann, 1904; Hinton, 1897, 1899; Stieglitz, 1892, 1899).

But as Stieglitz and his circle successfully moved away from amateur photography organizations and linked up with circles of painters and other fine artists, their influence on the larger world of pictorial photography faded. Stieglitz's attention turned increasingly to modernist developments in painting, drawing, and sculpture, so much so that many complained that there was no longer room for photography at Gallery "291" or in the pages of *Camera Work* (Doty, 1978; Norman, 1973). In fact, by 1912 *Camera Work* was devoted mainly to abstract painting. Having successfully broken away from the camera clubs, Stieglitz began to distance himself from fellow secessionists as well.

Steichen also drifted away from the photo-secessionists, venturing into commercial fashion photography as early as 1911. Following the outbreak of World War I, he enlisted in the U.S. Army and left for Europe, where he was placed in charge of aerial photography for the American Air Service. After the war he opened a commercial studio and became a leading magazine illustrator and fashion photographer for Conde Nast publications, particularly *Vogue*. Other prominent amateur salon exhibitors, such as Baron Adolf de Meyer and J.B.B. Wellington, also applied their penchant for still lifes and portrait photography to the na-scent field of advertising photography. By 1920 de Meyer had become one of the best-known fashion photographers in the United States.

Secessionists Clarence White, Gertrude Kasebier, and Alvin Langdon Coburn worked to preserve a tradition of serious amateur pictorialism by establishing the Pictorial Photographers of America in 1916; and White, through his influential Clarence H. White School of Photography in New York, fostered pictorialist no-tions of beauty and form among a new generation of professional and amateur photographers. By 1921 the Pictorial Photographers of America (PPA) had rees-tablished relations between many secessionists and the traditional amateur world, and PPA monthly print competitions were being reported alongside those of other camera clubs and pictorialist societies in the club news sections of the amateur journals. Although White died prematurely in 1925, PPA leaders Ger-trude Kasebier, Paul L. Anderson, and Edward Weston continued to be influential figures in the amateur world throughout the 1920s and 1930s.

As the "new school" of avant-garde pictorialists withdrew into increasingly ex-clusive and insular circles, the "old" pictorialism—motivated more by the simple visual beauty of a subject and the elegance of its rendering than by the expression of ideas—continued as the dominant philosophy of an expanding network of photographic organizations. When historians associate the death of pictorialism with the waning of the photo-secession, they are ignoring the tremendous persis-tence of amateur pictorialist activity and traditional pictorial codes long after 1913, confusing the dissipating influence of Stieglitz's fine-art movement with the demise of pictorialist philosophy and style (see Newhall, 1982: 171–174; Rosen-blum, 1984: 297–299).

In fact, pictorial photography was practiced more widely than ever after World War I. The crucial difference was that instead of pictorialism being a new move-ment associated with pioneering ideas about photographic art, it had become an established tradition marked by convention and imitation. Commenting years later on the photo-secession's impact on pictorialist practice, well-known ama-teur salonist J. Dudley Johnston wrote, "The adherents to tradition, who include the vast majority of practising photographers, continued on their way, undis-turbed by all the commotion (1946: 311)."

Margaret Harker (1979) regretted the fact that the influence of the photo-seces-sion was not more enduring and that the old pictorialism was carried forward with such strong institutional support.

> The majority of amateurs still worked within the framework of the old pictorialism, especially where the cult of the amateur was esteemed. . . . The blame for the perpet-uation of outmoded and derivative ideas in amateur photography must be attrib-uted to the societies and clubs whose advanced workers passed on to beginners the formulae for success which had become clichés, in particular the judges who went the rounds accepting the old and rejecting the new forms of photographic imagery. The influence they exerted was far too great. (p. 135)

Indeed, the history of amateur photography after World War I is not a history of a fading genre but one of a rapidly growing world of camera clubs, photo competitions, national and international salons and exhibitions, and pictorialist publications. The salon work that continued to appear in these journals and magazines is noteworthy both for the superior skill in photo technique and printing methods that is apparent and for its predictable subject matter and form. Pictorial photography continued to be dominated by picturesque landscapes, portraits, and genre pictures; and the amateur journals continued to publish oft-repeated prescriptions for technical perfection and compositional form.

This narrow distribution of pictorial genres and remarkable consistency of formal style continue to be apparent in the *American Photography* annual competitions between 1930 and 1950 and in the *American Annual of Photography* between 1931 and 1951. Formal portraits constitute 24 percent of the photographs exhibited in the contests over the twenty-year period (never less than 19 percent and never more than 29 percent in any given year). Landscapes average 24 percent in *American Photography* and 21 percent in the *American Annual*, with an even lower standard deviation from year to year. Genre pictures average 12 percent in *American Photography*, and 10 percent in the *American Annual*; still lifes average 7 percent in each. The consistency with which these subjects appear is matched by a consistency of form, with portraits routinely manifesting familiar and conventional studio settings and lighting, and landscapes and genre pictures regularly employing the conventional technique of s-curve composition and positioning subjects according to the frequently prescribed "rule of thirds."[5]

Part of the explanation for this phenomenon is that the picturesque and conventionalized photography of pictorialism was more accessible to large numbers of photographers than were newer modernist developments in art. This photography conformed to familiar and popular notions of beauty, with roots in nineteenth-century romanticism. And there were widely shared and clearly defined criteria for technical competence, good compositional form, and desirable subject matter, which had become established through decades of salon competitions and amateur debates. Further, pictorialist standards were widely shared by commercial photographers, many of whom were active members of camera clubs or wrote columns in the amateur photo journals and magazines. Landscapes, seascapes, portraits, and charming or quaint genre pictures dominated much professional as well as amateur work. Pastoral scenes featuring sheep or cows were especially popular for a long time, both in salon competitions and in commercial illustration. In both, explicit meaning was subjugated to the successful production of an "aesthetically pleasing" arrangement of recognizable forms. Whereas the world of fine art was characterized by elite memberships and often mystifying standards, amateur pictorial art was more broadly embraced, and as early as 1920, the photographic industry had thoroughly adopted it as its model of "beautiful photography" for promotional and instructional campaigns.

This stable world of pictorial practice mushroomed in the 1930s with the advent of 35mm "miniature" cameras and yet another wave of serious camera club amateurs. The Photographic Society of America (PSA), established in 1933 to serve as an overarching national association for thousands of new camera clubs, became an organizational link between amateur activity and the photographic industry. Funded largely by Eastman Kodak, PSA established uniform standards and practices for the judging and exhibition of photographic salons. The "salon mania" that resulted marked the zenith of amateur influence. Between 1930 and 1938 the number of internationally recognized salons in the United States rose from approximately forty-five to nearly one-hundred, with about five-thousand photographers having their work chosen for exhibition annually. In a recent catalog of the work of renowned salon pictorialist Max Thorek, Christian Peterson wrote, "The photographic salon, always a camera-club–sponsored event, was the focus of amateur activity during this period. Almost every major city in the United States had an annual salon, and some of them, such as the Pittsburgh Salon of Photographic Art . . . achieved an international reputation. Amateurs were passionate about submitting their work to salon juries all over the globe, for their standing as pictorialists was determined by the quantity of prints accepted for exhibition" (1984: 10).

Eastman Kodak Company and its chief competitor, the Ansco Company, joined the Photographic Society of America in offering any photographer free detailed information and instructions on organizing and running a camera club. Their Camera Club Departments also made available to all clubs free instructional materials and illustrated lectures promoting strategies and formulas for the successful pictorial photographer.

The increasingly entrenched codes for pictorial subject matter, compositional form, and technical execution—taught and reinforced through hundreds of amateur salons and scores of photo journal critiques—were echoed in all of the photo industry manuals and promotional literature. Professional portrait photography; nature, wildlife, and travel photography; and various forms of commercial and magazine photography implicitly accepted the same pictorialist assumptions about beauty and composition. In the 1930s the formidable world of camera club pictorialism represented an approach towards photographic picture making that was countered only by small groups of elite photo artists and political documentarians, some of whom (as discussed in "Amateurs and the Emerging Art World") were descendants of the pictorialist tradition themselves and never fully escaped its influence. Between World War I and the early 1950s, every major photography magazine and journal in the United States was linked to the camera club world, and each espoused the tenets of pictorialist photography.[6]

## AMATEURS AND
## THE EMERGING ART WORLD

In Beaumont Newhall's frequently cited history of photography (1982), he follows the chapter "Pictorial Photography" (chapter 9) with a chapter entitled "Straight Photography" (chapter 10). "Pictorial Photography" recounts the rise of pictorialism in the 1880s and 1890s and concludes with the final exhibitions of the photo-secessionists around 1910. "Straight Photography" begins by further examining the photo-secession, particularly the life and work of Alfred Stieglitz, before following the careers of photo-secession members Stieglitz, Steichen, Paul Strand, White, and their students as they increasingly adopted more direct and less manipulative techniques for photographic picture making.

The decision by Newhall and other photo historians to make the contrast between "straight photography" and "pictorial" work a major distinction and turning point in the history of photography represents an overriding preoccupation with technical style and largely ignores issues of subject matter, sentiment, and ideology—in other words, the overall conception of photography's role and purpose. Viewed in these terms, the transition from painterly pictorial work (emphasizing soft focus, handwork manipulation of negatives and prints, and derivative printing processes) to straight renderings of similar pictorial subjects seems a less significant change. Newhall's chapter "Straight Photography" is actually about some of the best-known names in the pictorialist tradition and addresses the influences that modified what remained essentially pictorial practice after World War I.

Edward Weston and Ansel Adams are good examples of proclaimed artistic "modernists" who never completely severed their contacts with the amateur pictorial world. For many years Weston supported himself as a commercial portrait photographer in California. In 1911, when he was in his mid-twenties, he began to expand his photographic interests by entering pictorialist salons. After several years of success as an amateur pictorialist he was elected a member of the London Salon of Photography, a group formed by traditional pictorialists in Britain following the dissolution of the Linked Ring, and he joined the newly formed Pictorial Photographers of America in New York. As a member of the PPA he came into contact not only with some of the traditional pioneers of pictorialism, such as Clarence White and Gertrude Kasebier, but also with the new generation of White's students, among them Anton Bruehl, Edward Dickson, Laura Gilpin, Paul Outerbridge, Margaret Watkins, Doris Ulmann, Ralph Steiner, Dorothea Lange, and a young Margaret Bourke-White.

In his Clarence H. White School of Photography, White cultivated pictorialist preoccupations with romantic imagery and pure visual appeal. This overriding interest in the picturesque and the beautiful is evident in Gilpin's commercial portraiture and landscapes; in the pioneering advertising and industrial photography of Bruehl, Outerbridge, Watkins, Steiner, and Bourke-White; in the portraits and genre pictures of Ulmann's and Lange's documentary work;[7] and even in Bourke-White's photojournalism.[8]

Nowhere is this interest more apparent than in the industrial photography that became the vogue in pictorial advertising and publicity in the late 1920s. Weston, Steichen, Outerbridge, Bruehl, and Bourke-White, like well-known camera club and salon pictorialists John Mudd and William Ritasse, sought out industrial

landscapes and settings from which to foreground elegant and pleasing composi-
tions.⁹ Machines, bridges, and skyscrapers became the new subject matter for
what was still essentially pictorialist practice; that is, the making of pictures that
are pleasant and visually appealing, that attempt to depict idyllic scenes and
graceful compositional arrangements drawn from our surroundings but which
stop short of modernist abstraction, that emphasize the beauty of surface, line,
form, and proportion but within the bounds of recognizable and accessible
representations.

Speaking of the development of advertising photography during this period
Rosenblum wrote, "One wellspring in the United States was the Clarence White
School of Photography. While little is known of its curriculum, the significance
of its contribution to the modernization of advertising photography can be seen
in the roll call of faculty and students who became active in the field during the
1920s and '30s. Bruehl, Bourke-White, Outerbridge, Ralph Steiner, and Margaret
Watkins translated the design precepts taught in the school into serviceable modernistic visual imagery" (1984: 490).

It is no coincidence, for example, that close-up "portraits" of hands were a familiar genre subject in the amateur pictorial journals following World War I
(hands working, hands praying), that Bruehl introduced the use of such close-
ups into advertising with his groundbreaking *Hands Threading a Needle* picture
produced for Weber and Heilbroner Advertising in 1929, that other commercial
and documentary photographers working in the late 1920s and early 1930s frequently used close-up portraits of hands (e.g., Aenne Bierman, Tina Modotti),
and that Steiner and Willard Van Dyke made the short film *Hands* in 1934 to dra-
matize the activities of the Works Progress Administration. Most of the motifs
common in the new, straight, precision photography were pictorialist motifs.
Rosenblum noted that "product pictures by Bruehl, Muray, Outerbridge, Steichen, and Ralph Steiner are essentially precise still lifes of recognizable objects.
Even the dramatic angles chosen by Bourke-White to convey the sweep and
power of large-scale American industrial machinery were selected with regard for
the clarity of forms being presented. . . . Most advertising images in the United
States (and elsewhere) were not conceived in the modernist idiom by any means"
(1984: 491–492).

Whereas canonical histories of photography identify the gradual replacement
of soft-focus, "fuzzy," or "dreamlike" images with precise, straight renderings as
the conquest of pictorialism by modernism, close scrutiny of photographic work
in the 1920s and 1930s reveals a persistent predominance of pictorialist attitudes
and forms within the new sharp-focused approach of straight photography. The
eschewing of overtly social or political subjects and the avoidance of potentially
disturbing imagery continued to characterize pictorialist work regardless of differing opinions on focusing techniques or printing processes. It is true that urban
and industrial subjects had held little attraction for traditional pictorialists and
that by the mid-1920s many photographers were turning their attention to the

rapidly growing urban and industrial environments of U.S. cities and factories.[10] But this potential conflict was resolved through the repeated assertion that the photographer could create "beauty" out of "ugliness," abstracting sanitized and aesthetically pleasing compositional arrangements from the urban or industrial landscape. By 1930 the notion of discovering beauty in ugliness had become a regular subject in the amateur photo journals.[11]

Although the range of acceptable subject matter was expanding to include locomotives, steamships, automobiles, skyscrapers, and factory machines, and the introduction of faster film stocks and higher-precision cameras and lenses was shifting technical preferences toward sharply focused, high-resolution images, the pictorialist philosophy of fashioning pleasing and picturesque views not only persisted but became increasingly predominant in various arenas of photographic activity. The new industrial photojournalism appearing in magazines such as *Fortune* and *Life* drew explicitly from the pictorialist approach to promote impressive and pleasing scenes of burgeoning corporate America: "Even during the nadir of the Depression, articles illustrated with well-reproduced, stylish photographs and signed artwork 'sold' the positive aspects of the American corporate structure; indeed, Bourke-White felt that 'the grandeur of industry,' which she pictured for *Fortune*'s pages, exerted the same appeal on manufacturer and photographer alike" (Rosenblum, 1984: 493). At the same time, interest in nature photography and panoramic landscapes of the American West grew, and photographers ranging from vacation snapshooters to commercial book, calendar, and postcard illustrators continued to rely upon pictorialist models of landscape and still life as templates for good picture making.

The ironic relationship between the amateur pictorialist tradition and emerging modernist forms of twentieth-century photography is apparent in the debates that took place between Edward Weston and William Mortenson in the amateur journal *Camera Craft* during 1938. Weston espoused the belief of his Group f/64 in high-resolution straight or "direct" photography, whereas Mortenson, the famous California commercial portraitist and amateur salon pictorialist, championed a more traditional preference for softly rendered pictorialist scenes. Mortenson was famous for his composite prints (sandwiching more than one negative to produce a combined image) and for his hand coloring and manipulation of finished prints. He encouraged handwork on prints or negatives as a means of enhancing pictorial effect. Yet in their debates both photographers clearly reveal their pictorialist roots, offering different means toward the same end—the exploration of visual beauty in representational art.[12] And both chose to hold their debate in the pages of *Camera Craft*, a San Francisco–based photo journal aimed at camera club amateurs and salon pictorialists nationwide.

Weston had previously contributed to amateur photo journals such as *Camera Craft* (he had also maintained a regular correspondence with noted amateur leaders such as Frank Roy Fraprie, the long-time editor of *American Photography*), and he clearly considered the growing world of amateur photography an important arena in which to propagate his new vision of pictorialist art. Group f/64, of which Weston, Imogen Cunningham, and Ansel Adams are the best-known representatives, tried to counter the sentimental and idealized manner of much pictorialist work with a more direct, sharply detailed, "pure" form of photographic rendering. But much of this new straight photography was little more than straight pictorialism—more direct, unmanipulated treatments of traditional pictorial motifs, especially landscapes, nature scenes, still lifes, nudes, and portraits. The degree to which straight photography represented a complete break with pictorialism has been greatly exaggerated.[13]

Because Weston is held up as a pioneer of straight photography and modernism in histories of photographic art, his long association with the amateur world (and the relationship of his work to the pictorialist tradition) tends to be overlooked or disregarded. Yet his career might best be described as one "between" art worlds, and he helps to illustrate the ongoing impact the amateur world enjoyed from its position at the margins of art.

Ansel Adams similarly preserved his amateur ties, maintaining a lifelong membership in the Photographic Society of America and occasionally contributing articles or photographic work to the amateur photo magazines. He enjoyed a long, somewhat ambivalent relationship with Stieglitz and Georgia O'Keeffe at the same time that he fraternized with many of the traditional pictorialists and camera clubbers Stieglitz had shunned. His work was also regularly featured in Eastman Kodak ads, especially those that ran in the amateur photo journals and magazines. These ads invariably featured Adams's scenic Western landscapes, landscapes that in many respects epitomized the pictorialist aesthetic.[14] Indeed, Adams long enjoyed great popularity among amateurs and camera club members, no doubt because his pictures so often exemplify camera club ideals of technical skill and pictorial beauty.

Of interest in this regard is an informal survey of PSA members done in 1978 by the *PSA Journal,* the official journal of the Photographic Society of America and the most widely read magazine among camera club members. Reported in an article entitled "Are PSA Members Photographic Isolationists? Or Is Ansel Adams Good at P.R.?" the poll questioned 211 PSA members on their familiarity with a list of forty-five twentieth-century photographers taken from the catalog, *Looking at Photographs: 100 Pictures from the Collection of the Museum of Modern Art* (MoMA).[15] Eighty-four percent of the sample said they were familiar with Adams's photography, a far greater number than those claiming to know the work of any other photographer in the MoMA collection; and 93 percent of those who claimed to know Adams's work said they admired it. The only other photographers for whose work 50 percent or more of the respondents claimed familiarity were Edward Weston, Edward Steichen, Margaret Bourke-White, Henri Cartier-Bresson, and Alfred Stieglitz. All but Cartier-Bresson have roots in early twentieth-century pictorialism, and all have successfully straddled different photographic worlds—amateur, commercial, photojournalistic, and fine art. By comparison, very few respondents knew the work of photographers whose reputations were built exclusively within the art world (e.g., Robert Frank at 9.5 percent, Lee Friedlander at 7.6, Ralph Meatyard at 6.2, Ken Josephson at 1.9). Some respondents felt some of the best twentieth-century photographers were not represented in MoMA's collection and submitted write-in votes for well-known salon pictorialists Max Thorek, Adolf Fassbender, Yousuf Karsh, William Mortenson, and John Mudd.

Because amateurs strive to emulate professional or commercial models, as well as to perpetuate traditional pictorialist standards, the amateur world occupies a unique space between art and industry—at the margins of both commercial photography (portrait studio work, professional wedding photography, corporate and industrial photography, photojournalism) and art (juried salons, community art centers, galleries, and even museums). Steichen, more than any single figure, symbolizes this bridging of many photographic worlds, moving during the course of the twentieth century's first fifty years from amateur society salonist to commercial fashion photographer to photojournalist and military photographer to art museum curator. His photographic work represents a kind of photographic middle ground, emphasizing as it does both pictorialist concerns for pleasing subject matter and formal visual appeal and professional photography's traditional faith in the verisimilitude and inherent value of photo recording.

Steichen's landmark *Family of Man* exhibit at the Museum of Modern Art in 1955 clearly reflects traditional amateur attitudes about picturesque, optimistic, and even "cute" imagery at the same time that it uncritically accepts the camera as a photojournalistic tool for "capturing" the world around us. Traditional pictorial subjects—romantic landscapes, genre pictures of village life, portraits of children, portraits of old, craggy faces filled with "character"—saturate the *Family of Man* catalog (although unlike salon photographs of an earlier era, these subjects are pictured by means of small, lightweight cameras and high-speed film stocks; thus many of the pictures are characterized by natural settings, sharp focus, and moments of stopped action). "Stars" of the exhibit include, not surprisingly, Adams, Weston, Bourke-White, Lange, Cartier-Bresson, and Steichen himself.

*The Family of Man* was a kind of last hurrah for pictorial photography in the fine-art world. But it was a sign of the continuing popularity of pictorial photography among the larger public. Conceived and directed by one of Stieglitz's original inner circle and consisting largely of magazine photographs characterized by a pictorialist attitude toward joyful people and pleasing subjects, *The Family of Man* was arguably the most popular photographic exhibit of all time (by 1978 the book had sold over 4 million copies). John Szarkowski, in his introduction to the Museum of Modern Art catalog *Mirrors and Windows: American Photography Since 1960* (1978), identified the exhibit as one of the three most important events marking the 1950s as a watershed decade for photography. For Szarkowski *The Family of Man* marked the end of an era, representing in his view a sentimental and popular form of photography whose time was coming to an end. In contrast, he argued that the founding of *Aperture* magazine by Minor White in 1952 and the publication of Robert Frank's *The Americans* in 1959 represented the new ambitions of younger, more innovative postwar photographers and signaled the totally modernist direction art photography was to take in the 1960s and 1970s. Still, even in the past thirty years, most amateur and professional photographers have continued to embrace the more traditional pictorialist approach, while fine artists have conscientiously separated themselves into more elite and esoteric memberships (Schwartz, 1986).

## A PHOTO WORLD
## BETWEEN ART AND INDUSTRY

Whereas legitimized fine-art photography has attempted to distance itself from the activities of amateurs, the world of camera club and salon photography has remained a substantial force at the margins of art. With considerable support from the photo industry, salon pictorialism has persistently confronted the art world with a more conventional aesthetic model, often serving as a foil against which to distinguish modern innovations. Throughout the 1920s, 1930s, and 1940s, the amateur photo journals were filled with essays and commentaries on photography's status vis-à-vis the fine arts. Sometimes these took the form of arguments for pictorial photography's special claim to artistic status; sometimes they were calls for greater artistic expression in pictorial work, sometimes reports on the growing acceptance of photography in art establishments, sometimes debates on the importance of specific art genres. Painters and other artists were often asked to judge amateur photo exhibitions, and many successful salon pictorialists authored books on art and photography (cf. Fassbender, 1937; Thorek, 1937 and 1947; Mortenson, 1936). Amateur photography was also occasionally accepted within the walls of the art establishment, particularly during the peak years of camera club activity between 1925 and 1950 (the Minneapolis Salon of Photography, for example, was exhibited at the Minneapolis Institute of Arts from 1932 through 1946).

The 1960s and 1970s saw the eventual establishment of fine-art photography throughout the institutional art world, but with it came a narrowing of artistic elites and a squeezing out of traditionalists. It was photography with a thoroughly modernist, exploratory sensibility, photography that disdained the "prettiness" and sentimentality of pictorialism and that opened the gallery doors once and for all to this long mistrusted mechanical medium. Although contact between the art world and the amateur world was not completely severed—George Tice rose from the camera club ranks in the early 1960s to become a noted U.S. photo artist—the two worlds have continued to move farther apart. Artists tend to snicker at camera club "postcard" photography, whereas club members shake their heads at the confusing and opaque explanations art photographers give for their work.

Photographers from these separate worlds no longer share evaluative criteria or conventions of meaning.[16] The split that began with Stieglitz and the photo-secession in 1902 was, perhaps, finally completed in the 1970s, as art photography gained an institutional foothold in the world of high art and no longer found much benefit in its traditional relationships with the institutions (e.g., camera clubs) that had nurtured it in the past.[17]

Amateur photography, then, is an arena of cultural production whose history has long existed "between" art and industry. For more than a hundred years photo journal articles and camera club minutes have revealed the competing influences of art and industry within amateur organizations. Debates between those striving to create serious photographic art and those more concerned with photo technology, professional techniques, and commercial formulas appear in the minutes and publications of every club and society. Amateur organizations were steadily drawn into factions: those more serious about working and experimenting in the darkroom to produce "fine prints" (prints displaying sophisticated technical competence and "aesthetic sensibility") and those more concerned with reproducing eye-catching travel pictures, scenic picture postcards, studio portraits, or "cute" domestic or genre scenes.

Between 1925 and 1940, at the same time growing amateur visibility led to more attention from the art world, the balance shifted decidedly toward more predictable and less innovative work. As camera club membership skyrocketed and salon entries multiplied enormously, pictorialist propensities solidified into increasingly rigid standards. More highly codified rules for appropriate subject matter, proper composition, and preferred technique were applied in order to establish consistent criteria for the hundreds of national and international salons and the thousands of club competitions and exhibitions. Choosing fifty acceptances from thousands of entries demanded quickly applicable and standardized methods of evaluation, methods that could be explained clearly to hundreds of thousands of amateurs investing their time and money to enter the competitions.

This codification of salon criteria paralleled industry efforts to encourage a stable and predictable use of photo products, film stocks, and paraphernalia. Not surprisingly, it was during the period of great amateur expansion between 1925 and 1940 that industry support (financial, material, and logistic) for amateur clubs and organizations became a major factor. Growing numbers of amateurs represented an expanding market for photo products, and camera club organizations provided ready-made marketing networks. Most important, the photo education and training promoted by club and salon participation augmented industry efforts to shape the nature of photographic practice. Early in the century the photo industry, led by Eastman Kodak Company, began to adopt and promote pictorialist aesthetics as a preferred style of photographic production.[18] By the 1930s and 1940s a formulaic, commercial form of pictorial photography had become an established standard in industry advertising and instructional literature and had come to dominate the amateur work exhibited in journals and salons.

Since World War II the amateur world has continued to receive substantial support from the photo industry, especially Eastman Kodak. As industry influence has increased, the number of amateurs dedicated to traditional print making and craft processes has dwindled. But the dedication to industry-defined genres of pictorial work persists. The growing popularity of color slide photography since the 1950s has produced a division in most camera clubs between slide makers and printmakers. Color slide makers—now the overwhelming majority—have abandoned the craftsmanship of darkroom work to more quickly and easily reproduce pictures like those in industry how-to manuals, aping commercial travel and nature photography, and striving for the look of Kodak's *How to Make Good Pictures, The Joy of Photography, More Joy of Photography*, or *The New Joy of Photography*. Small cliques of printmakers have, in most cases, survived as minority factions in the clubs. To some degree, these printmakers preserve a tradition of more serious pictorialist art. During my study of Philadelphia camera clubs I observed printmakers who were exhibiting their work at art centers and galleries and who were even attending lectures and symposia on photographic art at local colleges and universities. But many printmakers were attracted as much as slide makers to the more formulaic and commercial recipes for "good pictures" (Schwartz and Griffin, 1987).

Ironically, it was in the late 1970s, just as the divorce between the established camera club world and the official art world seemed final, that more traditional pictorial art photography received renewed attention from amateurs. A group dissatisfied with the dominant emphases of the Photographic Society of America and the camera club world formed the New Pictorialist Society, a group devoted to pictorialism and dedicated to the revival of vintage printing processes. This small organization circulates portfolios of its members' pictorial work and strives to refocus attention on the making of fine prints, employing the traditional artistic techniques of paper negatives, gum bichromate, and the application of handwork in the printing process. Although it is still unclear whether the new pictorialists will have any long-term impact, it seems evident that their attempt to renew a more traditional and rigorous standard for photographic art is a response to the gap left between the diverging worlds of amateur and fine-art photography.

Within the Photographic Society of America increased attention has also been paid to the PSA historical archives. Traveling exhibits of the work of Fassbender, Mortenson, and other renowned salon exhibitors of the past have been organized and circulated among clubs around the country. During the late 1970s and the 1980s retrospectives of pictorialist photography were organized at museums in Philadelphia, Los Angeles, San Francisco, Buffalo, and Minneapolis,[19] and a cluster of books, articles, and catalogs reexamining various aspects of amateur activity and pictorial photography appeared (Irmas, 1979; Bunnell, 1980; Coleman, 1982; Peterson, 1983 and 1984; Homer, 1984; Ruby, 1985; Seiberling, 1986). George Tice even wrote a book about one of his old camera club friends, *Artie Van Blarcum* (1977), in which Tice portrays the camera club world as routinized and

overly predictable but holds Artie up as one of the world's great nonconvention-
alists, a character whose personality is intriguing and whose amateur pictorial
work is worthy of consideration.

## CONCLUSION: CORPORATE PROMOTION
## AND MIDDLEBROW ART

The world of amateur photography is of particular historical and sociological interest given Howard Becker's (1982) conception of art worlds, Barbara Rosenblum's (1978) work on the social organization of photographic styles, and various
studies of middlebrow art and cultural production. In a series of essays and studies, Becker has demonstrated the value of understanding a broad range of artistic
and cultural production in terms of the social networks of people "whose cooperative activity, organized via their joint knowledge of conventional means of doing things, produces the kind of art works that art world is noted for" (1982: x). In
this vein Rosenblum (1978) explored and mapped the social networks, work
roles, and organizational routines and boundaries that structure the production
of different kinds of photography. Through meticulous long-term observation
and interviewing, she compared the work of newspaper, advertising, and fine-art
photographers and identified the relatively separate social worlds that shaped
photographic norms and practices in each case. Essentially, Rosenblum explained differing photographic styles as an inherent result of the different social
processes that constitute each world of cultural production.

Understanding "style as social process" in this way is indispensable to the recognition and description of amateur pictorialism as a cultural phenomenon. I
am convinced that the stable consistency of pictorialist aesthetics is a direct result
of the continuity of amateur-professional social networks and organizations. But
the case of amateur photography cannot be explained only as a stable and self-
perpetuating social world of specific expectations and work routines that distinguish it from other worlds of photo production (à la Rosenblum). Nor can it be
explained solely as an arena in which class status and social aspirations are played
out through aesthetic ambitions and taste cultures as Bourdieu, Castel, and
Schnapper suggested. The persistent tradition of simultaneously quasi-artistic
and quasi-commercial amateur photo production suggests the need for a more
historical analysis of social and economic interconnections and relationships.

Such a historical analysis reveals an amateur world that has long been a force
on the margins of art. As a social world of cultural production interdependent
with the photo industry, it has influenced and been influenced by both commercial photography and art photography. More than anything, it has provided social
and institutional support for certain notions about photographic aesthetics, notions rooted in the tradition of pictorialism. Once the birthplace of art photography, the amateur world has subsequently been rejected by an artistic elite intent
on separating itself from its less modern and less sophisticated forebears. Yet the

amateur networks have never died, and the pictorialist tenets they have espoused became an even more powerful (although usually unexamined) part of popular conceptions of "good" photography as amateur organizations collaborated in the establishment of industry-promoted pictorial standards.

Because over the years serious amateurs have constituted a major market for cameras, darkroom equipment, photographic film, supplies, and paraphernalia (in fact, a substantially larger market than professional photographers), the photo industry has had a long-standing interest in the amateur world. The interests and buying habits of serious amateurs generally paralleled and buttressed those of professional photographers, creating a combined professional-amateur market that expanded economies of scale for many products and lent stability and predictability to industry marketing and manufacturing.[20] Whereas growing masses of snapshot photographers soon constituted the largest consumer group for inexpensive cameras, film stock, and photofinishing, serious amateurs continued to provide the industry with models of photographic competence and success while also providing substantial markets for an entire range of advanced and specialized photo products unknown to the home-mode snapshooter.

Not only has the photo industry encouraged and financially supported amateur organizations as part of an ongoing attempt to amplify professional markets but for years photo companies such as Eastman Kodak have helped to direct amateur activities through educational and marketing programs, the sponsorship of contests and the awarding of prizes, and administrative and managerial interlocking with amateur organizations such as PSA. The close interconnections among PSA, Eastman Kodak, the Society of Photographic Scientists and Engineers, and the American National Standards Institute have helped to encourage a widely shared set of standards and common tastes for photographic work. Over time, the aesthetic codes of amateur pictorialism became indistinguishable from industry prescriptions for "good" photography—a middlebrow aesthetic that clearly set serious amateur photography apart from the mass of unskilled snapshooters yet remained a comprehensible and attainable goal for aspiring hobbyists and trade photographers.

Historically, the increasing influence of corporate marketing on photography paralleled the rise of commercial radio broadcasting, the establishment of the Hollywood movie industry, the transformation of baseball into a multimillion-dollar entertainment, and the rise of other corporate-sponsored cultural activities such as the Book-of-the-Month Club (founded in 1926, only a few years before the Photographic Society of America). As Joan Rubin (1992) discussed, the 1920s, 1930s, and 1940s (when the great explosion in camera club activity occurred) represented a period of cultural commercialization that produced many forms of middlebrow culture, including book clubs, women's study clubs, radio theater and literary programming, and community lecture circuits. Gladys Lang and Kurt Lang (1990), in their study of etching and artistic reputation, noted that it was during this waxing of middlebrow culture in the 1920s that an "etching

mania" occurred, with thousands of *amateurs d'estampes* compiling print collections with great fervor. Their account of the shift in etching from client-oriented
production, to please a patron, to a market-oriented production that traded on
artist reputations within networks of printmakers and print collectors closely re-
sembles the social and organizational context of clubs and salons that characterized pictorial photography. Both of these "minor" arts developed as attempts to
translate the aesthetics of painting into derivative and reproducible printing processes. And for support, both relied upon amateur-professional associations that
existed outside the established institutions of fine art. But etching never enjoyed
the support and sponsorship of a corporate giant such as Eastman Kodak and
thus remained more esoteric and more vulnerable to social and economic
change. Salon photography continued to enjoy a golden era after the financial
crash of 1929, but the market for etchings effectively collapsed.

The history of amateur pictorialism provides a prime example of the development of a mid-culture, a culture "betwixt and between," in the words of Virginia
Woolf, a culture Woolf or Dwight Macdonald would have condemned as corrupted by commercial interests. Indeed, "pictorial photography," defined by Fassbender as "nothing more or less than the making of beautiful pictures" (1952: 36),
provided the industry with a broadly appealing, completely noncontroversial approach to skillful picture making that proved salable to professionals, serious
amateurs, and the general public alike. And the extensive networks of organized
amateurs already committed to pictorialist standards offered the industry stable,
ready-made marketing and instructional outlets. The pictorialist aesthetic became the most widely shared standard of "good" photography for the millions of
photographers who consciously strive to produce competently crafted pictures.
For more than a century, as the art world of photography established its special
status by distancing itself from amateur activities, the social world of amateur
photography held the center of mainstream photographic practice.

## NOTES

1. Pictorial photography, a term coined in the amateur clubs of the nineteenth century, referred to the use of photography for the production of "pictorial art" and suggested that photographers, like painters, were in the business of making artistic *pictures*,
not mechanical records. Sieberling (1986) referred to this as "the aesthetic of the picturesque." See also Emerson, 1886: 138–139, and Stieglitz, 1899: 528–537.

2. The first Matisse exhibition in the United States was held at the Little Galleries in
1908 and the first Picasso exhibit in 1911; the work of Braque, Freuh, Picabia, Severini,
Brancusi, and Nadelman, among others, was first introduced to the United States at the
gallery. See Doty, 1978.

3. See, for example, the annual Wolfman Reports, routinely cited photo industry marketing surveys, in which distinctions among different types of nonprofessional photographers are absent.

4. Bourdieu, 1990, is a recent translation of *Un Art Moyen: Essai sur les Usages Sociaux*

*de la Photographie*, first published in France in 1965. Castel and Schnapper, students of Bourdieu, wrote chapter 3 on camera clubs.

5. A complete content analysis of subject matter and formal style in the photographs chosen for the salons and competitions of the *American Annual of Photography*, 1931–1951; *American Photography*, 1930–1950, the *Camera* annual camera club shows for 1946 and 1947; and the *Camera* print of the year contests, 1949–1952, are contained in chapter 11 of Griffin, 1987.

6. The prominent photo journals and magazines published between World War I and the 1950s included *Photo-era*, the *Camera*, *American Photography* (along with the *American Annual of Photography*), and *Camera Craft*. (In addition, there were industry publications such as *Kodakery*.) *Photo-era* merged with *American Photography* in 1932, and *Camera Craft* merged with *American Photography* in 1942. The *Camera* and *American Photography* continued until 1953, when they both ceased publication. *American Photography* and the *American Annual of Photography* were published by a circle of amateurs from the Boston–New England area under the leadership of Frank Fraprie. The *Camera* represented a similar circle of writers and salonists centered in Philadelphia. *Camera Craft*, published in San Francisco, was the major West Coast forum. Although each published articles and photographs for a national and even international audience, each reflected its different center of leadership.

7. Doris Ulmann, a New York studio portrait photographer who was trained at the Clarence White School, completed two documentary projects in the South and in Appalachia in the early 1930s. Jeffrey (1981) has described her work as "a form of pastoral documentary" and said she "pictured an idyll of the sort Emerson had originally set his heart on" (p. 162). N. Rosenblum (1984) wrote that her photographs were "in a style that invokes pictorialist ideas as much as social documentation" (p. 365). Dorothea Lange, like Ulmann and Weston, began as a commercial studio portraitist, and the pictorialist quality of much of her documentary work (portraits of migrant workers in California, sharecroppers and tenant farmers in the South) has been noted. (See especially Pepe Karmel's review of the *Aperture* monograph, 1983: 23–25, in which she said of Lange's work, "It is tempting to say that her best pictures are not really 'documents' of social problems at all but highly stylized portraits of strained beauty.")

8. Bourke-White's portraits for *Fortune* and *Life* and for books such as *You Have Seen Their Faces* with Erskine Caldwell (1937) tend to be posed, lighted, and stylized in a way that likely would have pleased her teacher, Clarence White. They would certainly look at home among the salon portraits exhibited at that time in the pages of *American Photography* or the *Camera*. (See her portraits of Patton, Stalin, Goehring, a French soldier, an Indian villager, and the like.)

9. Both Mudd and Ritasse were founding members of the Miniature Camera Club of Philadelphia, and Mudd later served as director of the Photographic Society of America. In addition to being top ranked internationally for their amateur salon work, they were both well-known for their industrial photography. Mudd, a vice president for employment and labor relations at Midvale Steel Company, did much of his industrial photography in Midvale's steel mills. Both photographers are described by Naomi Rosenblum as distinguished interpreters of the modern industrial landscape, without mention of their amateur backgrounds or camera club connections. (See her section "Photography and Industrialism," 1984: 422–430.)

10. Paul Strand is often cited as a noteworthy example of a pictorialist who moved

from the soft-focus pictorialist style to a more hard-edged, documentary rendering of machines, industrialism, and urban life (Stange, 1989).

11. See, for instance, Wilson, 1930; and Anderson, 1933, 1941. By the early 1930s photos of steamships, railroad locomotives, and automobile grills had begun to appear on the covers of amateur photo journals such as the *Camera* and *American Photography*.

12. Although Weston was clearly interested in the abstract qualities of nature, he resisted the modernist pull of abstract art. In his *Daybooks* he wrote, "The camera should be used for a recording of *life*, for rendering the very substance and quintessence of the *thing itself*, whether it be polished steel or palpitating flesh. . . . I shall let no chance pass to record interesting abstraction, but I feel definite in my belief that the approach to photography is through realism." *The Daybooks of Edward Weston: Vol. 1, Mexico*, edited by Nancy Newhall, 1973: 55.

13. This same point is suggested in an article written by Nancy Newhall for *Camera Craft* in November 1941 entitled "What Is Pictorialism?"

14. See, for example, the four page Kodak ad featuring *Ansel Adams' America . . . in Kodak Color* beginning on p. 169 of the March 1948 issue of *American Photography*, the leading postwar amateur photo journal.

15. A total of 462 questionnaires were mailed to a random sample of PSA members, and 211 were returned.

16. For a discussion of the importance of socially shared conventions for artistic communication and appreciation, see Gross, 1973. See also Baxandall, 1972.

17. On the forging of institutional ties between photography and art, see especially Christopherson, 1974; Becker, 1975 and 1982.

18. By 1916 Eastman Kodak Company had begun to publish a booklet entitled *How to Make Good Pictures*, which has continued to be revised and republished to the present day.

19. A 1984 show at the Minneapolis Institute of Arts exhibited work from the Minneapolis Salon of Photography, 1932–1946; a 1991 show exhibited the work of famed Czech-American salonist D. J. Ruzicka; and a retrospective, "The Pictorial Artistry of Adolf Fassbender," opened at the institute in July 1994.

20. More specialized companies such as E. Leitz and Carl Zeiss, with their high-priced 35mm cameras and lenses, or Weston Electrical Instrument Corp., which manufactured precision light meters, were particularly dependent upon expanding professional markets into the amateur sphere. In Rochester (Eastman Kodak) and Binghamton, New York (Ansco), many photographic researchers and marketing managers were avid camera club members themselves (Griffin, 1987: 513–621).

## REFERENCES

Anderson, Paul L. (1933). "Modernistic Reactionaries." *American Photography*, 27, no. 1 (January), pp. 34–37.
———. (1941). "Modern Trends in Pictorial Photography." *American Annual of Photography* 55, p. 28.
Baxandall, Michael (1972). *Painting and Experience in Fifteenth Century Italy*. New York: Oxford University Press.
Becker, Howard S. (1975). "Art Photography in America." *Journal of Communication* 25, no. 1 (Winter), pp. 74–84.

————. (1982). *Art Worlds.* Berkeley: University of California Press.

Bourdieu, Pierre (1965). *Un Art Moyen: Essai sur les Usages Sociaux de la Photographie.* Paris: Les Editions de Minuit.

————. (1990). *Photography: A Middle-Brow Art.* Stanford, Calif.: Stanford University Press.

Bourke-White, Margaret, and Erskine Caldwell (1937). *You Have Seen Their Faces.* New York: Modern Age Books. Reprint edition, New York: Dover, 1975.

Bunnell, Peter, ed. (1980). *A Photographic Vision: Pictorial Photography, 1889–1923.* Salt Lake City: Peregrine Smith.

Christopherson, Richard (1974). "Making Art with Machines: Photography's Institutional Inadequacies." *Urban Life and Culture* 3, no. 1, pp. 3–34.

Coleman, A. D. (1982). "Disappearing Act: The Photographs of William Mortensen." *Camera Arts* 2, no. 1 (January–February), pp. 30–38, 108–109.

Doty, Robert (1978). *Photo-Secession: Stieglitz and the Fine-Art Movement in Photography.* New York: Dover Publications.

Eastman Kodak Company (1920). *How to Make Good Pictures.* Rochester, N.Y.

————. (1938). *How to Make Good Pictures.* Rochester, N.Y.

————. (1982). *How to Take Good Pictures.* New York: Ballantine Books.

Emerson, Peter Henry (1886). "Photography, A Pictorial Art." *Amateur Photographer* 3, pp. 138–139.

Fassbender, Adolf (1937). *Pictorial Artistry: The Dramatization of the Beautiful in Photography.* New York: B. Westerman Company.

————. (1952). "Pictorialism Today." *American Photography* 46, no. 2, pp. 35–41, 54.

Frank, Robert (1959). *The Americans.* Introduction by Jack Kerouac. New York: Grove Press. Revised edition, Millerton, N.Y.: Aperture, 1978.

Griffin, Michael S. (1987). "Amateur Photography and Pictorial Aesthetics: Influences of Organization and Industry on Cultural Production." Unpublished Ph.D. dissertation, University of Pennsylvania.

Gross, Larry (1973). "Art as the Communication of Competence." *Social Science Information* 12, no. 5, pp. 115–141.

Harker, Margaret (1979). *The Linked Ring: The Secession Movement in Photography in Britain, 1892–1910.* London: Heineman.

Hartmann, Sadakichi (1904). "A Plea for Straight Photography." *American Amateur Photographer* 16, no. 3 (March), pp. 101–109. Reprinted in Peter C. Bunnell, ed., *A Photographic Vision: Pictorial Photography, 1889–1923,* pp. 148–150, 167. Salt Lake City: Peregrine Smith, 1980.

Hinton, A. Horsley (1897). "Methods of Control, and Their Influence on the Development of Artistic Photography." *Photographic Times* 29, no. 9 (September), pp. 439–443. Reprinted in Peter C. Bunnell, ed., *A Photographic Vision: Pictorial Photography, 1889–1923,* pp. 54, 71–73. Salt Lake City: Peregrine Smith, 1980.

————. (1899). "Individuality—Some Suggestions for the Pictorial Worker." *Photographic Times* 31, no. 1 (January), pp. 12–19. Reprinted in Peter C. Bunnell, ed., *A Photographic Vision: Pictorial Photography, 1889–1923,* pp. 74–78. Salt Lake City: Peregrine Smith, 1980.

Homer, William (1984). *Pictorial Photography in Philadelphia: The Pennsylvania Academy's Salons, 1898–1901.* Philadelphia: Pennsylvania Academy of the Fine Arts.

Irmas, Deborah (1979). *The Photographic Magic of William Mortensen*. Los Angeles: Los Angeles Center for Photographic Studies.

Jeffrey, Ian (1981). *Photography: A Concise History*. New York: Oxford University Press.

Johnston, J. Dudley (1946). "Pictorialism Then and Now." *Amateur Photographer* (May 8), pp. 309–314.

Karmel, Pepe (1983). Book review of *Dorothea Lange: Photographs of a Lifetime*, with an essay by Robert Coles and an afterword by Therese Heyman, in *Art in America* (November), pp. 23–25.

Lang, Gladys Engel, and Kurt Lang (1990). *Etched in Memory: The Building and Survival of Artistic Reputation*. Chapel Hill: University of North Carolina Press.

Mortensen, William (1936). *Monsters and Madonnas*. San Francisco: Camera Craft.

Newhall, Beaumont (1982). *The History of Photography*. New York: Museum of Modern Art.

Newhall, Nancy (1941). "What Is Pictorialism?" *Camera Craft* 48 (November), pp. 653–663.

Newhall, Nancy, ed. (1973). *The Daybooks of Edward Weston: Vol. 1, Mexico*. Millerton, N.Y.: Aperture.

Norman, Dorothy (1973). *Alfred Stieglitz: An American Seer*. New York: Random House.

Peterson, Christian A. (1983). *Pictorialism in America: The Minneapolis Salon of Photography, 1932–46*. Minneapolis: Minneapolis Institute of Arts.

———. (1984). *The Creative Camera Art of Max Thorek*. Chicago: Dr. Max Thorek Memorial Foundation.

Rosenblum, Barbara (1978). *Photographers at Work: A Sociology of Photographic Styles*. New York: Holmes and Meier.

Rosenblum, Naomi (1984). *The World History of Photography*. New York: Abbeville Press.

Rubin, Joan Shelley (1992). *The Making of Middlebrow Culture*. Chapel Hill: University of North Carolina Press.

Ruby, Jay (1985). "Francis L. Cooper, Spruce Hill Photographer." *Studies in Visual Communication* 11, no. 4, pp. 12–29.

Schwartz, Dona B. (1986). "Camera Clubs and Fine Art Photography: The Social Construction of an Elite Code." *Urban Life* 15, no. 2, pp. 165–195.

Schwartz, Dona B., and Michael Griffin (1987). "Amateur Photography: The Organizational Maintenance of an Aesthetic Code." In Thomas R. Lindlof, ed., *Natural Audiences: Qualitative Research of Media Uses and Effects*. Norwood, N.J.: Ablex Publishing.

Seiberling, Grace (1986). *Amateurs, Photography, and the Mid-Victorian Imagination*. Chicago: University of Chicago Press.

Stange, Maren (1989). *Symbols of Ideal Life: Social Documentary Photography in America, 1890–1950*. New York: Cambridge University Press.

Stebbins, Robert A. (1979). *Amateurs: On the Margin Between Work and Leisure*. Beverly Hills, Calif.: Sage Publications.

Steichen, Edward (1955). *The Family of Man*. New York: Museum of Modern Art.

Stieglitz, Alfred (1892). "A Plea for Art Photography in America." *Photographic Mosaics* 28, pp. 135–137. Reprinted in Peter C. Bunnell, ed., *A Photographic Vision: Pictorial Photography, 1889–1923*, pp. 24–25. Salt Lake City: Peregrine Smith, 1980.

———. (1899). "Pictorial Photography." *Scribner's Magazine* 26, no. 5, pp. 528–537. Reprinted in Peter C. Bunnell, ed., *A Photographic Vision: Pictorial Photography, 1889–1923*, pp. 124–127. Salt Lake City: Peregrine Smith, 1980.

Szarkowski, John (1978). *Mirrors and Windows: American Photography Since 1960*. New York: Museum of Modern Art.

Thorek, Max (1937). *Creative Camera Art.* Canton, Ohio: Fomo Publishing.

———. (1947). *Camera Art as a Means of Self-Expression.* Philadelphia: J. B. Lippincott.

Tice, George A. (1977). *Artie Van Blarcum: An Extended Portrait.* Danbury, N.H.: Addison House.

Wilson, Edward D. (1930). "Beauty in Ugliness." *Photo-Era* (June), p. 303.

# ❦ 10 ❧

# Trading Places in the Art World: The Reputations of Dorothea Lange and Walker Evans

CATHERINE L. PRESTON

Reputations fluctuate with fashions. Specifically, reputations persist insofar as people accept what is said about the character and abilities of others, including those with whom they are not personally acquainted. Whether or not the attributions and claims can be factually substantiated matters little. They still function as objective social facts with discernible consequences.

(Lang and Lang, 1990: 5–6)

IN 1973 ROY STRYKER, head of the Depression-era Farm Security Administration (FSA)–Office of War Information (OWI) photography section,[1] recalled Ansel Adams's words in 1938 regarding the FSA photographers: "What you've got are not photographers. They're a bunch of sociologists with cameras" (Stryker and Wood, 1973: 8). Adams's statement has struck an increasingly ironic note since the 1960s, as museum curators, directors, critics, and photographers have constructed and reconstructed an elastic boundary between "high-art" photography and more popular "middlebrow" (sociological, journalistic) photographic practice. The decision over where that boundary falls affects the reputations of photographers on both sides of the line. It makes a difference in everything from prices commanded at auction to the strength of one's lasting fame.

In this chapter I examine what happened to the reputations of two FSA-OWI photographers during the 1960s and 1970s when the evaluative categories by which photographers had been previously judged as art or "social documentary" or "journalistic" were collapsing. In place of such categories, strategies for evaluating photographs were erected that were intended to bring photographic interpretation more in line with an already established modernist art aesthetic. Through an examination of post-1960 critical and biographical writings about Walker Evans and Dorothea Lange, I investigate the process by which they more or less traded places in the eyes of the art world. Whereas Evans and Lange had both been recognized as "photographic artists" in the 1940s and 1950s, Edward Steichen, director of photography at MoMA (1948–1962), foregrounded Lange's committed social documentary in his exhibits and writings. Then, in the 1960s, John Szarkowski replaced Steichen as director and set about the reassessment of the photographic discourse. Evans's cool detachment and formalistic concerns were elevated to a central position in the new discourse, and Lange's work was judged as approximating photojournalism rather than art photography. She was therefore marginalized in references to the modernist concerns of the prevailing art establishment.[2]

Christopher Phillips has mapped out the process by which photography became tied to a modernist aesthetic discourse within the confines of the art museum during this period. Specifically, this occurred within MoMA largely through the efforts of John Szarkowski, director of the Department of Photography from 1962 to 1991 (Phillips, 1982). Phillips makes the point that whatever its value as a critical procedure for valorizing the work of one privileged sector of contemporary photographic practice (i.e., the documentary work of Gary Winogrand, Diane Arbus, Lee Friedlander, and Robert Frank), the application of a modernist aesthetic to photography also provides "a systematic re-reading along the same lines of photographs of the past" (1982: 39). It is this rereading and the kinds of distinctions that accompanied it that I argue explain the change in Evans's and Lange's reputations. I attempt to clarify some of the issues involved in this repositioning by focusing on the discursive strategies developed by Szarkowski and adopted by critics and scholars. The new aesthetic discourse effected the inclusion within the larger museum culture of the previously questionable medium of photography, but the application of a distinctly modernist aesthetic simultaneously created distinctions among photographs, and hence photographers, that hitherto had been linked under the general rubric *documentary*.

The inclusion of photography within the larger art museum culture created a situation in which photographers had to be reconstructed as *artists*. Even though Lange and Evans were considered photographic artists in the 1940s and 1950s, because of the assumption that the camera created the photograph, the label *artist* was nearly synonymous with craftsperson. As such, the photographed subject matter was more important than the photographer. In the 1960s and 1970s, as some photographers were accepted as artists on a par with painters and sculptors, the photographed subject matter became a reference for understanding the photographer as *creator* of the subject matter. The positioning of the "artist as the subject of the art work" (Pollock, 1980: 59) had particular repercussions for those photographs produced as social documentary prior to the late 1960s. Similar to the status of artifacts that end up in anthropological or history museums, when the title *art* was applied to photographs not intended as artworks, they were severed from their original context: "The image was once a way of acting as though the virgin were *there*, available for petition, conversation, repentance. In the museum the picture becomes a way of thinking as though Piero della Fransesca were *there*, as though the Renaissance were *there*, because from the picture we read out world view, style, moment—the 'problem' as art historians would say" (Fisher, 1975: 595; emphasis in original).

Szarkowski argued that attention to formal qualities was primary in the evaluation of all photographs. In other words, documentary photographs such as the FSA, which had been made according to a logic in which context was an important part of understanding the content, were now evaluated according to a strategy that sought to divorce subject from context in order to create a situation in which the photographs could be made to refer back only to the photographer. The social, political, economic, and even aesthetic meanings intended by the photographer at the time or read by the contemporary community for which they were made came to be replaced in the modernist agenda by "mysteries of creative genius and eternal value, mysteries whose meaning can only be interpreted to the art's public by the art dealers and the connoisseurs" (Phillips, 1982: 16).

## ART DEALERS AND CONNOISSEURS

Artistic reputation can be conceptualized as being built on two foundations, referred to as *recognition* and *renown* (Lang and Lang, 1990: 6). Recognition refers to how insiders (curators and other photographers) view the artist and has as one of its elements institutional legitimation. Renown refers to evaluations and other actions through which the artist is "served up" to the public. It refers to the artist's standing in the larger community made up of the public, specifically to the standing as created by critics and scholars who can be said to serve as guides for the general public concerning the artist's work. Renown does not necessarily follow from recognition, and the two do not necessarily proceed in lockstep once a reputation has been established.

Lange's and Evans's reputations were not redefined overnight. Each director of the photography department at MoMA left his mark on photographic discourse and in a real sense taught the growing legions of scholars and critics what to expect and how to think, interpret, and write about photographs. In this sense the directors have had a determining effect on the reputations of Lange and Evans. The ability to construct evaluative discourses that then support (or do not support) artistic reputations is a real power, one that is not exercised in a vacuum. It is based on the directors' subjective preferences, the needs of the institution, and the dominant political and economic tendencies in the larger society. By tracing two reputations that spanned the tenure of three directors at MoMA, I address the issue of how reputations founded according to a particular historical set of circumstances were redefined thirty years later when curators, critics, and scholars confirmed "the workaday photographer as creative artist" (Phillips, 1982: 28).

How photographs are received depends upon what function people (including critics) expect photographs to fulfill. Formation of expectations lies in the conjunction of historical, social, cultural, and political phenomena. The expectations of critics and scholars, largely because of their role as mediator between public and museum, are a function of the interpretive stance framed by the institution to which the critic responds, as well as of residual and emergent expectations operative in the larger environment.

## THE FORMATION OF EXPECTATIONS

Prior to Szarkowski's directorship at MoMA, the critical interpretation of photography tended to fluctuate between two poles—one interpreting the image as a mirror, or transparent window, on reality; the other approaching a photograph as a mediated expression of the scene (Sekula, 1975). Social documentary photography tended to occupy that part of the continuum interpreted as transparent images of reality, whereas art photography (that is, pictorialism) was read as mediated expression.

Beaumont Newhall, during his tenure as the founding director of the Department of Photography at MoMA (1935–1942), laid the groundwork for the study of photography as a scholarly activity. Within this agenda he grappled with defining *documentary* in relation to the other styles of extant photographic practice. Based on the example of the FSA-OWI, he argued that not only are documentary photographs direct records of things but that they are also records of the photographer's emotion in viewing the thing (Newhall, 1938: 3).

During the 1930s, when social realism was the dominant aesthetic, Newhall noted that documentary photographers interpret the world and also its social significance. He wrote, "It is undeniable that the documentary method, as opposed to the abstract desire to produce Fine Art, has resulted in significant photographic art" (Newhall, 1938: 4). Regardless of his preference for the documentary over pictorialism, he still had to negotiate the thorny problem of the technological ground out of which photography was produced. He anticipated Szarkowski's efforts when he wrote, "The documentary photographer is not a mere technician. Nor is he an artist for art's sake. Technically the documentary photographer is a purist. . . . Since the value of a photo-document lies in the directness of its technique, any intervention of hand-work is bound to be injurious" (Newhall, 1938: 4–5). Newhall attempted to define the aesthetic value of social documentary while maintaining that documentary "photographic art" is primarily pictorial report.

From 1942 to 1947, when Newhall was in the U.S. Navy, the Department of Photography was run by his wife, Nancy Newhall, and Willard Morgan. In 1948, rather than invite Newhall back to his previous position, Board of Trustees Chair Nelson Rockefeller appointed Edward Steichen to the directorship. The postwar years of corporate growth created a focus on the photographic industry. Steichen was appointed largely because of his prominence in commercial photography before the war and his continuing ties to this rapidly growing industry. In fact, his connections were such that members of the photographic industry pledged $100,000 to pay his salary at MoMA. In addition, during the war he had mounted two important exhibits at MoMA, *Road to Victory* (1942) and *Power in the Pacific* (1945), both of which were obvious propaganda vehicles for the war effort. In his capacity as director he was not as interested in photography as an expressive art as he was in its potential as a medium for mass communication that could dramatically interpret the world for a national and an international audience (Steichen, 1948: 69). In Steichen's exhibits and writings at MoMA, social documentary photography, photojournalism, and commercial photography were foregrounded.

John Szarkowski's agenda for establishing a distinct aesthetic realm for photography depended primarily upon a return to the post-Renaissance classical system of representation. Encompassing the two simultaneous and contradictory readings of the picture surface, photographs could be read as *both* transparent window and mediated expression. He returned to Newhall's aesthetic concerns, but unlike Newhall, who had based his evaluation of photography as art solely on the representational side of the equation, Szarkowski took a more synergistic approach. He asserted that the adoption of the unmanipulated and "invisible" style of documentary linked the photographer's work to that aspect of the classical system of representation that, through the single-point perspective, masks the mediation of human agency and makes it appear that reality itself is speaking. And as Phillips has noted, within the confines of the museum the critic-connoisseur must be on hand to certify "the presence of the artist and to provide expert guidance to the formal strategies of concealment through which the artist-photographer 'inscribes himself at the center of the world and transforms himself into things by transforming things into his representations'" (1982: 38). This strategy provided for the assumption of the artist's authorial voice in which the photographer became the creator of the reality seen through the "transparent window" as a result of creating the representation.

## TIES THAT BIND: EVANS AT MOMA

Evans was a likely candidate to launch as the embodiment of the new photographic aesthetic. He was a "self-conscious" artist photographer (Phillips, 1982: 63; Rathbone, 1993), whose temperament, style of working, and attitude toward his work fit the modern artist stereotype of a well-connected, moody, independent Bohemian (Wittkower and Wittkower, 1963). In 1933 and 1938, Lincoln Kirstein, a friend of Evans and an active member of MoMA's junior advisory committee, had sponsored one-man shows for Evans, and his photographs from those shows were among the first to become part of MoMA's permanent collection (Phillips, 1982: 30; Lynes, 1973: 107, 158). In the 1930s and 1940s he had consistently distinguished his work from that of the "creative" photographers such as Weston and Adams, whose work was then considered fine-art photography. He had known and lived with other modernist artists and authors, including Ben Shahn, Charles Sheeler, James Agee, Paul Grotz, and Hart Crane (Katz, 1979: 121).

Evans had connections with the men who made decisions at MoMA. He came from a similar background in the upper classes and was educated at the same schools. And he maintained those connections, assuming in 1965 a professorship of photography on the faculty for graphic design at the Yale School of Art and Architecture. Thus, Evans's promotion as exemplary American photographer based on claims of the intrinsic value of his work needs to be seen as related to his physical and intellectual proximity to the sources of those judgments.

## LANGE AND STEICHEN AT MOMA

Based on institutional recognition Dorothea Lange's reputation was similar to that of Walker Evans until approximately 1966, the time of her retrospective at MoMA. Her photographs had begun to be exhibited in 1934 in a San Francisco gallery owned by Willard Van Dyke. She had moved in artistic circles before working for the FSA, and at least two of her photographs (*Migrant Mother* and *White Angel Breadline*) were obtained by Beaumont Newhall for MoMA and exhibited as "Recent Acquisitions" in 1940. Much like Evans's connections with the leaders at MoMA, Lange's personal contacts encouraged her recognition. For example, Ansel Adams, a friend of Lange's from the West Coast f/64 Group, had gone from California to MoMA to help Newhall preside over the inception of a new Department of Photography in 1940 (Phillips, 1982: 35).

Lange was in one of Steichen's *Diogenes* shows at MoMA in 1951 and helped him select and organize photographs for both the *Family of Man* exhibit in 1955 and *The Bitter Years* in 1962, which contained nine and eighty-two of her photographs, respectively. Her friendship with Steichen had begun in 1938 through his interest in the FSA photographs.

Following her involvement with the FSA, Lange worked mainly for *Life* magazine doing photo-essays. It must be acknowledged that Steichen likely found Lange a more kindred spirit than he did Evans during his tenure at MoMA. He had respect for her as a photographer, and he believed she was sympathetic to his ideas about an "emotional response to life and photography's place in it" (Meltzer, 1978: 294). They also may have gotten along because of Lange's reticence to identify herself as an artist. Like Lange, Steichen viewed art photography as one "tiny band on the photographic spectrum" (Phillips, 1982: 50). They also both worked for the development of a government-funded contemporary photography project much like the FSA, referred to as "Project One," for which they both lobbied during the 1950s and 1960s.

Thus, during the 1940s, 1950s, and early 1960s, Lange was well-known within the art world and also in the larger community through her work for *Life* and the continued circulation of her FSA photographs in books and magazines. Furthermore, her work, like Evans's, had been legitimated within the art world not only through exhibitions but also through inclusion in Newhall's *History of Photography* (1982). And in 1958 she was one of two women, along with Julia Margaret Cameron, included in Newhall's *Masters of Photography*, in which Evans was also included. Newhall wrote about the FSA-OWI, specifically Lange and Evans, saying "*they* had created a style which influenced a generation of photographers and has since passed into the bloodstream of photojournalism" (Newhall, 1958: 140; emphasis added).

## CREATING REPRESENTATIONS

Reviews, biographies, and monographs represent the discursive structures through which the critic or scholar accomplishes the production of the artistic subject. They represent the space within which "art and artist become reflexive, mystically bound into an unbreakable circuit which produces the artist as the subject of the art work and the art work as the means of contemplative access to that subject's 'transcendent' and creative subjectivity" (Pollock, 1980: 59).

The discursive moves required to transform photographers into "artists" varied. The proximity of Lange and Evans to the art world during the 1960s when photography was being swept into the museum was similar in many ways, and historically both had been evaluated according to a similar standard of documentary photography. Expectations for their work and its meaning were determined by the material and critical frame that had been constructed around the FSA-OWI photographs in the years since 1943. As illustrated in a review written by George Elliott in 1962, interpretations of Lange's and Evans's photographs, like much critical writing on documentary photography in the early 1960s, displayed the influence of both Newhall and Steichen (Elliott, 1962).

Steichen, in fact, was an early publicist of the FSA-OWI photographs as representations of an American character. He used his influence as editor of *U.S. Camera Annual* in 1939 to reproduce in a special section of the magazine some of the photographs that had been exhibited at the First International Exhibition of Photography at the Grand Palace in New York City. He convinced Newhall to mount a traveling exhibition of that same selection of photographs in 1940, sponsored by the Museum of Modern Art. Newhall had been sufficiently impressed with the aesthetic quality (as he defined it) of some of Lange's and Evans's work that he obtained some pieces—notably *Migrant Mother* and *Washstand and Kitchen in the Burrough's House*—for MoMA's permanent collection. Steichen's last exhibit as director at MoMA in 1962 was a major retrospective of the photographs entitled *The Bitter Years: Rural America as Seen by the Photographers of the Farm Security Administration*. The title of the exhibit gives insight into Steichen's belief that photographs are pictures of what was *there* to see.

In 1962, prior to Szarkowski's series of writings that transformed the status of documentary photography, George Elliott (1962) wrote in a review of Walker Evans that the "art of photography" can be divided in two categories: the "compositional," in which belonged Edward Weston, Ansel Adams, and Alfred Stieglitz, and the "referential," which was not strictly interpreted on formal grounds and within which Elliott classed Evans and Lange. The referential category implied primarily that some kind of interest in and concern for the subject could be inferred from the photograph and secondarily that it could be appreciated as an act of personal expression.

The event that prompted Elliott's review was the republication of Evans's *American Photographs*, issued to accompany the 1962 rehanging of the original 1938 exhibition at MoMA. This exhibit signaled of Szarkowski's break with Steichen's directive and a return to Newhall's aesthetic concerns. However, it is clear that critics' expectations of what documentary photographs were and how they functioned were not yet so aesthetically bound, although Elliott implicitly acknowledged the arbitrariness of attribution in photographs. In describing a photograph Elliott wrote,

> The photograph is as little about social injustice as is Tom Sawyer, but it would be called documentary partly because it is *in a book of pictures of such intent* but mostly because we are given, both in the title and in the picture itself, the sort of circumstantial details about the girl which comment on her sociologically, or, *more accurately*, which could be thought of as commenting on her sociologically. Moreover, in this picture Evans has been successful, as he nearly always is, in the special *craft* of referential photography, a *craft* never more important than in documentary work. (1962: 541; emphasis added)

Based on the "teaching" of Newhall, the specificity of the subject was diminished through attention to the photograph's aesthetic expression, allowing for the effusion of nostalgia. And simultaneously, in a debt to Steichen's agenda, the instrumentality of the photographs was assumed, as evidenced in Elliott's expectation that Evans intended to "comment sociologically" on his subjects.

Elliott spends considerable space comparing Lange and Evans as the "two chief documentary photographers of the poor." He sees them as equally deserving of merit although differently involved with the subject: "Despite the difference between Evans and Lange his tone is not far from hers. He is disengaged where she is unmistakably involved with her subjects. . . . Nevertheless both communicate a sort of nostalgia which one must respect, a sense of valuable things scorned, broken, corrupted, cheapened, thrown away, badly replaced, gone" (Elliott, 1962: 543). This difference of involvement with the subject, which was significantly downplayed in 1962, soon became the foundation on which Evans's and Lange's reputations were distinguished.

## MARKING DISTINCTIONS

Formulated over the next few years, Szarkowski's theory of what makes a photograph art provided critics with a framework within which to gauge photographers as artists. The photograph was appreciated for its transparent relation to reality, but the artist-photographer was now endowed with the ability and the responsibility to see not simply the reality before him (or, rarely, her) but also the still invisible picture and to make his choices in terms of the latter (Szarkowski, 1966). It was no longer light and chemicals manipulated by the photographer that captured the real-life scene before the camera: It was the photographer who created it out of his true artistic vision. A corollary to this new positioning of photographers vis-à-vis reality was a redefinition of the correct position for the photographer to take vis-à-vis the subject.

Prior to 1965, and growing out of the documentary tradition of the 1930s and Steichen's humanistic directions at MoMA, the documentary photographer was the concerned photographer.[3] It was generally expected that those whose photographs exemplified the documentary style were involved with the subject, that there was a subtext, a statement being made about the subject, that could be and was intended to be read from the photograph.

Szarkowski's photographic aesthetic depended in part upon defining photography in terms of what it could do that the other arts could not. Thus it was necessary to appreciate photographs' apparently transparent view of reality. It is not surprising that the documentary and photojournalistic styles came to be favored within the new scheme, which equated notions of the camera's objectivity with dispassionate neutrality. But further distinctions were made between commercial or newspaper photographers and true documentary art photographers—distinctions that involved under what conditions and at whose bidding the images came to be made. In the article that was to frame the "logical" distinction to be made between Evans and the rest of the FSA photographers, Szarkowski wrote, "The basic effect of modern mass media on photography has been to erode the creative independence and the accountability of the photographer who has worked for them" (1967: 30). Szarkowski argued that as long as the photographer was making his own decisions about what and how to shoot, he was responsible for the meaning, and "he could look first and shoot afterward, showing that which he had already consciously edited" (1967: 30). Furthermore, Szarkowski argued that photographs ought to be looked at "without wondering how the picture might be made more 'effective' by tighter cropping and the addition of a good caption" (1967: 35). In other words, a "good" photograph should not be bound by words or context other than the immediate image within the frame. In this scheme the concern or compassion one has for one's subjects is completely beside the point, as is the political, social, or economic context in which the photograph was made.

This feeling ran contrary to what had been the working and exhibiting practices of the FSA-OWI. Stryker's shooting scripts had directed photographers as to what to shoot, and selections of captions and cropping had been primary tasks in the exhibitions of FSA-OWI photographs in the late 1930s and early 1940s. If any of the FSA-OWI photographs were to be incorporated into the new photographic order, something would have to change.

In 1962, before Szarkowski had disseminated his theory, the expectation that social documentary photography intended to comment socially and politically on the depicted subject matter was unavoidable, especially with regard to the FSA-OWI photographs. They had been framed within such an instrumental discourse from the late 1930s through 1962, as could be seen in *The Bitter Years.* Elliott wrote his review of Evans's one-man show, which ran concurrently at MoMA, in December of that year. In reference to Evans's and Lange's reputations, it is important to note the timing of both Steichen's and Szarkowski's commemorative exhibits.

Since 1960 Steichen had wanted to do a major retrospective of the FSA-OWI. He had always believed the photographs were important American documents, and the general popular awareness of poverty in the United States (beginning with *Harvest of Shame*, Edward R. Murrow's 1960 television documentary about the contemporary poverty of migrant workers) provided an opportunity to exhibit the FSA-OWI photos as relevant images for the U.S. conscience. Within *The Bitter Years* exhibit Lange's photographs made up nearly half of those displayed (82 of 204), reflecting Steichen's affinity with Lange as a photographer and friend and his desire to forward her reputation. Only 16 of Evans's photos were included. No letters exist that shed light on these selection decisions, but archival records of the progression of selection lists reveal that no more than 25 of Evans's photographs were originally considered. Whether this was a reaction to Szarkowski's impending exhibit is unknown (Edward Steichen Archives, Museum of Modern Art).

Similarly, Szarkowski had his own agenda in the decision to rehang Evans's 1938 show. He wanted to quickly establish a new direction for photography at MoMA upon Steichen's retirement and saw an opportunity to do so in a way that dovetailed with Steichen's last exhibit. He could provide a sense of continuity with the FSA photographs, but in the simultaneous Evans exhibit he claimed a special status for his own judgment of Evans as the exemplar of a newly defined U.S. documentary genre.

In critical writings about Evans and Lange after approximately 1963, although the two continue to share certain characteristics—such as an assertion of artistic independence and willful, temperamental personalities—they are "revealed" as differing on one fundamental aspect. In full conformity with modernist tenets, foregrounded in writings about Evans was his detachment from the subjects of his photographs and his insistence upon their apoliticalness, whereas qualities of involvement with and concern for depicted subjects come to mark critical writings about Lange.

Thus during the 1940s, 1950s, and early 1960s, Lange was well-known within the art world and also in the larger community through her work for *Life* and the continued circulation of her FSA photographs in books and magazines. Furthermore, her work, like Evans's, had been legitimated within the art world not only through exhibitions but also through inclusion in Newhall's *History of Photogra-*

*phy* (1982). And in 1958 she was one of two women, along with Julia Margaret Cameron, included in Newhall's *Masters of Photography* (in which Evans was also included). Newhall wrote about the FSA-OWI, specifically Lange and Evans, saying "*they* had created a style which influenced a generation of photographers and has since passed into the bloodstream of photojournalism" (Newhall, 1958: 140, emphasis added).

## COMPETING STRATEGIES

A selection of the critical writing reveals that the application of Szarkowski's modernist aesthetic set Lange and Evans on different trajectories of evaluation. Previously, they had been held up to a similar evaluative structure, one aspect of which assumed that they developed their style from a concern for their subjects. In the new scheme that became the generative quality of Lange's work, Evans was increasingly located at the center of Szarkowski's modernist aesthetic.

As noted, critical writing about the genre of documentary photography prior to the mid-1960s had no frame of reference in which to expect that Evans's or Lange's photographs were anything other than "referential" images, as Elliott had categorized them. Documentary might be an art of photography, Elliott wrote, but as with realism in fiction, it is "a servant art: it aims to create in the viewer the naive illusion, 'That's what things are really like'" (1962: 541). Rather than bemoaning this fact, he found it to be the strength of the work of both Lange and Evans and of any successful documentary photograph.

Like Evans, Lange was also characterized as having a unique vision and achieving transcendence in her photographs (Elliott, 1966). But her reputation— in terms of both institutional recognition and renown—was formed earlier, during Steichen's tenure and specifically, through the inclusion of her photographs in the *Family of Man* and *The Bitter Years*. During this period of declining influence and importance of picture magazines, there was still the expectation that documentary photographers were involved with the photographed subjects, but they were also expected to skillfully incorporate aesthetic qualities in their work.

Lange's transcendence was interpreted primarily as residing in her ability to reveal the "essence" of the objects she photographed. In the introduction to an interview with Lange in 1963, Nat Herz wrote that Lange is able to depict in "a rich mingling of simplicity and complexity the beauty that is present within the ugly, within the terrible. Within the particular object, a stack of cotton bales, for example, she gives us the universal, makes us sense the lives that went into those bales. . . . In looking at her photographs we know we are in the presence of a great artist. She is not a photographer of the Depression, she is an artist for all time" (1963: 8–9).

The particular aesthetic in operation during Steichen's tenure valued the revelation of the general, the universal, in the everyday specifics of the subject. This was the reigning standard by which both Lange and Evans were judged.

Critical writing about Lange in the mid-1960s and early 1970s increasingly cap-
italized on her concern and compassion for those she photographed, traits that
were considered responsible for the quality of her pictures. Steichen, using his
authority as curator, attempted to elevate Lange as the preeminent FSA photographer by exhibiting such a large proportion of her photographs in *The Bitter
Years*. To an extent, and for a short period culminating in her one-woman show
at MoMA, which opened in 1966 shortly after her death, the groundwork Steichen had laid for Lange held. After Szarkowski began to put forward his modernist aesthetic, her continued identification as a compassionate photographer resulted in her increased alienation from the institution that had sustained her
reputation within the art world for fifteen years.

The photographs that were said to be "classic Dorothea Lange's" were interpreted as demonstrating her ability to give evidence while she created pictures
"that have remarkable power as artistic statements as well" (1973: 90). "Given her
awareness of the distribution of light, which is the photographer's means of creating form, and her concern for the subject, her photographs take on the quality
demanded of all art, that it convey human feeling as vital experience" (Benson,
1965: n.p.). She was interpreted as being able to evoke a sense of the thoughts
running through the mind of her subject and hence to penetrate the surface and
reveal the essential, invisible humanity. Van Deren Coke described the strengths
of her work as revealing and informative but also felt there was another "ingredient of utmost importance." This other ingredient is an aesthetic quality of "un-
forced interplay of the formal elements, the foil of black by white passages, the
use of a low or high camera position to simplify her compositions to give emphasis" (1973: 90).

In addition to the diminished evaluation of concerned photography in the late
1960s, Lange's reputation was also affected by the anchoring of interpretations of
her photographs to her existence as a woman. The *Aperture* preview of her
MoMA retrospective made much of Lange as a *woman* photographer. It devoted
several pages to reproductions of her work, emphasizing that her photographs
were artistic creations but attributing the transcendence of her work to her "maternal concern for things of this world" (Benson, 1965: n.p.). The author emphasized the strength of feeling he saw communicated through her photographs and
identified this as her particular aesthetic quality. The emphasis was on the feeling
communicated in the photograph: "Photographs to be of continued interest
must transcend the specific event to become instruments for the conveyance of
feeling. . . . We would not look at a photograph long whether documentary or
'creative' unless the visual form commands our attention and interest, is lucid,
and [is] an articulate expression of feeling which is independent of its verbal
equivalent" (Benson, 1965: n.p.).

But again, her ability to feel strongly is tied to her "maternal" instinct, which
her photographs clearly "reveal." Citing the first two photographs one saw upon
entering the exhibit, Benson wrote that these two images reveal Lange at her

"most essential self." In the first, the texture of the limbs of *Sunlit Oak* are sensuous, warm, and inviting: "It is a maternal image in that the limbs growing diagonally from the central trunk reach out to embrace. One recognizes Dorothea's affection for the tree and her recognition of herself in the tree's maternal gesture" (Benson, 1965: n.p.). The second, a picture of her son holding her first grandchild as an infant wrapped in a blanket, is interpreted to convey a similar feeling of warmth and protectiveness. The review mentions that a "striking quality" of the exhibit is that it dispels the notion that Lange was only a photographer of the 1930s by also including her work from the 1940s and 1950s: "She documented whatever interested her, at the same time creating universal forms of human feeling through an instinctive artist's awareness of the fall of light and dark" (Benson, 1965).

The review is a tribute to Lange, but inasmuch as it interpreted her work as growing out of her existence as a woman, it undercut the application of the same evaluative strategies as those attributed to Evans's work. Within the modernist paradigm, in which qualities of cool detachment were desirable, the communication of feelings was not a priority. In addition, and perhaps more accurately, women were socially defined as being quite "naturally" incapable of achieving such disinterest. Unlike critical writings about Evans, especially after 1971, in which the images became his true creations and not merely expressions, Lange is constructed as the Mother of her photographs. She was not the creator in the generative sense, as was Evans, but rather in the sense that "no subject was beyond her woman's sense of care and tenderness" (Benson, 1965). Stryker also contributed to this interpretation of Lange in an interview for the exhibit catalog *Just Before the War*, a 1968 FSA-OWI retrospective: "I hadn't even met her yet, but I saw a sense—the Mother—the great feeling for human beings she had which was so valuable. She could go into a field and a man working there wouldn't even look up, and he must have had some feeling that there was a wonderful woman, that she was going to be sympathetic" (Garver, 1968: 5).

A degree of this interpretation must be considered as stemming from the fame of her photograph *Migrant Mother*, as it came to be "folded across the reading" of all her images (Fisher, 1987: 141). It prioritized certain images and effected the sense that could be made of them. Compared to what occurred with Evans, emphasis came to be placed on the sense that could be made of Lange herself, amid emerging assumptions of who an artist photographer was. Increasingly, Lange came to be acknowledged as having created great photographs, although not from any mystical instinct or calling, as was said of Evans. Rather, her abilities were revealed as related to the influence others had on her life and work, as well as to her natural motherly qualities.

Coke wrote that Lange was married to the artist Maynard Dixon: "Probably as a result of this experience she developed an eye for strong compositions" (1973: 90). Noting that it had often been said that Lange was little concerned about the aesthetic quality of her pictures, he stated that Lange was not a master printer and that she thought in terms of "photographs to be reproduced in books, newspapers, magazines, and reports" (Coke, 1973: 95). This conclusion is presumably based on the work she did after leaving the FSA (Newhall, 1958: 140). It excludes mention of the possibility that she also thought in terms of the display of photographs on museum walls, having played a large part in the selection and organization of three MoMA exhibits—*Family of Man, The Bitter Years,* and her own retrospective. Nor does he mention that she may have developed "an eye for strong composition" while studying with Clarence White in New York. Through exclusion of particular experiences in her life and an emphasis on others—as a woman, as a photojournalist—her work is discursively defined as being outside the purview of the art museum. Unlike Evans, in critical reviews she was not linked to previous photographers, and she had no disciples within the new tradition of photography.

In 1974 William Stott wrote an introduction for a book of Lange's "best photographs of the Depression." The book was never published, but the introduction was printed in the journal *Exposure* in 1984. Stott's article is a fine example of the way in which discursive strategies reverberate throughout a community and are enacted, unintentionally perhaps, by those in support of someone's work, just as such strategies are used purposefully by critics of that same work.

Stott argued that he "uses the *facts* of her life as we know them to speculate about how she came to make the pictures she did" (1984: 29; emphasis added). Maintaining that (unlike Evans) she had little influence on the neodocumentarians—Arbus, Winogrand, Friedlander, and Frank—he asked, of what interest is her work for today? In an indictment of concerned photography, already in decline in 1974, he stated that the interest was not historical, since the photographs impart little information and what information they do impart is "thrown into doubt because of the bias" from which they were made. Then, following the modernist aesthetic and implying that photographs do exist that are bias-free, he implied that the best photographs are those that do not inform us about the subject or about historical context. The best of her photographs "seem quite ahistorical which may be only to say that they are the best, they are transcendently pertinent, they are art" (Stott, 1984: 28).

The aspects of her "artistry" Stott brought to bear on the photographs had essentially become anathema to the art photography establishment of the time. He noted that Lange was the ideal *Family of Man* photographer and that her photographs succeeded too often for this success to be considered luck. But rather than attribute her success to, for example, her unique vision, he attributed it to her shooting technique, emphasizing a certain formula she used. Thus, her mastery was made up of a formulaic technique and her compassion. Even her supporters became her unwitting detractors. Acknowledging Lange as a "popular" art photographer, Stott felt that if Lange needed a precedent, it should be Gustave Courbet, who adapted studio technique to his social protest pictures of peasants, "whose hardship now is largely invisible to us, the beauty of their being is so great" (1984: 29). Thus Lange is not linked to the newly established photographic modernist canon of Atget, Brady, Frank, Arbus, Friedlander, and Winogrand as is Evans. Rather, her name is connected to that of another marginal art world figure, Courbet, who is known for his radical politics.

## CHANGING OF THE GUARD

Steichen had been brought to MoMA because of his contacts within the photography industry. In the postwar years the museum wanted to reach out to a broader audience. Steichen accomplished this, but he never believed in isolating photography as an art and separating it from a popular photographic practice. Szarkowski did have such beliefs. He felt such distinctions had to be made, and he sought to create an autonomous aesthetic sphere in which photographs could be singled out as "original" artworks—like painting or sculpture—and be judged, ranked, auctioned, and traded on that basis.

In 1971 MoMA exhibited a large retrospective of Evans's work. In conjunction with the exhibit, the museum issued a book of Evans's photographs with an introduction by Szarkowski. True to the classical paradigm of representation, he suggested that Evans had accomplished the transformation of the world into his own representation. Szarkowski concentrated first on those characteristics of artistic temperament and pedigree that would set Evans apart from social documentary photographers in general and from the other FSA-OWI photographers in particular. He stated that Evans's attempt to become a photographer was "almost a willful act of protest against a polite society," that he was a "conventional, if well-groomed, bohemian" (Szarkowski, 1971: 9). Szarkowski noted that he kept company with intellectuals, writers, and painters (1971: 11) and that his first occasional successes seemed to him to be "the product not entirely of his own intention but of a force that had chosen him as a vehicle," alluding to the possibility of some kind of mystical inspiration (1971: 13). Ralph Steiner was mentioned as an important photographer because he "anticipated in some respects the later work of Evans" (Szarkowski, 1971: 11). Evans was compared to Le Corbusier and Eugene Atget, but "the descriptive and elusive complexity, the richer ambiguity, the reticence of Evans's pictures result not in parody but in mystery" (Szarkowski, 1971: 16). And finally, in a move that placed Evans squarely in the center as mediator between reality and audience, Szarkowski wrote that "it is difficult to know now with certainty whether Evans recorded the America of his youth or invented it" (1971: 20).

Two reviews of the retrospective use this reifying paean as a springboard. Hilton Kramer's *New York Times* review states that Evans's photographs "embody the moral and esthetic *texture* of the Depression era" and that the issue of whether Evans's photographic "oeuvre" belongs to the realm of high art is beyond question. The fact that it is a forty-year retrospective allows the reviewer to appreciate his consistency, which is one of style rather than subject matter. Although he draws his subjects from many realms, his style always penetrates to the "utmost clarity and precision." The strength of his work lies in the "objective, almost abstract concreteness" with which he isolates a "motif," whatever it may be. The "purity" of his work serves a larger purpose in that whereas our experience of an Evans photograph might begin with admiration of the design and subject, it ends with an "overwhelming sense of the photographer's unmistakable temperament" (Kramer, 1971: 42). Although Kramer does not discuss what this temperament might be, he signals that it is the artistic temperament that is to be dealt with as a clue to the photographs' meaning. Kramer ends his review by quoting Szarkowski, saying it is difficult to know now whether Evans recorded or invented America in the 1930s. This obfuscation of past with present and confusion of the notion of photographs as transparent reality with representations is at the locus of Szarkowski's aesthetic theory.

Other reviewers fell in line behind Szarkowski's declarations. A. D. Coleman wrote a review of the show in which he equated Evans with Picasso. He noted that Evans recognized that "man had made the country into a work of art," and the photographs with which he recorded this "made the country his, just as Picasso made toy cars and bicycle handlebars by defining their context" (Coleman, 1971: 38). Like his "confreres" Lange and Ben Shahn, Evans was not indifferent to suffering, but there was always a "dispassionate curiosity and reverence for what is," and he never "relinquished his objectivity" (Coleman, 1971: 38). In a reference that implies the close proximity of Lange and Evans as late as 1971 while simultaneously marking their differences, and, incidentally, commenting on the extent to which the application of a high modernist aesthetic to photography had depoliticized the FSA-OWI photographs, Coleman stated that although he was as moved by Evans's portraits of the dispossessed as he was by Lange's, her pictures of the interiors of rural shacks made him aware of the squalor and poverty. But when he looked at Evans's he sometimes felt like moving right in because Evans made him "aware of how imbued with an *instinctive* artfulness they were" (1971: 38; emphasis added).

Unlike Elliott's review, in which he minimized the difference between Lange's and Evans's involvement with and choice of subject matter, critical writing began to solidify around that very issue. Whereas Lange had been ascendant in the museum under Steichen, and her work had been valued precisely for its ability to communicate involvement, subjectivity, and emotionalism, under Szarkowski those qualities had been removed from the formula of documentary photography and were no longer in favor.

Kramer had praised Evans's consistency of style as opposed to subject matter. And Lange's work came to be criticized for its privileging of subject over style. But the arbitrariness of Kramer's judgment is revealed if we consider the exhibit catalog *Walker Evans at Fortune, 1945–1965* (Baier, 1977), in which the content of the photographs is remarkably consistent with Evans's work of the 1930s: signs, candid street photographs obtained surreptitiously, buildings, and storefronts. It is possible that the catalog is not representative of the variety of photographic content in the exhibit and that the curators of the exhibit meant to publish only those photographs that were the most comparable to his best-known works. Nevertheless, Evans's published photographs, together with the reviews of his work, in which critics mirror the discourse of the museum's director, and including Evans's own characterizations of himself and his work, are what make up the "objective social facts" of his reputation (Lang and Lang, 1990: 5–6). Because of Lange's previous identity as a concerned photographer and her readiness to talk about her interest in the subjects of her photographs, her style was more difficult to separate from the content. She could not be passed off as disinterested.

In the introduction to *Walker Evans* Szarkowski wrote about the photographs taken later in Evans's life, "How surprising to find that documentary photographs (*cool, precise as a police report, emotionally aloof*) can be made in the apartments and weekend houses of one's friends, or in a child's bedroom in Stockbridge, Massachusetts" (1971: 19; emphasis added). The difference in critical expectation of what constituted documentary photography between the early 1960s and 1971 makes clear the extent to which Szarkowski's claims of an autonomous photographic aesthetic were communicated to the critical community. The "true nature" of a photograph in this case, as with a literary work, became a function of the critical perspective brought to bear upon it (Tompkins, 1984: 627).

In the 1976 commemorative book on the FSA (which accompanied a retrospective at the Witkin Gallery in New York City), Hank O'Neal, who served as curator and editor, wrote of Walker Evans that he occupied a "very special and eminent position" in the FSA photo section: "Within this group of extremely talented photographers, he was the artist with the camera; the man who set the standards of perfection for the others" (1976: 60). This is not the impression we get from earlier writing about the FSA or from some of the photographers themselves, allowing the obvious observation that O'Neal's interpretation—although it conveniently fit the present need to see Evans in that light—critically misrepresented the past.

In two earlier commemorative FSA-OWI exhibits, *The Bitter Years* and *Just Before the War* (the latter sponsored jointly by the Library of Congress and the Newport Harbor Art Museum in 1968), Evans had taken his place as one of several talented FSA photographers. Steichen, who curated *The Bitter Years*, highlighted Dorothea Lange. And in the book accompanying *Just Before the War*, Thomas Garver wrote, "Dorothea Lange, who had been documenting migrant labor camps in California, was to produce much of her finest, most passionate work for the FSA. Walker Evans, another early photographer for the FSA, was much more cool in his approach *but* made a splendid record of American buildings, signs and urban landscapes" (1968: iii; emphasis added).[4]

O'Neal's interpretation of Evans's importance within the FSA reflects the general critical response to Szarkowski's strategy. Between 1968 and 1976, simple recognition became widespread renown as critics and scholars stepped in to interpret for the wider audience what about Evans's photographs was so important: "He was a man unwilling to compromise his standards or beliefs on any level and had a unique vision of America that was fully developed by 1935. This vision, recognized by only a few in the early thirties, is now an accepted fact, a national resource, one might say . . . it was timeless, totally honest and constantly developed" (O'Neal, 1976: 60).

In his activities as reviewer and essayist on U.S. photography, Alan Trachtenberg has done much to generate continued renown for Walker Evans as the quintessential American photographer. Trachtenberg has taken an active role as expert guide to the formal strategies by which Evans can be interpreted to have transformed the world into his representations. Writing about Evans's transcendence, he tells us that Evans brought a "Jamesian fastidiousness" to his photographs, "a delicacy about the placement of the camera so as to allow objects and places to 'give out' their meanings in a manner utterly clear yet still mystic" (Trachtenberg, 1978: 22). He explains that these photographs do more than make statements that things exist. This "more" goes beyond the descriptive fact of the subject/object and is what Evans himself called "transcendence." Interpreting for us, Trachtenberg defines transcendence as "the unspeakable note of rightness in a picture" (1978: 24). As Abigail Solomon-Godeau has written, and as is overwhelmingly clear in the critical approach to Evans's work, "Ineffability becomes the fall back position at those moments when the modernist paradigm appears inadequate as an explanation for subjective preference" (1991: 44).

The late 1960s and 1970s were a period of widespread popular interest in photography in general but particularly in social documentary. The FSA-OWI photographs were widely published and exhibited as photographs that had made a difference socially and politically. Because this was also the period during which Evans was being fashioned as the father of a modernist American photography, the issue of his political and social involvement was unavoidable. The issue was addressed primarily in the form of denials. O'Neal maintained that Evans did not take any photographs for political purposes, that his point of view was aesthetic as opposed to wanting to bring about social change: "His images endure, quite apart from the circumstances of their time" (1976: 63). Alan Trachtenberg wrote, "In public statements Evans was at pains both to affirm the 'documentary' aspect of his work and to deny firmly *complicity* with New Deal politics . . . vigorously [denying] that he made pictures for the sake of positive social change, often arguing that belief in such efficacy is fatuous" (1979: 10; emphasis added). Complicity is an interesting word to use in this context, although it is unclear whether it was Trachtenberg's or Evans's choice. It implies that those who did make pictures for the New Deal in the hope of social change were somehow collaborationists.

After he left *Fortune* in 1965, Evans began to try to clear his reputation of the charge that during the Depression his works had "served a particular social and political goal. He wished, in short, to assert and explain his own autonomy" (Trachtenberg, 1979: 10). Trachtenberg did not deny that Evans's work had an implicit "political" message but felt this message, which Trachtenberg had gathered from his reading of *Messages from the Interior,* was that "art, the constructive energy of culture, inhabits the realms of everyday life" (1979: 15). More than this, "The book declares itself . . . the making of a space for the work of art (the only work that is also play) to show itself"(Trachtenberg, 1979: 16). Here we are encouraged to interpret Evans's photographs totally within the art realm and to read them, in keeping with the modernist paradigm, as referring only to themselves as art and not to the subjects of the images or the particulars of their lives.

## CONCLUSION

The new art of photography that emerged out of the rearticulation of photography within a modernist aesthetic did not interpret documentary photography to have the aims Elliott had written of in 1962. It served nothing so banal as reality or history. Rather, it served the institutional and personal desires, interests, and investments of those involved in revamping and reconstructing a new photographic canon, including curators, art dealers, and critics.[5] The transformation of what had been called social or concerned documentary photography into photographic art had, first, to remove the impurities of any political, social, or emotional investment from the evaluation of the photographs and, second, to subsume the subject fully as a creation of the photographer's own subjectivity, of his or her unique vision: "The quality of authenticity implicit in a photograph may give it special value as evidence, or proof. Such a photograph can be called 'documentary' by definition. . . . Thus any photograph can be considered a document if it is found to contain useful information about the specific subject under study" (Newhall, 1982: 235).

What can be said to have changed during the late 1960s and early 1970s in relation to documentary photography was the specific subject under study. This subject became the photographer rather than the subject pictured in the photograph. The end toward which the photograph was considered to have been made became the "art of the present" (Trachtenberg, 1978: 24). The "present" of the 1970s was judged to be best served by disassociating, when possible, the political, social, and historical detritus that lingered around that segment of documentary photography currently being elevated to the status of art masterpieces. What counted as authentic and useful information about the subject shifted from a concern for the immediate context of the subject within the frame to a concern for the aesthetic vision of the photographer *as extrapolated* from the subject within the frame.

MoMA's withdrawal of support for social documentary photography appeared complete in 1978 when Vicki Goldberg wrote that "concerned" documentary photography has "a bad name," to the extent that Szarkowski omitted it entirely from his 1977 show, *Mirrors and Windows, American Photography Since 1960* (Goldberg, 1978: 17). In the introduction to the exhibit catalog, Szarkowski asserted the value of the personal, apolitical vision by disavowing not only the work produced in the 1920s and 1930s but also the mass of social documentary photography produced during the 1960s: "The general movement of American photography during the past quarter century has been from public to private concerns. It is true that much of the most vital photography done in this country during the preceding period was also essentially private" (1978: 11). He continued, "Good photographers had long since known . . . that most issues of importance cannot be photographed" (1978: 14).

Although Szarkowski claimed the full photographic spectrum for the museum, in the practical application of that aesthetic distinctions were inevitably and strategically located. Lines were drawn to distinguish previously recognized creative photographers and concerned photographers from artist photographers. Weston and Adams were judged as being too preoccupied with the pure form and not enough with the "clear observation of significant fact," one of the newly defined intrinsic qualities of photography (Phillips, 1982: 55–56).[6] Interpretations of Lange's work became increasingly tied to notions of concerned photography at a time when such photography was on the decline. She was judged as overly attached to and interested in her subjects as subjects. And the interpretation of Evans's work became increasingly ephemeral as curators, critics, and scholars became more and more invested in a desire for him to be the "great white hope" of an American photography tradition.

Critics played a crucial role in the adoption of the new photographic aesthetic, as they at first struggled to grasp the distinctions Szarkowski was creating and then, in the interest of their careers, worked to communicate those distinctions to the public. Critics sought out the appropriate art world figures to compare and contextualize photographers within the larger sphere of art history. Whereas Evans was compared to the centrally placed modernist Le Corbusier, Lange was likened to the marginal realist Courbet.

Evans's reputation, built as it was primarily on recognition by the institution responsible for shifting expectations about documentary photography, became renowned, as critics and scholars fell in behind MoMA. His renown, therefore, has been limited to a small art public provided access to this viewpoint through art museums and the higher education system. The continued circulation of his photographs within this sphere has created a relatively secure place for him and his reputation within the art museum's canon of American photographic art.

Lange's reputation, on the other hand, was built on both her early renown, through widespread publication of her FSA and *Life* photographs, and her recognition by MoMA as early as 1940 and continuing through 1966. Following this period, her reputation was sustained by public renown, but institutional recognition diminished as her identification as a "compassionate" photographer led critics to minimize her previous relevance and status in the art world. Lange's reputation remains grounded in public renown through the continued circulation of her photographs and occasional small exhibits. Only one institution, the Oakland Museum, actively provides legitimation of her status as an eminent U.S. artist. Lange's reputation, as seen from the heights of fine art, is marginal. If her reputation extends today toward the high-art end of the American photographic canon, this position is based almost solely on the photograph *Migrant Mother,* which, in fact, reflects more accurately the surviving power of her popular renown than her history of institutional recognition within the art world.

## NOTES

1. The Farm Security Administration–Office of War Information photography unit operated from 1935 until 1943. From 1935 to 1942, as the FSA, it was charged with publicizing rural poverty and the New Deal programs set up to alleviate that poverty. As the Depression waned, the unit documented many aspects of everyday American life in the late 1930s and early 1940s. In 1942 and 1943, as part of the OWI, the unit produced photographic propaganda for the war effort.

2. This chapter is drawn from a more extensive study of the uses of the Farm Security Administration photograph collection in the construction of a national memory of the Depression. In addition to the authors directly quoted in the course of the chapter, I am also indebted to the work of Barbara Herrnstein Smith and Catherine Lord, among others.

3. See Stott (1973) for a discussion of this issue.

4. As mentioned earlier, curators have their own practical agendas that nonetheless have ideological consequences. Garver's *Just Before the War* was intended as a response to the negativeness of *The Bitter Years,* which displayed a preponderance of poverty-stricken and uprooted subjects. Thus more upbeat, positive images, most of which were taken after 1937, were selected for the exhibit. (Indeed, a comparison of titles signals the competing investment and selection of the images.) The focus of *Just Before the War* mitigated against the use of Evans's and Lange's photographs, since both had left the FSA by 1938.

5. See Abigail Solomon-Godeau's excellent article on the expediencies of photographic canon formation in the case of Eugene Atget (Solomon-Godeau, 1991).

6. See also Szarkowski, 1978, Introduction.

## REFERENCES

Baier, Lesley K. 1977. *Walker Evans at Fortune 1945–1965.* Wellesley, Mass.: Wellesley College Museum.

Benson, John. 1965. "The Dorothea Lange Retrospective." *Aperture* 12(4), n.p.

Coke, Van Deren. 1973. "Dorothea Lange: Compassionate Recorder." *Modern Photography,* May, 90–95.

Coleman, A. D. 1971. "Did He Find the Real U.S.A.?" *New York Times,* February 14, D38.

Elliott, George P. 1962. "American Photographs, by Walker Evans," book review. *Commentary* 34(6), 540–543.

———. 1966. "On Dorothea Lange." In *Dorothea Lange,* John Szarkowski (ed). New York: Museum of Modern Art, 6–14.

Fisher, Andrea. 1987. *Let Us Now Praise Famous Women, Women Photographers for the US Government 1935–1944.* New York: Pandora Press.

Fisher, Phillip. 1975. "The Future's Past." *New Literary History* 6(3), 587–606.

Garver, Thomas. 1968. *Just Before the War.* New York: October House.

Goldberg, Vicki. 1978. "Propaganda Can Also Tell the Truth," book review of *Russell Lee, Photographer. American Photographer,* December, 17–18.

Herz, Nat. 1963. "Dorothea Lange in Perspective." *Infinity,* April, 6–11.

Katz, Leslie. 1979. "Interview with Walker Evans." In *The Camera Viewed,* Peninah R. Petruck (ed). New York: E. P. Dutton, 120–132.

Kramer, Hilton. 1971. "An Era Lives in Photos at Evans Show." *New York Times,* January 28, 42.

Lang, Gladys Engel, and Kurt Lang. 1990. *Etched in Memory: The Building and Survival of Artistic Reputation.* Chapel Hill: University of North Carolina Press.

Lynes, Russell. 1973. *Good Old Modern: An Intimate Portrait of the Museum of Modern Art.* New York: Atheneum.

Meltzer, Milton. 1978. *Dorothea Lange, A Photographer's Life.* New York: Farrar, Straus, Giroux.

Museum of Modern Art Press Release. 1947. Edward Steichen Archive, Museum of Modern Art, July 15.

Newhall, Beaumont. 1938. "Documentary Approach to Photography." *Parnassus,* March, 3–6.

———. 1958. *Masters of Photography.* New York: Castle Books.

———. 1982. *The History of Photography from 1839 to the Present.* New York: Museum of Modern Art.

O'Neal, Hank. 1976. *A Vision Shared: A Classic Portrait of America and Its People, 1935–1943.* New York: St. Martin's Press.

Phillips, Christopher. 1982. "The Judgement Seat of Photography." *October* 22 (Fall), 27–64.

Pollock, Griselda. 1980. "Artists, Mythologies and Media—Genius, Madness and Art History." *Screen* 21(3), 57–96.

Rathbone, Belinda. 1993. Telephone Interview. April 30.

Sekula, Allan. 1975. "On the Invention of Photographic Meaning." *Artforum,* January, 37–45.

Soby, James Thrall. 1962. "The Muse Was Not for Hire." *Saturday Review,* September 22, 57–58.

Solomon-Godeau, Abigail. 1991. "Canon Fodder: Authoring Eugene Atget." In Abigail Solomon-Godeau, *Photography at the Dock: Essays on Photographic History, Institutions, and Practices.* Minneapolis: University of Minnesota Press, 28–51.

Steichen, Edward. 1948. "Photography and the Art Museum." *Museum Service, Bulletin of the Rochester Museum of Arts and Science,* June, 69–70.

Storey, Isabelle, and Alan Trachtenberg. 1978. *The Presence of Walker Evans.* Boston: Institute of Contemporary Art.

Stott, William. 1973. *Documentary Expression and Thirties America.* New York: Oxford.

———. 1984. "Introduction to a Never-Published Book of Dorothea Lange's Best Photographs of Depression America." *Exposure* 22(3), 22–30.

Stryker, Roy, and Nancy Wood. 1973. *In This Proud Land: America, 1935–1943, as Seen in the FSA Photographs.* Boston: New York Graphic Society.

Szarkowski, John. 1966. *The Photographer's Eye.* New York: Museum of Modern Art.

———. 1967. "Photography and the Mass Media." *Dot Zero* 3 (Spring), 30–35.

———. 1971. *Walker Evans.* New York: Museum of Modern Art.

———. 1978. *Mirrors and Windows: American Photography Since 1960.* New York: Museum of Modern Art.

Tompkins, Jane. 1984. "Masterpiece Theater: The Politics of Hawthorne's Literary Reputation." *American Quarterly* 36(5), 617–642.

Trachtenberg, Alan. 1979. "Walker Evans's *Message from the Interior:* A Reading." *October* 11, 5–29.

Wittkower, Rudolf, and Margot Wittkower. 1963. *Born Under Saturn: The Character and Conduct of Artists, A Documented History From Antiquity to the French Revolution.* New York: W. W. Norton.

# ❦ 11 ❧

# Graffiti as Public and
# Private Art

ROBERT S. DREW

GRAFFITI BEGAN TO APPEAR on the walls and subways of northeastern U.S. cities
in the late 1960s and early 1970s, and debates about graffiti's aesthetic merits date
almost as far back. Yet it was not until the early 1980s that critics, dealers, and
collectors within the mainstream art world first began to accept graffiti art; soon,
they eagerly sought it. Between 1980 and 1984, graffiti art moved from art collectives
and alternative spaces of the South Bronx and the East Village to Soho galleries, to
elite galleries in Midtown New York, and to other major U.S. and European cities.

If graffiti art's rise was meteoric, its decline was equally sudden and complete.
Although graffiti art has remained popular in Europe, there were almost no graffiti art exhibits in Manhattan by the end of the 1980s. Some of the artists whose
work had been in the highest demand had to suspend their artwork, holding
down full-time jobs as messengers and repairmen. In late 1992, graffiti art experienced a small revival, with several prominent New York exhibits, including a
well-received five-person show at the Klarfeld Perry Gallery in Soho. But for
years the work of graffiti artists has generally been sold out of the back room, if at
all; has rarely been mentioned in the art press; and has sold for a fraction of the
price demanded by most New York gallery art (Hess, 1987; Lippard, 1990).

The reasons for graffiti's precipitous fall from grace are complex and numerous. Some would no doubt argue (as some have all along) that graffiti art is unsophisticated in form and content and never deserved attention in the first place. I
disagree with this, but, more important, I would argue that all such judgments
are at least partially driven by social factors (Becker, 1982; Wolff, 1981). In fact, in
this chapter I largely avoid consideration of the inherent qualities of graffiti art—
which range from cursory signatures to elaborate renderings of natural, abstract,
and mass-mediated motifs—because such consideration was largely avoided by
the mainstream art world. Graffiti's rise and fall were, as much as the career path
of any art movement, "not simply individual and 'purely aesthetic' decisions, but
socially enabled and socially constructed events" (Wolff, 1981: 40).

Among sociological explanations for the failure of graffiti art to become institutionalized, Elizabeth Hess (1987) has attributed that failure to differences in
language and culture between the upper-middle-class art world and the working-
class artists. Graffitists were unable to talk and act "correctly" in the art world's
terms and to fit their work within the art world tradition. There is undoubtedly
some validity to this argument; however, it does not account for the fact that
many graffiti artists educated themselves in the art world tradition, adapted their
work to it, and were nevertheless rejected. Richard Lachmann (1988) blamed
graffiti's decline on the breakdown of the graffiti world's organizational base as a
result of the brief recruitment of some of its members into the mainstream.

Without denying the partial validity of these prior explanations, I suggest one
additional (and not inconsistent) factor. A clue to graffiti's life course is contained in Hess's paraphrase of a statement by New York graffiti king Lee Quinones: "Quinones says dealers were able to 'romanticize' graffiti on subways because
the images were transitory, offering only a glimpse of the work. Later it became
clear that dealers only *wanted* a glimpse" (Hess, 1987: 37). I argue, along with
Quinones, that graffiti's ultimate rejection by the mainstream art world was assured in part by the terms upon which it was initially accepted. Graffiti was represented by the art world as an essentially *public* art form, and its publicness was an
important part of its allure. As a result, from the start graffiti on canvas constituted an uncomfortable paradox for the art world. By citing articles, interviews,
and reviews of graffiti art from art magazines and newspapers, I show that arguments about the inappropriateness of graffiti art in a private context were consistently deployed in its dismissal.[1] These articles and reviews are not only indicative
of art world thinking about graffiti art at the time but also were extremely influential in determining graffiti art's market value. The second part of this chapter is
devoted to an analysis of interviews I conducted with Philadelphia graffitists in
1986. I demonstrate that graffiti artists (or "writers," as most prefer to be called)
do not always consider their art to be an essentially public practice and that in
many ways graffiti is best analyzed as private art.

My intention is not to address the issue of whether graffiti writers deserved to
be accepted into the mainstream art world, which is too complex to consider
here. I only mean to point to one set of assumptions I feel was pivotal in the art
world's initial acceptance and eventual rejection of graffiti and to show that this
set of assumptions was inconsistent with the graffitists' own construction of their
world. I hope a study such as this can promote a better understanding between
art world elites and "popular," "folk," or "subcultural" artists and help to facilitate
and reward good art.[2]

## GRAFFITI AS PUBLIC ART

Graffiti art first began to appear on public walls at a time when many members of
the mainstream art world were themselves experimenting with various forms of

nongallery art. Under the influence of 1960s luminaries such as Andy Warhol and Joseph Beuys, conceptual art, performance art, street works, and happenings all shared a utopian desire to liberate art from museums and galleries, dealers and critics, and their economic supports; to expand participation in both the production and reception of art; and to call into question the officially sanctioned, commercial allocation of public space (Alloway, 1975; Lippard, 1973, 1984). Thus Lucy Lippard has written of street works and performances, "One of the major virtues of such work is that it requires no dealer or sponsor other than the artist himself or herself, and that it commands a ready-made audience when it takes place in a naturally crowded area" (1984: 57). At the same time, she warned that often such work is easily reintegrated into the system it purports to challenge: "All too often, however, no real alternative to the marketplace is offered. Tiptoeing out of the gallery and into the streets, then rushing back to exhibit documentation, only parodies the need to form a 'dialectic' between the real and art worlds" (1984: 57). Despite the lofty intentions of the period, artists essentially remained tied to the traditional commerce of gallery and dealer and became even more dependent upon such commerce during the art market boom of the 1980s.

It was under these circumstances that the art world turned to graffiti, and it was on these terms that graffiti was provisionally accepted by some art world members. Here was a truly public art form—illegal, transgressive, and participatory. These themes were central to Norman Mailer's early and influential book on graffiti, which called it "the impulse of the jungle to cover the walled tombs of technology" and compared it to the shock tactics of conceptual artists like Chris Burdon (1974: 8). In the early 1980s, when graffiti began to draw some serious attention from the art world, the focus of analysis was often less its content than its context, its violation of spatial and legal borders. For instance, Richard Goldstein (1980) praised graffiti for "rais[ing] the heady possibility that art can happen anywhere. Like conceptual art and Pop, graffiti questions the context in which art is appreciated. It renews the dream of work for its own sake, the idea of creation as a democratic process—in short, radical humanism" (1980: 55).

The specific styles, motifs, and methods of graffiti art were overshadowed in art world discourse by the facts of its visibility and illegality. Suzi Gablik wrote, "Paradoxically, it is crossing the border into criminality that gives graffiti its ethical quality and its note of authenticity. Just as skulls on sticks serve as a warning to initiates in certain cannibal tribes of New Guinea that a territory has been demarcated and taken possession of, so have graffiti artists . . . staked out their claim on this mechanical, late-industrial Underworld" (1982: 34).

Tim Rollins, who has since devoted himself to artistic collaborations with young people in the Bronx, was director of an East Village art collective that was one of the first to display graffiti art. In an interview with Gablik, he referred to graffiti as "radical art with a radical methodology because it's illegal" (1982: 37). And Mel Neulander, owner of a small gallery devoted solely to graffiti, was quoted by Anna Quindlen on the marketability of graffiti as radical chic: "New

York is a city where many of the same things that are criminal are also chic—cocaine, for example, and Jack Henry Abbott—and Mr. Neulander says that in a fashion, that makes the art at his gallery easier to market. 'As long as it has this bandito image, we're going to sell paintings,' he said" (1982: 27).

Ironically, then, the art world legitimated graffiti using the same reasoning by which most everyone else condemned it: because of its infringement on public space. Although their opinions of graffiti were diametrically opposed, the art world and the policymakers concurred in viewing graffiti as, before all else, public and illegal.

The art world's fascination with graffiti's transgressive aspect typifies the romantic notion of the artist as an inspired criminal or madperson unencumbered by social norms. Just as, according to Janet Wolff, "work done by artists . . . becomes seen as an ideal form of production, because it appears free in a way in which other production is not" (1981: 17), the work of graffiti writers was apparently seen as free in a way other forms of art were not. As Arnold Hauser (1951) showed, this view of the artist as an ideally sovereign individual originated in the Renaissance and was historically tied to painters' release from the guild system and from traditional forms of patronage. Although it remains powerful, the ideology of autonomous art fails to recognize the many financial imperatives that have always guided and constrained artistic production. In recent decades, art world members have often gestured symbolically against the dealer-critic system even while remaining beholden to that system. Graffiti art, too, as I show later, has never been illegal or public or particularly "free" by nature. Nevertheless, the art world's understanding of graffiti art has been determined by its own contradictory ideology.

Even as graffiti was brought indoors and began to be exhibited in prestigious Soho and Midtown galleries, the occasion was surrounded by constant reference to graffiti's public self. At the Sidney Janis Gallery's 1983 *Post-Graffiti* show, widely regarded as the apex of graffiti artists' rise through the art world, photographs of graffiti on subway trains were exhibited alongside the artists' work on canvas (as was the practice at several graffiti art exhibitions). The Janis catalog (1983) assured patrons that the artists had not given up working on public space and that the show was only "post-graffiti" by virtue of "an extension in scope and concept of their spontaneous imagery." Even the magnificent books of graffiti art, *Subway Art* (Cooper and Chalfant, 1984) and *Spraycan Art* (Chalfant and Prigoff, 1987), are confined to photographs of publicly executed works; to my knowledge, there are no published collections of graffiti artists' work on canvas. As with conceptual art, the only documentation considered appropriate for graffiti was a photograph of its appearance as a transient event in the public world.

In some cases, the graffiti writers who were picked up by the art world participated in this equivocation themselves. For instance, artist Leonard McGurr (also known as Futura 2000) told Suzi Gablik, "I see the paintings more as a documentation of what goes on in the subways, a memento. Obviously, nobody can have an actual train, although in a few years time, some museum will probably buy one" (1982: 36). (As he predicted, in 1991 a Japanese collector purchased a ten-car New York subway covered with graffiti from New York's transit authority [Raynor, 1991].) McGurr's view of his studio work as a mere "memento" may seem to trivialize it but more likely succeeded in elevating it to the mediation of his public work that his sponsors desired. At the same time, studio graffiti artists were sometimes dismayed to find their personae being defined by their public work at the expense of their more recent work on canvas: "Most of the press that mention me speak of the things I did two or three years ago. What I'm doing now they're not even up on.... I haven't been painting trains! I've been making paintings" (Fred Brathwaite, also known as Fab 5 Fred, quoted in Moufarrege, 1982a: 88).

Even as the art world embraced graffiti on these contradictory terms, there were signs that the fragile alliance could not be sustained. Nicolas Moufarrege asked, "Would not the legitimacy of the graffiti lead to a certain kind of death? Do we not get a rush from the danger and illegality of it all?" (1982b: 70. The author suggested as a solution that East Village gallery owners "pirate" a down-town subway station for a one-night exhibition during which graffitists would perform on public space for the attendees.)

The death anticipated by Moufarrege arrived in the form of reviews of the ma-jor graffiti art exhibitions, which were almost uniformly negative and which overwhelmingly made reference to the "failure" of graffiti art's transition from walls and trains to canvas, suggesting that the art lost something in the process. The first such review in a major art journal, which was of an isolated 1975 exhibi-tion, claimed that "the consequences of the displacement [from walls to canvas] are enfeebling" (Goldin, 1975: 102). The more numerous reviews in response to the *Post-Graffiti* show and subsequent shows often compared the work on canvas unfavorably to the public work, not on the basis of content but of context.

What had had a raw vitality, a rugged vibrancy in its native locale, acquired a forced immediacy and studied nonchalance; the translation onto unstretched or often stretched canvas neutralized it into a sequence of effects. (Linker, 1984: 92)

It is *context* . . . that characterizes the transition in graffiti art from New York subways, through the downtown scene, and up to prestigious 57th Street. And this shift in context signals a loss of graffiti painting's initial impact and meaning. . . . The work has lost in the transition. (Saul, 1984: 38)

Clearly the good old days of authentic graffiti throwaway art are over. I hope the gallery takeover doesn't destroy the quality of subway decor. (Kuspit, 1985: 138)

All of these critics expressed admiration for public graffiti art and disappoint-ment with its studio version. What is perhaps still more telling is that even the critics who disliked (or hated) graffiti on subways and walls believed public space was the "appropriate" milieu for graffiti art and reacted vehemently against its arrival in the galleries. For instance, Grace Glueck considered public graffiti to be "offensive" and "an eyesore" and yet preferred it to private graffiti: "The very idea of enshrining graffiti—an art of the streets impulsive and spontaneous by nature—in the traditional, time-honored medium of canvas, is ridiculous" (1983: 22). Addison Parks referred to public graffiti as "the visible manifestations of a system gone wrong" and "the skin cancer of our civilization" but admitted that at least "in its context it's real," whereas gallery graffiti was "artistically produced anti-art" (1982: 73). And Edward Sozanski, who wrote that public graffiti was "more often than not profoundly ugly," nevertheless decided that "taking graffiti off the wall is like taking the tiger out of the jungle and caging him: he doesn't put the fear of God into you anymore. . . . Putting these designs on canvas doesn't make them art, it only depletes them of their most endearing qualities, animal vitality and energy" (1984: D3).[3]

What these recurrent critiques of graffiti art leave unsaid is that *all* art is necessarily "enfeebled," "neutralized," or "depleted" by virtue of its containment within the four walls of a museum or gallery. It is in the nature of museums and galleries to isolate works of art from their conditions of production; to detach them from whatever social, political, or religious functions they may have served; and to subordinate them to the constructed history of art (Adorno, 1967; Fisher, 1975; Crimp, 1983). Theodor Adorno compared museums to mausoleums, calling them "the family sepulchres of works of art." Galleries also diminish the works they shelter, not through embalmment but through commodification: "Their market value leaves no room for the pleasure of looking at them" (Adorno, 1967: 175).

The art world was abundantly familiar with these arguments when graffiti art was brought indoors in the early 1980s. The question is not why they were deployed in the critique of graffiti but why they were applied so selectively to graffiti when so much other art was being commodified without objection. In fact, throughout the twentieth century, museums and galleries have without fail accomplished the appropriation of what was previously considered unappropriable (Duncan, 1983: 114–116; Hughes, 1980: 365–369).

One of the most recent such accommodations involved a number of artists such as Keith Haring, Jean Michel Basquait, and Kenny Scharf, who became associated with the graffiti writers because they worked on public space before they achieved any recognition in the art world, although they did not originate from the working-class conditions of most graffitists and did not paint on subways. Haring and Scharf were both white and art school–trained; Basquait was half Haitian and half Puerto Rican and was involved in the downtown art and music scenes from early on. In short, these artists differed from the Bronx and Upper Manhattan graffiti artists in terms of both their class background and their initial relationship with the art world.

These artists, particularly Haring and Scharf, were initially interviewed and packaged together with the graffiti writers in art magazines (Gablik, 1982; Moufarrege, 1982a; Alinovi, 1983), and their work was often exhibited side by side. The association seems to have been designed to lend the graffitists an art world pedigree while lending the art school graduates street credibility, but it ended up being more beneficial to the latter group. Reviews of these artists' work were mixed (their reviews and exhibitions throughout the 1980s were much more numerous than those of the graffiti writers), but they never suggested that the work belonged in the streets or lost something in the gallery. Early reviews often referred to the artists' illegal public work, but as they became successful an effort was made to distance them from public territory and from the graffiti writers with whom they had been associated. Generally, for the middle-class art school graduates, the illegal public work was treated as part of the brief period of youthful insurrection expected of any soon-to-be art world practitioner.

I would argue that the art world's labeling of graffiti as an essentially public, transgressive art form actually succeeded in fulfilling the traditional exclusion of working-class and ethnic art from the mainstream art world's mechanisms of power and profit. Graffiti was represented as a natural element of the city's tableau, appropriate to provide inspiration for the wandering middle-class flaneur but excluded from the sanctuaries of the middle class's "real" art. Working-class art has always been defined as public art or folk art and, consequently, been condemned to the margins of the market. Just as the relegation of traditional blues songs to the public domain has resulted in the original musicians being denied royalties (Chapple and Garofalo, 1977: 255–256), so the framing of graffiti as essentially public art precludes the artists from benefiting financially from their work within the art world.

Lucy Lippard, much of whose work comments acutely on the issues raised in this chapter, has written of graffiti writers' experience with the art world.

> In some parts of the artworld . . . the intruders were reminded that their real place was in the streets. They were . . . often seen as "primitives" taken out of their element to play for a while in the "civilized" artworld. The very real danger and extralegality of graffiti made in the subway and the streets . . . were considered "natural" for young artists of color. God forbid they be allowed too comfortable circumstances within which to work, sell their art, and learn the ways of these new contexts so their work could continue to grow. (1990: 161)

As a result, Lippard continued, "The great parties, trips to Europe, and cross-class flirtations were short-lived. Most of the gifted, powerful artists 'discovered' during that brief heyday were ushered out when the party was over" (1990: 162).

Graffitists were represented by the art world not only as public and illegal but as democratic to the point of lacking any differentiation. Among the beliefs most damaging to graffiti's chances of survival in the art world was that expressed by Tony Shafrazi, a gallery owner asked by Elizabeth Hess why he stopped exhibiting graffiti art: "Real graffiti is done by kids 11 to 14 in public places. Some of the artists incorporated graffiti images into their work the same way environmental artists used dirt. . . . It's a populist idea, I have no interest in it" (1987: 39). Here graffiti is viewed not only as essentially public but as dirt (natural, authentic raw material) and as populist—in a word, as folk art. The folk artist is typically equated with nature, egalitarianism, and collectivism; the professional artist with culture, individualism, and hierarchy.[4] Sensitive analyses of folk art worlds reveal them to be just as disciplined and discriminating as those of the fine arts, yet because the so-called folk arts allow for a wider scope of participation, they tend to be devalued (financially and aesthetically) by the mainstream art world. As Howard Becker expressed, folk art "is stigmatized . . . as being too connected with the everyday life of common people to be treated as the special work of gifted people" (1982: 368).

The depiction of graffiti writers as undifferentiated folk artists ignored the fact that graffiti's art world, like the mainstream art world, involved competition for limited recognition and resources. The handful of graffiti writers who were briefly picked up by the mainstream art world were indeed unusual: They were among the few who had dedicated the most time and effort to the form and produced some of its finest examples, and they were admired throughout graffiti's art world. This is why comments such as the one by Shafrazi quoted earlier are insidious: In the guise of supporting popular art, they disauthenticate the work of some of the most talented and respected graffitists, the few who had gained some real reward from their work.

## GRAFFITI AS PRIVATE ART

In contrast to the art world's construction of graffiti as essentially public, illegal, and undifferentiated, I argue that graffiti writers often conceived of what they did as private art. Graffiti can be seen as private art in three senses. First, graffiti art was often circulated among writers through nonpublic media, such as papers and books. Second, writers often sought opportunities to perform their art legally and for profit. Third, even when graffiti was done publicly and illegally, there were many proprietary, restrictive aspects to this practice.

In making this argument, I refer to interviews I conducted with twenty-one Philadelphia graffiti writers in summer 1986. I met most of these individuals through my work with the West Philadelphia Improvement Corps (WEPIC), a neighborhood beautification project that worked with about sixty high school students at three sites in West Philadelphia. When I got to know the students and began to ask about graffiti writers, I found that many students on the project admitted to having written graffiti and agreed to discuss their activities with me. A few other writers were contacted through the Philadelphia Anti-Graffiti Network (AGN). The sample ranged from local, little-known writers to some of the most prolific, well-known writers in the city. This was not a random sample, but I have no reason to believe it was severely biased toward any particular type of graffitist.

I prepared a list of questions for the interviews concerning the graffiti writers' social network, message system, and intended audience. Most of the interviews, however, were semiconversational, with much probing and often much continued conversation after the formal interview. An objection might be raised about my use of interviews with Philadelphia graffitists to make an argument about an art world that was largely centered in New York City, but a reading of prior ethnographies of New York graffitists (Castleman, 1982; Lachmann, 1988) shows that the patterns of behavior in the two cities are similar, and I cite these past studies at appropriate points to corroborate my own claims.

## Circulation of Work

It must first be admitted that graffiti writers highly value public visibility and quantity. A prime measure of "rep," or status, among writers is how often one gets one's name around—that is, one's sheer prolificity or output, particularly in visible and hard-to-reach locations. This is one side of the issue, the side most often stated. The other side, usually ignored, is how often graffitists work on paper. First, there is an interaction between private and public work. Often the public work is practiced and blueprinted on paper, especially if an elaborate piece or a mural is planned. Younger writers develop their style on paper before they begin writing on walls (many begin experimenting with graffiti art in their preteens).

But work on paper does not merely serve as preparation or template for work on walls; paper is itself an important medium for graffiti art. Public graffiti writing is fraught with obstacles. Executing a piece publicly requires a huge amount of paint and more time than writers can spare without risk of arrest. If one does manage to procure the paint and avoid the police long enough to complete a public piece, it's likely to be painted over by cleanup crews from groups such as the AGN or crossed out by rival graffitists.

For these reasons, most of the writers I spoke with told me they did most of their pieces in miniature on notebook paper or in "piece books" (cf. Castleman, 1982: 21). One writer said, "If you really wanted to catch all the graffiti writers, you could—you just grab up all the notebooks in the school." Piece books and notebooks serve not only for individual practice but also for circulation of work among writers: "You pass it down from group to group, and everybody's hits be in there." Writers sometimes carry out challenges, or "verses," in their books, executing pieces side by side and consulting a third writer to judge whose is best. A piece book can also serve as a portfolio or a book of references in graffiti's status game: "You get all the autographs you can, then show it to somebody who has a lot of rep." The importance of the work on paper is evidenced by two interviewees who wrote exclusively on paper and still considered themselves graffiti writers.

Graffiti on paper can be seen as backstage communication among writers, allowing them to hone their styles and work out status distinctions out of the public's sight. Interestingly, even graffiti on public walls often has a backstage character. Although visibility in public graffiti is prized, open spots involve added risk of being caught. For this reason, much of the public piecing takes place at inconspicuous locations; for instance, I was told of an abandoned warehouse in North Philadelphia that served at one time as a base for writers and a locale for "piece parties" and competitions. (New York writers, who worked primarily in the subway train yards and layups, had the advantage of both low visibility for themselves and high visibility for their work.)

Graffiti styles also circulate through other private media in addition to the writers' work on paper—specifically through books, movies, and schools. When asked how they got into graffiti, a number of writers said they realized they had artistic talent and began practicing in graffiti style in art class at school. Writers are generally aware of graffiti's historical development and are familiar with the work of the more renowned New York writers. Philadelphia writers could not acquire this knowledge firsthand; it came by way of books such as *Subway Art* (Cooper and Chalfant, 1984) and *Spraycan Art* (Chalfant and Prigoff, 1987) and movies such as *Wild Style, Beat Street,* and *Style Wars.* A supposedly public, mobile, and unfixed form, by the mid-1980s graffiti was in fact centered largely on fixed, commercial texts. One writer said, "Most pieces in Philadelphia have been techniques taken from New York since the big splurge of books came out." At the same time, writers were eager to individualize themselves, to distance themselves somewhat from the New York scene and avoid accusations of "biting" from New York writers.

### Legal, For-Profit Graffiti

There is much evidence to support the view that graffiti is an essentially illegal activity. Graffiti writers often proudly portray themselves as outlaws. They brag of their prowess in evading the police and in stealing paint and markers (cf. Lachmann, 1988: 235). Indeed, for some writers legal graffiti is a contradiction in terms. One writer told me that if graffiti were legal, "It wouldn't be no more fun. Then everybody could be able to do it." He disparaged those who wrote on paper or any medium other than public walls as "bookworms."

But this view is countered by endless examples of legal, profitable graffiti. Almost all of the writers I interviewed had either made money through graffiti at some point or knew others who had (cf. Castleman, 1982: 70–71, 116–133; Lachmann, 1988: 244). It would be difficult to argue that this was any less legitimate or authentic a practice than the illegal work.

Some of the writers' activities resembled those of mainstream artists of the high-art and commercial art worlds. One writer in my sample, Donald Ameci ("Prink"), had been paid to do a record cover and a magazine cover and had attended art school briefly until financial problems forced him to drop out. There were a few exhibits of local graffitists in Philadelphia in the early 1980s, and a number of local writers appeared in Chalfant and Prigoff's *Spraycan Art* (1987). The writers I spoke to considered graffiti to be a legitimate art form and resented the lack of attention accorded graffiti artists, especially those in Philadelphia, by the mainstream art world. When asked about graffiti in the art galleries, one writer said, "When they do that, they get paid for it. And once they do it, we want to do it. But we can't, because we don't know the right people." Another "king" of Philadelphia graffiti, Randall Sykes ("Ran"), asserted that "spray paint is a new art . . . we should be rich off it."

But work obtained through mainstream commercial and gallery channels represents a fraction of graffitists' for-profit efforts. Most such activities are part of a local economy that has remained invisible to many of graffiti's critics. Many of my interviewees had been paid to decorate clothing, party invitations, stereo equipment, and the interiors of homes with graffiti art. Some, like Ran, considered this a serious business and intended to expand their efforts.

> I'm gonna always do things for people on the side, continue doing artwork, people's basements, patios, whatever, on a house, the side of a van, t-shirts, stores. And as it builds up, I'll get better and better stuff, and my art will get better, and maybe I can get inside a shopping mall, inside of a warehouse or something, mac trucks—which I will do, because I have that much confidence, and I have a way of giving a person what they want. No matter what their race, color or whatever, I can give them a picture that they'll like.

Another source of income for some graffitists comes from murals outside of businesses and private homes. In the mid-1980s, some sections of Northeast and West Philadelphia were scattered with legal graffiti-style murals. Business and home owners often commission these works because they feel they discourage other graffiti, particularly the quick signatures, or "tags," the public finds so loathsome. Although this art is public in a literal sense, it is not the illegal, transgressive form of public art usually associated with graffitists. Writers such as Eric Furness ("Sub"), who had done several signs for businesses, preferred it this way: "The best piece you can do is a legal piece, broad daylight, have all your equipment and stuff, then you don't gotta worry about nobody running behind you and chasing you or nothing like that."

Only a few of my interviewees had acquired this type of work, but many others aspired to do so. Graffiti writers, even as they work illegally, concoct all sorts of publicly and privately funded schemes for legal murals. They dream up city-wide competitions for mural commissions judged by local art experts. They persistently claim that legal, paid murals would eliminate graffiti, especially tags, which they readily see as the dark side of graffiti.

> If they would focus a place for it, if they would take a building downtown and say, "Alright, you want a spot? Alright, Zare," and give it to him, and give him the cans, I swear, they could stop so much graffiti. (Dean)
>
> If you get the main graffiti writers to do murals and pay them to do murals, when they put the mural up and tag their names at the bottom, you won't see no other graffiti writer touch that. (Tane)

Proposals by graffiti writers for paid public murals can be viewed as attempts to circumvent the established channels of public arts funding, through which the writers would have little chance of succeeding because of lack of contacts, lack of familiarity with the proposal process, and lack of access to the vocabulary of the mainstream art world. (Compare Castleman's [1982: 132, 177] description of proposals submitted by New York graffiti writers to the Metropolitan Transit Authority for legal, paid murals on subway trains.) Occasionally, writers have succeeded in convincing public authorities to fund their work, as when Randall Sykes was paid to do graffiti-style murals outside the James Rhodes School in West Philadelphia, and the murals have remained free of tags.

A final source of income that must be mentioned in connection with graffiti includes publicly funded beautification and anti-graffiti projects such as WEPIC and AGN. From the perspective of those who view graffiti as essentially public and illegal, writers who join these groups can only be described as traitors and sellouts, yet many are happy to join. The Anti-Graffiti Network was innovative in recognizing that city government could work with graffiti writers. Those who credit AGN with wiping out graffiti (or drastically reducing it) fail to mention that many young people gained something from the arrangement that they would not have had otherwise: summer jobs.

Even when they were employed by them, the writers regularly criticized AGN and WEPIC on two points. First, the organizations refused to allow graffiti-style murals. One writer employed by WEPIC complained that the project supervisor "wants me to write 'Lea School,' he's talking about box letters. Box letters were played out a long time ago. . . . At least do a New Yorker graffiti 'Lea,' have it in cursive and all that, and they probably won't go over that." Graffiti styles were anathema to the supervisors, who claimed they would encourage more graffiti. (Writers claimed the opposite, that project murals were written over because they were "corny.")[5]

The writers' second grievance was that the projects had no respect for graffiti's status system. Two professional artists were employed full time by AGN to supervise all murals, whereas in the graffiti world high-status writers would often supervise low-status writers, the former doing the outlines and the latter filling them in. Writers criticized AGN's employment and job assignment policies. One writer complained, "They hire people like Knife, who's never done any painting in his life," and another, a former AGN employee, said, "They never really put me nowhere where I could use my talent; it was always like sweeping streets clean." Nevertheless, for many writers AGN, which treated them as an undifferentiated group of laborers, was at least a step up from being treated as an undifferentiated group of criminals.

## Proprietary Aspects of Public Graffiti

Even when graffiti appears on public walls illegally, it is by no means a completely unrestricted or undifferentiated practice. Public graffiti is not considered to be public domain by the writers; they are extremely possessive about the styles and designs they create. Almost every writer informed me of the prohibition against "biting" in the graffiti world: "Some writers get real offended if you just copy a letter of theirs or something and use it for your name." In response to biting, the person whose style is appropriated will cross out the offender's work (cf. Castleman, 1982: 24).

In view of their possessiveness about their work, it is not surprising that one of the graffitists' favorite symbols is the copyright sign. Graffiti writers like to represent their world as a self-regulating system in which derivative work is immediately checked: "Automatically, in the graffiti world, they'll be like 'that looks like one of Prink's letters,' or 'that looks like Sub's style. You better make up your own style.'" There are certain circumstances in which the appropriation of another writer's style or content is sanctioned; for instance, among writers who belong to the same graffiti club. In one isolated but interesting example, a writer told me he would "sell letters" written on paper to younger graffitists who needed help with their style.

The trouble is that despite the ban on biting, there is no way to enforce intellectual property on public graffiti. One young writer, describing a design of which he was particularly proud, said, "If I was to write that on the wall, you can't hide it, you know? Somebody else is gonna do it, and you can't prove that you made it up." This is another reason some writers chose to keep their designs under wraps: "Soon I'm gonna make something else up, but I'm gonna just keep it to myself on paper, and . . . if somebody wants to hold my book, I'll just go over to their house and let them see it, and then I'll take it back so he can't get the vivid imagination that he wants." Another writer, this one well-known, showed me his sketchbook and told me, "Everybody in the city saw my stuff, but they never saw my *best* stuff. I never pulled out any of this stuff for the writers."

Graffiti writers are much more discriminating than the model of graffiti as homogeneous folk art portrays them. In fact, they have a highly differentiated status system. Graffiti writers range from those who occasionally pick up a can and write if one is available to those who eat, sleep, and breathe graffiti. Writers who have invested time and effort in graffiti are quick to distinguish the "kings" and "masters" of graffiti from the "toys" and "wanna-bes" (cf. Castleman, 1982: 78ff; Lachmann, 1988: 242). Status distinctions are often worked out through formal competition, which usually takes the form of a challenge, or verse.

Writers will only accept challenges from others who are nearly equal to them in status: "Certain kids, they see my name and they want to verse me. The majority of times, I don't even waste my time, but with somebody real good, I'll probably give them a go on a verse." Competition is often encouraged between up-and-coming writers in order to settle status distinctions: "There was Klik and this boy named Jack. I said, 'Klik, come here a minute,' and he came over, and I called Jack. They said, 'Prink, what do you want, man?' I said, 'I think you two should have a little battle.' They looked at each other like, 'Oh, man.' But see, I knew they wanted to battle each other."

Although I would not want to argue this point conclusively on the basis of the available evidence, it can be suggested that public graffiti and the status system associated with it function not only to apportion fame within the community of graffiti writers but also to prepare and validate them for the wider, more profitable fame that can accrue from private, commercial work outside the graffiti community. Top writers consider it important that graffitists be authorized by their peers before they go on to outside work. As Prink said, "You can't just learn graffiti; you've gotta learn it the hard way. I came up through the ranks; it was rough." The term *bookworm* is applied disapprovingly not to any graffitist who writes on paper but to those who move on to private and commercial media before proving themselves on public walls, where their work is accessible to the entire community of writers.

Once writers have so proven themselves and have distinguished themselves as kings of graffiti, however, they often move on to a wider audience with the backing of the graffiti community. Among the writers I interviewed, the ones who had been the most successful in acquiring remuneration for artwork, murals, clothing decoration, and similar activities were those most often mentioned as kings of graffiti by fellow writers—people like Ran, Prink, and Sub. Other writers spoke of the achievements of these individuals with pride. Among the Philadelphia writers who appeared in the 1984 Kennel Club exhibition and in Chalfant and Prigoff's *Spraycan Art* (1987) were other acknowledged kings and masters of the local graffiti scene—writers with names like Espo, Pep, Parish, MB, Pez, and Mr. Blint, all of whom were mentioned as kings by some of my interviewees. In New York City as well, the graffitists who received commercial work and were courted by the art world were all acknowledged masters—writers like Lee Quinones, who, according to Castleman, "appears to be respected and admired by all of the writers in the city" (1982: 20).

Hence, even public, illegal graffiti can be viewed as functional in distinguishing those worthy to move on to private, paid work. It provides writers with an opportunity to develop their technique in a forum visible to their peers and to acquire authorization to serve as the graffiti community's liaisons to a wider audience. However, this system, insofar as it can be called a system, is far from perfect. Laborious pieces are often whitewashed by AGN or crossed out by fellow writers soon after completion. Styles are appropriated, and disputes over status abound. If a writer does succeed in surmounting all of these difficulties and joining the ranks of graffiti's masters, often the rewards aren't there. Graffiti writers are still labeled criminals by the majority of the public, and the few rewards that can be gained from graffiti art sometimes go to people who have not come out of the writers' community.

These were the points cited by those who worked for AGN and had given up public writing. Generally, they decided graffiti was wasteful, pointless, and simply did not pay:

> They can think they're kings all they want, but there's nobody there to crown them, so they're nothing; they're just another person. If they had a name like DuPont, I'd give them some respect, but come on. (Rocco)

I was like, "Man, I gotta meet him because he's a king," and all that. But now it's not like that. I don't write on walls, so he ain't benefiting my life, he ain't putting money in my pocket. . . . Who I consider king now is when you get a job and you got money in your pocket, that's the king. (Drak)

## CONCLUSION

In this chapter I have attempted to contrast the art world's perspective on graffiti with that of graffiti writers themselves. Many art world members read graffiti as an attempt to aestheticize everyday life, democratize art production, and challenge the dominant culture's property boundaries. Consequently, they dismiss graffiti art on canvas as a betrayal of graffiti's street life. In contrast, graffiti writers often work on private media and attempt to deploy their skills for profit; even their public work has a proprietary character and, I would argue, serves in part to validate the most deserving envoys to a larger public.

The view of graffiti as essentially illegal public art has been espoused not only by critics in the art press and the popular press but also by academic theorists of art and the social sciences. For instance, Susan Stewart has argued:

Graffiti attempts a utopian and limited dissolution of the boundaries of property. Within the manufactured environment of the city, it points to the false juxtaposition by which the artistic is made part of the private and domestic while its figure or referent stands outside in nature. . . . Graffiti may be a petty crime, but its threat to value is an inventive one, for it forms a critique of the status of all artistic artifacts, indeed a critique of all privatized consumption. (1987: 175)

Similarly, Hal Foster (1985) followed Jean Baudrillard (1976) in representing public graffiti as "code scrambling," an attempt to interfere with the sign system of private property. He condemned graffiti art in galleries as "the subversion of the subversive" (p. 49): "Like the cartoons and comics in much East Village art, graffiti art is concerned less to contest the lines between museum and margin, high and low, than to find a place within them" (p. 52). Here again, graffiti artists' proprietary inclinations are regarded as evidence of the watering down of graffiti's initially pure, public instincts.

The implicit model behind most critics' and theorists' responses to graffiti seems to derive from subcultural theory. By virtue of its public context, graffiti is viewed as an expression of resistance to the dominant culture by working-class youth, and any attempts by graffiti writers to turn a profit from their labors are seen as commodified appropriations of this oppositional impulse. Such a reading denies legitimacy to the few graffiti writers who were able to gain some marginal control over the economic value of their work for a short time. No one would deny that there is an element of resistance behind much graffiti—with good reason, considering the material circumstances from which most writers originate. But there is much more to their art than this and to so reduce it belittles it. If anything, it is the art critics and theorists who have "appropriated" graffiti to fulfill their fantasies of a radical public art form.

I would suggest that it is more realistic and constructive to view graffiti writers not as a subculture but as a group of amateur artists, comparable to the amateur musicians studied by Ruth Finnegan (1989) in Milton Keynes, England. The term *amateurs* is not limited to musicians or artists who work without pay. Many of Finnegan's musicians had profited from live performances and recordings, and she reminds us, crucially, of the *continuum* between amateur and professional art worlds. But what most distinguishes this group is not their achievements but their aspirations, because Finnegan makes a point of rebutting the subculture theorists' view of rock and pop as primarily protest music:

> Most bands did not seem to see protest as in any sense their main purpose, even though they were keen to express their own personal views through their music. Again and again they stressed the comradeship of playing together in a band, the great feel of being on stage, "giving people pleasure and excitement," self-expression, an outlet for their energy and expertise, making people think about their views and their music, getting some public recognition and, for some but not all, one day becoming professional musicians. (p. 127)

These same rewards—sociability, aesthetic display, recognition, status, and possible financial gain—were the ones mentioned to me by graffiti writers far more often than any form of protest. The art world could do more good by helping graffiti writers and other amateur artists achieve these goals than by imposing its own agenda upon them.

## NOTES

1. My analysis of the art world's representations of graffiti art does not claim to be systematic or exhaustive. I have been selective in my choice of evidence, if only because of space limitations, yet I am convinced that the evidence I cite coheres into one common view of graffiti art that was important in deciding its institutional path.

2. None of these terms seems quite right, precisely because all of them tend to be devalued or marginalized by the world of high art.

3. Although this issue is not my principal concern, the racial stereotypes in some of these quotations are too blatant to let pass without noting.

4. John Michael Vlach (1986) listed adjectives frequently used to identify folk art: "primitive, naive, amateur, grass-roots, outsider, country, popular, backyard, spontaneous, unsophisticated, innocent, provincial, anonymous, visionary, homemade, vernacular, isolate, ethnic, non-academic" (p. 14). Also see Henry M. Sayre (1992) for a brief history of the application of another common folk art term, *authentic*, to graffiti. He stated, "Graffiti seemed to many completely unmediated" (p. 142).

5. Cf. Jeff Ferrell (1993: 178–186) for an extended account of a similar stylistic conflict between artists and authorities over public murals in Denver.

## REFERENCES

Adorno, T. E. (1967). Valery Proust Museum. In T. E. Adornor, *Prisms*. London: Neville Spearman, pp. 173–186.

Alinovi, F. (1983). Twenty-First Century Slang. *Flash Art* 114 (November), pp. 23–27.

Alloway, L. (1975). The Expanding and Disappearing Work of Art. In L. Alloway, *Topics in American Art Since 1945*. New York: Norton, pp. 207–212.

Baudrillard, J. (1976). Kool Killer ou l'insurrection par les signes. In J. Baudrillard, *L'echange symbolique et la mort*. Paris: Editions Gallimard, pp. 118–128.

Becker, H. S. (1982). *Art Worlds*. Berkeley: University of California Press.

Castleman, C. (1982). *Getting Up: Subway Graffiti in New York*. Cambridge, Mass.: MIT Press.

Chalfant, H., and J. Prigoff (1987). *Spraycan Art*. London: Thames and Hudson.

Chapple, S., and R. Garofalo (1977). *Rock and Roll Is Here to Pay*. Chicago: Nelson-Hall.

Cooper, M., and H. Chalfant (1984). *Subway Art*. New York: Henry Holt.

Crimp, D. (1983). On the Museum's Ruins. In H. Foster, ed., *The Anti-Aesthetic*. Seattle: Bay Press, pp. 43–56.

Duncan, C. (1983). Who Rules the Art World? *Socialist Review* 13(4) (July/August), pp. 99–119.

Ferrell, J. (1993). *Crimes of Style: Urban Graffiti and the Politics of Criminality*. New York: Garland Publishing.

Finnegan, R. (1989). *The Hidden Musicians: Music-Making in an English Town*. New York: Cambridge University Press.

Fisher, P. (1975). The Future's Past. *New Literary History* 6(3) (Spring), pp. 587–606.

Foster, H. (1985). Between Modernism and the Media. In Hal Foster, *Recodings: Art, Spectacle, and Cultural Politics*. Port Townsend, Wash.: Bay Press, pp. 33–57.

Gablik, S. (1982). Report from New York: The Graffiti Question. *Art in America* 71 (October), pp. 33–39.

Glueck, G. (1983). On Canvas, Yes, but Still Eyesores. *New York Times*, December 25, sec. 2, p. 22.

Goldin, A. (1975). United Graffiti Artists at Artists Space. *Art in America* 63 (November), pp. 101–102.

Goldstein, R. (1980). The Fire Down Below. *Village Voice*, December 30, pp. 55–56.

Hauser, A. (1951). *The Social History of Art*. New York: Alfred A. Knopf.

Hess, E. (1987). Graffiti R.I.P.: How the Art World Loved 'Em and Left 'Em. *Village Voice*, December 22, pp. 37–41.

Hughes, R. (1980). *The Shock of the New*. New York: Alfred A. Knopf.

Janis, S. (1983). *Post-Graffiti*. New York: Sidney Janis Gallery.

Kuspit, D. B. (1985). Crash and Daze at Janis. *Art in America* 73 (February), p. 138.

Lachmann, R. (1988). Graffiti as Career and Ideology. *American Journal of Sociology* 94(2) (September), pp. 229–250.

Linker, K. (1984). "Post-Graffiti," Sidney Janis Gallery. *Artforum* 22 (March), p. 92.

Lippard, L. (1973). *Six Years: The Dematerialization of the Art Object from 1966 to 1972*. New York: Praeger.

———. (1984). The Geography of Street Time: A Survey of Streetworks Downtown. In Lucy Lippard, *Get the Message? A Decade of Art for Social Change*. New York: E. P. Dutton, pp. 52–66.

———. (1990). *Mixed Blessings: New Art in a Multicultural America*. New York: Pantheon.

Mailer, N. (1974). *The Faith of Graffiti*. New York: Praeger.

Moufarrege, N. (1982a). Lightning Strikes (Not Once But Twice): An Interview with Graffiti Writers. *Arts Magazine* 57 (November), pp. 87–93.

———. (1982b). Another Wave, Still More Savagely Than the First: Lower East Side, 1982. *Arts Magazine* 57 (September), pp. 69–73.

Parks, A. (1982). One Graffito, Two Graffito. *Arts Magazine* 57 (September), p. 73.

Quindlen, A. (1982). About New York: The M.T.A.'s Poison Becomes a Gallery's Art. *New York Times*, February 6, p. 27.

Raynor, V. (1991). "Hip Hop" Moves Closer to Respectability. *New York Times*, March 3, p. 22.

Saul, J. (1984). Post Graffiti, Sidney Janis. *Flash Art* 116 (March), pp. 38–39.

Sayre, H. M. (1992). Pursuing Authenticity: The Vernacular Moment in Contemporary American Art. *South Atlantic Quarterly* 91(1) (Winter), pp. 139–160.

Sozanski, E. (1984). Art: Bringing Graffiti Inside. *Philadelphia Inquirer*, April 27, pp. D1, D3.

Stewart, S. (1987). Ceci Tuera Cela: Graffiti as Crime and Art. In J. Fekete, ed., *Life After Postmodernism:Essays on Value and Culture*. New York: St. Martin's Press, pp. 161–180.

Vlach, J. M. (1986). "Properly Speaking: The Need for Plain Talk About Folk Art. In J. M. Vlach and S. J. Bronner, eds., *Folk Art and Art Worlds*. Ann Arbor: UMI Research Press, pp. 13–26.

Wolff, J. (1981). *The Social Production of Art*. New York: New York University Press.

# 12

# Animation Art:
# The Fine Art of
# Selling Collectibles

### WILLIAM MIKULAK

IN 1984 CHRISTIE'S EAST in New York City held an auction devoted solely to art used in the production of Disney features and shorts from the 1930s and 1940s. The nearly four hundred pieces, all from the collection of retired Disney animator John Basmajian, grossed $543,620, far in excess of the preauction estimates (Mehren, 1984). This sale became legendary in animation art collecting circles as the pivotal event that legitimated animation as an art form worthy of serious consideration and monetary investment (Solomon, 1989: 299; Tumbusch, 1989: 65; Zamora, 1990). Since that time, a series of record-breaking auction bids has stimulated press coverage, as pieces of art that had once sold as souvenirs at Disneyland for under $2 were suddenly commanding thousands of dollars, and prices were rising at an annual rate of 25 percent to 30 percent according to animation dealer Howard Lowery (quoted in O'Brian, 1990).

News stories on the animation art market peaked after two long-standing records were set in 1989: the private-sale record of $450,000, paid for artwork from the production of the 1934 Disney short, *Orphan's Benefit*, as well as the auction-house record of $286,000 for production art from another scene in the same cartoon (Egan, 1990; Hadad, 1991; O'Brian, 1990; Peers, 1991; Reif, 1992; Rohter, 1990; Wasserman, 1992; Zamora, 1990). Although the latter piece sold for only $88,000 when it was returned to auction in 1992, the lower end of the market has continued to grow in volume despite the recession as more dealers and collectors enter the market. The broad market sells pieces that range in price from less than $100 to tens of thousands of dollars.

The term *animation art* encompasses a wide range of artwork that is created for the production of animated films as well as related art designed expressly for sale. The primary type of production art sold is the clear plastic cel (short for celluloid), on which characters, foreground objects, and special effects are painted. As animated films are photographed frame by frame, up to twenty-four incremental paintings of each character are required to produce a single second of film. The transparent plastic allows the same background painting to be used underneath thousands of cels over the course of a scene. Prior to the creation of the camera-ready art, many preparatory sketches, paintings, and sometimes sculptures are made. Model sheets are created to offer animators consistent guides to drawing characters in different perspectives and positions. Animation teams then create the drawings from which the cels are traced and painted.

Until the escalation of prices, studios saw production art as a by-product of their primary commodity, the animated films, and they destroyed most of the art as a matter of course after the films were completed. Enough art survived through a variety of art marketing ventures, studio artists' personal collections, and adventurous trash pickers to feed collector interest prior to the boom. Given the mode of production, cels are much more common than background paintings and have been marketed without backgrounds, with hand-prepared backgrounds, and with reproduction backgrounds. When cels are overlaid on the production backgrounds against which they were originally photographed, the backgrounds are called "master backgrounds," and the ensemble is a "key setup." Both of the record-breaking *Orphan's Benefit* pieces were key setups.

The increased demand for animation art is being met by the creation of non-production art. Numerous companies have gained licenses from character copyright holders to produce new art to supplement the dwindling supply of vintage production art. The most prevalent form of new art is the limited edition hand-painted cel, usually with a reproduction background. Other nonproduction art ranges from unlimited scene cels to serigraph cels to lithographs. The images depicted may be re-creations of particular film scenes or new presentations of recognized characters. Other ancillary art includes cels created for publicity purposes and artwork for posters, books, theme parks, comic strips, and similar uses.

## FINE ART OR COLLECTIBLE?

With such a booming market, the emphasis on top prices can easily obscure issues of aesthetic evaluation. To determine how the sale of animation art is related to the legitimation of animation as art, I compare this particular market to those of fine art and popular collectibles. In many ways, animation art is circulated much as fine art is—within a network of dealers, collectors, investors, galleries, auction houses, and museums. In some cases the same organizations function in both markets; for example, the Circle Gallery chain displays animation art amid other aesthetic objects, and the auction houses Christie's and Sotheby's place animation art with collectibles in their specialty departments (Dobrzynski, 1990; interview with Arfer, 1992; interview with Hawkes, 1992). Certain art museums also consecrate animation art along with other art, whether through temporary exhibitions, such as the Museum of Modern Art's Warner Bros. exhibit in 1985 (Corliss, 1985), or by permanent acquisition, such as the Metropolitan Museum of Art's purchase of Disney art (Maltin, 1982). This institutional approbation occurs both by bestowing the museum's considerable prestige on each piece it collects and by increasing the scarcity of similar works once a piece is off the market (Becker, 1982: 116; "More Money Than Art," 1987).

Additionally, several criteria for evaluation obtain for both animation art and fine art: artistic reputation, scarcity, authenticity, medium, and condition of the work. Of these, scarcity, authenticity, and condition are also integral to the collectibles market. Most highly sought are Disney production artworks from the early 1930s shorts because they combine the magic name of Disney at a most vibrant era of creativity with the rarity of these old black-and-white paintings (Egan, 1990; Rohter, 1990; Zamora, 1990). Although the animation art market generally accords artistic reputation to studios rather than individuals, some artists such as Chuck Jones of Warner Bros. (Altyn, 1991) and Carl Barks of Disney Studios (Blum, 1992) are recognized for their distinctive work. Thus, their names and signatures are a marketing advantage for limited edition art they produce involving the characters of their respective studios.

For both animation art and fine art, the value attributed to scarcity is double-edged; it must be coupled with reputation to contribute to an artwork's stature. For example, works from the Depression-era Van Beuren Studio gain little from their rarity because of the studio's relative obscurity (Maltin, 1987: 199–208; Solomon, 1989: 93). However, when scarcity of artwork is combined with continual exposure to the films and increased critical acclaim, prices rise. This confluence of factors has affected vintage Warner Bros. art—a great majority of which was burned in the early 1960s to gain warehouse space—thus boosting prices of vintage cels, drawings, and model sheets above those of all rival studios except Disney (Egan, 1990; "Jones Returning to Animation," 1990; "Warner Goes Wacky!" 1991).

As prices climb, the concern over authenticity has grown. Dealers regard outright forgeries to be much less common than misrepresentation, in which a piece is claimed to be older, rarer, or in better condition than it actually is. Disney alone among major animation studios maintains an archive that offers historical production information crucial to authenticating artwork. Archivist David R. Smith and his staff are often cited for their expertise at answering such questions as which peg-hole registry system was in use at a particular time, what water bond marks should appear, what sequence numbers correspond to which scenes, or what colors were used to paint each character (Brooks, 1990; interview with Leigh, 1990). Additionally, Disney art originally sold by the Courvoisier Galleries from 1937 to 1946 and at Disneyland from 1955 to 1973 comes with labels of authentication.

The lack of authenticating resources from other studios has led to reliance on unofficial experts for identification of artwork. For example, avid Warner Bros.

art collector Stephen Ferzoco is regularly consulted as to what production a piece is from or whether an item is a forgery (interview with Ferzoco, 1992). Thus the current market relies upon disinterested assessments made by interested parties, whose very interest has gained them expertise beyond that of most dealers. However, numerous dealers seek no such assessments because of the risk that their art will lose historical importance, which translates into lower prices.

One attempt to rectify the lack of uniform professional standards among dealers is the founding of the Animation Art Guild in 1990, which serves as a central clearinghouse of information about prices, legal issues, and ethics. Unaffiliated with any gallery or studio, the guild builds collector awareness of unscrupulous business practices, issues bulletins about stolen art, and provides fair-market range estimates for particular pieces. It is run by collectors Michael and Pamela Scoville, who keep their collecting separate from the services they provide and who accept no advertisements in the guild's newsletters (interview with Scoville, 1992). This growth of standards of authentication and professional ethics parallels the development of systematic techniques of attribution in the fine-arts world that are, in the words of sociologist Howard Becker, "a standard part of the value-creating activity" of art worlds (1982: 115).

Paralleling the issue of authentication is that of restoration. Older cels are particularly vulnerable to deterioration because they were made of cellulose nitrate rather than today's standard acetate. They have a tendency to shrink, wrinkle, and yellow. Additionally, paint and ink can crack, chip, and become discolored. Some early cels were laminated to prevent dehydration, but this caused a variety of damaging chemical reactions to occur. Vintage Disney art benefits from the studio's choice of a gum arabic paint binder, the expense and durability of which starkly contrast with the cheap acidic casein binder that erodes the surviving vintage Warner Bros. cels (Halbreich and Worth, 1990).

Several restoration experts have garnered reputations for quality work both for their use of the latest conservation technology to analyze damage and for their knowledge of past production methods to re-create exact paint, ink, and coating formulas. Animation art dealer Heidi Leigh and others claim such restoration does not lower the value and can even raise it (interview with Leigh, 1990; Worth and Stude, 1990). As restorer Janet Scagnelli put it, "Restoration can be a great asset to a piece of artwork when it is done correctly by professional art conservators" (1990: 2). The collectibles market, on the other hand, generally accords a price reduction to items that have been restored (Hughes, 1984: 27–33).

One might argue that restoration serves aesthetic integrity at the expense of collectible integrity, for the visual experience takes precedence over the historical authenticity of the ingredients. Conversely, the historical importance of certain key setups from cherished films places them in the position of benefiting the most from restoration. They are unique embodiments of what Christie's animation expert Joshua Arfer called "magic moments" during a film's narrative, moments that capture the essence of the characters in memorable scenes (interview with Arfer, 1992). According to Sotheby's animation expert Dana Hawkes, the value of restoration is reduced for lesser, more ubiquitous vintage art, such as the many *Snow White* Dwarf cels originally sold by Courvoisier in the 1930s. She claims their availability parallels that of mass-produced collectibles, whose market operates on the assumption that an identical item in better condition may appear in the future (interview with Hawkes, 1992).

Another correspondence to the fine-art market lies in the hierarchy of values accorded to different media. Curator John Carlin reflected a widely held sentiment when he placed painting and sculpture above drawing and the various methods of printmaking and photography, in part because he called the former "the flagship media . . . of the history of art from the Middle Ages through the present time" (1990: 44). This judgment incorporates such criteria as size, cost of materials, investment of time and labor, as well as an endorsement of uniqueness over multiplicity. The general tendency in the animation art market is to rank paintings above drawings, but such a dichotomy fails to account for specific conditions of animation production that have no counterpart in the fine-art market.

## ANIMATION ART AS ARTIFACT

Fine artists produce finished works that are meant for display and consumption. In contrast, the most valuable animation art being sold is that which was meant to be a miniscule portion of a much larger work, the film itself. It is the greatness of the film as a whole that enriches the individual cels and backgrounds as art objects in their own right. As collector Bob Bennett stated, "Aside from its artistic value, cartoon art that is essential or important in making an animated cartoon or strip can have tremendous value" (1987: 16). This is the value of the artifact, the time capsule from the initial filmic experience that first captivated audiences. Vintage animation art embodies this history with its indications of age, resulting in what Janet Scagnelli called a "beautiful warm patina . . . created by the yellowed cel and faded colors" (1990: 2).

This artifactual criterion of value is based on an existential relationship between artwork and film rather than a representational one that iconically maps a sign to its referent. Animation art dealer Pam Martin expressed the lure of production art: "It is historical, a slice of an actual film. You wouldn't have the buttons and pins and all the other animation memorabilia if you didn't have the cartoon first" (interview with Martin, 1990). In the collectibles field, dealer Ted Hake made a similar claim of cultural origination for what he sells: "I only deal in original collectibles; I just like to handle the real thing" (interview with Hake, 1990).

All artworks that are part of the animation production process are tinged with the reflected glow of the entire film, be they inspirational sketches, storyboards, layout drawings, character model sheets or statues, animation drawings, painted cels, or backgrounds. Joshua Arfer stated, "Part of collecting animation [art] is freeze-framing your VCR and finding your cel or concept [sketch] or drawing in there" (interview with Arfer, 1992). Those elements that are actually photographed—the matching cels and master backgrounds—are most highly prized, for they contribute directly to the cinematic spectacle. The emotional bond formed between the audience and the characters plays a central role in the high value placed on cels, the ownership of which is like "buying a heartbeat of Mickey Mouse," according to Disney art collector Peter Merolo (quoted in Zamora, 1990: B1).

The popularity of cels counters the fine-art market's preference for works created by artists over those made by craftsworkers. The staffs of the ink and paint departments that prepare cels are historically among the lowest paid in the animation production hierarchy and have remained anonymous throughout the growth of the animation art market. The work done by the inkers was turned over to xerographic machines in the early 1960s, and Disney feature films since 1990 have replaced cels with computer technology.

The animation art market's pricing structure reveals much less emotional attachment to characters in the form of production drawings than in the form of cels. Lacking the vibrant color of cels, animation drawings do not sufficiently match the character's filmic appearance to warrant such high prices. However, several dealers and high-end collectors share the sentiment expressed by dealer Toni Volk: "The artwork of the drawings is going to be what is here two hundred years from now, what the museums will collect as we go into the future. The cels are a by-product" (interview with Volk, 1992).

These sophisticated members of the market know about the hierarchy of artistic talent within the animation departments, from head animators at the top down through assistant animators, in-betweeners, and cleanup artists. The head animators create the extremes of character motion or emotion, and successively less-skilled artists fill in the positions between extremes. Finally, cleanup artists draw the exact character outlines based on the rough animation drawings. Certain animators, such as the famed Nine Old Men whom Walt Disney anointed, are sought by the knowledgeable collectors, but the production methods in use did not record who did each drawing. Thus the market has difficulty privileging individual artists even when collectors are interested in them.

Background paintings have been accorded much greater monetary validation in the market than have drawings, for reasons that fit both fine-art and collectible evaluative criteria. The high ratio of cels to backgrounds allows much more detail to be included in background art than would be economical for cels. This encourages wider stylistic variations in background paintings than are available for character designs, especially in a studio such as Disney with its adherence to naturalistic animation. Thus it is easier to identify individuals in the layout and background departments who are responsible for specific paintings. In addition, the scarcity of backgrounds in comparison to cels makes an unadorned background a target for a buyer who hopes to find a matching cel in the future.

Among sophisticated collectors who have studied the Disney productions, particular backgrounds by such well-regarded artists as Gustaf Tenggren, Sam Armstrong, Eyvind Earle, and Claude Coats will stir considerable interest, but the cel's marriage to a master background still gives that background a degree of desirability it would not otherwise attain.

## PRODUCTION ART VERSUS
## NONPRODUCTION ART

The animation art market has made room for nonproduction art as the base of collectors has grown and supplies of vintage production art have dwindled. Many studios and character copyright holders have either produced their own limited edition cels or have licensed publishers to do so. Disney, the pioneer of selling animation art in galleries, also produced limited edition cels in the early 1940s before other studies did so. After three of these cels, the studio discontinued the practice until 1974, when it began to re-create scenes from its early classic films (Altyn and Altyn, 1991). Chuck Jones followed suit in 1977, producing portraits of Bugs Bunny and other characters from Warner Bros. cartoons in new poses under license from the studio. The field burgeoned to include artwork by other Warner Bros. directors and their offspring and retired animators from Fleischer studios, MGM, Walter Lantz, Hanna-Barbera, Jay Ward, and smaller studios (Halbreich and Halbreich, 1989). A number of sold-out limited editions have brought considerably more than their initial price upon resale, prompting numerous unscrupulous dealers to promise buyers a high return on their investment in limited edition art.

A number of dealers have expressed preferences for production art but carry limited editions because collectors desire them. Dealer Pam Martin condoned limited editions issued in the absence of surviving material from a notable film, in which case fidelity to the original was the criterion of worth. Whereas she praised the works coming from Bob Clampett Productions for their high-quality evocations of old scenes, she had reservations about the presentation of characters in situations alien to their established personalities (interview with Martin, 1990). Dealer Susan Spiegel expressed concern that collectors might ascribe more importance to the famous signature on the limited edition than to the art itself (interview with Spiegel, 1992).

Disdain for limited edition cels and other nonproduction art increases among market participants at the high end of collecting. These individuals view limited editions as products of "the pop end of the scale, [which] serious collectors scrupulously avoid" (Egan, 1990: 77). Collectibles dealer Stephen Hughes called such limited editions "instant collectibles" that bypass two critical stages through which an item must pass to be a true collectible. Initially, an item must be valued for its utilitarian purpose only; then there must be a steady buildup of collector interest, which increases demand relative to supply. Only after these conditions have been met and there is a broad base of collector support can the item be generally regarded as a collectible; otherwise Hughes feels it lacks "collectible soul" (1984: 13–16).

Yet the limited editions may find redemption as art rather than as collectibles. For instance, now that animation fans recognize Chuck Jones as a consummate artist, his limited editions are current evidence of his artistry. Chris Surico, a dealer and publisher of Fleischer Bros. limited editions, defended Jones's fanciful new interpretations of characters: "When you have someone as talented as [Chuck Jones and Friz Freleng] and they create a scene, it's almost as if they are directing another cartoon" (interview with Surico, 1992). Regarding Disney limited editions, Hake stated, "Disney is a magic name; you're able to call it art. It has the potential of attracting more people, as opposed to Hopalong Cassidy memorabilia. No matter how nice the design, no one calls that art" (interview with Hake, 1990).

What is shared by both production and nonproduction animation art is that whether a piece is ascribed aesthetic value, artifactual value, or both, that piece is a beneficiary of, more than a contributor to, reputation. In other words, the sale of animation art relies on reputations that were previously established as a result of films and characters already created. Whereas fine-art dealers discover new talent, animation art dealers require collectors to recognize the depicted characters through prior exposure to films, television, and ancillary media. Thus the animation art market is dependent upon the institutions of mass-media production, distribution, and exhibition.

This dependence prevents animation art dealers from nurturing animators who are little known, independent, or foreign. Catalogs rarely include works by artists such as Robert Breer, Sandy Moore, Sally Cruikshank, or Suzan Pitt, even though these very names were mentioned by curator John Carlin as artists whose work "may well be among the best art values around" (1990: 41). His advice was intended for neophyte fine-art collectors rather than memorabilia collectors, yet he urged investment in "artists whose work you may admire but which does not fit within currently accepted notions of fine art—i.e., work by animators, cartoonists, graphic artists, and craftspeople" (Carlin, 1990: 41).

In contrast, Bob Bennett's advice to collectors of original cartoon art was to "purchase the works of the most respected cartoonists or animators, not the unknown or neglected" (1987: 13). The basis of this difference in strategy rests on the collector's role promoted within each market. In the context of the fine-arts market, such an investment may be valued as an act of daring in that it attempts to redefine the boundaries of what is considered legitimate art. Sociologist Pierre Bourdieu argued that the success of such an act hinges on the investor's self-assurance in imposing legitimacy upon the artwork (1984: 92). No such aesthetic gambling is rewarded in the animation art market.

Critics play a prominent role in fine-art markets by exhibiting this very self-assurance when pronouncing their judgments upon various artworks displayed in galleries and museums. Their words carry the weight of the highly cultivated taste that reflects their extensive experience with art. In performing a gatekeeping function at the border of the fine-arts world, critics contribute to decisions regarding the allocation of limited resources within that world (Becker, 1982: 135). Given the ever-shifting terrain of avant-garde conventions, critics distinguish the charlatans from the visionaries by divining artistic sincerity and novelty in the absence of such obvious measures as skill, labor, or complexity (Gross, 1973: 135–136).

Animation criticism abounds as well, but critical discourse focuses almost exclusively on the animated productions rather than the artwork that contributes to them. Often reviewers of museum exhibits of animation briefly mention the exhibited graphic materials before focusing on the main subject, the represented studio's films, as was the case with the MOMA Warner Bros. exhibit in 1985 (Burden, 1985; Corliss, 1985; Gelmis, 1985; Givens, 1985; Kaplan, 1985; Putzer, 1985). Museum reviews that discuss the graphics at any length consider them primarily in terms of whether they contribute to an understanding of how animation is created. For example, Steve Schneider's critique of a 1981 touring exhibit *The Moving Image* went so far as to claim "the display is marred by a 'suitable-for-framing' orientation," which he felt negated animation's unique interest as a kinetic art (1981: 123).

This type of judgment contributes to the distinction between animation graphics as artifacts and films as aesthetic objects. One critic, Regina Cornwell, countered this view in her review of the 1981 Whitney Museum exhibit *Disney's Animations and Animators.* Although she paid more attention to the ideology of the installation design than to the images depicted, she praised the display of sketches and drawings because "they reveal a vitality and sense of playfulness very often missing from work from the later stages" (1981: 116). Ironically, Disney Productions was reluctant to exhibit such preliminary work on the theory that the films' mystique would be destroyed. Now, these drawings are coveted works in their own right and are reproduced in coffee-table art books (e.g., Abrams and Canemaker, 1982).

With the exception of these few reviews, much of what passes for aesthetic discussion in the animation art market is limited to broad generalizations regarding the recognition of animation as a legitimate field of art. For example, dealer Luigi Goldberg claimed, "Animation is to art as jazz is to music, one of the few original American art forms" (quoted in O'Brian, 1990: 5), a statement that reflects the ethnocentricity of the market as a whole. Specific aesthetic judgments often consist of nothing more than the declaration that a particular cel or drawing came from a classic cartoon, but what makes it classic is left to others to define.

A few writers do attempt to link the graphics and production methods of animation art. Arlene Shattil made the case that the animation artist operates within a more restricted format than does the painter, because every line must count to define character emotion and action (1988). Another argument along these lines posited that animation art benefits from its initial disposability, because the artists labor as egoless, anonymous craftspeople to create unpretentious works (Schneider, 1990). One more aesthetic judgment stated, "A good production cel is not necessarily one which has the look of a posed portrait, but instead is similar to a candid photograph, capturing the spontaneity of life at a given moment" (Halbreich and Halbreich, 1990).

These arguments are based on the existential relationship between cel and film that accords the film primacy in setting value. Artwork that is produced in the service of a film is judged on no grounds other than its contribution to that film, even though it has been removed from its initial context into a new world of circulation. Animation art market participants essentially ignore the opportunity this relocation provides for reevaluating the artworks as independent entities. Instead, they constantly look backward to what has already been constituted as the golden era of classics, using conventions of the past to assess contemporary animation art being released.

Unremarkably, these are timeworn conventions of representation that offer easily recognizable characters whose emotional appeal is contingent upon the experience of viewing them in theaters or on television. One example of this contingency within the market is the lack of enthusiasm for production cels from the Don Bluth film, *All Dogs Go to Heaven*, although dealers Michael and Jackie Halbreich were not alone when they stated, "The artistry, color, and vitality of these cels will impress the most discriminating animation art collector" (1989: 17). Pam Martin contended that even the extensive art marketing program conducted by the Sullivan-Bluth Studio could not overcome the fact that the film failed to live up to box-office expectations despite the favorable comparisons of its artwork to that of Disney (interview with Martin, 1990).

## PRICING AS AESTHETIC EVALUATION

Another aspect of the animation art market that bears examination is the manner in which dealers routinely discuss value in terms of current and future pricing of pieces. In this chapter I have followed their lead by referring to the pricing hierarchies as a measure of evaluation that often operates in lieu of aesthetic discourse in the market. Because prices have risen so rapidly in recent years, this topic is of central concern to all participants. Several animation art dealers have mixed feelings about the price escalation. Collectibles dealer Ted Hake complained that media publicity caused an influx of investors to drive up prices, making it difficult for him to restock and inhibiting the bulk of collectors of more modest means from obtaining the pieces they want (interview with Haker, 1990). Heidi Leigh claimed that a small circle of investors is actually responsible for most of the record-breaking bids, and she mentioned two effects of the media coverage of their purchases: "On the one hand it's good because the market is getting attention, and it gives substance to claims that this is really valuable art. The downside is that with such heavy hitters, no one else can get close to the best pieces" (interview with Leigh, 1990). Pam Martin was most concerned about the growing number of unscrupulous people entering the market because of the astounding price increases, a concern echoed by Jackie and Michael Halbreich. They suggested that a collector should establish a continuing relationship with a reputable dealer who is authorized by a particular studio to market its artwork (interview with Martin, 1990; Halbreich and Halbreich, 1990).

In general, dealers seem happy to accept price increases as evidence of aesthetic legitimation of animation; thus they prefer to consider their customers as collectors who buy for love rather than as investors speculating on an expanding market. Collectors and dealers alike extol the virtues of displaying the artworks rather than hiding them in a vault while they appreciate. As Disney collector Peter Merolo put it, "Although many of the works that I own have skyrocketed in value, too often the artistry, creativity and imagination of the cels is lost to cold and antiseptic consideration of value" (1990: 1).

As long as the current boom in the animation art market continues, it offers substantial short-term economic gains that are generally absent in the field of fine-art investment. Bourdieu argued that the fine-art market operates on a long-term cycle of economic profit in which only a small proportion of emerging artists will experience a dramatic rise in reputation. In the interim, dealers must disavow economic gain, cultivating instead the symbolic capital of prestige and authority by which they select artists who will eventually be recognized by the art world as geniuses. Thus they engage in euphemized promotional practices to interest critics and important collectors in their stable of artists (Bourdieu, 1986).

The practice of animation art dealers is fundamentally different because their clientele has a general knowledge of the cartoons and characters that are represented in the artworks. Collectors experience an emotional gratification through viewing the cartoons that is easily transferred to the artworks they purchase. This is in direct contrast to the disinterestedness Kant claimed was necessary for aesthetic judgments. The interest of neither pleasure nor moral reason can interfere with such pure judgments in his scheme, and the repercussions of his constraints are felt in the disavowals of interest Bourdieu identified in the fine-art market. By candidly discussing price as a contributor to aesthetic value but also noting the effects of speculation and fraud, animation art dealers may actually subvert the Kantian isolation of aesthetics from its historically contingent social practices.

The history within which the animation art market operates is one that begins with the broad popularity of the films and shows, which is indicated by box-office or ratings-based advertising revenues. This popularity need not occur immediately upon initial release but may grow over successive rereleases, as in the case of *Fantasia*. Over time this economic capital is translated into accumulated cultural capital: Perennial favorites are deemed classics. Thus what was once merely popular is now seen as something more for withstanding the test of time, which indicates intergenerational popularity rather than faddish fashionability.

In contrast, the avant-garde artists of the fine-art market spurn mass popularity, which would mark them as too accessible and as lacking the innovation that will set them apart from previously recognized artists. Additionally, a preoccupation with popularity would indicate an interest in material and social success, which the fine-art market ideology forbids serious artists to have. These constraints have been flouted by many artists and movements in the past three decades, most notably by pop art, conceptualism, neo-pop, and neo-geo (Carlin, 1990: 86–87). However, Bourdieu argued that those artists who challenge established artistic hierarchies by acknowledging such interests make their challenge an artistic act and thus claim for themselves "the monopoly in legitimate transgression of the boundary between the sacred and profane" (1986: 155). Thus fine artists who appropriate popular culture are applauded by the art world for their postmodern aesthetics, but popular culture producers or commercial artists who find inspiration in elite cultural works are accused of creating kitsch. This is the thrust of most criticisms of *Fantasia*; its attempt to make classical music accessible was considered too highbrow by the mass audiences of 1940 and too vulgar for the elite (Cornwell, 1981).

The necessary fact of the animation art market is that it exalts commercial art originally produced for immediate economic returns as popular entertainment. Although the individual pieces hang in galleries, framed like those in the fine-art market, they were created in a different field of cultural production that emphasizes collective contributions to the overall project. This frustrates attempts to seek out the lone artistic genius responsible for the works, as is customary in the fine-art market. The continual violation of conventions that drives the fine-arts market also is lacking in the animation art market, for commercial animation is widely distributed and must operate within the aesthetic conventions shared by a broad audience. Thus a wide portion of the public can feel competent in the aesthetic codes that are utilized in animation; it can communicate meaning to them in a way that much avant-garde art does not.

## ANIMATION ART AS A HYBRID MARKET

In the final analysis the animation art market accentuates aesthetics more than the popular collectibles market does and recognizes artifactual evaluation more than the fine-art market does. Thus it is most comprehensible as a hybrid, an elite collectible market and a popular art market, most of whose investors mean to satisfy nostalgic cravings rather than break the boundaries of aesthetic convention. As Joshua Arfer, the animation art specialist at Christie's East, stated, "Many big buyers collect this material not because they consider animation an art form, but because the Disney films mean something to them" (quoted in Solomon,

1989: 299). This conflicts with the order of events described by Larry Gross regarding an audience's response to an artwork. He claims that their first concern is whether to grant the work legitimacy as art and thus whether to respond to it aesthetically. Only when they have resolved that it is art do they begin to make judgments of quality as well as of personal taste (Gross, 1973: 122). In contrast, most animation art collectors begin to know what they like and proceed to buy it, unconcerned with whether they have bought art.

The animation art market caters to those who wish to purchase a piece of their childhood, memories of which require no aesthetic justification from critics. Thus art depicting 1960s television characters such as the Flintstones is quickly rising in price not only because the cost of the older works of Disney is climbing out of reach but also because younger collectors grew up watching the Hanna-Barbera shows. However, the animation market's price scale shows that collectors continue to bid highest on vintage art from such Disney works as *Snow White*, *Pinocchio*, *Fantasia*, *Dumbo*, *Bambi*, and the 1930s shorts—all of which are routinely grouped together as acclaimed contributors to Disney's "Golden Era" (Lotman, 1990; O'Brian, 1990; Solomon, 1989: 43). Below Disney come such second-tier studios as Warner Bros., MGM, and Fleischer; Walter Lantz, Jay Ward, Hanna-Barbera, and the rest follow, with the usual price distinctions favoring vintage over contemporary art and production over nonproduction art. Thus the animation art market reaffirms prior mainstream canonization, whereas the activity of the market as a whole may serve to focus more attention on animation as an artform. Whether this renewed interest spills over to independent and foreign animation remains to be seen, but presently too many institutional barriers exist for these categories to get the widespread distribution that benefits every piece of animation artwork now being sold.

The manner in which collectors covet their vintage production cels reflects the desire to retain the aura of the original work of art that Walter Benjamin predicted would wither in the face of mechanical reproduction (1979: 855). Because the original is a mass-produced film, he claimed it is endowed with "exhibition value," whose reproducibility makes it universally accessible. However, the animation art market reclaims the film's "cult value" by sacralizing the few remaining prefilmic constituents that can be called unique and handcrafted. As these techniques give way to computer animation, the once-discarded artifacts of cel animation will be subject to even greater bouts of speculative investment than is now the case.

Just as the pinnacle of the fine-art market drowns out aesthetic discourse with exchanges of vast amounts of wealth, so too might the animation art market succumb to capitalist excess at the expense of the art form itself. However, if we can separate our aesthetic responses from those based on owning artifacts, we may consider nonproduction art as consisting of objects that yield similar aesthetic experiences as the vintage production art at a lower cost. Nonproduction artworks are akin to the reproductions Benjamin advocated, and Edward Banfield suggested that when their quality approaches that of the original, it threatens an art world that fetishizes the original as the site of capital accumulation (1982).

## REFERENCES

Abrams, Robert E., and John Canemaker. (1982). *The Treasures of Disney Animation Art.* New York: Abbeville Press Publishers.

Altyn, John. (1991). "Unlimited Editions: Chuck Jones." *In Toon!* 2 (Fall): 6–7, 18–19.

Altyn, John, and D. L. Altyn. (1991). "Unlimited Editions: The Disney Company." *In Toon!* 2 (Summer): 4–5, 22.

Arfer, Joshua. (1992). Assistant Vice President, Collectibles and Animation Art Department, Christie's East. Personal interview with the author in New York City. 13 May.

Banfield, Edward C. (1982). "Art Versus Collectibles." *Harper's*, August, 28–34.

Becker, Howard S. (1982). *Art Worlds.* Berkeley: University of California Press.

Benjamin, Walter. (1979). "The Work of Art in the Age of Mechanical Reproduction." In *Film Theory and Criticism*, ed. Gerald Mast and Marshall Cohen. New York: Oxford University Press, 848–870.

Bennett, Bob. (1987). *Collecting Original Cartoon Art.* Lombard, Ill.: Wallace-Homestead.

Blum, Geoffrey. (1992). "The Disney Art of Carl Barks." *Inside Collector* 2 (July–August): 40–44.

Bourdieu, Pierre. (1984). *Distinction.* Cambridge, Mass.: Harvard University Press.

———. (1986). "The Production of Belief: Contribution to an Economy of Symbolic Goods." In *Media, Culture, and Society*, ed. Richard Collins et al. Beverly Hills: Sage, 131–163.

Brooks, Leslie. (1990). "The Hole Idea: Walt Disney Studios (1928–1986)." *In Toon* 1 (Summer): 2, 4.

Burden, Martin. (1985). "Be Ve-wy, Ve-wy Quiet, It's Wabbit Time at MoMA." *New York Post*, 13 September, 22.

Carlin, John. (1990). *How to Invest in Your First Works of Art.* New York: Yarrow Press.

Corliss, Richard. (1985). "Warnervana." *Film Comment* 21 (November–December): 11–13, 16–19.

Cornwell, Regina. (1981). "Emperor of Animation." *Art in America* 69 (December): 113–120.

Dobrzynski, Judith H. (1990). "A Bigger Canvas for Sotheby's." *Business Week*, 21 May, 134–136.

Egan, Jack. (1990). "The Extremely Lucrative Life of a Cel." *U.S. News and World Report*, 21 May, 76–77.

Ferzoco, Stephen. (1992). Animation art collector. Telephone interview with author. 23 March.

Gelmis, Joseph. (1985). "Ehhh, What's Up, MoMA?" (New York) *Newsday*, 13 September, Part 3, 1, 3.

Givens, Ron. (1985). "Honoring a Daffy Auteur." *Newsweek*, 21 October, 11–12.

Gross, Larry. (1973). "Art as the Communication of Competence." *Social Science Information* 12: 115–141.

Hadad, Herbert. (1991). "Collecting Cartoon Art Is Drawing Enthusiasts and Profits." *New York Times*, 29 September, Section 12, 25.

Hake, Ted. (1990). Proprietor, Hake's Americana and Collectibles. Telephone interview with author. 24 July.

Halbreich, Jackie, and Michael Halbreich. (1990). "Question and Answer Session." *Animation Magazine* 3 (Winter–Spring): 19.

Halbreich, Michael, and Jackie Halbreich. (1989). "What's Up, Doc? The Latest Animation Art Releases." *Animation Magazine* 3 (Fall): 17.

Halbreich, Michael, and Stephen Worth. (1990). "Collecting Animation Art." *Animation Magazine* 3 (Summer): 12.

Hawkes, Dana. (1992). Vice President, Collectibles Department, Sotheby's. Personal interview with author in New York City. 14 April.

Hughes, Stephen. (1984). *Pop Culture Mania: Collecting 20th Century Americana for Fun and Profit.* New York: McGraw-Hill.

Kaplan, Peter W. (1985). "Bugs Bunny at the Modern—Is That All, Folks?" *New York Times,* 11 September, Section C, 25.

Leigh, Heidi. (1990). Director, Animazing Gallery. Telephone interview with author. 25 July.

Lotman, Jeff. (1990). *A Salute to Walt Disney Animation Art: The Early Years: 1928–1942.* Exhibit Catalog, Philadelphia Art Alliance.

Maltin, Leonard. (1982). "The Art of Animation." *Museum* (July–August): 57.

———. (1987). *Of Mice and Magic.* New York: Plume.

Martin, Pam. (1990). President, Cel-ebration! Gallery. Telephone interview with author, 17 July.

Mehren, Elizabeth. (1984). "Disney Art Brings Out the Buyers." *Los Angeles Times,* 10 December, Part 6, 1, 6.

Merolo, Peter. (1990). "Collecting Original Disney Art." *In Toon* 1 (Summer): 1.

"More Money Than Art." (1987). *Economist,* 23 May, 95.

O'Brian, Dave. (1990). "Cartoon Cachet." *New York Daily News,* 7 January, 5.

Peers, Alexandra. (1991). "TV's Simpsons Stir Controversy as They Seek Entry to Art World." *Wall Street Journal,* 6 June, Section C, 1, 17.

Putzer, Gerald. (1985). "Bugs, Porky, Daffy and the Rest Getting Museum Retro Treatment." *Variety,* 17 July, 6, 22.

Reif, Rita. (1992). "Are Cartoons Stills Still a Hot Ticket?" *New York Times,* 12 April, Section 1, 33.

Rohter, Larry. (1990). "Once Movie Trash, Now Worth a Fortune." *New York Times,* 26 May, Section 2, 11, 16.

Scagnelli, Janet. (1990). "Restoration of Vintage Cels." *In Toon* 1 (Spring): 2.

Schneider, Steven. (1981). "The Animated Alternative." *Art in America* 69 (December): 123.

———. (1990). "But Is It Art?" *Bugs Bunny Magazine,* Time-Warner, 16.

Scoville, Michael. (1992). Director, Animation Art Guild. Telephone interview with author. 26 April.

Shattil, Arlene. (1988). "Circle Galleries." *Animation Magazine* 2 (Fall): 13.

Solomon, Charles. (1989). *Enchanted Drawings.* New York: Knopf.

Spiegel, Susan. (1992). Director, Animation Art Resources. Personal interview with author in Philadelphia. 14 March.

Surico, Chris. (1992). Director, Animation Plus! Gallery. Telephone interview with author. 19 March.

"That's Not All, Folks!" (1990). *Variety,* 18 April, 47.

Tumbusch, Tom. (1989). *Tomart's Illustrated Disneyana Catalog and Price Guide.* Radnor, Pa: Wallace-Homestead.

Volk, Toni. (1992). Proprietor, Zip's Toys to Go. Personal interview with author in Ardmore, Pa. 26 March.

"Warner Goes Wacky!" (1991). *In Toon!* 2 (Summer): 14.

Wasserman, Elizabeth. (1992). "What Price Mickey?" *Newsday,* 16 April, Part 2, 64–65.

Worth, Stephen, and Lew Stude. (1990). "The Care and Restoration of Vintage Animation Cels: Vintage Ink and Paint." *Animato!* no. 20 (Summer): 50–51.

Zamora, Jim Herron. (1990). "Cartoon 'Cels' Animate a Sellers' Market." *Wall Street Journal,* 13 August, Section B, 1, 6.

# 13

# Native American Art and Artists in Visual Arts Documentaries from 1973 to 1991

### STEVEN LEUTHOLD

IN THIS CHAPTER I EXAMINE a selection of films and videos that represent nearly twenty years of documentation of Native American visual arts and artists by both natives and nonnatives. A number of issues have emerged in recent writing about Native American visual art and artists that helped frame the analysis of the documentaries. One issue involves the different understanding of art as a social activity and artists as social actors in native cultures versus contemporary Western culture. Over the past five hundred years the role of artists in Western cultures has shifted from an understanding of artists as mere craftspeople to the level of inspired artist or even genius. By way of contrast, many Native American artists, even those working within contemporary styles, often view art as a form of work closely integrated into the flow of everyday life (Eaton, 1989). What underlying assumptions and actual statements about the relationship among art, artists, and life do we find in visual arts documentaries?

A second issue is the breakdown of visual patterns that indicate tribal identity as native artists innovate and also explore ideas from Western art; this development relates to the problematic status of Indianness for artists caught between two worlds. Traditional art forms, with their conventional stylistic elements, provided highly visual markers of identity in times of cultural contact and change. For example, Castle McClaughlin (1987) demonstrated the way stylistic variations in beadwork functioned as a system of boundary marking that indexed a complex series of social realignments among nineteenth-century Plains Indian tribes. Stylistic aspects of artifacts symbolized and supported social boundaries between groups (McClaughlin, 1987: 55). Many of these stylistic properties and other references to traditional aesthetic expression were carried over into Native American painting as it developed during the first half of the twentieth century (Highwater, 1976).

Since the establishment of the Institute of American Indian Arts (IAIA) in Santa Fe in 1962, the youngest generations of Indian artists, many of whom were trained at IAIA, have developed innovative styles and an openness toward subject matter not seen in the work of earlier generations (Strickland, 1985: 39). This does not mean that recent Indian painters have rejected their Indian identity but that the way some artists express identity differs from the highly conventionalized styles and subject matter of their ancestors.

Marketplace influences further complicate the discussion of native art and identity. Early in the development of Indian art markets, conventional aspects of artistic activity—related to both style and subject matter—were read as the traditional visual language of a group. Clearly identifiable visual patterns were a marker of belonging and authenticity. As the market for Indian art and artifacts developed during the early twentieth century, the assumption that Indian art should be "traditional" or "authentic" by readily reflecting the conventional styles or subject matter of a given tribe became embedded in market economics. This development and the related definition of much Indian art as craft within the Western aesthetic system—following from its categorization of media such as pottery, textiles, wood carving, and so forth—has, in many cases, limited the type of art that Indians can successfully market. Native American artists are pressured in the craft marketplace to produce several identical pieces of less monetary value rather than unique, one-of-a-kind pieces that may sell for more in the fine-art marketplace (Eaton 1989). Alternatively, some contemporary Indian artists value innovation in art and hope to make unique pieces rather than produce for a craft market. The question of Indianness can become problematic from both an economic and a conceptual perspective as Indian artists seek to balance their heritage and community identity with their artistic and economic goals.

Visual arts documentaries, then, have been created in an era of active discussion about the relationship between Indian art and identity. These issues—assumptions about the relationship between art and life in native cultures, aesthetic tradition and innovation in relation to artists' understanding of Indianness, and social aspects of artistic production including marketplace forces—serve as touchstones for this discussion of visual arts documentaries. Although the filmmakers' and video makers' conceptual frameworks for presenting native art and artists must be addressed, I downplay stylistic analysis of the films and videos themselves in order to focus on larger issues of Indian art and identity.

## VISUAL ARTS DOCUMENTARIES
## PRODUCED BY NONNATIVES

As a background to the documentation of their own art by Native Americans, I first consider several examples of films by nonnatives. *Oscar Howe: American Indian Artist* (1973), directed by Joan and Sanford Gray, explores the art and career of this pioneer native abstractionist. The film conveys Howe's general philosophy, artistic goals, and methods and includes sketchy biographical material and a lengthy sequence devoted to his paintings. As in the *American Indian Artist Series* produced three years later, the filmmakers concentrate on a single artist. We are exposed to Howe's own explanation of his complex art theory, but his work isn't placed in the context of other Native American art of the period. As is often the case with accounts that focus on a single artist, the director intimates that Howe was especially motivated or endowed with artistic ability almost from birth. Early in the film we see a dramatization of a story told by Howe about his youth when his father, angry about his son's constant drawing, took away his drawing tools, forcing Howe to draw in the earth.

In the film Howe describes his motivation to record Sioux culture as the source of his inspiration. He grounds his contemporary working method of "painting the truth" in traditional hide-painting ceremonies, which employed a technique of imaginary dots to develop the composition. Howe discusses the symbolism of lines, shapes, and colors in Sioux culture and the alignment of art with nature. We learn little about the source of Howe's academic art theory—he was one of the few members of the early generation of painters to obtain an M.F.A.—or of his relationship to other artists, to art history, and to his audience, but the film conveys his unique theory and artistic motivation.

A contrasting orientation of nonnative filmmakers is evident in the series *American Indian Arts at the Phoenix Heard Museum* (1975). This series was produced at KAET-TV, Phoenix, by Jack Peterson and was filmed by Tony Schmitz and Don Cirillo, all of whom worked on the *American Indian Artist Series* that appeared a year later. Surprisingly, for two series of films created by similar personnel within a short span of time, these two series vary widely in approach. The narrated text is weighed down by specialized terms and questions about dates, origins, and attribution, making the script sound like passages read from a textbook.

The survey format of the series approaches the artwork according to medium. As with many traditional surveys, the films strongly emphasize technique and the succession of important artists or styles within a given medium but attend less to the social or cultural function of art. The film perpetuates one traditional Western art historical approach recognized through its survey organization; it is the counterpart to the approach taken in *Oscar Howe: American Indian Artist* (1973), which highlights the achievements of one individual. Some episodes in the Heard Museum series, such as the one about painting, focus on a succession of individuals and styles that is consistent with an art historical approach to "high art." Others, such as the episode on pottery, analyze techniques that were developed and applied by specific tribes, which is consistent with archaeological approaches often applied to crafts or material culture.

In contrast to the largely descriptive, academic approach of the Heard Museum series, Peterson, Schmitz, and Cirillo take a poetic turn in their *American*

*Indian Artists* series of films. Here, they single out well-known figures in American Indian art for individual profiles and evocatively photograph the artists' working environments and art to convey a sense of each artist's character.

The artists featured in the first series are Allan Houser, Fritz Scholder, Medicine Flower and Lonewolf, Helen Hardin, Charles Loloma, and R. C. Gorman. As with the earlier film about Howe, these individual portraits focus on the current work and ideas of the artists and limit biographical details to information offered by the artists themselves. For instance, we learn that Houser's father, who was on the "warpath with Geronimo," influenced his work through his ability to "put a song or story over." Houser explains that telling stories in his own art is the "basis of what I'm all about." Thus a small amount of biographical material emerges through the discussion of art and ideas. Generally, there is an attempt to encapsulate the artist's relation to his or her culture or peers in poetic form rather than through detailed explanation, as seen in an excerpt from James McGrath's poetry in the Houser episode: "My Apacheness is the mountain, the bird, the stone, the drum that I am: all of them together . . . I am what I do."

Many of these films open with a striking graphic image. In the Medicine Flower and Lonewolf episode, the opening frames depict their exquisite pottery displayed in an outdoor setting of old Pueblo ruins, evoking the timelessness of the pottery art form. Similarly, the episode featuring the painter Helen Hardin opens with a shot of dawn over a Southwest landscape and cuts to visuals of ancient structures, cliffs, and petroglyphs. The Loloma episode also opens with a landscape filled with warm morning light and shots of petroglyphs. The text reinforces this evocation of the past: "I touch the face and heart of myself when I touch the stone." Elizabeth Weatherford and Emelia Seubert, scholars and bibliographers of native media, noted that "sometimes the opening sequences lend a romantic atmosphere which is at odds with the straight-forward documentary style of the body of the programs" (Weatherford, 1981: 14). The romantic style of some of the openings does seem oddly inflated. However, romanticism in text and imagery is a characteristic that runs throughout the series, even in the body of the programs. Perhaps the romantic treatment is justified in many cases, but the artists themselves tend to speak more matter-of-factly about their lives and work.

Less outwardly romantic in approach is the episode about Fritz Scholder, a painter at the heart of the debate between traditional and contemporary native artists. This film conveys Scholder's status as a symbol of mainstream success, with a major reputation in leading art cities: a painter who has been validated by the larger art world of galleries and museums. In this episode, as in other forums such as gallery catalogs and interviews, Scholder distances himself from the label "Indian artist." Scholder says in the film that he isn't interested in "making statements" as much as in exploring "new visual experiences." The year before this film was made Scholder stated, "I'm not directly involved in the whole way that Indians are thinking currently [1975]. It's, for one thing, very nationalistic, and, for another, very ingrown" (quoted in Highwater, 1976: 181). But his paintings are taken as visual statements by Indian artists and the Indian community at large. Some viewers take Scholder's art as a disparagement rather than a celebration of Indian culture, whereas others feel his expressionistic style has freed Indian art from the formulaic expression of Indianness found in traditional art. The traditional Indian emphasis on painstaking control and clarity of detail does seem lost in the expressionistic style of Scholder, who has stated that he is more influenced by the British painter Francis Bacon than by traditional Indian art styles.

Those who have found his influence liberating include younger artists such as T. C. Cannon and Jaune Quick-to-See Smith. Cannon, who studied at IAIA and the San Francisco Art Institute, takes a Scholderesque approach to the place of Indianness in art: "First of all, let me say that an Indian painting is any painting that's done by an Indian. Today, however, I don't think there is such a thing as an Indian painting.... I believe there is such a thing as Indian sensibility. But I don't believe it necessarily has to show in a person's painting" (quoted in Highwater, 1976: 177).

It is clear from this early series of films that many contemporary Indian artists value innovation in traditional patterns and styles and hope to make unique pieces rather than produce for a craft market. Even those who are traditionalists have moved away from an understanding of art as craft—objects that can easily be reproduced and marketed as crafts—toward a unique, one-of-a-kind understanding of art objects. For instance, the Hopi jeweler Loloma designs custom jewelry for clients based upon his intuition of their "inner feeling." His gemstone designs function as visual metaphors of the "gems within people," as expressions of the client's inner self. Loloma has consciously developed a style and sought an audience for custom jewelry through his travels to Europe and to the U.S. cultural centers. His motive has been to "experience what fine is" in order to do "work that is fine." Although the filmmakers and Loloma himself ground his work in the land and people of Hopi, his consciousness of the need to appeal to the wider art marketplace is clearly evident.

This straddling of two worlds is also evident in videos from the second *American Indian Artist Series* (1983), which features the artists Jaune Quick-to-See Smith, Dan Namingha, and Larry Golsh. The series was produced by the Native American Public Broadcasting Consortium (NAPBC), but the episodes on Smith and Golsh were produced, directed, and filmed by the same crew that was behind the first series. The narration in the Smith piece is by noted native author N. Scott Momaday and the writer is Joy Harjo (Creek).

From the film we learn that Smith's exposure to Western art practices, including the gallery system, and to ideas such as those that emphasize formal training has led to her increased valuation of formal innovation and originality in her own work. Smith's abstract art still relates to her Indian experience. In the film she describes her *Prairie Series* of paintings in which a Bauhaus grid (a design principle developed at the Bauhaus School in Germany during the 1920s) becomes an abstract image of a travois (an Indian sledge designed to be dragged by a horse). Triangular tipi-like designs also reveal the play between geometric forms and Indian cultural references. Smith states that the *Prairie Series* is "bound together by my formalist training and caring about things in the Indian world." Later, shots of her studio's interior include shelves filled with books about Klee, Gottlieb, Hesse, Schwitters, and so on, which reinforce this reference to an international formalist tradition.

At the same time she feels it is important that her imagery isn't "arbitrarily abstract." Thus, in addition to the travois and tipi references, Indian-like figures and strong, bright colors lend a sense of Indianness to the pieces. Perhaps more important is the openness of her composition and the frequent reference to landscape forms. Smith's art is shaped by her relationship to the land and to animals. Her home and studio are located in a remote rural location; the adobe-style structures seem to emerge from the surrounding open land. Shots of the artist at work are intercut with images of her riding or holding animals—she states at one point her conviction that animals have souls—to impart her strong sense of connectedness to her environment.

The issue of Indianness in art is an underlying concern in the film. At one point Smith is shown in conversation with two other Native American artists. The other, unidentified woman artist (Emmie Lou Whitehorse) comments on the expectation of people that Native American art "look Indian." The trio agrees that it is important to be an artist first, that the "brotherly feeling of being an Indian shouldn't limit the art." Although the film reveals values common to Indians, such as the spiritual value of the land and animals, it emphasizes artistic vision. Smith states that art has always been important for her: "The obsession was always there . . . but now art gives me great harmony in my life—it is my life." Smith's art and her attitudes toward art, then, are definitely a product of two cultures. For her, art is a nonutiltitarian activity in its own right. Formal concerns are central to her work, and she seems to derive as much inspiration from European and American modernists as from traditional Indian themes. As revealed in a gallery scene in the film, the audience for her art is the non-Indian art world. And the viewpoint of the film itself emphasizes the solitary, creative, poetic aspects of art making.

What, then, is the collective aspect of this portrait of an artist? The social basis for her group identification seems to derive from educational and professional association as much as from a tribal or generational basis. The film gives few clues to the social function of Smith's art, focusing instead on the private nature of the artistic process for her, which is consistent with humanist or romanticist aesthetic conceptions that emphasize the autonomous artist. However, Smith's affinity for the land and animals acquires a spiritual cast and points to a common source of collective identification in the Native American community.

The issue of *formal* change, so prominent in the films about Smith and Scholder, has social and economic consequences for individual artists. One of the important issues addressed here is the degree to which a highly individualistic view, which is a consequence of an emphasis on formal innovation in art, is being absorbed by artists whose cultures' traditional aesthetic outlooks may have been quite different from that innovation.

Another episode in the second *American Indian Artists* series, *Dan Namingha*, addresses similar issues. *Namingha* is unique because it is the only film in the series largely produced, directed, and written by Native Americans. (The producer is Frank Blythe, director of NAPBC; Larry Littlebird participated in the writing.) This film about a Hopi artist opens similarly to the films from the first *American Indian Artists* series, with landscape shots of places the artist finds special—in this case, Chaco Canyon in New Mexico, which Namingha feels conveys a sense of mysticism and magic. He explains, "I visualize things that were probably here at one time" and find a "sense of design among the ruins." Architectural and mesa-like landscape forms, along with the warm reds, oranges, and earth colors of the Southwest, permeate Namingha's art.

Namingha states, "I live in two worlds." One is represented in native land, Hopi ceremony, and ties to family; the other is the outside world of the successful, modernist gallery artist. In the video, Namingha emphasizes creativity, variety, and experimentation above other aesthetic values: "As an artist, one creates for himself," not for the public. Like Smith, he values spontaneity and an emphasis upon personal creativity over adherence to any socially defined guidelines for artistic style. But Namingha also claims that his family has "molded me into who I am" and feels that he has balanced traditional ideas with a modern approach.

Is Namingha, then, like Oscar Howe, a modernist obviously influenced in part by Western art theory in his art but a conservative in his view of society? If so, this arrangement prefigures adjustments recently made by the entire Hopi culture, as documented in *Winds of Change: A Matter of Choice* (1990). In this video we see a culture in transition, striving to maintain an essential core while continually integrating aspects of modern life—from individual housing unit arrangements to Western-style schools—that threaten to divorce the culture from its core. Perhaps this is one reason why native producers and writers chose to document Namingha's art themselves; he represents the elusive synthesis of two ways of life that entire cultures are currently trying to achieve.

## RECENT NATIVE AMERICAN–PRODUCED VISUAL ARTS DOCUMENTARIES

*Visions* (1984), produced by Indian News Media of the Blood Reserve in Alberta, Canada, reveals a diversity of opinions about the role of Indian artists, although the video makers emphasize the role of tradition and culture in the visual arts. Their introduction reads, "Indian artists in the 1980s are making a strong impression on art circles around the world. Traditions and culture play an important part in the inspirations and expression of their works." As with the *American Indian Artists* series, the video makers open with landscape shots and images of a buffalo herd and skull that are visual references to the Northern Plains culture. The opening statement of the first artist interviewed, John Webber (Blackfoot), contrasts with the individualist and modernist positions of some Southwest-based Indian artists: "Indian art to me is just ideas, beliefs put on something tangible, that someone can understand and relate to, rather than just makin' their own idea or own picture of something." For Webber the importance of art is its roots in Blackfoot culture; it provides "something to hold onto" in an area where "much of the culture is lost."

Ironically, in the same statement he notes that "a lot of Indian artists were influenced by Russell," referring to the realistic, illustrative art of Charlie Russell, the late-nineteenth-century Montana "cowboy artist." In another interview sequence Everett Shoop (Blood) disagrees: "We [Indian artists of southern Alberta and Montana] aren't merely copying Charlie Russell. . . . Russell copied the Blackfoot confederacy because he admired them so much, and he thought they were majestic." Glenn Eaglespeaker, also Blood, feels that the realism of the area derives from the "recording of legends" and sees the realistic illustration of legends from the past as the basis of the "Plains style."

Notably, the native video makers chose to compare and contrast a number of artists rather than focusing on one well-known or "great" artist. This may be a result of the relative obscurity of Northern Plains artists compared to the highly successful Southwesterners, but it may also result from a cultural tendency among some Indians to not single out individuals within a group for special exposure. At a conference on Indian art in Helena, Montana (1991), Salish writer, poet, and video maker Vic Charlo noted that it is a "hard task for Indian people to get themselves out there" in order to promote their work. An Indian woman participant added, "It's even harder if you're an Indian woman; you're not brought up to brag about yourself." In this type of culture, which values blending in with the group, traditional art is a natural path because "traditional art is its own voice." It doesn't have to be explained like contemporary art, which demands that the artists articulate what they are trying to say (author's notes from Montana Indian Arts Conference, 1991).

Of the artists interviewed in *Visions*, Alfred Youngman (Cree), a college teacher of Indian art, and Everett Shoop (Blood) are the most contemporary in style, but they have opposite ideas about the role of Indianness in art. Youngman feels that there is a difference between Indian art and the art of other ethnic groups. However, he feels the most popular forms of Indian art are determined by the people and institutions that collect it, and he singles out museums in this regard. Museums' primary interests are in ethnography—the collection of war bonnets, vests, moccasins, and so forth, as "ethnographical material"—more than in fine art. Youngman feels this doesn't reflect the reponse of Indians to contemporary reality that concerns him as an artist. Shoop also feels it is important to respond to contemporary issues, which he does through the art of editorial cartooning. However, he rejects the idea of "Indian art," explaining that the desire to distinguish Indian art as special emerges from a fear of cultural homogenization. He states that the background of all art is in nature and that "how people relate to nature reflects on how they relate to their deity." For Shoop, art is a product of its time and place, but there is not a core of Indianness that runs through all art produced by members of that ethnicity.

Another native video, *Native American Images* (1985), parallels *Visions* by featuring artists from the Southern Plains region. Like many of the Northern artists, the subjects of this video are "untrained" in a formal academic setting. Palladine H. Roye (or Pon se se) said he never cared about art but was approached by his brother's agent and asked to paint. After selling his first painting, his career was launched. Roye attributes his artistic influences to his grandparents, for whom traditional arts such as beadwork were "just another part of life," and to the shared cultural symbolism of the Southern Plains. Donald Vanne also had little formal training but enjoyed great success in the first formal competition he entered, sponsored by the Museum of the Five Civilized Tribes (Oklahoma). Roye's and Vanne's work falls well within the Southern Plains style—which is especially strong in Oklahoma—which evolved from an earlier flat, outlined traditional style into a highly illustrative mode. Illustrative, nostalgic, popular, and romantic in vision, Oklahoma artists, like their Northern counterparts, use art to document tradition. However, they depart from the Northerners in their fondness for theatrical, exaggerated motion, as seen in the art of painters such as Dick West and Rance Hood. These two videos by and about Native Americans seem rare in their concentration on the two-dimensional art of painting. Most videos about the visual arts by Native Americans have focused on traditional expressive forms that often predate Western contact.

## TRADITIONAL VISUAL ARTS VIDEOS

*Eyes of the Spirit* (1984), written and produced by Corey Flintoff and directed, photographed, and edited by Alexie Isaac (Yup'ik), exemplifies coproduced documentaries that draw on the talents of both natives and nonnatives and on the close cooperation of local civic organizations—in this case the Bethel Native Dancers group. *Eyes of the Spirit* addresses issues of cultural loss and renewal centered around the revival of ceremonial carved masks. Early missionaries looked on the masks with disfavor as being superstitious; because of outside pressure, masks and even dancing were neglected. Masks were still carved but were used as wall decorations and works of art for collectors. They no longer followed the form of a man's face and with this "loss of original purpose . . . lived on as models, toys, or stylized representations" (*Eyes of the Spirit*, 1984). As they evolved into a new art form, a kind of sculpture, "the masks lost their eyes." In the older art form holes were cut for the eyes, which symbolize the mask's spirit.

Mask making was a point of aesthetic and spiritual locus for the Yup'iks, whose masks were the most complex and imaginative of those made by Eskimos. Ralph Coe described this link between spirituality and identity in the mask makers' art.

> The concept of soul was the only thing that was somehow stable and permanent—an ice floe, a polar bear, a piece of driftwood, a whale, a rock, everything animate or inanimate, had a soul or *inua*. Any mask with an inner face or carved with a fragmentary part of another face—an additional mouth or partial nose, for example—represented not an individual animal but the collective *inua* of the whole species: a reincarnative force. . . . The plural of *inua* is *inuit*, meaning people, which is the name by which the Eskimos referred to themselves as a group. (Coe, 1977: 110)

Masks represent humans, animals, stories, and things of the unseen world seen only in dreams and visions. The video makers stress the importance of the "mind's eye" as a source of inspiration and as a guide to the actual carving process, since no formal plan is used. Masks magically transform the physical into the mythic and spiritual.

*Eyes of the Spirit* documents the technical process of making a mask, traditionally passed directly from master carver to apprentice. The videographers explain the traditional Eskimo learning process based on careful observation—"the Eskimo way of watching"—and its difference from Western educational methods.

At the end of the video, viewers see excerpts from the performance in which the masks were used. In this way the videographers document the need for a "return of the mask maker's art to a community purpose," including the relationship between masks and traditional spirituality, ways of learning, and traditional stories. Socially, masks function as mnemonic aids that trigger narratives about animals, sources of livelihood such as sealing, family relations, shamanism, and the first contact with whites. For those who saw the performance, the effect of seeing the masks after so many years of neglect was electrifying.

Another locally based organization, the Muscogee Creek Nation Communication Center in Oklahoma, has produced videos about traditional Creek culture since the early 1980s. Titles include *Folklore of the Muscogee People, Stickball: Little Brother of War, The Strength of Life, 1,000 Years of Muscogee Art,* and *Turtle Shells.* One of these videos, *Strength of Life* (1984), tells the story of an individual artist, Knokovtee Scott (Creek-Cherokee), and a traditional art form, Creek shellworking. Although he was trained at IAIA, where Indian art was catapulted into the modern art world, Scott is primarily a traditionalist who looks deep into the past for his inspiration. His formal training fueled an interest in Cherokee jewelry making and ancient designs, which Scott learned from books about the Southeastern ceremonial complex culture. Of shellwork, Scott says, "If something good lives, it never dies" and adds that shellwork has been done for the past two thousand years. Scott strives to capture the strength, vitality, and power of the old work.

Although its subject is one artist, this video is similar to *Eyes of the Spirit* in its coverage of historical subject matter, technical processes, the social function of the "gorget" art form, and educational processes. It emphasizes the historical role of shell jewelry in the Creek tribe and in Southeastern Mound Cultures. Technical passages highlight Scott's use of contemporary machine tools, whereas *Eyes of the Spirit* dwells on the traditional curved carving knife. The Yup'ik video documents the Eskimo way of seeing as an educational form; *Strength of Life* shows Scott in a classroom, teaching young children basic shapes and designs based on a curriculum of Indian art. The video details the collective social function of gorgets in the historical section through contemporary footage of the Green Corn dance and in gallery scenes in which Scott mingles with the opening-night crowd. This coverage of historical, educational, and other social factors such as ritual performance contexts reinforces the community purpose of traditional art forms.

Part of the reason for these videomakers' emphasis on the collective function of traditional art may be the problematic notion of Indianness in contemporary art. This problem can be formulated by asking whether Indianness is simply a result of the ethnicity of the artist or whether it is a function of both the art object and the artist's ethnicity. Contemporary artists have tended toward the former position, whereas traditionalists have emphasized the latter. For instance, in the video profile, Knokovtee Scott defines Indian art in this way: "Indian art is that art done of an Indian subject matter by an Indian artist. . . . Indian subject matter should pertain to that particular artist's tribal background." By contrast, Indian modernists often distance themselves from the role of Indian artist.

Two hour-long documentaries by nonnative outsiders, *Seasons of a Navajo* (1984) and *Hopi: Songs of the Fourth World* (1983), demonstrate fully the integration of traditional art practices into the total life of the community. *Seasons of a Navajo* documents the cycle of seasons and activities in the lives of one Navajo family, the Neboyias. As part of a rich portrait of a pastoral lifestyle in the Canyon de Chelly area of northeastern Arizona, the video details the close integration of Navajo weaving with the land. Many shots of Dorothy Neboyia and her family carding, spinning, weaving, and dying wool, boiling flowers for natural dyes, and hanging wool to dry in the trees near her hogan demonstrate that the weaving process begins long before the weaver sits at the loom. These activities are carefully woven into a holistic portrayal of the Neboyia's annual life cycle rather than being isolated into demonstration sequences. The video is less concerned with explaining techniques than with documenting a way of life. The most striking result of this approach is that weaving isn't artificially singled out as an activity; rather, it truly emerges as an integral part of everyday life. Dorothy weaves throughout the year. She's seen at the loom outdoors on a bright summer day and indoors by firelight and gas lamp during the heart of winter. The video's breadth evokes a sense of connectedness less apparent in profiles of individual artists or techniques.

A connectedness of art, ritual, nature, and daily life, rooted in ancient spiritual traditions, is also the keynote of *Hopi: Songs of the Fourth World* (1983), directed by Pat Ferrero. In this vital film about the people of the oldest continually inhabited settlements on the North American continent, Ferrero presents a culture largely intact nearly five hundred years after contact with Europeans. The filmmaker emphasizes the continuity of Hopi philosophy and ways of life, in contrast to the recent film *Winds of Change: A Matter of Choice* (1990), which places greater emphasis on social changes in Hopi land. Without ignoring the changes wrought through cultural contact, Ferrero gives us a visual and verbal essay about a culture that collectively values tradition and spirituality.

The visual arts in the Hopi culture express, record, or participate in a primarily spiritual understanding of life. The filmmakers rely heavily on other visual traditions: paintings of traditional weddings and other ceremonies by Hopi artist Fred Kabotie; wonderful historical stills, especially portraits; and short interview sequences with various visual artists. In one particularly powerful sequence, Kabotie's *kachina* paintings are paired with the intense music of ceremonies in which *kachina* dancer's appear. Hopis believe that death, the last breath—or spirit—of a person, becomes a cloud, a *kachina* spirit. Wherever there is breath or moisture, there is the spirit life of a *kachina*, an idea that has inspired Kabotie: "As I painted the *kachina* dances, I would hum that particular *kachina* music because you're just involved with all that and you're bound with it and you can't help singing very softly as you paint." Kabotie started painting while away at school in Santa Fe. He thought of his people and "heard the *kachina* music among the trees. . . . It's the music that inspires you to start painting" (all quotes from the video, *Hopi: Songs of the Fourth World*).

Many Native American artists, both traditional and contemporary, find artistic inspiration in visions and emphasize the role of spirituality in their art. A recent video by the contemporary Indian artist Susan Stewart raises questions about the role of visions and rituals in contemporary Native American art. Stewart's video documents a "personal ceremony," her contact with the Mapuche Indians of Patagonia, Argentina, and her painting process and philosophy. It prompts us to ask whether the ritual functions of art can be successfully combined with contemporary art forms.

*The Crow Mapuche Connection: The Art of Susan Stewart* (1991) begins with a solitary drumbeat and opening shots of clouds, mountain landscapes, and bird-like sounds. Estonian director and editor Arvo Iho then intercuts among shots of a circular drum, a circular ring around the sun, and a ceremonial ring of sand. These visual references to nature and the classic Native American symbol of the circle or medicine wheel introduce the major theme of the video: land and ceremony as a source of connection for all indigenous peoples of the Americas.

Stewart's vision surfaced through a dream: "Over two years ago I had a dream; I was taken above a medicine wheel in the Bighorn Mountains. . . . An old woman said to me, 'This is your connection; this is how you are connected to the earth.'

She took me even higher and the earth was a ball and it was rotating and I could see points of light and they were all connected . . . these are the sacred spots all over the earth." This vision led Stewart to visit the Mapuche Indians twice and participate in ceremonies with them.

As she tells the story in voice-over narration, Stewart places different colors of powder—symbolizing the directions—in each quadrant of the ceremonial circle along with symbols of the indigenous peoples from each region. Placing symbols of all the Indian cultures within the same circle expresses connection: "I was seeing the Indians of the South and they were like brothers and sisters to me. . . . We did not need any words to know who we were. . . . There was so much familiarity; it was like a dream." Using a slide transfer technique, Stewart and Iho document her experience as the first Indian from the North to participate in Mapuche ceremonies. In the final sequence of the video, Stewart paints a large canvas with a circular form, a combined reference to the Mapuche drum and the earth. She effectively combines traditional symbolism with contemporary art-making processes including performance, painting, and the video itself.

Susan Stewart's video expresses the commonly held native values of land stewardship and spirituality. The theme of a special attachment of indigenous peoples to the land pervades documentaries about contemporary and traditional artists and Native American media in general. The expression of reverence for nature unites various regions, tribes, and artistic approaches. In the video, Stewart often mentions a special feeling for the land as the motivational force behind her painting and performance art. A number of the visual arts documentaries open with landscape sequences that root the art and the artist in a specific location. Many of the artists speak of the influence of place in their artistic expression.

For Stewart, technology plays a positive role in contemporary art. The video camera with its immediacy and accessibility is an important tool for exposing contemporary art to a wider audience. She recognizes that it is more difficult for contemporary artists to be validated within their community; newer art forms such as installations may not even be recognized as art by some community members (Montana Indian Arts Conference, 1991). Contemporary arts speak in a different language, and these innovative forms threaten change in cultures that value continuity. Stewart's solution is a merging of contemporary and traditional forms and issues in video.

However, from the contemporary artist's perspective, cultural preservation can have a stifling effect. When preservation is the overriding motive, "culture becomes mummified," and people run the danger of living in the past instead of the present (Charlo, 1991). Artists such as Stewart try to blend contemporary and traditional influences within the visual arts in order to address a larger audience, but many Native Americans find the strongest expression of their collective identity in the traditional performance arts, especially on the powwow circuit. Some contemporary visual artists are concerned, however, that the powwow and visual art worlds don't cross over; that the songs, dances, and art of the powwow circuit are not integrated into the mainstream art world (Montana Indian Arts Conference, 1991).

Traditional visual artists feel differently about this issue. The rapid growth of the powwow scene has created a marketplace for their art; most traditional art is now made for use in powwows (Montana Indian Arts Conference, 1991). Pow-wows are highly symbolic celebrations of collectively held values and are poten-tial commercial bonanzas for traditional artists. However, many traditional art-ists creating for the powwow trade may not view themselves as artists but as craftspeople and may devalue their work when compared with that of artists pro-ducing for galleries (HorseCapture, 1991).

## DIFFERENCES BETWEEN
## TRADITIONAL AND CONTEMPORARY ART

Films and videos documenting contemporary and traditional Native American visual art point out differences in the expression of Indianness by native artists. Native American art is changing rapidly. Some artists might describe this transi-tion as progress, others as loss.

Traditional artists view art as a way to hold on to culture, an activity that pre-vents even greater cultural losses. In painting, the emphasis of their art is illustra-tion or documentation, but rarely are their paintings exact replicas of life; instead they paint myths, legends, and history from the imagination and memory. These paintings of myth and history may become documentary material in their own right for filmmakers and video makers, as in Ferrero's use of Kabotie's paintings.

Many traditional arts are land based. The potter collects clay in a nearby field, and the weaver shears sheep and prepares the wool as a prelude to weaving. Through this dependence upon locally available material that must be carefully prepared, art blends into daily life rather than standing out as a separate activity. This material connectedness is echoed in the social and spiritual functions of tra-ditional art forms, which often incorporate key symbols, patterns, and myths central to the entire culture. The art form acts as a bridge between material as-pects of life and collectively held values.

In contrast to videos documenting traditional arts, videos and films about contemporary artists tend to focus upon the individual artists' creativity and per-sonal artistic philosophies, but they do so in the context of balancing Indian and Western influences. Documentaries about individual Indian artists are often cre-ated by non-Indians. Although there are exceptions, Native Americans tend to document a particular technique or a group of artists rather than an individual artist. Native-produced videos usually emphasize the collective or ritualistic functions of art.

For the traditionalist, art may be recognized as Indian in several ways: through the medium of expression (shellwork, quillwork, basketry, and similar mediums); designs that clearly relate to tribal, clan, or other group identity; or subject matter pertaining to Indians (Montana Indian Arts Conference, 1991). Although all of these elements may not be present in a given work, the underlying assumption is that something in the artwork, not just in the artist, makes an artwork Indian.

Contemporary artists' location of Indianness in the ethnicity of the artist rather than in the artwork frees artists from formulaic expressions of Indianness but risks excluding those audience members who do not understand new visual languages that result from formal innovation. Thus artistic progress, understood as technical and stylistic development and rooted in the transition to an economic market that values uniqueness, has its price: the problematic relationship of contemporary art with a Native American audience. Artistic progress affects audience understanding or misunderstanding, the latter of which may lead to social exclusion. For example, cultural assumptions (progress, innovation, technological and formal development), acquired by some Indian artists through contact with the non-Indian art world, lead to specialization and individualization (in technical ability, individualized forms of expression), which in turn lead to social exclusion.

The relationship between native progress in art and social exclusion must be addressed within the context of competitive social relations. Native artistic progress is driven partially by a desire to succeed in the competitive non-Indian art world. Competition is the exercise of power by one person over another. Progress in competitive societies ultimately depends upon subjugation, which is consistent with a view that progress in art inherently leads to social exclusion. For many traditional Native American cultures, the endurance of the social structure depends upon consistency with the past and cooperative decisionmaking rather than subjugation. Very different criteria for artistic evaluation arise in the two types of societies. The traditional society allows for individual styles and artistic development but legitimates art through recognition of a communicative code that has endured across time. Perseverance takes precedence over progress and innovation. The goal of the artist in a competitive society is differentiation through innovation; artwork is legitimized through its creativity or novelty, which has led to increasingly rapid changes in style. The highly individualized and socially isolated nature of some contemporary art, a product of art world competition and progress, has in some cases led to interpretive confusion.

From these and related documentaries emerges a portrait of two very different sets of assumptions about the role of art and artists. Documentaries about traditional arts emphasize the *integration* of art into daily life and collective ritual. In some cases this integration may be so complete that art is undistinguishable from work or religion. Although individual style is recognized, formal and thematic consistency with the past is most highly valued. Indianness in traditional art is clearly located in the artwork itself and receives its strongest expression in participatory events such as powwows.

Documentaries about contemporary artists emphasize the creative, personal, and relatively *autonomous* aspects of art making. Many contemporary Indian artists are trying to synthesize an Indian worldview with participation in the highly competitive, non-Indian art world. Mainstream values such as formal innovation shape contemporary native artists' work. Since formal innovation eventually leads to the loss of common artistic languages, contemporary artists tend to locate Indianness in the artist's ethnicity rather than in the artwork itself.

I have focused here on the different social functions of traditional and contemporary art. But there are undercurrents common to much Native American expression. A large percentage of the visual arts documentaries I have viewed open with landscape sequences that ground the art and the artist in a specific location. Many of the artists, traditional and contemporary alike, speak of the influence of place on their artistic expression. This, perhaps, is one of the greatest advantages of film and video documentaries about art over written expositions of art and culture. Film and video give us a sense of context that can be achieved only through a visual familiarity with the artist's native environment. From this body of documentaries I gained an appreciation for the importance of place in all Native American artistic expression. The documentaries' emphasis on a special attachment of indigenous peoples to the land is such a pervasive theme that it can be considered the factor that unites various regions, tribes, and even artistic approaches.

## REFERENCES

Charlo, Vic. 1991. Participant. Contemporary Arts Workshop, Montana Indian Arts Conference, Helena.

Coe, Ralph. 1977. *Sacred Circles: Two Thousand Years of American Indian Art*. Kansas City: Nelson Gallery Foundation.

Eaton, Linda. 1989. "The Only One Who Knows: A Separate Vision." *American Indian Art Magazine* 14, no. 3: 46–53.

Highwater, Jamake. 1976. *Song from the Earth: American Indian Painting*. Boston: New York Graphic Society.

HorseCapture, George. 1991. Participant. Montana Indian Arts Conference, Helena.

McClaughlin, Castle. 1987. "Style as a Social Boundary Marker: A Plains Indian Example." In Reginald Anger, ed., *Ethnicity and Culture: Proceedings of the 18th Annual Conference of the Archaeology Association of the University of Calgary*. Calgary.

Montana Indian Arts Conference. 1991. Helena. Author's notes.

Strickland, Rennard. 1985. "Where Have All the Blue Deer Gone? Depth and Diversity in Post-War Indian Painting." *American Indian Art Magazine* 10, no. 2: 36–45.

Weatherford, E., and Emelia Seubert. 1981. *Native Americans on Film and Video, Volume I*. New York: Museum of the American Indian, Heye Foundation.

## FILM-VIDEOGRAPHY

*Allen Houser, American Indian Artists Series*. 1976. Directors: Tony Schmitz and Don Cirillo; producer: Jack Peterson. KAET-TV, Phoenix, National, Distributed by PBS.

*American Indian Artists Series: Hardin, Loloma, Houser, Gorman, Lonewolf, Scholder.* 1976. Directors: Tony Schmitz and Don Cirillo; producer: Jack Peterson. KAET-TV, Phoenix, National, Distributed by PBS.

*American Indian Arts at the Phoenix Heard Museum.* 1975. Director: Rick Thomson; film: Tony Schmitz and Don Cirillo. KAET-TV, Phoenix.

*Charles Loloma, American Indian Artists Series.* 1976. Directors: Tony Schmitz and Don Cirillo; producer: Jack Peterson. KAET-TV, Phoenix.

*The Crow Mapuche Connection: The Art of Susan Stewart.* 1991. Producer: Susan Stewart; director and editor: Arvo Iho. KUSM, Bozeman, Mont.

*Dan Namingha, American Indian Artists Series.* 1983. Producer: Frank Blythe; writer: Larry Littlebird. Native American Public Broadcasting Consortium, Lincoln, Nebraska.

*Eyes of the Spirit.* 1984. Producer/writer: Corey Flintoff; Director/camera: Alexie Isaac. KYUK-TV, Bethel, Alaska.

*Fritz Scholder, American Indian Artists Series.* 1976. Directors: Tony Schmitz and Don Cirillo; producer: Jack Peterson. KAET-TV, Phoenix.

*Hopi: Songs of the Fourth World.* 1983. Producer/director: Pat Ferrero. Independent.

*Jaune Quick-to-See Smith. American Indian Artists Series.* 1983. Director: Tony Schmitz; producer: Jack Peterson. Native American Public Broadcasting Consortium, Lincoln, Nebraska.

*Larry Golsh. American Indian Artists Series.* 1983. Director: Tony Schmitz; producer: Jack Peterson. Native American Public Broadcasting Consortium, Lincoln, Nebraska.

*Native American Images.* 1985. Director: Carol Patton Cornsilk, S.W. Texas Public Broadcasting Council.

*Oscar Howe: American Indian Artist.* 1973. Directors: Joan and Sanford Gray. University of South Dakota, Vermilion, South Dakota.

Scott, Knokovtee. 1984. In *Strength of Life.* Producer/director/writer/editors: Scott Swearingen, Gary Robinson, Sheila Swearingen. Muscogee Creek Nation Communication Center, OK.

*Seasons of a Navajo.* 1984. Producer/camera: John Borden; associate producer/sound: Joanna Hattery; executive producer: Tony Schmitz. Produced by Peace River Films for KAET-TV, Tempe, Ariz.

Sekauaptewa, Emory. 1983. In *Hopi: Songs of the Fourth World.* Producer/director: Pat Ferrero. Independent.

*Strength of Life.* 1984. Producers/directors/writers/editors: Scott Swearingen, Gary Robinson, Sheila Swearingen. Muscogee Creek Nation Communication Center, Okmulgee, Okla.

*Visions.* 1984. Producer/director: Rick Tailfeathers; editor, Duane Mistaken Chief. Indian News Media, Bullhorn Productions, Alberta, Canada.

*Winds of Change: A Matter of Choice.* 1990. Producer/writer: Carol Cotter; advisers: Frank Blythe, Roger Buffalohead, Phil Lucas. WHA-TV, Madison, Wis. PBS Home Video.

# About the Book and Editor

The concept of the art world confronts and undermines the romantic ideology of art and artists that is still dominant in Western societies. By treating the production of art as work and artists as workers and examining the conditions under which these activities take place, this sociological perspective illuminates much that remains obscured by romantic individualism.

The art worlds analysis represented in this collection of original studies questions the social arrangements that determine the recruitment and training of artists, the institutional mechanisms that govern distribution and influence success, the processes of innovation within art worlds, and the emergence of new formations around new media or new players. These studies share a focus on borderline cases and questions—on actions, transactions, and transitions at the margins of art worlds.

Controversies and critical incidents expose many of the otherwise invisible rules and procedures that determine art world practices. Examining transitions across the border into art worlds has much to tell us about aesthetic values and biases obscured by the romantic ideology of artistic genius. Looking at art worlds organized around marginal media—amateur photography, video, graffiti—reveals patterns of interaction and evaluation strikingly reminiscent of those found in the fine art mainstream.

The research reflected in this volume was conducted at the Annenberg School for Communication of the University of Pennsylvania. By approaching the study of art worlds from within the framework of communications studies, these scholars were free from the disciplinary boundaries that separate the study of art into social, historical, and aesthetic domains. At the same time, they were obliged to follow the threads of their questions wherever they led without resorting to the security of those same disciplinary constraints. These studies reflect the rich potential, indeed the necessity, of interdisciplinary approaches that combine empirical investigation and theoretical analysis for a deeper, more nuanced understanding of the workings of art worlds.

Larry Gross is professor of communications at the Annenberg School, University of Pennsylvania. He is editor of *Studying Visual Communications* (1981), coeditor of *Communications Technology and Social Policy* (1974) and *Image Ethics* (1988), associate editor of *The International Encyclopedia of Communications* (1989), editor of Between Men/Between Women: Lesbian and Gay Studies book series, and author of *Contested Closets: The Politics and Ethics of Outing* (1993).

# About the Contributors

Robert S. Drew teaches and writes about the sociology of art and popular culture. He is currently visiting assistant professor of communications at the State University of New York at Albany.

Michael Griffin is an assistant professor in the School of Journalism and Mass Communication at the University of Minnesota. He has published articles on visual media and is completing a book on the visual construction of TV news. In spring 1995 he is a visiting professor at the University of Amsterdam.

Lisa Henderson is assistant professor of communication at the University of Massachusetts, Amherst, a lesbian activist, and the author of studies in cultural production and reception. Her current project is about call-in radio and the public sphere.

Pamela Inglesby is a doctoral candidate in communication at the Annenberg School, University of Pennsylvania. She is currently conducting research on the historical relationship between popular culture and institutions of higher education.

Bette J. Kauffman is assistant professor of communications at Pennsylvania State University. Her areas of specialty include critical cultural studies, social identity and media, visual communications, and qualitative research methods. She is currently writing *"Woman Artist": Communicating Social Identity*.

Steven Leuthold is assistant professor in the School of Art and Design, Syracuse University, and is working on a book about Native American media.

Moira McLoughlin is assistant professor of communication at Santa Clara University. Her research centers on the nature of public art and history exhibition, with a particular interest in the representation of First Nations' culture in the Canadian museum context.

William Mikulak is a doctoral candidate in communication at the Annenberg School, University of Pennsylvania, where he is completing his dissertation on the legitimation of animation as an art form in museums and art galleries.

Catherine L. Preston is currently a lecturer in women's studies and American studies at the University of Kansas.

Ruth Slavin is museum educator at the Ackland Museum of the University of North Carolina at Chapel Hill.

Krystyna Warchol is assistant professor of media studies at Widener University. She is writing a book on the entry of new artists into the art market in New York and Philadelphia in the 1980s.